PROGRAMMING AN RTS GAME WITH DIRECT3D

PROGRAMMING AN RTS GAME WITH DIRECT3D

CARL GRANBERG

CHARLES RIVER MEDIA
Boston, Massachusetts

Cover Design: Tyler Creative
Cover Images: Carl Granberg

CHARLES RIVER MEDIA
25 Thomson Place
Boston, Massachusetts 02210
617-757-7900
617-757-7969 (FAX)
crm.info@thomson.com
www.charlesriver.com

This book is printed on acid-free paper.

Carl Granberg. *Programming an RTS Game with Direct3D.*
ISBN: 1-58450-498-6
ISBN-13: 978-1-58450-498-6

Library of Congress Cataloging-in-Publication Data
Granberg, Carl.
 Programming an RTS game with Direct3D / Carl Granberg.
    p. cm.
 Includes index.
  ISBN 1-58450-498-6 (pbk. with cd-rom : alk. paper)
 1. Computer games--Programming. 2. Direct3D. I. Title.

 QA76.76.C672G752 2007
 794.8'1536--dc22

2006027366

Printed in the United States of America
06 7 6 5 4 3 2 First Edition

CHARLES RIVER MEDIA titles are available for site license or bulk purchase by institutions, user groups, corporations, etc. For additional information, please contact the Special Sales Department at 800-347-7707.

To Aino

Contents

Preface

AUDIENCE

Obviously, this book is not directed at beginners of Direct3D®, nor is it directed to the professionals, but somewhere in-between. You will need a solid understanding of object-oriented programming using C++. You should also preferably have completed an introductory book on Direct3D before you continue on with this book. We will jump straight into fairly complex code and create things like terrains, dynamically.

For an excellent book covering the basics of Direct3D, refer to Frank Luna's *Introduction to 3D Game Programming with DirectX 9.0.* The examples that accompany the DirectX SDK are good as references, but for learning they tend to be a bit overly complex. Instead, I would suggest going through the many tutorials available online.

USING THIS BOOK

This book has been divided into 16 chapters; each chapter usually focuses on one or a few related components and has a very practical approach to the problems we face when making a Real-Time Strategy (RTS) game. Much time will be spent explaining actual source code rather than just covering high-level theories. The book is best read from beginning to end, since each chapter builds on previous chapters. I've also tried to maintain a logical workflow throughout the book as much as possible.

Many parts in this book are pretty generic, like code for sound, network, and skinned meshes, for example. These can easily be used as they are in your own projects even if they are not real-time strategy games. However, for some of the more RTS-specific examples covered in this book, you are encouraged to write your own code, rather than just use the examples provided. In general, I would suggest you use the example code provided only as a guideline, or as help whenever you are stuck. If you rely too much on it, you will miss the most important lesson this book is trying to teach: Always code as much as you can by yourself. It is the only way to become better at it. Having said that, some things are always better left to the professionals. Therefore, we will rely heavily on the Standard Template Library (STL) as well as the D3DX library throughout this book.

The examples in this book are numbered according to chapter number and example number. For instance, Example 2.3 refers to the third example in Chapter 2. You can find the source code and executables for these examples on the CD-ROM. Many of the examples demonstrate just one small concept. But as the book progresses, the examples become increasingly more complex, including more components, until finally, our last example is a fully functional real-time strategy game.

SYSTEM REQUIREMENTS

- Microsoft Windows® XP
- DirectX SDK 9.0c
- Graphics card that supports vertexshaders and pixelshaders version 2.0
- 1,200 MHz processor
- 512-MB RAM

Throughout this book, we will write many advanced shader effects that require a graphic card that supports vertexshaders version 2.0 and pixelshaders version 2.0. Many of the examples in this book will not work at all on older graphic cards.

Acknowledgments

Throughout this project I have had a lot of help from many different people. First off, I would like to thank Jenifer Niles and Lance Morganelli at Charles River Media for their patience while helping me throughout this process. I would like to thank Paul Houseman for supplying some epic music to this project and Markus Tuppurainen for drawing some excellent concept art. A big thanks goes out to Andrew Tather for letting me use his Panda DirectX Exporter for this book as well as supplying it on the companion CD-ROM. I would also like to thank Tom Cadwell for lending his expertise on game balancing during the writing.

I would like to send a warm and personal thank you to all the people sharing their game-programming hobby with others by writing and publishing articles online. Without you, I would never have been able to learn what I know now about game programming.

I would also like to thank my good friend Simon Djerf for giving me the idea of writing a book in the first place.

Finally, thank you to my family and my fiancé, Aino, for the support they have given me through this rather hectic period of my life. A special thank you also goes out to my little brother Emil for zealously testing the games I've made, as well as for being my biggest fan.

1 Introduction

O kay, so we have established the fact that you want to make a Real-Time Strategy (RTS) game. Real-time strategy games are as close as most of us will ever get to assuming the role of a military commander. In RTS games, the player must form and carry out long-term strategies, just like in a game of chess. However, in RTS games, the player must also be able to quickly adapt his strategies to a very dynamic environment. The player does not always have a perfect picture of what is happening in the game world (unlike in a game of chess). Therefore, a plan that seemed sound a minute ago might have to be planned anew, or even scraped totally. Maybe it is just this that makes RTS games so complex and fun to play. However, in this book we will try to do something even more fun than just playing a real-time strategy game—we will make one. Throughout this book, we will build our own real-time strategy game from the ground up. Each chapter in this book works like a tutorial covering one or more of the components needed to make a real-time strategy game.

BRIEF HISTORY OF REAL-TIME STRATEGY GAMES

Before we start looking at all the details necessary to implement our own RTS game, let us take some time to admire what has already been done in this genre. You most likely have played at least some of these games in the past. In Chapter 2, when we cover the design of a real-time strategy game, keep in mind what has already been done. When you sketch out your own game, you can always "borrow" good ideas from existing games. If you try to do something completely new, you are less likely to end up with something that works.

Real-time strategy gaming as a genre is fairly young; in fact, the genre as we know it today is less than 20-years old. In 1989, the game *Herzog Zwei*™ was released for Sega Genesis by Technosoft. Even though this is the first game to resemble what we now call real-time strategy, the game that defined this genre was *Dune II: The Building of a Dynasty*™.

Dune II defined the RTS genre as what it is today. It had all the general game elements that you find in more modern real-time strategy games—things like multiple teams, different unit types, base building, fog-of-war, resource gathering, and different terrain types. It was also the first RTS game to use the mouse to control units. *Dune II* was released in 1992 by Westwood studios and spawned many successors, such as *Warcraft*® (1994), *Command & Conquer*™ (1995), *Total Annihilation*™ (1997), *Starcraft*® (1998), and many more. *Warcraft* was also the first of these games to support multiple players doing battle over a network, something that today is considered a necessary component in any real-time strategy game. Until today, the genre hasn't changed much since these early days. *Starcraft*, for instance, still remains a benchmark against which new games are compared. *Starcraft* is excellently balanced, despite the fact that the user can play with three very different races. (We will take a closer look at game balancing in the next chapter.) Of course, each new RTS game has more units, larger maps, and better graphics, but the core of most new RTS games still remains the same. We will cover the core of RTS games in the next chapter when we dissect an RTS game into its basic components.

In 1997, the RTS game *Total Annihilation* (created by Cavedog Entertainment®) was released. This was the first RTS game done in 3D, which was quite an achievement considering that graphic cards with 3D acceleration weren't that common back then. Perhaps more well known than *Total Annihilation* is the real-time strategy game *Homeworld*™ (Sierra™). This game was released in 1999 and was one of the first really successful 3D RTS games. After that, it took four years before another successful title was released. This time it was *Warcraft III*®: *Reign of Chaos*™, released in 2003 by Blizzard®. A screenshot of *Warcraft III* is shown in Figure 1.1. After this, most real-time strategy games have been produced in full 3D (even though camera movements usually are pretty limited). It is clear that the future of real-time strategy games is in the realm of 3D.

FIGURE 1.1   A screenshot from *Blizzard's Warcraft III*. *(Warcraft screenshots provided courtesy of Blizzard Entertainment, Inc.)*

WHAT WILL YOU LEARN?

Can one person really learn how to make a whole RTS game in 3D? These days, making RTS games takes many thousands of dollars, as well as a very large crew of talented people. Making a commercial RTS game is certainly outside the reach of a single person, but luckily, that is not our goal here. We will make a very simple RTS game with only the very core of what is needed. But don't be fooled, getting this core up and running will take a lot of knowledge and hard work. So to answer the initial question: Can one person really learn how to make a whole RTS game? The answer is definitely: Yes! And in the process of making the core of an RTS game in 3D, we will also need to learn many general game programming skills, like:

- Terrain generation,
- Skinned meshes,
- Pathfinding,
- Visual effects,
- Sounds,
- Networking,
- And much, much more.

These are all complex topics that will take a lot of effort to learn completely. Because we need to cover so many topics in such a rapid pace, you will often be referred to online resources, books, and articles where you can read more about a certain subject. You are greatly encouraged to do this. It will increase your knowledge about a subject and make other concepts easier to understand. Once you get used to searching for online information, it will become one of your primary sources of information, as well as serving as a helping hand in tight spots.

STRUCTURE OF THIS BOOK

The goal of this book is to help you understand the underlying components of an RTS game well enough for you to build your own. The hope is that by the end of this book, you will be more intrigued by making your own games than by playing others'.

This book aims to follow a logical project work flow, starting with concept, creating 3D art, then working through each of the necessary components until, at the end, we have a finished game. This book also has a heavy emphasis on coding, so be prepared to exercise your fingers. With so much theory to cover, most of the code will be found in the example applications on the companion CD-ROM rather than
ON THE CD in this book. In order to make the most of this book, you should probably spend a lot of time working with the examples.

NOTE

ON THE CD

Half of this book is in printed form; the other half is on the companion CD-ROM. There you'll find all the code and example projects. It is important that at the end of each chapter, you go through the examples and make sure that you understand them all. As the book progresses we will cover increasingly more code; if you move ahead too quickly, you might find yourself having to go back quite often.

Building an RTS game is quite a daunting task, but like most daunting tasks, it can be divided into several less-daunting tasks. Keep dividing the task until the resulting, smaller chores are easy to perform—divide and conquer. When building an RTS game, we need to solve the following primary tasks:

- Define the rules and restrictions for the game.
- Construct a game board to play the game on.
- Create a user interface.
- Construct player teams consisting of unit and building entities.
- Create artificial opponent(s).
- Create sound effects.
- Network game play.

Each chapter of this book deals with one or more specific components necessary to build a real-time strategy game. Many of these components are of course not specific to the RTS genre, but can be used in many other game projects, as well. The books starts by laying the theoretical framework and discussing RTS game design, such as various implementation issues. Then we move on to implement component after component, until we are finally ready to put them all together to form an RTS game. The chapters of this book are organized as follows:

- **Chapter 1—Introduction:** We introduce the task of creating a real-time strategy game.
- **Chapter 2—Concept and Design:** We talk about issues we need to address *before* we start coding. We cover the basic concepts of RTS games, such as rules, game balancing, technology trees, and so on.
- **Chapter 3—Direct3D Primer:** Here we finally start looking at some code. We cover Direct3D initialization, creating windows, the Standard Template Library, and more. Here we also introduce the application framework that we will use throughout the book.
- **Chapter 4—Terrain:** In this chapter, we address the first vital component needed to create an RTS game: the terrain. We cover the creation of a terrain mesh from heightmaps and a few different texturing techniques. We also have a look at the A* pathfinding algorithm in this chapter.
- **Chapter 5—Camera and Mouse:** We create a camera and a mouse class, and look at several related topics. We cover topics like level-of-detail rendering, picking, culling, and much more.
- **Chapter 6—Creating 3D Models:** This chapter takes a break from coding and briefly looks at how to create 3D content for our games, using 3Ds Max®. We look at modeling, texturing, skinning, animating, and exporting 3D models.
- **Chapter 7—Skinned Meshes:** We import some of the models created in the previous chapter into our game, and create the bone structure (i.e., the skeleton) of a character, animate it, and finally apply it to the character mesh.
- **Chapter 8—Team Colors:** To separate units from different teams, we apply a team color to the units (and buildings) using a pixelshader. For this pixelshader to work, we must also create a texture with an alpha channel that describes what parts of the units should be painted in the team color.
- **Chapter 9—Players:** In this chapter, we look at building a team consisting of multiple units and multiple buildings. We also look at the complex problem of doing pathfinding with multiple units.
- **Chapter 10—Fog of War:** This chapter takes a look at how to create the important fog-of-war effect for our RTS game. We also look at an optimization that culls units and buildings residing in the unexplored parts of the terrain.

- **Chapter 11—Minimap:** Another standard component in the RTS toolbox is the minimap. It helps the player move the camera quickly to a certain part of the terrain. The minimap can also be used to order units to locations outside the current camera view.
- **Chapter 12—Effects:** All games need visual effects. In this chapter, we look at how to create fireballs, lens flares, dynamic fires, particle systems, and more.
- **Chapter 13—The Sound of Music:** We now add sound to our game, and look at how to play WAV, MIDI, and MP3 files using DirectMusic® and DirectShow®.
- **Chapter 14—AI:** Here we add some brains to our game. In this chapter, we try to construct an artificial opponent, building on the "chain of command" model used in most military organizations.
- **Chapter 15—Network:** After playing an AI opponent for a while, it might be fun to go up against a real human opponent. In this chapter, we look at how to set up a client-server application in DirectPlay®.
- **Chapter 16—Putting It All Together:** Finally, we put all the building blocks together and (hopefully) end up with something resembling a real-time strategy game.

PROGRAM STRUCTURE

As you can see, there are many things we need to implement in order to complete our real-time strategy game. As mentioned, we will use a divide-and-conquer approach to solve any problems we encounter. Luckily, object-oriented programming fits well into the picture. Throughout this book, we will implement about 50 classes and structures, each designed to solve a specific problem. A very simplified overview of how the most important classes interact with each other can be seen in Figure 1.2.

However, we are getting a little bit ahead of ourselves. Don't worry about the individual classes shown in Figure 1.2. The important thing here is the relationship between the classes; we will use this notation throughout the book. A tilted square means that an object of this class has one or more objects of whatever class the line is pointing to. An example of this is our terrain class, which has a heightmap object. Next we have the triangle symbol. This means that whatever class the line points to is an extension of the class the triangle points to. Both our BUILDING and UNIT classes are examples of this. These two classes inherit from the MAPOBJECT class—or in other words, they extend this class. Last we have the dotted arrow, meaning that a class knows another class by reference. For example, the classes MESH and SKINNEDMESH are both resources that can require quite a bit of memory to store. Instead of storing a copy of these resources for each object that wants to use them, it is more efficient to allow multiple objects to have a reference to the same resource.

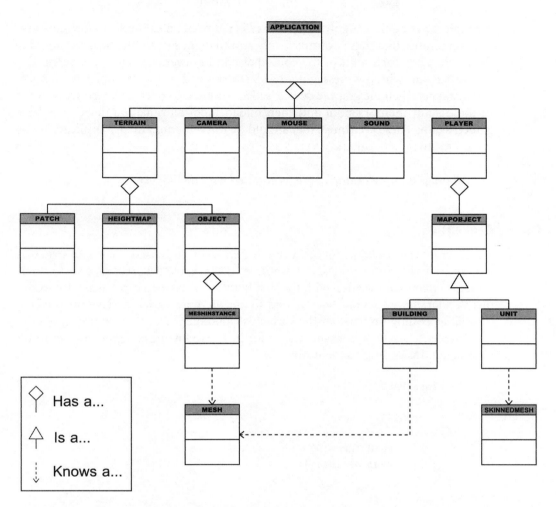

FIGURE 1.2   The program structure overview.

It is suggested that you read "Being a Better Programmer," an article by Danny Burbol [Burbol01], if you are new to managing large projects. This article contains some general programming tips that you would do well to adhere to.

Example Code

On the companion CD-ROM, you will find all the examples referred to in this book. Examples are labeled according to chapter number and example number. Go through the code thoroughly whenever referred to in an example, before continuing. Remember that these examples only aim to demonstrate the topics covered in the book. Therefore, a lot of the code that handles events, such as losing/gaining the device and window messaging, has been skipped in the examples for brevity. For instance, when the graphic device is lost, you need to release all resources stored in the default memory pool and then reload them all once the device has been gained again. These are things that should be implemented in any application you intend to share with others.

All programming examples are terminated with the ESC key.

Coding Convention

Throughout the book, the following coding convention is used. Class and structure names are written in capitals, for example: TERRAIN, UNIT, BUILDING, and so forth. Function names are written with the first letter of each word capitalized, for example: Render, SetAnimation, MoveTo, and so on. Member variables have the prefix m_ or m_p, depending on whether the variable is a pointer or not, for example: m_time, m_animationSequence, m_pParent, and so forth. The following code shows an example class using this coding convention:

```
class BALL
{
    public:
        void Bounce(int numTimes);
        void Throw(D3DXVECTOR3 toPos);
        bool Deflate();

    private:
        D3DXCOLOR m_color;
        D3DXVECTOR3 m_position;
        BASKETBALLCOURT *m_pCourt;
};
```

DirectX 9 Versus DirectX 10

Throughout this book, we will be using the Microsoft DirectX API to render our 3D RTS game to the screen. DirectX is a collection of useful classes, interfaces, and functions that make it easy for a developer to create graphical applications, such as games. DirectX does not only help us render 3D objects, it also has interfaces for sound playback, creating network applications, external device input, and much more.

As this book was being written, Microsoft had already released a preview of DirectX 10. DirectX 10 is only supported by Windows Vista, which presents a problem for Windows XP users. Therefore, we'll use DirectX 9 in this book (which will run on Windows Vista, as well). However, most of the techniques presented in this book are independent of what version of DirectX you use. You should have no trouble porting the code to DirectX 10 if that's your preferred Application Programming Interface (API).

WHAT TOOLS WILL BE USED?

To create a real-time strategy game, we will of course need a lot of tools to help us. At the very least, you will need access to the following programs and tools:

- **Microsoft Visual Studio 6.0 or greater:** This is the developing tool we will use to create and compile our Direct3D projects. Visual Studio version 7.0 or greater is recommended. You can download a trial version at *http://msdn. microsoft.com/vstudio/products/trial/.*
- **Microsoft DirectX SDK 9.0c:** This is a collection of headers, libraries, runtime files, samples, and everything else needed to create Direct3D applications. You can download the latest version of the DirectX SDK at *http://msdn. microsoft.com/directx/sdk/.*

NOTE

Microsoft DirectX SDK (June 2006) was used to compile the examples in this book.

- **Autodesk® 3ds Max® 6.0 or greater:** A tool is used for the creation of 3D models, such as game characters and buildings, this program is not absolutely necessary for you to enjoy this book. Only one chapter will focus on the use of 3ds Max. However, to understand the entire process of game creation, you will need to familiarize yourself with 3ds Max or a similar 3D program. You can download a trial version from Autodesk at *http://usa.autodesk.com/adsk/servlet/ index?id=5659302&siteID=123112.*
- **Panda® DirectX Exporter:** This is a plug-in for 3ds Max that exports 3D models to the .x format. An .x file can then be used by the Direct3D application we are going to create. You can download the exporter for free at *http://www. andytather.co.uk/Panda/directxmax.aspx.* You can also find a copy of this plug-in on the companion CD-ROM.

ON THE CD

- **Adobe® Photoshop®:** We also need a program to help us create and edit needed 2D content, such as textures. For this purpose we use Adobe Photoshop. You can download a trial version at *http://www.adobe.com/products/ photoshop/.*

- **NVIDIA® DDS Plug-Ins:** There is a collection of useful plug-ins for both 3ds Max and Photoshop that allow you to save images in the DDS (DirectDraw Surface) format. You can find these plug-ins free online at *http://developer. nvidia.com/object/nv_texture_tools.html.* You will need the plug-ins for both 3ds Max and Photoshop.
- **NVIDIA Transmogrifying Textures, Vol. I:** NVIDIA has a collection of general-purpose, tileable textures that you can download for free. You can find these textures at *http://developer.nvidia.com/object/IO_TTVol_01.html.*

SUMMARY

This chapter presented an overview of what will be covered in this book. We also looked briefly at some games released in the RTS genre, and which have made RTS what it is today. We also covered the structure of this book and how to use it. The tools necessary to make the most out of this book were also presented. It is strongly recommend that you try to get your hands on as many of these tools as possible, because we will soon put them to use. However, before that, the next chapter will take a closer look at the different components of an RTS game, as well as how to do an initial design.

REFERENCES

[Burbol01] Burbol, Danny, "Being A Better Programmer." Available online at: *http://www.flipcode.com/articles/article_betterprogrammer.shtml,* 2001.

2 | Concept and Design

	Damage	Movement	Armor	Health	Cost
	2	2		2	4

Y ou most likely already have a fair idea of what a real-time strategy game is, and parts of this chapter will probably just tell you what you already know. Despite this fact, we do need to define some basic concepts that will be referred to throughout the book. So we'll start this chapter by looking at RTS games in general. Then we'll try to break RTS games into components and analyze these. We'll talk about prototyping and defining a core idea for an RTS game. We will also look at the important concept of balancing an RTS game.

You most likely already know how you want your finished game to look and behave. Design is the process of figuring out how to achieve this goal before you actually start the implementation. Often you can catch yourself thinking, "I wish I had thought of this earlier." Becoming better at planning ahead during the design process is done in the same way you become better at anything else—by practice . . . lots of it.

CONFLICT!

That's right! Conflict. This of course is the essence of any real-time strategy game. Without conflict, it is impossible make a proper RTS game. Consider the following two scenarios:

> **Scenario 1:** Two bunny families share a sunny glade in the forest. The sun is shining and all is nice and friendly. There are plenty of wild carrots growing in the glade, enough to feed everyone.
>
> **Scenario 2:** Two rivaling bunny families violently struggle over control of the previously mentioned glade and its diminishing supply of carrots.

Not much conflict in Scenario 1, now is there? Certainly not enough to base a good RTS game on. Scenario 2, on the other hand, contains all we need for a good RTS. We have different teams—the two bunny families. We also have a resource to fight over—the wild carrots. How does the player create more bunnies to aid in the struggle? Well, that part is left up to your own imagination.

An Idea Takes Shape

Throughout this book, we are going to implement a real-time strategy game, piece by piece. But it all starts here, with an idea. Coming up with an idea really isn't that hard. All you really need are two or more factions wanting something bad enough to fight the other(s) for it. Whether it is galactic empires battling among the stars, nations fighting over global control, or two ant hills fighting over the local waste bin—these are all good ideas worthy of their own RTS game. These three examples all answer the following questions:

- Who is fighting?
- Where and when are they fighting?
- Over what are they fighting?

We've established that we need two or more factions fighting each other. Galactic empires, nations, or ant communities are all good examples of factions that could fight each other. Next, we need a setting that will answer the where and when questions. Again in our examples, this can be a futuristic interstellar setting, a World War II setting, or a Tuesday morning in someone's backyard setting. The final question we need to answer is: Over what are they fighting? Galactic control? Global control? Or the squishy bits at the bottom of the trash bin? You probably get the idea by now. A good idea for an RTS game can usually be described in just one or two sentences.

REAL-TIME STRATEGY GAME 101

Strategy games in general are games where the goal is to outsmart your opponent(s). The best and most classic example is chess, where nothing is left up to chance. Games like poker and Monopoly could also be considered strategy games with a varying degree of chance involved. However, all of these games are all turn-based, which means that only one player will affect the game state at a time. In real-time strategy games, all the players can affect the game state at the same time, and often the speed with which a player can play the game is a big factor in who is successful and who is not. In most real-time strategy games, the player takes the role of a general (or similar entity) overseeing the battlefield. He directs his soldiers on the battlefield and engages the opponent's soldiers in combat. He manages resources, and decides what buildings and soldiers are going to be allocated, and so on. Most real-time strategy games share these common components:

A Terrain: This is the battlefield or the game board on which the game takes place. The terrain usually consists of many connected map tiles with different attributes. Tiles may be of different types, such as grass, rock, water, or swamp. The type of a tile may affect how fast a unit can cross it. We will cover terrains in more detail in Chapter 4.

Units: A unit is an entity roaming the terrain under the control of a player. Some unit attributes could be, for instance, attack strength, movement speed, and health. We will talk more about how to set and adjust these attributes further on in this chapter.

Buildings: Building in general share many similarities and attributes with units. Usually, buildings are static object constructed by the player. The role of the building is foremost to generate more units or upgrade technology. Some buildings, like turrets or guard towers, can also attack enemies that come within range.

Teams: Two or more players each control a team of units and buildings. The different teams usually have their own color or appearance so the players can tell them apart.

Resources: This is the currency of the game. Resources are in most cases gathered somehow from certain locations on the terrain and are usually depleted by generating more units or constructing new buildings.

UNITS

As previously explained, a unit is an entity that roams the terrain under the control of a player. Units come in many different flavors, some of which we'll have a look at in this section. Each unit type has its own unique appearance, making it easy for the player to tell what type a certain unit is. Units also have different attributes, strengths, and weaknesses. In general, units in real-time strategy games have these four primary attributes:

Damage: The amount of damage a unit can do during an attack.

Health: The amount of damage a unit can take before it dies.

Movement Speed: The speed with which the unit can move around the terrain.

Attack Range: The minimum distance to a target required for a unit to be able to attack.

These primary attributes define the overall effectiveness of the unit. But to make things more complicated, most RTS games add a long list of secondary attributes, as well. Here are some common secondary attributes a unit may have:

Attack Rate: The rate with which the unit can attack enemy targets.

Sight Range: The distance the unit can see across the terrain.

Armor: A unit with a higher armor value reduces the incoming damage to its health attribute.

Mana: Some units have spell-casting abilities. The mana measures how much "magical energy" the unit has available for casting spells. (Variations of mana could be stamina, electric energy, and so on.)

Regeneration Rate: Attributes like health or mana can be regenerated over time, depending on the regeneration value of a unit.

This is just a short list of some common unit attributes. When playing RTS games, you will find that there are many more. Later in this chapter, we will have a look at how to weigh these attributes in order to make a balanced game.

Now that you know what types of attributes can be assigned to units, you can select what unit attributes you want to support in your game. Then you create the units you want and assign different attribute values to these unit types. The unit types usually fall into different categories, as well. Here are some common unit categories:

Engineering Units: The engineering unit's foremost task is to construct and/or repair buildings. They might also be capable of repairing neutral terrain objects, like bridges. Usually, the engineering unit has a nonexistent or very limited fighting capability, as well as weak armor. Examples of engineering units are engineers, farmers, workers, or construction yard units.

Resource-Gathering Units: The resource-gathering unit category is, in many games, combined with the engineering unit category. The job of the resource-gathering unit is to gather resources from the terrain. It can be anything from cutting lumber to harvesting minerals. Just like the engineering unit, the resource-gathering unit has limited range, armor, and attack capability. Examples of this type of unit could be a harvester vehicle or a worker unit.

Short-Range Units: These units are usually the first type of offensive unit a player can produce in an RTS game. The short-range unit has medium or heavy armor, good attack capabilities, but limited range. Examples of these units are infantry units or foot soldiers.

Long-Range Units: These units are more lightly armored than short-range units, but they have a longer attack range. Long-range units provide attack support from a distance for the short-range units on the front line. Examples of these units are archers, snipers, grenadiers, bazooka men, and offensive spell casters.

Supporting Units: These units do not pose a big threat by themselves. Their purpose is to support other nearby units. These units usually have limited attack capabilities and lighter armor. Examples of supporting units are medics, supporting spell casters, and banner men.

Mounted Units: Mounted units usually have an increased movement capability compared to normal infantry units. In the medieval setting, mounted units are often knights or archers on horses, while in the World War II (WWII) setting, it can be soldiers on motorbikes, cars, or trucks. In theory, you can mount any of the previously mentioned unit types to create new combinations.

Siege Units: These are very slow-moving units (e.g., machines, vehicles) with the long-range capability to do a lot of damage. These units are good at destroying static targets from a distance, but are less effective against close or fast-moving targets. Usually, siege units are machines like catapults, ballista, or heavy tanks.

Stealth Units: Stealth units have a cloaking ability that make them invisible to the enemy, and usually only for a limited period of time. These units are a great addition to an RTS game because they allow strategic surprise attacks to be made. Once stealth units start to attack an enemy unit, they automatically become visible to the enemy. To compensate for the great advantage of being unseen, these units usually pay a penalty in armor or firepower. Examples of stealth units are spies, thieves, assassins, or stealth vehicles. (Stealth units could also be normal units under some sort of "invisibility" spell.)

Air Units: While all of the previously mentioned unit types move on the ground, we can also have airborne units. These units cannot be attacked by short-range units while airborne. They are capable of moving independently of the terrain below them. This means that air units can cross terrain types that normal ground units can't. Examples of air units are planes, helicopters, space-craft, and birds.

Transport Units: These units traditionally don't have any attack capabilities. They are generally fast moving and can transport other units over great distances. They can also often travel over terrain types that normal units are unable to cross. An example is a transport ship that can carry land units over water. While other units are inside the transport unit, they are inaccessible to the player. Examples of transport units are ships, trucks, and planes.

Heroes: One of the latest additions to RTS games is the hero unit. These units are unique, and a player can only have one of each hero at a time. A hero is capable of more damage, has more armor, and also an appearance that makes him stand out from other units. A hero's mere presence in a battle can give other units a moral boost or other bonuses. Heroes can also have certain abilities, like unique spells.

Strengths versus Weaknesses

You are, of course, not limited to these standard categories when you create your game. You could break tradition and create a heavy armored spell-casting unit, but it's important to realize that units need both strengths and weaknesses. For instance, a heavily armored unit needs to be slow, while a magician usually has low health points. This way it is up to the player to use his units strategically, taking both strengths and weaknesses into account. If you make an all-powerful unit without any weaknesses, then (unless it is ridiculously expensive to produce) this unit makes other units obsolete.

For the RTS demo that we will create throughout this book, we will have the following three units: the worker, the soldier, and the magician.

The Worker

The worker (Figure 2.1) is our engineering unit, whose main purpose is to construct new buildings. He's unarmed, has a short attack range, and doesn't do much damage. The worker would also be the unit that collects resources from the terrain. The worker unit is quite fast and can easily outrun other units, like soldiers. The worker unit will be produced in the town hall building; it will be the cheapest unit to produce.

The Soldier

The soldier (Figure 2.2) is a heavily armored short-range unit. He's quite slow, but makes up for it with attack power and health. The soldier is meant to be the unit that is on the front line, guarding the player's base or attacking his enemies. The soldier will be produced in the barrack building.

FIGURE 2.1 The worker.
(Copyright 2006 by Markus Tuppurainen.)

FIGURE 2.2 The soldier.
(Copyright 2006 by Markus Tuppurainen.)

The Magician

The magician (Figure 2.3) is a medium-range support unit. He can conjure up fireballs with his staff and throw them at enemy units. The magician is a fairly weak but fast unit that is best kept away from the center of the battle. The magician can also cast a heal spell that heals any wounded friendly units (including himself). The magician is produced in the tower building. The magician takes the longest to produce and also costs the most.

FIGURE 2.3   The magician. (Copyright 2006 by Markus Tuppurainen.)

BUILDINGS

Buildings in real-time strategy games usually exist to produce more units, upgrade technologies, and so on. Some buildings have other special functions, like the radar building in *Dune II* that allows the player to see the minimap. In *Warcraft*, the number of farm buildings the player has determines how many units he can produce. Other buildings, like watch towers or turrets, defend the base against enemy attack from the ground or the air. Many games have the feature that buildings require power to operate. This means that the player must also construct buildings like power plants (or similar) to produce sufficient power for all his other buildings.

You can, of course, decide the exact purpose of your buildings, yourself. The buildings don't even have to be static, as can be seen in *Starcraft* or *Warcraft III*. Players usually build several buildings in a cluster near resources or in a secure location. A cluster of buildings like this is often referred to as a "base." In some games, the objective is to destroy the other players' bases and/or all of their units.

GAME BALANCE

Many RTS games allow the user to select a faction or a team to play the game with from a couple of different options. These factions may be countries in a WWII game, for instance. These factions may also differ from each other. They may have different types of units, different costs, and so on. A game is unbalanced when one of these factions (and/or unit types) is notably better than another. Achieving balance in an RTS game is absolutely essential for fair gameplay. The cost of a unit must equal its effectiveness; it represents the amount of resources the player needs to pay in order to create a new unit of this type. If we make a "super-unit," we must also make sure that the price tag of this unit matches its abilities. As we add more units to the game, maintaining this balance becomes harder to do. We must be careful that when we add a new type of unit, we don't render an old unit type useless.

Here are two useful formulas to help weigh initial attributes and costs of units and buildings. They are the "effectiveness formula" and the "cost-effectiveness formula":

$$Game\_impact \times Durability = Effectiveness$$

$$\sqrt{\frac{Game\_impact \times Durability}{Cost^2}} = Cost\_Effectiveness$$

Now what exactly is the *Game_impact* of a unit? The impact a certain unit has on the game world depends on all the different unit attributes we covered in the previous section (both primary and secondary attributes). The *Durability* of a unit stands for how long the unit can be effective in combat. We usually calculate this value from the amount of health points the unit has, taking into account things like armor and so forth.

By dividing the *Effectiveness* of a unit by its *Cost²*, we get the *Cost_Effectiveness* of a unit, or how much *Effectiveness* you get for your *Cost*, according to the cost-effectiveness formula. Since the cost effectiveness should be roughly equal for all units, we can set it to one and calculate the cost of a unit using the following cost formula:

$$\sqrt{Game\_impact \times Durability} = Cost$$

Take the following very simple example of three WWII units, as shown in Figure 2.4.

	Damage	Movement	Armor	Health	Cost
 🪖	2	2	1	2	4
 🪖	3	3	4	3	8
 ✈	6	4	2	4	14

FIGURE 2.4 An example diagram of unit attributes and cost.

In Figure 2.4, three different WWII units—the infantry unit, the tank, and the plane unit—are listed with their attributes and cost. The cost of the units in this diagram is just an initial guess that we now shall attempt to verify. We will begin by defining the *Game_impact* of a unit for this simple example as a unit's *Damage* multiplied by its movement. The *Durability* of a unit will be calculated by multiplying its health value with its armor value. If we calculate the *Game_impact* and *Durability* for the three units, and insert these values into the cost formula, we get the actual cost, as shown in Figure 2.5.

	Guessed Cost	Actual Cost	Difference
 🪖	4	2.8	+1.2
 🪖	8	10.3	-2.3
 ✈	14	13.8	+0.2

FIGURE 2.5 The actual cost of the units shown in Figure 2.4.

As you can see in Figure 2.5, the cost of the tank differs quite a lot between the guessed cost and the actual cost. If we use the guessed cost, we would have a perfect example of an unbalanced game. A player building his army of only tanks would always win over a player building his army of mixed units. We can also see that the infantry unit costs more than 40 percent more than it actually should, which effectively renders it useless compared to the tank.

This was, of course, an extremely simplified example where the units only had four attributes—damage, movement, armor, and health. In most RTS games, you have many more than four attributes to take into account. You also have to consider other issues, like the fact that planes can travel over water, tanks can't traverse swamp terrain but infantry can, and so on. Getting a perfectly balanced RTS game is nearly impossible, but we can at least attempt to reduce the more-obvious flaws using methods like the one described above. The moral of this story is that you shouldn't just guess the initial cost of a unit because this will most certainly lead to an unbalanced game. Start with assigning attributes to your units, then define the *Game_impact* and *Durability* from these. It then becomes easy to calculate a rough cost using the simple cost formula presented in this section. (See [Cadwell01] for a more detailed discussion about balancing a game.)

Obviously, the initial attribute values you assign to a unit won't be perfectly accurate, either. Once your game has been implemented and you can actually test your ideas, you will have to spend a lot of time tweaking these values to make sure that no unit's cost effectiveness is higher than any others.

TECHNOLOGY TREE

We've covered the concept of real-time strategy games and how a player constructs his base and army. Usually, there are rules governing when and where units and buildings can be built. One building type might require that you have already built another building of a certain type first. This is called a "technology tree," and it defines the requirements that must be met for each building and unit. Figure 2.6 shows an example of a technology tree for a hypothetical RTS game with a World War II setting.

The technology tree example in Figure 2.6 should be read from top to bottom. A line drawn from a specific unit or building represents the requirements for that unit or building. To build a tank, for example, you must first have constructed both a factory and a research center. The factory, in turn, first requires the barrack to be built, and so on. Sketching a technology tree is another thing you should do in the design stage of your game. This can quickly make it clear if there are any flaws or areas that need improvement.

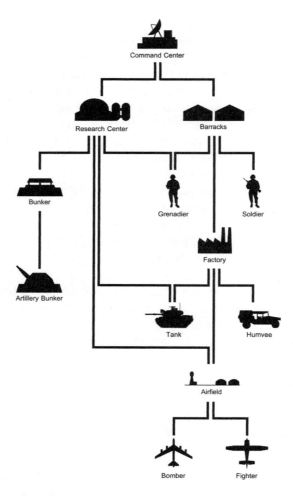

FIGURE 2.6   Example of a technology tree.

SUMMARY

If you're thinking: "I don't know what I want to do. I'll just start coding and then figure out all game-specific details later," then you've already reduced your chances of completing your game by magnitudes. Why? Well, when you start designing your program structure, you do it with a specific goal in mind. Are you going to have flying units in the game or not? If so, then it will perhaps affect how you design your pathfinding system. Trying to add support for flying creatures after you have already finished a pathfinding system for ground units might cause more pain than you think. It's a lot better to figure out what you want your game to do before you start coding, and then design your game with this in mind. Make sure that you have at least defined most of the following things before continuing:

- The setting of the game
- Unit/building attributes supported
- Unit types
- Buildings
- Rough balancing of the unit/building attributes and costs
- Technology tree
- Concept art
- Story

You may be about to write your largest piece of software, ever. Most of us attack the problem by opening up our editor, and we start coding away. But if this chapter is meant to teach you anything, it is that the more time you spend defining your game before you start, the more time (and brain cells) you will save in later stages of the process. Things like drawing concept art and writing a story for your game will help you define the idea. The physical act of putting art and ideas on paper can do a lot of good in this stage of the process. It will, for example, help you remember that great idea you had a week or so ago. Doing this will also increase your chances of actually finishing your game.

REFERENCES

[Cadwell01] Cadwell, Tom, "Techniques for Achieving Play Balance." Available online at: *http://www.gamedev.net/reference/design/features/balance/,* 2001.

3 | Direct3D Primer

We have now covered some necessary background information concerning real-time strategy games. In this chapter, we will start programming something. However, before we can start with the fun programming parts of this book, we must first cover the little bit boring, but necessary tasks. We will cover the application framework that will be used for the remainder of this book. We will also cover some classes that will be used a lot—methods for debugging, the Standard Template Library, and much more. As mentioned earlier, before you attempt to tackle the content in this book, you need some C++ experience and basic knowledge about DirectX and Direct3D. It would be best to complete one of the many basic books about Direct3D, and then you will be ready for your next challenge.

To save space, throughout this book the descriptions of some function parameters, class members, and so on have been omitted. You can easily find the full description of functions, classes, and structures in the DirectX documentation for C++ (hereafter referred to as the DirectX documentation). You will do well to familiarize yourself with this reference documentation, since you will definitely need it during the course of this book. The most useful function here is the search function, with which you can search for the full description of functions, classes, and structures. A screenshot of the DirectX documentation is shown in Figure 3.1.

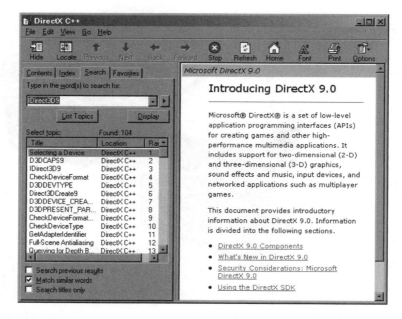

FIGURE 3.1   The DirectX documentation.

Add a DirectX documentation shortcut to your quick launch bar or on your desktop so you can fire it up quickly whenever you need it.

APPLICATION FRAMEWORK

Most programming books provide an application framework, and this book is no exception. This section covers the application framework we will use for all the examples throughout this book. We will briefly cover the program loop, creating windows, and so on. We create a simple class to maintain our application as follows:

```
class APPLICATION
{
    public:
        APPLICATION();
        HRESULT Init(HINSTANCE hInstance,
                     int width, int height,
                     bool windowed);

        HRESULT Update(float deltaTime);
        HRESULT Render();
        HRESULT Cleanup();
        HRESULT Quit();

    private:
        IDirect3DDevice9* m_pDevice;
        HWND m_mainWindow;
};
```

Init(): The Init() function takes a handle to the application instance, a width and height, as well as a Boolean indicating whether the application should be full screen or not. In this function, we create a window and initialize the Direct3D components. It is also in this function that you will load any application-specific resources that you will need.

Update(): The Update() function has only one parameter, and that is the delta time in milliseconds since the last time this function was called. The Update() function is always called before the Render() function in each frame, and in it you should update your scene.

Render(): In this function you render all the objects in your scene.

Cleanup(): This function releases all resources.

Quit(): This function destroys the window and sends the quit message that terminates the application.

Before we take a closer look at the implementation of the APPLICATION class, let's take a look at the WinMain() function.

The WinMain() Function

All Windows programs must have an entry point. You need to include the windows.h header file in your code before you can use any of the functions defined in this section. The program entry point is defined by the WinMain() function, as follows:

```
int WINAPI WinMain(
    HINSTANCE hInstance,            //Handle to current instance
    HINSTANCE hPrevInstance,       //Handle to previous instance
    LPSTR lpCmdLine,               //Command line
    int nCmdShow                   //Show state
);
```

We don't care about most of these parameters. The only important one is the current instance handle because we need this one to register a new window class (more on this later). In the WinMain() function, we must create an infinite loop that runs until the user quits our game. The following is an example of a WinMain() function that creates such a loop and runs our application using the APPLICATION class:

```
int WINAPI WinMain(HINSTANCE hInstance,
                   HINSTANCE prevInstance,
                   PSTR cmdLine,
                   int showCmd)
{
    //Create new application object
    APPLICATION app;

    //Init the application object
    if(FAILED(app.Init(hInstance, 640, 480, true)))
        return 0;

    MSG msg;
    memset(&msg, 0, sizeof(MSG));
    int startTime = timeGetTime();

    //Start Message loop
    while(msg.message != WM_QUIT)
    {
        //Handle messages
        if(::PeekMessage(&msg, 0, 0, 0, PM_REMOVE))
        {
            ::TranslateMessage(&msg);
            ::DispatchMessage(&msg);
        }
        else
        {
            //Delta time between frames in milliseconds
            int t = timeGetTime();
            float deltaTime = (t - startTime) * 0.001f;
```

```
            //Update application
            app.Update(deltaTime);

            //Render application
            app.Render();

            startTime = t;
        }
    }

    //Release all resources
    app.Cleanup();

    return msg.wParam;
}
```

You are hopefully already familiar with how to write Windows programs; if not, then there are plenty of more in-depth articles available online on the subject. The main loop runs until it receives a WM_QUIT message. Otherwise, we calculate the delta time for each frame, update our application, and render it.

Creating a New Window

Before we can start rendering, we must create a target window for our application. In the APPLICATION::Init() function, we create a new window before we set up any Direct3D components. To create a new window, we must first create a new window class and register it. We define a window by filling out the WNDCLASS structure:

```
struct WNDCLASS {
    UINT        style;              //Window Style
    WNDPROC     lpfnWndProc;        //Window Procedure function
    int         cbClsExtra;         //Used to extend the class
    int         cbWndExtra;         //Used to extend the instance
    HINSTANCE   hInstance;          //Application Instance
    HICON       hIcon;              //Application Icon
    HCURSOR     hCursor;            //Application Cursor
    HBRUSH      hbrBackground;      //Background Brush
    LPCTSTR     lpszMenuName;       //Menu Name
    LPCTSTR     lpszClassName;      //Class Name
};
```

We just set most of these members to zero because we won't use them. The following code creates a new window class and registers it.

```
//Create a new Window Class object
WNDCLASS wc;

//Set all members to 0
memset(&wc, 0, sizeof(WNDCLASS));

//Fill out the useful members
wc.style         = CS_HREDRAW | CS_VREDRAW;
wc.lpfnWndProc   = (WNDPROC)::DefWindowProc;
wc.hInstance     = hInstance;
wc.lpszClassName = "D3DWND";          //Window Class Name

//Register Class
RegisterClass(&wc);
```

Once a window class has been registered, we can create a new window of this type. Note here that we specify the window class name as D3DWND. Later, when we create a new window, we must also specify that we want to create a window of the D3DWND class. To create a new window, we use the CreateWindow() function:

```
HWND CreateWindow(
    LPCTSTR lpClassName,          //Class name
    LPCTSTR lpWindowName,         //Window name
    DWORD dwStyle,                //Window style
    int x,                        //X
    int y,                        //Y
    int nWidth,                   //Width
    int nHeight,                  //Height
    HWND hWndParent,              //Parent window
    HMENU hMenu,                  //Menu handle
    HINSTANCE hInstance,          //Application instance
    LPVOID lpParam                //Window-creation data
);
```

This function returns a window handle (HWND) that we need later when we initialize the Direct3D components. So remember to store this window handle because you may need it throughout your application's life span. We use the CreateWindow() function like this:

```
HWND aWindow = CreateWindow("D3DWND", //Window Class
                "Framework",           //Title
                WS_EX_TOPMOST,         //Style
```

```
                   0, 0,               //X, Y
                   width, height,      //Width, Height
                   0,                  //Parent Window
                   0,                  //Menu
                   hInstance,          //Application Instance
                   0);                 //Window-creation data

   //Also show and update the window
   ShowWindow(aWindow, SW_SHOW);
   UpdateWindow(aWindow);
```

Now that we have a window that we can render our application to, we can continue with the initialization of Direct3D.

INTRODUCING DIRECT3D

In this section, we will take a very brief look at what is necessary to set up and initialize Direct3D. Again, most of the steps in this section should already be familiar to you. To do any type of 3D rendering, we first need to create an IDirect3D9 interface. This interface allows us to find different devices (e.g., graphics cards) installed on a specific computer. Through the IDirect3D9 interface, we can retrieve the IDirect3DDevice9 object we need to render our 3D game with. You could, of course, retrieve more than one IDirect3DDevice9 object if there's more than one graphics card installed. The IDirect3D9 object can also be used to retrieve the capabilities of a specific device. This information is useful during the initialization of your game because it allows you to set up the application differently according to things like maximum texture size, video memory, supported shader versions, and so on. Include the d3dx9.h header in your code, and then you can create your IDirect3D9 interface like this:

```
   //Create the IDirect3D9 interface
   IDirect3D9* d3d9 = Direct3DCreate9(D3D_SDK_VERSION);

   if(d3d9 == NULL)
   {
       //Creating the IDirect3D9 interface failed...
       //Exit application
   }
```

The `Direct3DCreate9()` function creates a new `IDirect3D9` interface for us. Should this function fail for some reason, it will return `NULL`. Before we can create a device that we can render things with, we must first define how we want the scene to be rendered. For this, we fill out a `D3DPRESENT_PARAMETERS` structure:

```
struct D3DPRESENT_PARAMETERS {
    UINT BackBufferWidth, BackBufferHeight;  //Width & Height
    D3DFORMAT BackBufferFormat;              //16, 24, 32 Bit
    UINT BackBufferCount;                    //Num backbuffers
    D3DMULTISAMPLE_TYPE MultiSampleType;     //Anti-aliasing
    DWORD MultiSampleQuality;                //AA quality
    D3DSWAPEFFECT SwapEffect;                //Buffer swap behavior
    HWND hDeviceWindow;                      //Window to draw to
    BOOL Windowed;                           //Fullscreen yes/no
    BOOL EnableAutoDepthStencil;             //Manage depth buffer?
    D3DFORMAT AutoDepthStencilFormat;        //Depth/Stencil buffer
    DWORD Flags;                             //Device flags
    UINT FullScreen_RefreshRateInHz;         //Fullscreen Refresh rate
    UINT PresentationInterval;               //when to present the image
};
```

Next, we create a new `IDirect3DDevice9` object using the `IDirect3D9::CreateDevice()` method:

```
HRESULT CreateDevice(
    UINT Adapter,                     //Display Adapter
    D3DDEVTYPE DeviceType,            //Hardware/Software rasterization
    HWND hFocusWindow,                //Window to draw to
    DWORD BehaviorFlags,              //HW/SW vertex processing
    D3DPRESENT_PARAMETERS *pPresentationParameters,
    IDirect3DDevice9** ppReturnedDeviceInterface      //Output
);
```

This is all pretty easy. The following code creates a new `D3DPRESENT_PARAMETERS` object, fills it out, and then creates a new device using the `IDirect3D9` interface:

```
//Set D3DPRESENT_PARAMETERS
D3DPRESENT_PARAMETERS d3dpp;

d3dpp.BackBufferWidth  = width;
d3dpp.BackBufferHeight = height;
...
```

```
//Fill other members of the d3dpp object here as well...

//Create the IDirect3D9 interface
IDirect3D9* d3d9 = Direct3DCreate9(D3D_SDK_VERSION);

//Create the IDirect3DDevice9
IDirect3DDevice9 *Device = NULL;

if(FAILED(d3d9->CreateDevice(D3DADAPTER_DEFAULT,
                             D3DDEVTYPE_HAL,
                             mainWindow,
                             D3DCREATE_HARDWARE_VERTEXPROCESSING,
                             &d3dpp,
                             &Device)))
{
    //Creating new device failed!
}

//Release IDirect3D9 interface
d3d9->Release();
```

That takes care of initializing an IDirect3DDevice9. Be sure to check the DirectX documentation for all possible parameters and variations. As you also may have noticed, we release the IDirect3D9 interface because we don't need it for anything else than acquiring the device.

Rendering a Scene Using the IDirect3DDevice9 Interface

After initializing a device, we can use it to render a scene. This process is best explained with the following example:

```
//Clear the viewport
Device->Clear(OL, NULL, D3DCLEAR_TARGET | D3DCLEAR_ZBUFFER,
              0x00000000, 1.0f, OL);

//Begin the scene
Device->BeginScene();

//Render scene here...

//End the scene.
Device->EndScene();
```

```
//Present the result on the screen
Device->Present(0, 0, 0, 0);
```

The IDirect3DDevice9::Clear() function clears the viewport we are about to render to. We will have a closer look at this function later on. The scene must be rendered between the two functions BeginScene() and EndScene(). Once we have rendered our scene, we call the Present() function, which presents the result to the screen. The parameters of this function specify the source rectangle of the back-buffer to use as well as the destination rectangle. In most cases, we want to use the entire backbuffer and project it to the entire window, in which case we set all the parameters to zero.

Checking the Capabilities of a Device

As mentioned before, we can use the IDirect3D9 interface to check the capabilities of a specific graphic card. The capabilities of a specific device are stored using the D3DCAPS9 structure. This structure has too many members to list all of them here (see the DirectX documentation). However, we can retrieve the capabilities of a graphic card like this:

```
D3DCAPS9 caps;
d3d9->GetDeviceCaps(D3DADAPTER_DEFAULT,      //Display adapter
                    D3DDEVTYPE_HAL,          //Device type
                    &caps);                  //Output
```

All the information about the device is now stored in the caps variable. We can now use the caps variable to check what features a device supports. For example, the following code checks that the device supports pixelshaders version 2.0 or greater:

```
if(caps.PixelShaderVersion < D3DPS_VERSION(2, 0))
{
    //The card does not support PS 2.0
}
```

To see the capabilities of your current display device, try the DirectX Caps Viewer program that accompanies the DirectX SDK. This is the same information available in code using the D3DCAPS9 structure.

CAUTION

Several of the examples in this book require a graphic card that supports vertexshaders and pixelshaders version 2.0 or greater.

THE STANDARD TEMPLATE LIBRARY

Novices in the field of game programming tend to reinvent the wheel. If you need a binary tree structure, for instance, you create one from scratch. The problem with this is that it takes a lot of time and tends to be far from optimal, if it works at all. Creating complex structures for handling objects is, after all, not what we want to spend our time doing. We want to make a game! Therefore, let's use the efficient, "one-implementation-fits-all" data structures of the Standard Template Library (STL). If you learn to use the STL, creating things like queues, stacks, arrays, binary trees, maps, sets, and so on become very easy. In addition to useful data structures, STL also contains several useful algorithms for sorting, editing, and traversing the different data structures. In this section, we will take a quick look at creating some common data structures, using the Standard Template Library.

The Vector Structure

The most used STL structure in this book is without doubt the vector class. This class maintains a list of objects that we can traverse, add new objects to, and remove objects from. All STL data structures are defined in the `std` namespace. The following piece of code creates a vector of integers:

```
#include <vector>
...

//Create a new vector of integers
std::vector<int> intVector;

//Add the square of i to the vector (0, 1, 4, 9, 16)
for(int i=0;i<5;i++)
    intVector.push_back(i * i);
```

This code creates a new vector that holds integers. Then, five numbers are pushed onto the vector using the `push_back()` function. This example might not be so exciting, but imagine we have a vector of user-defined objects—say, for example, monsters. We can then store all monsters in a vector and traverse it when we want to render all the monsters:

```
//Create monster vector
std::vector<MONSTER> monsters;
```

```
//Add some monsters
monsters.push_back(MONSTER(TROLL));
monsters.push_back(MONSTER(GOBLIN));
monsters.push_back(MONSTER(DRAGON));

...

//Render all monsters in the vector
for(int i=0;i<monsters.size();i++)
{
    monsters[i].Render();        //Render the i'th monster
}
```

Here we create a new vector holding monsters and add new monsters to the structure just like we did with simple integers. Then we traverse the vector using the size() function of the vector class. (This function returns the current number of items in the vector.) To access a certain item we use the overloaded []-operator. Surely you can see how easy-to-use data structures like this can benefit any game programmer.

The Queue Structure

The queue structure is a little bit different from the vector structure. In the vector structure, we can access any item in the vector at any time. However, in the queue structure, we can only access the item that is in the front of the queue. The queue operates according to the First In, First Out (FIFO) rule. A queue works just like a regular, real-life queue—there's no limit to the number of people that can stand in queue, but it is always the person who came first that gets served first, then the second person, and so on. In code, the STL queue can be used like this:

```
#include <queue>

//Create a new action queue
std::queue<ACTION> actionQueue;

//Add some actions
actionQueue.push(ACTION(WAKEUP));
actionQueue.push(ACTION(EAT));
actionQueue.push(ACTION(SLEEP));

//Carry out all actions
while(!actionQueue.empty())
```

```
{
    //Retrieve next action
    ACTION nextAction = actionQueue.front();

    //Carry out action
    nextAction.CarryOut();

    //Remove action from queue
    actionQueue.pop();
}
```

This piece of code creates a new queue that holds objects of the user-defined type ACTION. Some actions are added to the queue using the push() function. Then we perform the actions as long as the empty() function of the queue returns false. We retrieve the first item in the queue using the front() function and then remove that same item from the queue using the pop() function. The actions were added in the order: WAKEUP, EAT, SLEEP, and they will be performed in the same order.

The Stack Structure

The stack structure is very similar to the queue structure. But instead of the FIFO rule, the stack uses the rule Last In, First Out (LIFO). Imagine that you were to code the program for a dish-washing robot:

```
//stack of dirty plates...
std::stack<int> plates;

//Add some dishes
plates.push(1);                 //Plate #1
plates.push(2);                 //Plate #2
plates.push(3);                 //Plate #3

while(!plates.empty())
{
    //Get next plate to wash
    int plateToWash = plates.top();

    //Remove plate from stack
    plates.pop();

    //Wash the plate
    Wash(plateToWash);
}
```

The dirty plates get added to the stack in the order `plates.push(1)`, `plates.push(2)`, and `plates.push(3)`. When it's time to actually wash the dishes, it doesn't make sense to start with plate number one since it's underneath plates two and three. Using a stack structure will force the plates to be washed in the order three, two, and one.

These are only some of the many structures available in the Standard Template Library. If you ever have to build a collection of objects, chances are that there's already a better structure in the STL, whether it be priority queues, trees, or sets. This section has only scratched the surface of what can be done with the STL. For a good introduction to the STL see [Josuttis99].

THE D3DX LIBRARY

Another helping hand that is more specific to game programming is the D3DX library, which accompanies DirectX. The D3DX library contains functions and structures to help us with the most common problems we have when developing 3D games. This can be anything from loading meshes and textures to drawing lines or sprites, or performing 3D math—and much more. In fact, the project we will cover throughout this book could never have been completed if it weren't for the D3DX library. You can recognize functions and structures that belong to this library by the D3DX prefix. Table 3.1 shows some of the most commonly used data structures in the D3DX library

TABLE 3.1 Some Common D3DX Structures

D3DXVECTOR2	2D Vector, contains the members x, y
D3DXVECTOR3	3D Vector, contains the members x, y, z
D3DXVECTOR4	4D Vector, contains the members x, y, z, w
D3DXCOLOR	Color vector, contains the members r, g, b, a
D3DXMATERIAL	A material, contains texture filename, colors, etc.
D3DXMATRIX	A 4×4 matrix
D3DXPLANE	A plane, contains the members a, b, c, d
D3DXQUATERNION	A quaternion rotation, contains the members x, y, z, w

These are only some of the most-used data structures in the D3DX library. There are an even greater number of helper functions that use these structures— too many to list here, but we will have a closer look at some of the most common D3DX functions throughout this book. See the DirectX documentation for the full list of D3DX helper functions (type in D3DX in the index search).

DEBUGGING

In any large project you attempt to tackle, you will need some means to debug your code. In a full-screen, 3D application, you generally have two options: output debug information to the screen or output it to a separate file. If you choose to output your debug information to the screen, remember that the screen is only updated once every frame. This might mean that a serious bug crashes the program before it can run the part of the program that updates the screen. Therefore, the safest way to get your debug information is to dump it into a text file. The problem with this approach is that you have to wait until after your program has finished executing before you can read your debug information. However, the advantages of this method outweigh its downsides. We will, therefore, implement a class called DEBUG, which we will use to output debug information to a text file:

```
class DEBUG{
    public:
        DEBUG();
        ~DEBUG();
        void Print(char c[]);
};


static DEBUG debug;
```

In the debug.h header file, we define the DEBUG class, as shown, and also declare a static DEBUG object. Any other files that include the debug.h header file can now access the same debug object. The DEBUG class is implemented like this:

```
std::ofstream out("debug.txt");

DEBUG::DEBUG(){}

DEBUG::~DEBUG()
{
    //Close text file
    if(out.good())
```

```
                out.close();
        }

        void DEBUG::Print(char c[])
        {
            out << c << std::endl;
        }
```

Any other class can now include the debug class and use it like this:

```
        #include "debug.h"

        void SOME_CLASS::SomeFunction()
        {
            try
            {
                //Do some complicated calculations etc...
            }
            catch(...)
            {
                debug.Print("Something went wrong
                        in SOME_CLASS::SomeFunction()");
            }
        }
```

If our program crashes or behaves in unexpected ways, we can check the debug text file and see where our program crashed or what went wrong. Debugging is an art as old as coding. Learning how to isolate and find bugs is an essential skill for any programmer. No one writes perfect code on their first attempt. Having a class to handle all debugging makes it pretty easy to output information to a text file (or to the screen). Later, if you decide to change where your debug information is sent, you only have to edit the DEBUG class. For example, you might want a message box to appear with the error instead of writing it to a file.

THE ID3DXFONT CLASS

Often in a game we need to write simple 2D text messages to the screen. There are a few different ways we can do this, but then again, why reinvent the wheel? Accompanying the DirectX SDK, there's already a class called ID3DXFont for this purpose. Include d3dx9.h in your project to use this class. Then we can create a new ID3DXFont object, using the D3DXCreateFont() function:

```
ID3DXFont *pFont = NULL;

D3DXCreateFont(Device,                       //D3D device
               48,                           //Height
               0                             //Width
               FW_BOLD,                      //Weight
               1,                            //MipLevels
               FALSE,                        //Italic
               DEFAULT_CHARSET,              //CharSet
               OUT_DEFAULT_PRECIS,           //OutputPrecision
               DEFAULT_QUALITY,              //Quality
               DEFAULT_PITCH | FF_DONTCARE,  //PitchAndFamily
               "Arial",                      //Font Name
               &pFont);                      //output
```

Simply replace the font name with whatever font you would like to create. (See the DirectX documentation for a complete list of the parameters to this function.) Use an initiated font to render a text message to the screen, like this:

```
RECT r = {0, 0, 640, 480};

pFont->DrawText(NULL,                        //Sprite to use
                "Hello World!",              //Text
                -1,                          //Text length
                &r,                          //Destination rect
                DT_CENTER | DT_VCENTER,      //Flags
                0xffffffff);                 //Color
```

This function draws the supplied text in the destination rectangle, using the font. You can determine where in the rectangle you want the text to be drawn using a combination of the flags DT_LEFT, DT_TOP, DT_RIGHT, DT_BOTTOM, DT_CENTER, and DT_VCENTER. When you are done with a font object, simply release it by calling:

```
pFont->Release();
```

ON THE CD

Example 3.1

Have a look on the CD-ROM for the first sample program of this book. In it, we implement the application framework, initialize Direct3D and then use the ID3DXFont class to type the famous "Hello World!" message to the screen.

THE INTPOINT CLASS

Despite all of the functionality provided by the Standard Template Library, the D3DX library, and the DirectX common classes, there are some things we need to do on our own. Throughout this book, we will need a simple place to store an integer *x*- and *y*-coordinate, as well as all the related functionality. For this purpose, we have the INTPOINT class:

```
class INTPOINT{
    public:
        INTPOINT();
        INTPOINT(int _x, int _y);

        void operator=(const POINT rhs);
        bool operator==(const INTPOINT rhs);
        bool operator!=(const INTPOINT rhs);
        void operator+=(const INTPOINT rhs);
        void operator/=(const int rhs);
        INTPOINT operator/(const int d);
        INTPOINT operator-(const INTPOINT &rhs);
        INTPOINT operator+(const INTPOINT &rhs);
        INTPOINT operator-(const int &rhs);
        INTPOINT operator+(const int &rhs);

        float Distance(INTPOINT p);
        bool inRect(RECT r);
        void Set(int _x, int _y);

        int x,y;
    };
```

As you can see, the INTPOINT is nothing more than an *x*- and *y*-coordinate with added functionality. We overload all math and comparison operators that will help us write good-looking code using the INTPOINT class. For example, by overloading all these operators, we can do the following using our own INTPOINT class:

```
INTPOINT a(10, 10);
INTPOINT b(5, 5);

a /= 2;
b += 5;

INTPOINT c = (a + b / a + b * a);

if(c != a)
{
    //Do something...
}
```

As you can see, we use INTPOINT objects with all manners of mathematical and comparison operators (as long as they are defined, of course). This will let us do complex operations with INTPOINT objects, using very little code. We've also added functions for calculating the distance between two INTPOINT objects, checking if an INTPOINT object is within a rectangle, and so on. Creating small, general-purpose classes like this and defining all thinkable operators for them can greatly simplify your code. You could, for practice, implement your own rectangle and/or circle class, as well.

VERTEXSHADERS AND PIXELSHADERS

Shaders are very small programs that execute directly on the Graphical Processing Unit (GPU) of a computer. Shaders, at the time of this writing, come in two flavors: vertexshaders or pixelshaders. Vertexshaders perform per-vertex calculations, like vertex lighting, transformations, and so on. Pixelshaders, on the other hand, perform per-pixel calculations. This usually involves sampling pixels from different textures, blending pixels, alpha transparency calculations, and much more. In DirectX 10, the fixed function pipeline will be completely removed and replaced by shader programs. So it is prudent to start moving in this direction, and write more of our games using vertexshaders and pixelshaders.

A shader program can be stored as a separate file or simply as a character array inside our program. The benefit of storing the shader as an external text file is that we don't have to recompile our game to change it. The shaders can be compiled during the runtime of the game. We can then simply edit the text file and restart the game to edit a shader program. Being able to quickly edit a shader is, of course, good during the production of the game. But usually the shaders are hidden away inside the program before the game is released to prevent users tampering with them.

Throughout this project, we will cover more than 10 unique shader programs, all saved in individual text files using the .vs extension for vertexshaders and the .ps extension for pixelshaders. DirectX also supports effect files, where both vertexshaders and pixelshaders are stored in the same file (more on this later). However, in order to keep things simple and focused on the actual shaders, we separate vertexshaders from pixelshaders throughout this book. We will be writing the shaders using the Microsoft High-Level Shading Language (HLSL). HLSL allows us to write instructions for the GPU using syntax similar to C++.

Compiling a Shader

To read into and compile a vertexshader or pixelshader from a text file, we use the following D3DX library function:

```
HRESULT WINAPI D3DXCompileShaderFromFile(
    LPCTSTR pSrcFile,                    //Filename
    CONST D3DXMACRO* pDefines,           //Macros
    LPD3DXINCLUDE pInclude,              //Additional Includes
    LPCTSTR pFunctionName,               //Entry Function
    LPCTSTR pTarget,                     //Target Shader Version
    DWORD Flags,                         //Compile flags
    LPD3DXBUFFER* ppShader,              //Output
    LPD3DXBUFFER *ppErrorMsgs,           //Error messages
    LPD3DXSHADER_CONSTANTTABLE *ppConstantTable //Constant table
);
```

This is quite a powerful function. We can supply our own defined macros and additional include files to it. However, we won't use this functionality, and so just supply NULL to these parameters. The parameters we will use are:

pSrcFile: The source text file containing the shader program.

pFunctionName: The entry function in the shader (most often Main).

pTarget: Shader version to compile to. Vertexshaders use either vs_1_1 or vs_2_0. Pixelshaders can use ps_1_1, ps_1_2, ps_1_3, ps_1_4, or ps_2_0.

ppErrorMsgs: This returns a list of errors that occurred during the compile.

ppConstantTable: This is a list of handles to all variables defined in the shader. From the constant table, you can retrieve a handle to a specific variable. This handle can then be used to change the value of a shader variable.

This function can be used like this:

```
HRESULT hRes;
LPD3DXBUFFER Code = NULL;
LPD3DXBUFFER ErrorMsgs = NULL;
ID3DXConstantTable *ConstantTable = NULL;
IDirect3DPixelShader9 *PixelShader = NULL;

//Compile Shader
D3DXCompileShaderFromFile("someShaderFile.ps",
                          NULL,
                          NULL,
                          "Main",
                          "ps_2_0",
                          D3DXSHADER_DEBUG,
                          &Code,
                          &ErrorMsgs,
                          &ConstantTable);

//If an error occurred
if(ErrorMsgs != NULL)
{
    debug.Print((char*)ErrorMsgs->GetBufferPointer());
}
else
{
    //Create Shader
    Device->CreatePixelShader(
                (DWORD*)Code->GetBufferPointer(),
                &PixelShader);
}
```

This piece of code compiles a shader from an external file to a version 2.0 pixelshader. The exact same process is used for a vertexshader. Once the code has been compiled, we either type out compile errors or we create the new shader using the CreatePixelShader() function of the IDirect3DDevice9 interface. To activate a shader, we must call either the SetPixelShader() function or the SetVertexShader() function of the IDirect3DDevice9 interface, like this:

```
Device->SetPixelShader(somePixelShader);
```

Any rendering done after this call will use the provided shader. To remove an active shader, simply provide NULL to the SetPixelShader() function or the SetVertexShader() function.

Setting Shader Variables

In the shader program, we can have many different types of variables stored. Some of these variables we have to be able to change from our program code. We do this by first retrieving a handle to the specific variable from the constant table of the shader. (The constant table was created during the compile of the shader in the previous section.)

```
D3DXHANDLE varHandle;
varHandle = ConstantTable->GetConstantByName(
                        NULL,        //Root
                        "varName");       //Variable name
```

We can now use the handle to set the variable used in the shader program, like this:

```
//Set a Float value
ConstantTable->SetFloat(Device, varHandle, 0.3435f);

//Set a Matrix variable
ConstantTable->SetMatrix(Device, varHandle, &someMatrix);
```

The constant table has several of these functions to set different types of variables. Some other common ones are: SetFloatArray(), SetInt(), SetVector(), and SetValue(). For a complete list of these functions, see the DirectX documentation.

To help us encapsulate the low-level details of reading in a shader program and activating it, we have created the SHADER class. Vertexshaders and pixelshaders are represented differently inside this class, but for anyone using a SHADER object, the interface for both vertexshaders and pixelshaders is the same. We will use this class throughout this book whenever we deal with shaders.

SETTING UP A PROJECT IN VISUAL STUDIO® 7.0

This final section is meant to help you set up a project in Visual Studio. Hopefully, it will help reduce the frustration of getting the various sample projects to compile.

Adding Include Directories

For the samples in this book to compile properly on your computer, you must first add some search paths in Visual Studio to the DirectX include files. This is something you only have to do once, after you've installed the DirectX SDK.

Click Options in the Tools menu. This opens up the window shown in Figure 3.2. Select Projects and VC++ Directories (Figure 3.2, marked 1). In the Show Directories for drop-down box (Figure 3.2, marked 2), select Include Files. Create new entries by using the button in Figure 3.2 marked 3. Add the following directory if it is not already there:

C:\DXSDK\Include

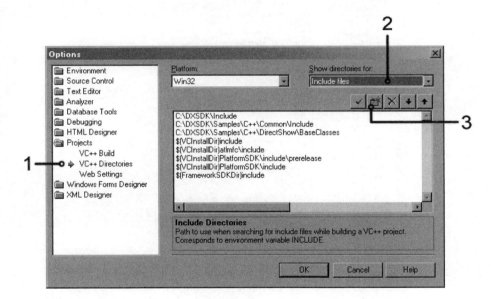

FIGURE 3.2   Adding include directories.

Also, select Library Files in the Show directories for: drop-down box. In the same way as before, add:

C:\DXSDK\Lib

This section assumes that you have installed the DirectX SDK at the location C:\DXSDK\. If this is not the case, then alter all the paths accordingly.

Linking Libraries to a Project

To link library files to your project, open the Solution Explorer window. Either click Solution Explorer in the Views menu or press CTRL+ALT+L. Right-click your current project and select properties. This will bring up the window shown in Figure 3.3.

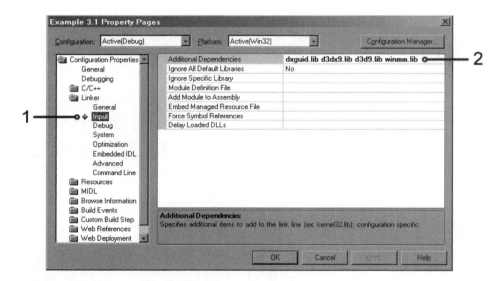

FIGURE 3.3   Project properties.

Click Linker, then Input in the list to the left (Figure 3.3, marked 1). In the Additional Dependencies field (Figure 3.3, marked 2), enter any libraries you wish to link to the project.

You have to link libraries manually for each project that you create. Here's a list of the libraries used throughout this book:

■ d3d9.lib (Direct3D9)
■ d3dx9.lib (D3DX Library)
■ dxguid.lib (DirectX Interfaces)

- dsound.lib (DirectSound)
- strmiids.lib (DirectShow)
- dinput8.lib (DirectInput)
- winmm.lib (Windows Multimedia)
- vfw32.lib (Video for Windows)

SUMMARY

This chapter is meant to provide the practical base on which we will build the rest of our game. We have covered the application framework—how to initialize Direct3D. We had a brief look at the Standard Template Library and the D3DX library. We've also covered some general-purpose structures, like the INTPOINT structure and the ID3DXFont class. We've had a brief look at creating and maintaining vertexshaders and pixelshaders, and finally we covered some common pitfalls related to setting up a project in Visual Studio.

Remember that you are strongly encouraged to use the DirectX documentation to look up flags, function parameters, and structure members that aren't covered in this book. Another thing to keep in mind throughout this book is that often the code presented is written with the purpose of clarity, not optimization. We will talk some more about optimization later on. Also, in order to keep the code as short as possible, error-checking has been kept to a minimum. It is, for example, always good practice to perform the FAILED() or SUCCEEDED() test on any function that returns a HRESULT variable. Don't assume that everything will work as planned. Check to make sure it actually did. In the next chapter, we will start our journey toward building a real-time strategy game by having a look at generating terrains.

EXERCISES

- Make your own RECTANGLE class. Give it member functions to determine if two rectangles intersect, if an INTPOINT is within it, and so on.
- Extend the DEBUG class to also output debug information to the screen, using the ID3DXFont class.

REFERENCES

[Josuttis99] Josuttis, Nicolai, *The C++ Standard Library, A Tutorial and Reference.* Addison-Wesley, 1999.

4 Creating the Terrain

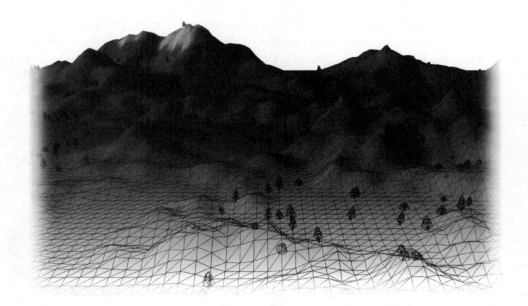

E ven though you might not think of it as such, the terrain is one of the most important and most complex objects of any real-time strategy game. The terrain is the chess board on which the battles are fought. Creating terrains is not a small subject, and there are entire books written on it. Unfortunately, this chapter cannot cover all possible aspects of terrain generation. So if you feel that you need more information, you can refer to any of the articles listed at the end of this chapter.

As mentioned in previous chapters, performance is one of the key aspects when making an RTS game. Therefore, we must have a terrain that can be created and rendered, and handle pathfinding at a minimum of CPU cost. The terrain class we cover in this chapter will do all this and more. It is a massive piece of the puzzle, one that's worth spending some extra time on before moving on. Having a good, solid terrain class will help you when you are creating things like your AI system.

The most common way of creating terrains is by constructing a regular mesh from a heightmap (i.e., a 2D array of height values). In this chapter, you will learn how to create different heightmaps by loading them from a file, generating them at random, or editing them in a map editor. Then you'll learn how to create a regular mesh from these heightmaps and how to texturize that mesh using advanced techniques, such as texture splatting. We won't create one big mesh for the entire terrain because this is rather inefficient. It's better to split the terrain up into smaller, rectangular patches. This allows us to render larger terrains. There are many methods to deal with rendering very large terrains in multiple levels of detail. These methods are often used for Massively Multiplayer Online Role-Playing Games (MMORPG), for instance. However, for real-time strategy games where the terrain size is always limited, these methods are a little bit overkill. We will also take a look at populating the terrain with objects such as stones and trees. To do this, we need to learn how to effectively load meshes and render them using the X-file format. We will also take a look at the functional side of a terrain and see how to integrate a unit pathfinding system using the same map nodes we used to create the terrain mesh. In short, to generate a terrain, there are four steps we need to implement, as shown in Figure 4.1.

| Step 1 | Step 2 | Step 3 | Step 4 |

FIGURE 4.1   Four general steps needed to create an RTS terrain.

Step 1: Create/Load a Heightmap. First we generate the heightmap by reading it in from an image file, creating it at random, or reading it in from a map file created with a map editor. The important thing is that at the end of this step, we have a 2D array of heights.

Step 2: Create Terrain Patches. From the heightmap, we create our terrain patches. A patch is a rectangular subset of the entire terrain mesh. Instead of creating one large mesh covering the entire terrain, we create these subsets because they are much more efficient to render. It also allows us to have much larger terrains.

Step 3: Terrain Texturing. Once we have created our patches, we generate or apply textures to the terrain to make it look more visually pleasing. There are several ways we can do this. We will cover techniques ranging from using precreated textures to advanced texture splatting using pixelshaders.

Step 4: Add Terrain Objects. Next we want to add things like trees, stones, and debris to the terrain to break the monotony. To do this, we need to learn how to load X-file models with textures and how to render them.

These are the four steps we need to implement in order to create a nice-looking terrain. However, there is another important thing we need before we can use our terrain in a real-time strategy game, and that is pathfinding. Our units need to be able to find their way across the terrain, and at the same time avoid doing impossible things like walking on water or through trees, and so on. But first, let us define some terrain lingo.

Map Node: A certain point on the terrain connected in a grid-like fashion to other map nodes. Together they form the map or terrain. Figure 4.2 shows a map with 5 × 5 map nodes.

Map Tile: The rectangular area whose four corners are marked by map nodes. Note that in Figure 4.2, the map has 5 × 5 map nodes but only 4 × 4 map tiles.

Heightmap: A 2D array holding the heights in the y-direction of the different map nodes. By varying the values in the heightmap, many different-looking terrains can be generated. If all the values in this array are equal, then this results in a completely flat terrain.

Pathfinding: The processes of finding a path between two map nodes on the map while avoiding obstacles (both static and dynamic).

FIGURE 4.2   Interconnected map nodes, together forming the terrain.

HEIGHTMAPS

Usually, heightmaps are created from an image file or at random, using some sort of noise function. Some people prefer to store heightmaps using a BYTE for each height to save memory. This gives you 0–255 possible heights for each map node, which is enough for most applications, especially if some smoothing is done before creating the terrain mesh. In the terrain examples, we use float values for the heightmaps to get some extra precision. Here's how we define our HEIGHTMAP structure:

```
struct HEIGHTMAP
{
    //Functions
    HEIGHTMAP(INTPOINT _size);
    ~HEIGHTMAP();
    void Release();

    HRESULT LoadFromFile(char fileName[]);
    HRESULT CreateRandomHeightMap(int seed, float noiseSize,
                                  float persistance, int octaves);

    //variables
    INTPOINT m_size;          //Size of heightmap
    float m_maxHeight;        //The height of the highest peak
    float *m_pHeightMap;      //Array with height values
};
```

This is our basic HEIGHTMAP structure. In the next three examples, we are going to add functionality to this structure to handle all our heightmap needs. Here's how we set up the m_pHeightMap array:

```
//Create a new 2D array with m_size.x * m_size.y height values
m_pHeightMap = new float[m_size.x * m_size.y];

//Set all heights to 0.0f
memset(m_pHeightMap, 0, sizeof(float) * m_size.x * m_size.y);
```

When we want to query a specific value from the m_HeightMap array, we do it like this:

```
float height_x_y = m_pHeightMap[x + y * m_size.x];
```

Loading a Heightmap from an Image

As noted in the previous section, each map node has its own height. The easiest way to set these heights up is to load them from an image file. This can be done very easily using a D3DX library function. First, we need to create a heightmap texture that we want to load. This file can be a bitmap, JPEG, DDS, or any of the other format supported by Direct3D. We then use the following D3DX function to load the texture:

```
HRESULT D3DXCreateTextureFromFileEx(
        LPDIRECT3DDEVICE9 pDevice,              //Device
        LPCTSTR pSrcFile,                       //Image filename
        UINT Width, UINT Height,                //target width & height
        UINT MipLevels,                         //Miplevels
        DWORD Usage,                            //Texture usage
        D3DFORMAT Format,                       //Image format
        D3DPOOL Pool,                           //memory pool
        DWORD Filter,                           //Image filter
        DWORD MipFilter,                        //Mipmap filter
        D3DCOLOR ColorKey,                      //Transparent color?
        D3DXIMAGE_INFO *pSrcInfo,               //Output image info
        PALETTEENTRY *pPalette,                 //Palette
        LPDIRECT3DTEXTURE9 *ppTexture           //Texture Output
    );
```

For a complete list of the parameters and the different formats, pools, and so forth, see the DirectX documentation. The following code implements the HEIGHTMAP::LoadFromFile() function:

```
HRESULT HEIGHTMAP::LoadFromFile(char fileName[])
{
    //Reset the heightMap to 0.0f
    memset(m_pHeightMap, 0,
            sizeof(float) * m_size.x * m_size.y);

    //Initiate the texture variables
    IDirect3DTexture9 *heightMapTexture = NULL;

    //Load the texture (and scale it to our heightMap size)
    D3DXCreateTextureFromFileEx(
                    Device, fileName, m_size.x, m_size.y,
                    1, D3DUSAGE_DYNAMIC, D3DFMT_L8,
                    D3DPOOL_DEFAULT, D3DX_DEFAULT,
                    D3DX_DEFAULT, NULL, NULL, NULL,
                    &heightMapTexture);

    //Lock the texture
    D3DLOCKED_RECT sRect;
    heightMapTexture->LockRect(0, &sRect, NULL, NULL);
    BYTE *bytes = (BYTE*)sRect.pBits;
```

```
//Extract height values from the texture
for(int y=0;y<m_size.y;y++)
    for(int x=0;x<m_size.x;x++)
    {
        BYTE *b = bytes + y * sRect.Pitch + x;
        heightMap[x + y * m_size.x] =
            ((*b / 255.0f) * m_maxHeight;
    }

//Unlock the texture
heightMapTexture->UnlockRect(0);
}
```

That was easy. First we reset our 2D array holding our height values. The use of the memset() function is a fast way of setting all the values in the array to 0.0f without having to loop through them. Then we create and load our texture using the size INTPOINT variable to indicate how large we want the resulting texture to be. Note that we set the Format to D3DFMT_L8, which stands for 8-bit luminance, only. This transforms any image into a black-and-white 8-bit image, which is perfect for describing a heightmap. Each height is now stored as a single byte in the image whether the original was a color image or not.

The heightmap could also be stored as an 8-bit RAW file in Photoshop and then read in with a normal binary reader. However, using the D3DXCreateTexture-FromFileEx() function to load heightmaps gives us a bit more flexibility and allows us to store heightmaps using the JPEG file format, which saves a whole lot of disk space. It also allows us to scale the image to any size. For example, we can load a 100 × 100-pixel image and create a 1000 × 1000-node heightmap, or vice versa. After the texture has been loaded, we lock the texture to be able to access the byte information within it. The m_maxHeight variable controls how high our highest peak will be. Use this variable to scale the heightmap in the *y*-axis.

ON THE CD

Example 4.1

The HEIGHTMAP structure in this example reads in a heightmap from a file, and creates and renders a particle cloud according to the heightmap file. We have extended the HEIGHTMAP structure to render a particle cloud according to the height values. Don't worry about how the particles are created at this stage. We will cover particles and other effects in more detail in Chapter 12.

Random Heightmaps

Another way to create heightmaps is to generate them at random. This approach is, of course, less predictable to deal with, but on the other hand, you can get more variation in your game. We're going to implement a Perlin noise function to create our random heightmaps. Perlin noise was invented by Ken Perlin [Perlin99], and it is one of the most common ways of creating procedural noise. Perlin noise works by adding together noise of different frequencies. To do this, we first need a number generator that returns the same random number for a specific seed. Here is a noise function that does just that:

```
float Noise(int x)
{
    x = (x<<13) ^ x;
    return (1.0f - ((x * (x*x * 15731 + 789221)
            + 1376312589) &
            0x7fffffff) / 1073741824.0f);
}
```

All you need to know about this function is that it returns a float value in the range −1.0f to 1.0f. Next we need to be able to interpolate between two random values. Linear interpolation is a bit to crude, so use either cosine interpolation (faster) or cubic interpolation (more accurate, but also more expensive).

```
float CosInterpolate(float v1, float v2, float a)
{
    float angle = a * D3DX_PI;
    float prc = (1.0f - cos(angle)) * 0.5f;
    return v1*(1.0f - prc) + v2*prc;
}
```

This CosInterpolate() function interpolates between the two values v1 and v2 using the cosine angle rather than just the percentage (a = 0.0 to 1.0), as is used in a linear interpolation. This gives us a smoother interpolation that will result in a nicer looking Perlin noise. Now, let's use these two functions to generate a noise curve. Generate a few random numbers using the Noise function and then create a curve by interpolating between these numbers using the CosInterpolate() function. The result might look like the curves shown in Figure 4.3.

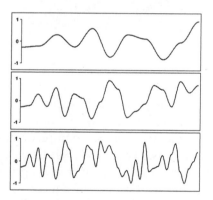

FIGURE 4.3 Three different noise curves.

The first curve was generated with 10 random numbers, the second with 20, and the third with 40 numbers. For each curve, the number of random numbers used (or frequency) is doubled. Each doubled frequency is called an octave. To create 1D-Perlin noise, we need to add these curves together. But as the frequency of each curve increases, we want that the amplitude (or influence) of each curve to decrease. We control how much the amplitude decreases per octave using persistence.

$$\text{Amplitude} = \text{Persistance}^{Oct}$$

If we have a persistence value less than 1.0, then the amplitude will be increasingly less for each octave. If the persistence value is greater than 1.0, then we will end up with a very spiky curve, since the amplitude of each consecutive octave will increase. The Perlin-noise curve in Figure 4.4 was created by adding together the three noise curves from Figure 4.3, with a persistence value of 0.5. (This means that the amplitude is cut in half for each octave.)

FIGURE 4.4   The resulting Perlin noise curve.

This exact same thing can be done in 2D, 3D, or any other number of dimensions, as well. Figure 4.5 shows how this looks in 2D, using nine octaves of noise.

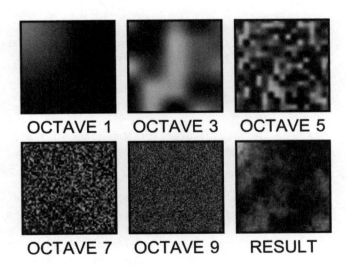

OCTAVE 1   OCTAVE 3   OCTAVE 5

OCTAVE 7   OCTAVE 9   RESULT

FIGURE 4.5   Perlin noise in 2D.

The resulting 2D Perlin noise is excellent to use for heightmaps. We can regulate the noise size, the persistence, and the number of octaves used to get some control over how the final noise will look. The following function extends our HEIGHTMAP structure to create random heightmaps using Perlin noise.

```
HRESULT HEIGHTMAP::CreateRandomHeightMap(int seed,
                                         float noiseSize,
                                         float persistence,
                                         int octaves)
{
    //For each map node
    for(int y=0;y<m_size.y;y++)
        for(int x=0;x< m_size.x;x++)
        {
            //Scale x & y to the range of [0.0, noiseSize]
            float xf = ((float)x / (float)m_size.x) * noiseSize;
            float yf = ((float)y / (float)m_size.y) * noiseSize;
            float total = 0.0f;

            // For each octave
            for(int i=0;i<octaves;i++)
            {
                //Calculate frequency and amplitude
                //(different for each octave)
                float freq = (float)pow(2, i);
                float amp = (float)pow(persistence, i);

                //Calculate the x,y noise coordinates
                float tx = xf * freq;
                float ty = yf * freq;
                int tx_int = (int)tx;
                int ty_int = (int)ty;

                //Calculate the fractions of x & y
                float fracX = tx - tx_int;
                float fracY = ty - ty_int;

                //Get noise per octave for these 4 points
                float v1, v2, v3, v4;
                v1 = Noise(tx_int + ty_int * 57 + seed);
                v2 = Noise(tx_int + 1 + ty_int * 57 + seed);
                v3 = Noise(tx_int + (ty_int+1) * 57 + seed);
                v4 = Noise(tx_int + 1 + (ty_int+1) * 57 + seed);
```

```
            //Smooth noise in the X-axis
            float i1 = CosInterpolate(v1, v2, fracX);
            float i2 = CosInterpolate(v3, v4, fracX);

            //Smooth in the Y-axis
            total += CosInterpolate(i1, i2, fracY) * amp;
        }

        //Save to heightMap
        m_pHeightMap[x + y * m_size.x] =
            total * m_maxHeight;
    }
}
```

The inputs to this function (e.g., `seed`, `noiseSize`, `persistence`, and `octaves`) control how the final noise will look. These input values are the ones you can play with to generate different heightmaps.

Example 4.2

Have a look at Example 4.2 on the CD-ROM. If you try to create heightmaps with low persistence, you will tend to get rolling landscapes, while if you have a high persistence, you get a more "mountainy" look. In this example, the result of the total noise is clamped to [-1.0, 1.0]. This can produce some nice effects, such as a canyon landscape (high noise size, high persistence). Any specific seed value will generate a specific terrain for a given size and persistence value. This means we can recreate any heightmap by simply feeding this function with the same seed, size, and persistence values.

A Heightmap Editor

Your third choice would be to create an editor and edit the heightmap yourself. As with most games these days, RTS games use a level editor to create the different terrains, to place initial units, and so on. When you create your RTS game, a map editor is a great tool for creating maps to test your game with. In this section, we will have a quick look at how heightmaps can be generated using a very simple map editor. We add the following function to the HEIGHTMAP structure:

```
void HEIGHTMAP::RaiseTerrain(RECT r, float f)
{
    for(int y=r.top;y<=r.bottom;y++)
        for(int x=r.left;x<=r.right;x++)
        {
            m_pHeightMap[x + y * m_size.x] += f;

            if(m_pHeightMap[x + y * m_size.x] < -m_maxHeight)
                m_pHeightMap[x + y * m_size.x] = -m_maxHeight;
            if(m_pHeightMap[x + y * m_size.x] > m_maxHeight)
                m_pHeightMap[x + y * m_size.x] = m_maxHeight;
        }
}
```

This function is very simple; it adds the value f to all map nodes within the rectangle r and caps the result to [-m_maxHeight, m_maxHeight]. This, of course, creates a very blocky and unnatural-looking terrain, which brings us to the next operation we need to perform—smoothing. There are a number of different filters you could apply to make your terrain look the way you want it. Smoothing is one of them. The following function smoothes the entire heightmap:

```
void HEIGHTMAP::SmoothTerrain()
{
    //Create temporary heightmap
    float *hm = new float[m_size.x * m_size.y];
    memset(hm, 0, sizeof(float) * m_size.x * m_size.y);

    for(int y=0;y<m_size.y;y++)
    {
        for(int x=0;x<m_size.x;x++)
        {
            float totalHeight = 0.0f;
            int noNodes = 0;
```

```
        for(int y1=y-1;y1<=y+1;y1++)
        {
            for(int x1=x-1;x1<=x+1;x1++)
            if(x1 >= 0 && x1 < m_size.x &&
                y1 >= 0 && y1 < m_size.y)
            {
                totalHeight +=
                    m_pHeightMap[x1 + y1 * m_size.x];
                noNodes++;
            }
        }

        hm[x + y * m_size.x] =
            totalHeight / (float)noNodes;
        }
    }

    //Replace old heightmap with smoothed heightmap
    delete [] m_pHeightMap;
    m_pHeightMap = hm;
}
```

This piece of code takes all surrounding map nodes for each map node, sums up the total height, and then divides by the number of nodes. You can apply this filter to any of the previous examples, as well, to smooth out the result.

ON THE CD

Example 4.3

Check out Example 4.3 on the CD-ROM, in which a simple heightmap editor has been implemented. There's also a rudimentary camera implementation in this example, as well—a preview of Chapter 5.

One last thing to mention about random heightmaps is that better results are often produced if you multiply two or more heightmaps. Consider the random maps in Figure 4.6.

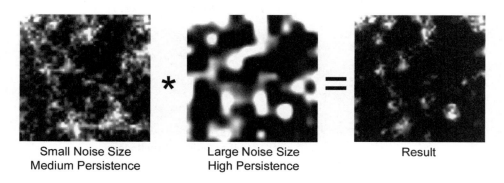

Small Noise Size   Large Noise Size   Result
Medium Persistence   High Persistence

FIGURE 4.6 Multiplying two random heightmaps.

Figure 4.7 shows a mesh created from the resulting heightmap in Figure 4.6.

FIGURE 4.7 A mesh created from the resulting heightmap in Figure 4.6.

Using the resulting heightmap produces a much better effect than using either one of the original heightmaps. You must make sure that your map has enough flat areas to build buildings on, and so forth. A too-noisy map doesn't provide enough flat land to play the game on and is therefore useless for an RTS game. Get to know your noise functions and filters. They are a great tool when creating random maps; and as you'll see later, we will use them to place trees, rocks, and other objects, as well. There's a lot of literature online and in print about procedural textures, which are very helpful when creating random terrains.

Here's some code that overloads the `*=` operator of our HEIGHTMAP structure and enables easy multiplication of two heightmaps:

```
void HEIGHTMAP::operator*=(const HEIGHTMAP &rhs)
{
    for(int y=0;y<m_size.y;y++)
        for(int x=0;x<m_size.x;x++)
        {
            //Scale heightmaps to the range of [0.0, 1.0]
            float a;
            a = m_pHeightMap[x + y * m_size.x] / m_maxHeight;
            float b = 1.0f;
            if(x <= rhs.m_size.x && y <= rhs.m_size.y)
                b = rhs.m_pHeightMap[x + y * m_size.x]
                    / rhs.m_maxHeight;

            //Multiply heightmaps and scale to [0.0, m_maxHeight]
            m_pHeightMap[x + y * m_size.x] =
                a * b * m_maxHeight;
        }
}
```

This piece of code scales each entry in the two heightmaps to the range [0.0, 1.0] and multiplies them. The result is then scaled back to the original heightmap's range and stored. After overloading the `*=` operator, all you need to do in order to multiply two heightmaps is the following:

```
//Create 2 heightmaps
HEIGHTMAP h1(sizeA, maxHeightA), h2(sizeB, maxHeightB);

//Initiate them
h1.CreateRandomHeightMap(seed1, size1, persist1, oct1);
h2.CreateRandomHeightMap(seed2, size2, persist2, oct2);

h1 *= h2;       //Multiply them... Done (result stored in h1)
```

There are many articles online about procedural terrain generation and random terrain generation. Check out [Olsen04] for a really interesting article on procedural terrain generation. Also, be sure to see [Shoemaker04] for an article about how terrains for RTS games can be "grown" to produce equal and fair terrains for all players. Now let's take a look at how to create a mesh like the one shown in Figure 4.7.

CREATING THE TERRAIN MESH

Now we know what we need in order to generate heightmaps in a few different ways. In the previous examples, we've used a simple particle cloud to visualize our heightmaps. Now it's time to generate a mesh from our heightmaps. Whether you want to load your heightmaps from a file, generate them at random, or use a heightmap editor, the mesh is created in the same way. At the beginning of this chapter, it was mentioned that we would create many mesh patches, rather than one big mesh. The reason we do this is that it is much more efficient, since we only need to render those patches that are within the viewing volume (more on this in the next chapter). Having patches also allows us to render a larger terrain than one big mesh would allow. This is because we use 16-bit WORD instances to index vertices in the index buffer of a mesh. Sixteen bits allows us a maximum of 32,768 vertices, which gives us a terrain mesh with roughly 180×180 vertices. To create our terrain mesh, we need three things: a vertex declaration, a patch structure, and a terrain class.

> **Vertex Declaration:** The vertex declaration is used to declare what information is stored within each vertex. Each vertex can contain one or more of the following: a position, a normal, a color, or texture coordinates.
>
> **Patch Structure:** This creates and renders a single mesh covering a small part of the entire terrain.
>
> **Terrain Class:** The terrain class creates and contains all the patches of the entire terrain.

So, let's first define the vertex structure that we will use to create our terrain mesh.

```
struct TERRAINVertex
{
    TERRAINVertex(){...}
    TERRAINVertex(D3DXVECTOR3 pos, D3DCOLOR col)
    {
        position = pos;
        color = col;
        normal = D3DXVECTOR3(0.0f, 1.0f, 0.0f);
    }

    D3DXVECTOR3 position, normal;
    D3DCOLOR color;
    static const DWORD FVF;
};
```

```
const DWORD TERRAINVertex::FVF = D3DFVF_XYZ | D3DFVF_NORMAL |
                                 D3DFVF_DIFFUSE;
```

If you aren't familiar with creating your own vertex formats, then you should read up on it. This particular vertex format contains a position, a normal, and a color. At the moment, we won't worry about things like texture coordinates. (We'll cover these in more detail later.) The Flexible Vertex Format (FVF) variable tells the fixed function pipeline how large our vertices are. Note that at the moment we just set the vertex normal to point straight up, but if you want to calculate it yourself, then just add a parameter to the constructor, like the position or the color. Next is our PATCH structure definition.

```
struct PATCH{
    PATCH();
    ~PATCH();
    void Release();
    HRESULT CreateMesh(HEIGHTMAP &hm, RECT source,
                    IDirect3DDevice9* Dev, int index);
    void Render();

    IDirect3DDevice9* m_pDevice;
    ID3DXMesh *m_pMesh;
};
```

We will build on this structure to handle everything related to a single patch, generating the mesh as well as rendering it. At the moment, we are going to create a vertex colored, nontexture mesh from a heightmap. We have an ID3DXMesh interface to hold our mesh structure. (See the Microsoft DirectX documentation for more information.)

If you are manually creating a mesh in code, there are three important things to consider about a mesh: the vertex buffer, the index buffer, and the attribute buffer. The vertex buffer holds the vertices, and the index buffer describes which vertices create which triangles. Finally, the attribute buffer can be used to split a mesh up into different parts. We will use the attribute buffer later on when we do tile-based terrain texturing. But first, let's see how we create the vertices for the terrain:

```
HRESULT PATCH::CreateMesh(HEIGHTMAP &hm, RECT source,
                    IDirect3DDevice9* Dev)
{
    Device = Dev;
```

```
int width = source.right - source.left;
int height = source.bottom - source.top;
int nrVert = (width + 1) * (height + 1);
int nrTri = width * height * 2;

D3DXCreateMeshFVF(nrTri, nrVert, D3DXMESH_MANAGED,
                  TERRAINVertex::FVF, Device, &m_pMesh);

//Create vertices
TERRAINVertex* ver = NULL;
m_pMesh->LockVertexBuffer(0,(void**)&ver);
for(int z=source.top, z0 = 0;z<=source.bottom;z++, z0++)
    for(int x=source.left, x0 = 0;
        x<=source.right;x++, x0++)
    {
        // Generate color & position for each vertex
        D3DCOLOR col = {...};
        D3DXVECTOR3 pos;
        pos = D3DXVECTOR3(
                x,
                hm.m_pHeightMap[x + z * hm.m_size.x],
                -z);

        ver[z0 * (width + 1) + x0] =
            TERRAINVertex(pos, col);
    }

m_pMesh->UnlockVertexBuffer();

//To be continued...
```

This function creates a terrain patch from a subset of the heightmap described by the source rectangle. We create color and position as a function of the height value, just like with the particle clouds in previous examples. Between the LockVertexBuffer() call and the UnlockVertexBuffer() call, you can use the pointer ver[index] to read/write from the vertex buffer as you like. Take care though not to read/write beyond the vertex limit because this will generate a runtime error. Once we have filled our vertex buffer with the correct vertices, it's time to have a look at the next step—the index buffer:

```
//PATCH::CreateMesh() Part II
```

```
//Calculate Indices
WORD* ind = 0;
m_pMesh->LockIndexBuffer(0,(void**)&ind);
int index = 0;

for(int z=source.top, z0 = 0;z<source.bottom;z++, z0++)
    for(int x=source.left, x0 = 0;x<source.right;x++, x0++)
    {
        //Triangle 1
        ind[index++] =   z0   * (width + 1) + x0;
        ind[index++] =   z0   * (width + 1) + x0 + 1;
        ind[index++] = (z0+1) * (width + 1) + x0;

        //Triangle 2
        ind[index++] = (z0+1) * (width + 1) + x0;
        ind[index++] =   z0   * (width + 1) + x0 + 1;
        ind[index++] = (z0+1) * (width + 1) + x0 + 1;
    }

m_pMesh->UnlockIndexBuffer();

//To be continued... again...
```

Right after our vertices have been created, we lock the index buffer and start making our triangles. This code will create a regular grid using our vertices. As before, once we have locked our index buffer with a WORD pointer, we can use it to read/write to the buffer as we want. Finally, we need to set the attribute buffer before we can start using our mesh.

```
//PATCH::CreateMesh() Part III

//Set Attributes
DWORD *att = 0;
m_pMesh->LockAttributeBuffer(0,&att);
memset(att, 0, sizeof(DWORD)*nrTri);
m_pMesh->UnlockAttributeBuffer();
```

Here we lock a DWORD pointer to the attribute buffer and the use the memset() function to set the whole buffer to zero, simultaneously. This means that the whole mesh will be part of group zero. Further on when we talk about tile-based texturing, we will set different triangles of the mesh to different groups. The last thing to do before the mesh is complete is to calculate the vertex normals.

```
//Compute normals
D3DXComputeNormals(m_pMesh, NULL);
```

That's it! Let the D3DX library do all the hard work. The D3DXComputeNormals() function sums up all triangle normals of those faces connected to a specific vertex and stores the average value as the vertex normal. Now that we've created a mesh patch, all we need to do is render it.

```
void PATCH::Render()
{
    //Draw mesh
    if(m_pMesh != NULL)
        m_pMesh->DrawSubset(0);        //Renders Group 0
}
```

The ID3DXMesh::DrawSubset() function takes an attribute ID as a parameter. Remember how we set the whole attribute buffer to zero? When we call Draw Subset(0), it means we will draw the whole mesh. Only one more component left to go: the TERRAIN class.

```
class TERRAIN{
    public:
        TERRAIN();
        void Init(IDirect3DDevice9* Dev, INTPOINT _size);
        void Release();
        void GenerateRandomTerrain(int numPatches);
        void CreatePatches(int numPatches);
        void Render();

    private:
        IDirect3DDevice9* m_pDevice;
        INTPOINT m_size;
        HEIGHTMAP *m_pHeightMap;
        std::vector<PATCH*> m_patches;
};
```

The TERRAIN class handles the creation and rendering of all the patches. Over the next couple of examples, we will be adding functionality to the vertex declaration, PATCH structure, and TERRAIN class. Later in this chapter, the TERRAIN will handle things like texturing, pathfinding, saving and loading terrains, and more. However, at the moment, the most important function in the TERRAIN class is the CreatePatches() function:

```
void TERRAIN::CreatePatches(int numPatches)
{
    //Clear old patches here...

    //Create new patches
    for(int y=0;y<numPatches;y++)
        for(int x=0;x<numPatches;x++)
        {
            // Source Rectangle for this patch
            RECT r = {x * (m_size.x - 1) / (float)numPatches,
                      y * (m_size.y - 1) / (float)numPatches,
                      x+1) * (m_size.x-1) / (float)numPatches,
                      y+1) * (m_size.y-1) / (float)numPatches};
            PATCH *p = new PATCH();
            p->CreateMesh(*m_pHeightMap, r, Device);
            m_patches.push_back(p);
        }
}
```

This function assumes that the HEIGHTMAP pointer m_pHeightMap contains the address to a valid heightmap. This function first clears away all the old patches and then calculates the source rectangle for each patch. Then a new patch is created for each source rectangle and added to the patches vector.

ON THE CD

Example 4.4

Have a look at Example 4.4 on the CD-ROM. This example creates patches covering the whole heightmap and then renders them either as a solid mesh or as a wireframe.

Example 4.4 contains the finished HEIGHTMAP *structure with all the unnecessary bits shaved away.*

TERRAIN TEXTURING

The previous section covered how to create a terrain mesh from a heightmap. Now it's time to look at how we can apply a texture to this mesh to make it a bit more pleasing to the eye. There are a lot of different approaches on how to texture a terrain. I'm sure you'll find more ways than those we'll cover here. Before we get started on the different ways to do this, we need to have a look at UV, or texture coordinates. A UV coordinate is a two-dimensional coordinate that maps a vertex to a position in a texture, as shown in Figure 4.8.

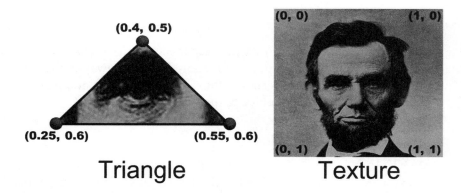

FIGURE 4.8 The relationship between a UV-mapped triangle and a 2D texture.

The three vertices of a triangle have their own UV coordinates that are used to describe how to map a texture onto the triangle. Let's have another look at our terrain vertex declaration and see how we add a UV coordinate to it.

```
struct TERRAINVertex
{
    TERRAINVertex(){}
    TERRAINVertex(D3DXVECTOR3 pos, D3DXVECTOR2 _uv)
    {
        position = pos;
```

```
        normal = D3DXVECTOR3(0.0f, 1.0f, 0.0f);
        uv = _uv;
    }

    D3DXVECTOR3 position, normal;
    D3DXVECTOR2 uv;

    static const DWORD FVF;
};

const DWORD TERRAINVertex::FVF = D3DFVF_XYZ | D3DFVF_NORMAL |
                                 D3DFVF_TEX1;
```

The constructor takes a D3DXVECTOR2 that holds the UV coordinate and stores it for each vertex. Note that you also have to add the D3DFVF_TEX1 flag to the FVF for this to work. The color variable has also been removed from our vertex structure because we will be getting our color information from a texture, instead. So from now on when we create vertex buffers using this vertex declaration, we have to calculate the UV coordinates and use these to initiate the vertices.

Tile-Based Texturing

Tile-based texturing assigns a specific texture to each map tile. The major problem with this approach is that the seams between tiles of different textures becomes very clear. Tile-based texturing can be a good approach in environments like city streets and so on, but for outdoor landscapes, this is generally not a good method. When texturing a terrain, make sure that the textures you use are tileable. With tileable textures, you can't see the seams when tiling the texture, as shown in Figure 4.9:

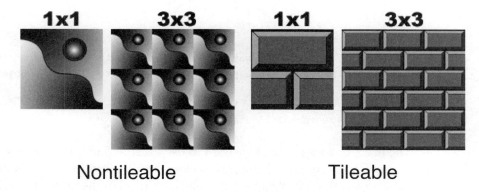

FIGURE 4.9 The difference between tileable and a nontileable textures.

Tile-based texturing uses the attribute buffer to divide the terrain mesh into different subsets. In the previous examples, we set the whole attribute buffer to zero, which means that the whole mesh belongs to subset zero. Now we will divide the mesh into different subsets according to what texture we want to render. Here is one way in which you can divide the mesh into different subsets according to the heights in the heightmap (excerpt from the PATCH::CreateMesh() function):

```
//Create vertices
for(int z=source.top, z0 = 0;z<=source.bottom;z++, z0++)
    for(int x=source.left, x0 = 0;x<=source.right;x++, x0++)
    {
        D3DXVECTOR3 pos = { ... }     // position as usual...
        D3DXVECTOR2 uv = D3DXVECTOR2(x * 0.2f, z * 0.2f);
        ver[z0 * (width + 1) + x0] = TERRAINVertex(pos, uv);
    }

//Calculate Indices... as usual...

//Set Attributes
DWORD *att = 0, a = 0;
m_pMesh->LockAttributeBuffer(0,&att);

for(int z=source.top;z<source.bottom;z++)
    for(int x=source.left;x<source.right;x++)
    {
        int subset;         //Calculate subset
        if(hm.m_pHeightMap[x + z * hm.m_size.x] == 0.0f)
            subset = 0;
        else if(hm.m_pHeightMap[x + z * hm.m_size.x]
                <= hm.m_maxHeight * 0.6f)
            subset = 1;
        else subset = 2;

        att[a++] = subset;    // Assign both triangles of the
        att[a++] = subset;    // map tile to the same subset
    }

m_pMesh->UnlockAttributeBuffer();
```

The first thing we do when we want to use a textured mesh is to create vertices containing UV coordinates. Here we calculate the UV coordinates as a function of the x and z variables. Then we loop through each quad in the mesh and assign it to a subset, depending on what height the map tile has. This code divides the mesh into three subsets, one where the heightmap is zero (water), one where the heightmap is below 60 percent of the m_maxHeight (grass), and one where it is above 60 percent of the m_maxHeight (stone). All we need to do now is set the correct texture and material, and render the specific subsets of the patches in our TERRAIN class.

```
void TERRAIN::Render()
{
    //Set render states here...

    //Create and set white material
    m_pDevice->SetMaterial(&m_white);

    //Render Patches
    for(int t=0;t<3;t++)
    {
        m_pDevice->SetTexture(0, m_textures[t]);

        //Render subset t in patch i.
        for(int i=0;i<m_patches.size();i++)
            m_patches[i]->Render(t);
    }
}
```

Example 4.5

ON THE CD

This is what the result of tile-based terrain texturing looks like. As you can see, the line between water and grass is a little bit too visible.

Pre-Rendered Textures

So how do we fix the problem of having sharp edges between tiles? One way is to stretch a single, pre-rendered texture over the entire terrain. This is one of the easiest ways to texture a terrain. The first thing we need to do is create the vertices with the correct UV coordinates. Here's the line in our PATCH::CreateMesh() function that determines our UV coordinate:

```
D3DXVECTOR2 uv = D3DXVECTOR2(x / (float)hm.m_size.x,
                             z / (float)hm.m_size.y);
```

We create the position and so forth just like before. The UV coordinate is now calculated by dividing the vertex position by the size of the heightmap (i.e., terrain size). This puts all UV coordinates in the range of 0.0–1.0; or in other words, it stretches the texture exactly once over the whole mesh. The next thing we need to do, of course, is to load a texture and activate it before we render the patch:

```
HRESULT D3DXCreateTextureFromFile(
    LPDIRECT3DDEVICE9 pDevice,
    LPCTSTR pSrcFile,
    LPDIRECT3DTEXTURE9 *ppTexture
);

//Use this function like this
IDirect3DTexture9* texture = NULL;
D3DXCreateTextureFromFile(Device, "example.jpg", &texture);
```

The following piece of code shows the TERRAIN::Render() function. We assign the terrain texture to stage zero and then render all our patches.

```
void TERRAIN::Render()
{
    //Set render states here...

    //Set Texture and Material
    m_pDevice->SetMaterial(&mtrl);
    m_pDevice->SetTexture(0, texture);

    //Render Patches
    for(int i=0;i<m_patches.size();i++)
        m_patches[i]->Render();
}
```

Example 4.6

Create a heightmap in Photoshop or another picture editor, but this time also create a diffuse map containing the color information. When combining a heightmap and a diffuse map, we get the following result.

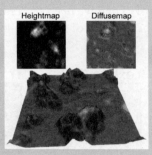

Have a look at Figure 4.10. Pre-rendered textures look good in the Overview image, don't they? The problem with this particular method appears when you zoom in and have a closer look. There's not much detail per pixel in the Zoomed In image, is there? If you still want to texture your terrain like this, make sure to have as large diffuse maps as is supported by your video card to reduce this effect as much as possible.

Overview   Zoomed In

FIGURE 4.10   The problem with pre-rendered textures.

Texture Splatting

Texture splatting is a method designed to deal with the "zoom" problem covered in the previous section and also allows for fuzzy edges between tiles. Texture splatting works by assigning an alpha map to each terrain type (e.g., grass, mud, snow, rock). This alpha map is stretched over the entire terrain like the diffuse map in the previous example. The diffuse maps, on the other hand, are textures tiled to increase the texture detail. During the rendering, the diffuse map is multiplied by its alpha map, and the result is added to the final rendering. We load in the diffuse maps and store them in a vector. Then we need to create an alpha map for each diffuse map. Figure 4.11 shows the concept of texture splatting.

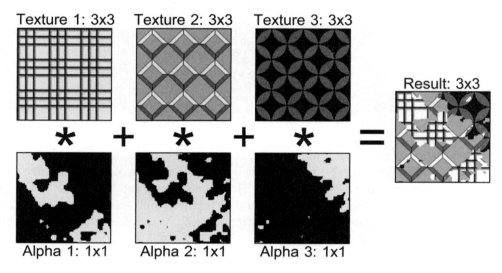

FIGURE 4.11 The concept of texture splatting.

Note how the textures (diffuse maps) are tiled 3×3, but the alpha maps are stretched to cover the same size as all the tiled diffuse maps. We multiply the textures with their corresponding alpha maps and add the product to the final result. This way the texture detail can be increased by simply tiling the diffuse maps more. To do this, we need two separate UV coordinates for the terrain vertices—one UV coordinate for the tiled textures (e.g., mud, grass, etc.) and one UV coordinate for the alpha maps. So let's once again have a look at our vertex declaration and see how we can do this:

```
struct TERRAINVertex
{
    TERRAINVertex(){}
```

```
TERRAINVertex(D3DXVECTOR3 pos,
              D3DXVECTOR2 _uv1,
              D3DXVECTOR2 _uv2)
{
    position = pos;
    normal = D3DXVECTOR3(0.0f, 1.0f, 0.0f);
    uv1 = _uv1;
    uv2 = _uv2;
}

D3DXVECTOR3 position, normal;
D3DXVECTOR2 uv1, uv2;
static const DWORD FVF;
};

const DWORD TERRAINVertex::FVF = D3DFVF_XYZ | D3DFVF_NORMAL |
                                 D3DFVF_TEX2;
```

All we've added is another texture coordinate and replaced D3DFVF_TEX1 flag in the FVF variable for the D3DFVF_TEX2 flag. The D3DFVF_TEX2 flag tells the pipeline that this vertex just has two texture coordinates, rather than one. Otherwise, we create the vertices as usual with the addition of the new UV coordinate (excerpt from the PATCH::CreateMesh() function):

```
...
D3DXVECTOR3 pos = { ... };                 //Position as  usual...

D3DXVECTOR2 alphaUV = D3DXVECTOR2(x / (float)width,
                                  z / (float)height);

D3DXVECTOR2 colorUV = alphaUV * 8.0f;

ver[z0 * (width + 1) + x0] =
    TERRAINVertex(pos, alphaUV, colorUV);
...
```

The alphaUV is calculated in the same way as we calculated the UV coordinate in the previous example. It stretches a texture once over the entire terrain. We set colorUV to be eight times larger than alphaUV; this means that we will tile the diffuse texture 8 × 8 times over the terrain. The next step is to create the actual alpha textures. In this example, we assign each terrain type a height range. For example, grass (0–1), mountain (1–15), and snow (15–20), and so on. We then check for each terrain type and what areas of the heightmap are within this range, and paint the corresponding alpha map white in these areas. The following function has been added to our TERRAIN class to create these alpha maps:

```
void TERRAIN::CalculateAlphaMaps()
{
    //Clear old alpha maps here...

    //height ranges...
    float min_range[] = {0.0f, 1.0f, 15.0f};

    //Create one alpha map per diffuse map
    for(int i=0;i<m_diffuseMaps.size();i++)
    {
        //Create new texture
        IDirect3DTexture9* newTexture = NULL;
        D3DXCreateTexture(m_pDevice, 128, 128, 1,
                    D3DUSAGE_DYNAMIC, D3DFMT_A8R8G8B8,
                    D3DPOOL_DEFAULT, &newTexture);

        //Lock the texture
        D3DLOCKED_RECT sRect;
        newTexture->LockRect(0, &sRect, NULL, NULL);
        BYTE *bytes = (BYTE*)sRect.pBits;

        //For each pixel in the alphaMap
        for(int y=0;y<sRect.Pitch / 4;y++)
        for(int x=0;x<sRect.Pitch / 4;x++)
        {
            //Extract height for this pixel
            int hm_x = hm->m_size.x *
                    (x / (float)(sRect.Pitch / 4));
            int hm_y = hm->m_size.y *
                    (y / (float)(sRect.Pitch / 4));
            float height =
                hm->m_pHeightMap[hm_x + hm_y*hm->m_size.x];

            //Paint white if height is within correct range
            BYTE *b = bytes + y * sRect.Pitch + x * 4;
            if(height >= min_range[i])
                memset(b, 255, 4);
            else memset(b, 0, 4);
        }
```

```
        //Unlock the texture
        newTexture->UnlockRect(0);

        m_alphaMaps.push_back(newTexture);
    }
}
```

We create the alpha texture with the D3DFMT_A8R8G8B8 format, even though all
we are going to use is the alpha channel. Next, we get the corresponding height for
each a pixel in the alpha map from the heightmap. Then we compare this height
against the terrain type's height range. If it is within the range, we paint the pixel
white, otherwise we paint it black. With that done, now we have one vector containing the diffuse maps and one vector containing the alpha maps. All that's left is
to render the mesh:

```
void TERRAIN::Render()
{
    //Set render states
    m_pDevice->SetRenderState(D3DRS_LIGHTING, false);
    m_pDevice->SetRenderState(D3DRS_ZWRITEENABLE, true);

    //Alpha from alphaTextures, stage 0
    m_pDevice->SetTextureStageState(0, D3DTSS_ALPHAOP,
                                    D3DTOP_SELECTARG1);
    m_pDevice->SetTextureStageState(0, D3DTSS_ALPHAARG1,
                                    D3DTA_TEXTURE);

    //Color from Diffuse textures, stage 1
    m_pDevice->SetTextureStageState(1, D3DTSS_COLOROP,
                                    D3DTOP_SELECTARG1);
    m_pDevice->SetTextureStageState(1, D3DTSS_COLORARG1,
                                    D3DTA_TEXTURE);
    m_pDevice->SetTextureStageState(1, D3DTSS_ALPHAOP,
                                    D3DTOP_SELECTARG1);
    m_pDevice->SetTextureStageState(1, D3DTSS_ALPHAARG1,
                                    D3DTA_CURRENT);

    m_pDevice->SetRenderState(D3DRS_ALPHABLENDENABLE, true);
    m_pDevice->SetRenderState(D3DRS_SRCBLEND,
                              D3DBLEND_SRCALPHA);
    m_pDevice->SetRenderState(D3DRS_DESTBLEND,
                              D3DBLEND_INVSRCALPHA);

    m_pDevice->SetMaterial(&mtrl);
```

```
//Draw mesh once for each terrain type
for(int i=0;i<m_diffuseMaps.size();i++)
{
    m_pDevice->SetTexture(0, m_alphaMaps[i]);
    m_pDevice->SetTexture(1, m_diffuseMaps[i]);

    for(int p=0;p<m_patches.size();p++)
        m_patches[p]->Render();
}
```

The two textures—the diffuse and alpha map—are multiplied and then added to the final image. We take the alpha information from the alpha maps (texture stage 0) and the color information from the tiled diffuse maps (texture stage 1). One downfall of this method is that the patches have to be rendered once for each terrain type. So if we have five terrain types, that means we need five rendering passes to render them all.

Example 4.7

Have a look at Example 4.7 on the CD-ROM. Here, texture splatting using the fixed function pipeline is implemented. There is a big difference between the previous example and this one because now we can again have random maps and still generate high-quality terrain texturing. If you zoom in, the quality of the texture is still good because we now can tile the diffuse texture as much as needed.

Texture Splatting Using a Pixelshader

Texture splatting using a pixelshader produces the same result as the previous example. However, instead of storing the alpha textures in separate textures, we combine them into one texture. This saves us a multitude of rendering passes, and we can now perform texture splatting in one pass (as long as the number of terrain types isn't more than the channels of our alpha texture). The terrain pixelshader presented here requires a graphics card that supports at least pixelshader version 2.0. As before, one alpha texture is created for each terrain type; but this time they are stored in one single texture, rather than in multiple alpha textures (excerpt from the TERRAIN::CreateAlphaMaps() function):

```
//height ranges...
float min_range[] = {0.0f, 1.0f, 15.0f};
float max_range[] = {2.0f, 16.0f, 21.0f};

D3DXCreateTexture(m_pDevice, 128, 128, 1, D3DUSAGE_DYNAMIC,
            D3DFMT_A8R8G8B8, D3DPOOL_DEFAULT, &m_pAlphaMap);

//Lock the texture
D3DLOCKED_RECT sRect;
m_pAlphaMap->LockRect(0, &sRect, NULL, NULL);
BYTE *bytes = (BYTE*)sRect.pBits;
memset(bytes, 0, 128*sRect.Pitch);        //Clear texture to black

for(int i=0;i<m_diffuseMaps.size();i++)
    for(int y=0;y<sRect.Pitch / 4;y++)
        for(int x=0;x<sRect.Pitch / 4;x++)
        {
            int hm_x = m_pHeightMap->m_size.x *
                    (x / (float)(sRect.Pitch / 4.0f));

            int hm_y = m_pHeightMap->m_size.y *
                    (y / (float)(sRect.Pitch / 4.0f));

            float height =
                m_pHeightMap->m_pHeightMap[hm_x + hm_y *
                                    m_pHeightMap->m_size.x];

            BYTE *b = bytes + y * sRect.Pitch + x * 4 + i;
            if(height >= min_range[i] &&
                height <= max_range[i])
                *b = 255;
            else *b = 0;
        }

//Unlock the texture
m_pAlphaMap->UnlockRect(0);
```

Now that we have one single texture to store the alpha maps for the different color channels, all we need is a pixelshader to perform the actual texture splatting. For this we use our SHADER class to load and handle the following pixelshader code (see Chapter 3 for more details on our SHADER class):

```
sampler alpha;               //Stage 0
sampler texture1;            //Stage 1
sampler texture2;            //Stage 2
sampler texture3;            //Stage 3

float4 Main(float2 alphaUV : TEXCOORD0,
            float2 colorUV : TEXCOORD1) : COLOR
{
    //Sample the textures
    float4 a  = tex2D(alpha, alphaUV);
    float4 c1 = tex2D(texture1, colorUV);
    float4 c2 = tex2D(texture2, colorUV);
    float4 c3 = tex2D(texture3, colorUV);

    //Calculate the inverse
    float inverse = 1.0f / (a.r + a.g + a.b);

    //Multiply texture with alpha value
    c1 *= a.b * inverse;
    c2 *= a.g * inverse;
    c3 *= a.r * inverse;

    //Return result
    return c1 + c2 + c3;
}
```

The pixelshader takes two texture coordinates, alphaUV and colorUV. It samples all the textures and scales the values of all the alpha channels so that when added together, the result is always 1.0. Then the alpha channels are multiplied by their corresponding diffuse maps, and the result is returned. This pixelshader is loaded and maintained by our TERRAIN class. Finally, we modify our TERRAIN::Render() function:

```
void TERRAIN::Render()
{
    //Set render states
    m_pDevice->SetRenderState(D3DRS_LIGHTING, false);
    m_pDevice->SetRenderState(D3DRS_ZWRITEENABLE, true);
```

```
//Set texture stages & material
//Stage 0  (alpha)
m_pDevice->SetTexture(0, m_pAlphaMap);
//Stage 1-3  (grass, mountain, snow)
m_pDevice->SetTexture(1, m_diffuseMaps[0]);
m_pDevice->SetTexture(2, m_diffuseMaps[1]);
m_pDevice->SetTexture(3, m_diffuseMaps[2]);
m_pDevice->SetMaterial(&m_mtrl);

//Start the texture splatting pixelshader
m_terrainPS.Begin();

for(int p=0;p<m_patches.size();p++)
    m_patches[p]->Render();

m_terrainPS.End();       //and then end it...
}
```

The texture stages are set to match the order in which the textures appear in the pixelshader. We then simply start the pixelshader and render the patches. The result will look just as it does in Example 4.7, but the difference is that now we perform the texture splatting all in one pass. It is also a good thing to do the texture splatting with a shader because we will soon do all our advanced graphical rendering using vertex and pixelshaders, anyway. However, there are limitations to this method, as well. One thing is that the number of terrain types is limited to as many channels as there are in the alpha map. It is, of course, possible to send more than one alpha texture to the pixelshader, but as the number of operations per pixel increases, the frame rate will steadily decrease.

Example 4.8

ON THE CD

In Example 4.8 on the CD-ROM, texture splatting is implemented using a pixelshader. There's not much visual difference between using a pixelshader and the fixed function pipeline, but now the texture splatting can be done in a single pass.

TERRAIN OBJECTS

Okay, the terrain is done, textured, and ready to go. The next issue we need to address is terrain objects—that is, loading meshes from a file. At the moment the terrain is fairly basic. We have hills, mountains, and valleys, but that's pretty much it. To break the monotony, let's place some trees, rocks, and other things on it to make it seem more "alive." What we need is a way to create, store, load, and render complex "objects." The creation and storage part of objects will be covered in more detail in Chapter 6: Creating 3D Models. For now, let's use the two example objects in Figure 4.12, instead—the tree and the stone.

Tree.x
36 Vertices, 35 Faces

Stone.x
18 Vertices, 28 Faces

FIGURE 4.12   The tree mesh and the stone mesh.

For objects like trees, which are going to be scattered across the terrain, try to keep the vertex and polygon count to a minimum.

Object meshes are stored in the DirectX X-format. These can, for example, be created by converting 3ds Max files (*.3ds) using the "conv3ds.ex·" converter that comes with DirectX, or by exporting a model from any other 3D software to the .x file format. Once you have an X-file that you want to load, let's have a look at the function and structures supplied by the D3DX library.

Loading X-Files

The most important function we need in order to load a mesh is the D3DXLoadMesh FromX() function. It takes care of almost everything. The only little thing we need to do ourselves is to load any textures used by the mesh.

```
HRESULT D3DXLoadMeshFromX(
    LPCTSTR pFilename,
    DWORD Options,
    LPDIRECT3DDEVICE9 pDevice,
    LPD3DXBUFFER* ppAdjacency,
    LPD3DXBUFFER* ppMaterials,
    LPD3DXBUFFER* ppEffectInstances,
    DWORD* pNumMaterials,
    LPD3DXMESH* ppMesh
);
```

pFilename: The filename of the target .x file.

Options: Flags describing how the mesh should be created. We use D3DXMESH_MANAGED in our examples. (For a complete list, see the DirectX documentation.)

ppAdjacency: A pointer to an adjacency buffer (three DWORD instances for each face storing the indices of its neighboring faces).

ppMaterials: A buffer containing the materials used by the mesh. The materials are stored using the D3DXMATERIAL structure.

ppEffectsInstances: A list of effect filenames (not used).

pNumMaterials: The number of materials used by the mesh.

ppMesh: The mesh itself.

From this function, we get a mesh, all its materials, and the filenames of the textures used by the mesh.

The MESH Class

The MESH class encapsulates the ID3DXMesh structure and the D3DXLoadMeshFromX() function. The MESH class also contains all textures, materials, and so on needed to render the mesh, and is defined as follows:

```
class MESH{
    public:
        MESH();
        MESH(char fName[], IDirect3DDevice9* Dev);
        ~MESH();
        HRESULT Load(char fName[], IDirect3DDevice9* Dev);
        void Render();
        void Release();
```

```
        private:
            IDirect3DDevice9 *m_pDevice;
            ID3DXMesh *m_pMesh;
            std::vector<IDirect3DTexture9*> m_textures;
            std::vector<D3DMATERIAL9> m_materials;
            D3DMATERIAL9 m_white;
    };
```

The most important function in this class is the MESH::Load() function. It loads the mesh, and all its textures and materials:

```
HRESULT MESH::Load(char fName[], IDirect3DDevice9* Dev)
{
    ...

    //Load new mesh
    ID3DXBuffer * adjacencyBfr = NULL;
    ID3DXBuffer * materialBfr = NULL;
    DWORD noMaterials = NULL;

    //Load the mesh...
    D3DXLoadMeshFromX(fName, D3DXMESH_MANAGED,
                      Device, &adjacencyBfr,
                      &materialBfr, NULL,
                      &noMaterials, &m_pMesh);

    //Get materials and textures
    D3DXMATERIAL *mtrls = NULL;
    mtrls = (D3DXMATERIAL*)materialBfr->GetBufferPointer();

    for(int i=0;i<noMaterials;i++)
    {
        m_materials.push_back(mtrls[i].MatD3D);

        if(mtrls[i].pTextureFilename != NULL)
        {
            IDirect3DTexture9 * newTexture = NULL;
            D3DXCreateTextureFromFile(m_pDevice,
                             mtrls[i].pTextureFilename,
                             &newTexture);
```

```
            m_textures.push_back(newTexture);
        }
        else m_textures.push_back(NULL);
    }

    adjacencyBfr->Release();
    materialBfr->Release();
}
```

This function retrieves the mesh object, as well as all the materials and textures used by it. Now all we have to do in order to load and render a precreated mesh is the following:

```
//Load it like this...
MESH mesh;
mesh.Load("meshes/tree.x", Device);

//Render it like this...
mesh.Render();
```

Example 4.9

Meshes are loaded and rendered simply. Have a look at the Example 4.9 for the full source code and implementation of the MESH class.

ON THE CD

The MESHINSTANCE **Class**

However, on a terrain we want hundreds of trees and stones, not just one. It would be very inefficient to load one mesh, and one set of textures and materials for each tree we wanted to render. Therefore, we need a way of rendering multiple instances of the same object using a different location, rotation, and/or scale. The MESHINSTANCE class will not hold a mesh itself, but merely a pointer to a MESH object, as well as additional information on how to transform the mesh. With the MESHINSTANCE class, we can control the position, rotation, and the scale of how we want a MESH object to be rendered.

```
class MESHINSTANCE{
    public:
        MESHINSTANCE();
        MESHINSTANCE(MESH *meshPtr);
        void Render();

        void SetMesh(MESH *m)          {m_pMesh = m;}
        void SetPosition(D3DXVECTOR3 p){m_pos = p;}
        void SetRotation(D3DXVECTOR3 r){m_rot = r;}
        void SetScale(D3DXVECTOR3 s)   {m_sca = s;}

    private:
        MESH *m_pMesh;
        D3DXVECTOR3 m_pos, m_rot, m_sca;
};
```

As mentioned, the MESHINSTANCE class simply holds a pointer to the actual mesh and information on how to create the world transformation matrix for rendering. Let us have a look at the MESHINSTANCE::Render() function.

```
void MESHINSTANCE::Render()
{
    D3DXMATRIX p, r, s;
    D3DXMatrixTranslation(&p, m_pos.x, m_pos.y, m_pos.z);
    D3DXMatrixRotationYawPitchRoll(&r, m_rot.y,
                                       m_rot.x,
                                       m_rot.z);
    D3DXMatrixScaling(&s, m_sca.x, m_sca.y, m_sca.z);

    D3DXMATRIX world = s * r * p;
    m_pMesh-> m_pDevice->SetTransform(D3DTS_WORLD, &world);
    m_pMesh->Render();
}
```

The MESHINSTANCE::Render() function creates the matrix using the object's position, rotation, and scale vectors, and then renders it. Note how we create the world matrix by first multiplying the scale, then the rotation, and last the position. If you multiply these matrices in any other order, you will end up with weird results. This happens because matrix multiplication is not commutative— that is, the matrice A * B is not the same as B * A.

Example 4.10

The MESHINSTANCE class is implemented in Example 4.10. In this example, a lot of instances of the same object are created with different positions, rotations, and scales. By using the MESHINSTANCE class, we can to do this without loading the necessary resources more than once.

The OBJECT Class

You may have thought that we would be done with mesh objects by now. Alas, no; we need to take it one step further and implement the OBJECT class. The OBJECT class is going to hold all other needed information about a map object, such as pathfinding information. For instance, if you would like to create trees as a resource that can be gathered, you might want to save information, like how much wood a certain tree will yield, and so forth. The point is that instead of saving all this extra functionality and information in the MESHINSTANCE class, we create an OBJECT class. This helps keep the MESHINSTANCE class nice and uncluttered (which we will need later on because we will use this class for things like buildings, projectiles, as well). So the OBJECT class is simply a wrapper class for the MESHINSTANCE structure, where we realize any game-specific functionality. For instance, we often want our units to find a path around our map objects, and to do this we need to store information like the object's map position, size, and so forth.

```
class OBJECT{
    public:
        OBJECT();
        OBJECT(int t,D3DXVECTOR3 pos,
                        D3DXVECTOR3 rot,
                        D3DXVECTOR3 sca);
        void Render();

    private:
        MESHINSTANCE m_meshInstance;
        int m_type;
        INTPOINT m_mappos, m_mapsize;
};

...



std::vector<MESH*> objectMeshes;

//fill objectMeshes here...

...

OBJECT::OBJECT(int t, D3DXVECTOR3 pos,
                        D3DXVECTOR3 rot,
                        D3DXVECTOR3 sca)
{
    m_type = t;
    m_meshInstance.SetPosition(pos);
    m_meshInstance.SetRotation(rot);
    m_meshInstance.SetScale(sca);
    m_meshInstance.SetMesh(objectMeshes[m_type]);
}

void OBJECT::Render()
{
    m_meshInstance.Render();
}
```

ON THE CD

Example 4.11

Have a look at Example 4.11 on the CD-ROM. The OBJECT class is used to create forests and stones on a terrain. In this example, a random heightmap is used to determine where the trees and stones should be placed. An array of objects have been added to our TERRAIN class, along with a TERRAIN::AddObject() function that creates a new object at a certain location.

TIP

If you have many similar objects in a scene, you can gain a few frames per second by batching them together into larger meshes. Another method to increase efficiency is to reduce the draw calls by using as few textures per object as possible.

PATHFINDING

Until now, this chapter has dealt with how to make a terrain look "pretty." Now it is time to have a look at the functional side of a terrain. What goes on behind the curtains, and what else does our TERRAIN class have to be capable of? One of the most important features (and one of the greatest challenges in an RTS game) is the pathfinding system. In an RTS game, you have multiple units, all running around the terrain, and all wanting paths calculated for them. Achieving this without using too much CPU power takes a whole lot of effort and does not come easy.

The terrain must contain information about which tiles are connected to which tiles. So far, the only map node information we have worked with is the height (i.e., the heightmap). Now we are going to add information such as type, time to walk across the tile (i.e., tile cost), and any other things you will need for your particular game. For this purpose, we introduce the MAPTILE structure:

```
struct MAPTILE{
    MAPTILE();          //Set everything to 0

    int m_type, m_set;
    float m_height, m_cost;
    bool m_walkable;
    MAPTILE* m_pNeighbors[8];

    //... more to come later ...//
};
```

Type: This variable sets the terrain type (e.g., grass, marsh, mountain, etc.) from here on. We also use this variable to calculate the alpha maps for the texture splatting.

Set: This variable keeps track of what set this map tile belongs to. (This will be explained in more detail in the next section).

Height: This is the tile's height that was previously stored in the HEIGHTMAP class. From this height value, we generate the terrain patches.

Cost: This is the cost for a unit to cross the specific map tile.

Walkable: If true, then units may cross this tile, otherwise they may not.

Neighbors[8]: This contains pointers to the eight potential neighbors of a map tile.

The cost could, for example, be calculated from the "steepness" of the tile. It could also be directly related to what type of terrain you have—for example, crossing a marsh tile would take longer than crossing a grass tile.

When you have a finished map with interconnected map tiles (i.e., a graph), this can be used to search a path from one map tile to another. When we search for a path between two map tiles, we are in most cases looking for that path whose sum of costs is as low as possible. But first we need to extend our TERRAIN class to hold the map tiles and provide us with an interface that we can use for pathfinding.

```
class TERRAIN{
    public:
        TERRAIN();
        //Generate Terrain and Render Functions goes here...

        //Pathfinding Functions
        bool Within(INTPOINT p); //Test if point p is within
                                 //the terrain bounds
```

```
        void InitPathfinding();
        MAPTILE* GetTile(int x, int y);
        MAPTILE* GetTile(INTPOINT p);

        //Public variables
        MAPTILE *maptiles;

    private:
        INTPOINT m_size;
        IDirect3DDevice9* m_pDevice;
        HEIGHTMAP *m_pHeightMap;
        //Variables such as patches, textures,
        //objects etc goes here...
};
```

An array of map tiles has been added to the TERRAIN class (containing m_size.x
* m_size.y map tiles). The map tiles are created in the TERRAIN::Init() function
and can be accessed with the GetTile() function. The InitPathfinding() function
calculates the cost and type of the map tiles, as well as sets all the neighbor pointers.
First the terrain should be created from a heightmap. Then the InitPathfinding()
function should be called; this connects all the map tiles and creates a graph that we
can use for pathfinding.

Connecting the Map Tiles

Here's a short outline of what we need to do in the InitPathfinding() function:

1. Copy node heights from a HEIGHTMAP object to our array of map tiles.
2. Calculate the cost of all the tiles and whether they are walkable or not.
3. Connect walkable tiles using the m_pNeighbors[] pointers.

In this example, we calculate the cost of map tiles as a function of the height
variance of its surrounding tiles. There are many ways you could calculate the cost
of a tile: as a function of the map tile's type, setting the cost manually, or having a
constant cost. Again, pick the one that fits your game best. Also, we need to set the
m_walkable variable of any map tiles that have an object on it to false. This prevents
any units from walking through trees, and so forth.

```
        void TERRAIN::InitPathfinding()
        {
```

```cpp
//Read maptile heights & types from heightmap
//and copy them into our maptile array

//Calculate tile cost as a function of the height variance
for(int y=0;y<m_size.y;y++)
    for(int x=0;x< m_size.x;x++)
    {
        MAPTILE *tile = GetTile(x, y);
        if(tile != NULL)
        {
            //Possible neighbors
            INTPOINT p[] = {/*possible neighbors*/};

            float variance = 0.0f;
            int nr = 0;

            //For each neighbor
            for(int i=0;i<8;i++)
            {
                MAPTILE *neighbor = GetTile(p[i]);

                if(neighbor != NULL)
                {
                    float v = neighbor->m_height -
                                tile->m_height;
                    variance += (v * v);
                    nr++;
                }
            }

            //Cost = height variance
            variance /= (float)nr;
            tile->m_cost = variance + 0.1f;
            if(tile->m_cost > 1.0f)tile->m_cost = 1.0f;

            //If the tile cost is less than 1.0f,
            //then we can walk on the tile
            tile->m_walkable = tile->m_cost < 1.0f;
        }
    }
```

```
//Make maptiles with objects on them not walkable here...

//Connect maptiles using the m_pNeighbors[] pointers
for(int y=0;y<m_size.y;y++)
    for(int x=0;x<m_size.x;x++)
    {
        MAPTILE *tile = GetTile(x, y);
        if(tile != NULL && tile->m_walkable)
        {
            //Clear old connections
            for(int i=0;i<8;i++)
                tile->m_pNeighbors[i] = NULL;

            //Possible neighbors
            INTPOINT p[] = {/* possible neighbors*/};

            //For each neighbor
            for(int i=0;i<8;i++)
                if(Within(p[i]))
                {
                    MAPTILE *neighbor = GetTile(p[i]);

                    //Connect tiles if the
                    //neighbor is walkable
                    if(neighbor != NULL &&
                        neighbor->m_walkable)
                        tile->m_pNeighbors[i] = neighbor;
                }
        }
    }
}
```

This function initializes the map tiles for pathfinding. It calculates the cost of all tiles and finds their neighbors. If a valid path doesn't exist between two tiles, then the corresponding neighbor pointer is set to NULL. Another way you could define the cost would be to assign a cost value to each neighbor pointer. So instead of saying how costly it is to cross this specific tile, we say how much it costs to go from this tile to a specific neighbor. This can be used to give different cost values, depending on which way a unit is walking. This would, for example, allow us to have a pathfinding system where it costs more to climb a mountain than to descend it.

Example 4.12

Example 4.12 on the CD-ROM implements the `TERRAIN::InitPathfinding()` function and displays the cost of a tile using particles. In this example, you might also want to have a look at how we calculate the texture-splatting alpha map using map tile types, rather than height ranges. In Example 4.12, note how tiles with low-height variance have a green color, while tiles with high-height variance (unwalkable tiles) have a bright red color. Also note that tiles with an object on them is also unwalkable.

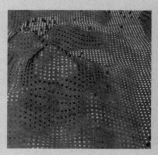

Now we have a graph of interconnected tiles that each have a cost value assigned to them. This is all we need to search a path from any point on the map to any other point, but first . . .

Dividing the Map into Sets

One thing that we need to do before searching a map for a path between two points is to divide the map into sets. We do this to rule out the worst-case scenario when there is no path existing between two points on the map. In this case, the pathfinding algorithm will search all possible tiles that are accessible from the starting point. Of course, this will all be in vain, because the goal point won't be one of them. This is a very slow process that we want to avoid (especially for large maps). So the solution is to divide the map tiles into sets. Simply put, a set of tiles is all those tiles that have a valid path between them, as shown in Figure 4.13.

When a path between two points is queried, we first check to see whether those two points belong to the same set or not. If they do, then we start the search; otherwise, we know without the expensive search that there is no valid path. The set of a map tile is stored as an integer value at each tile. The following function in the TERRAIN class calculates the tile sets.

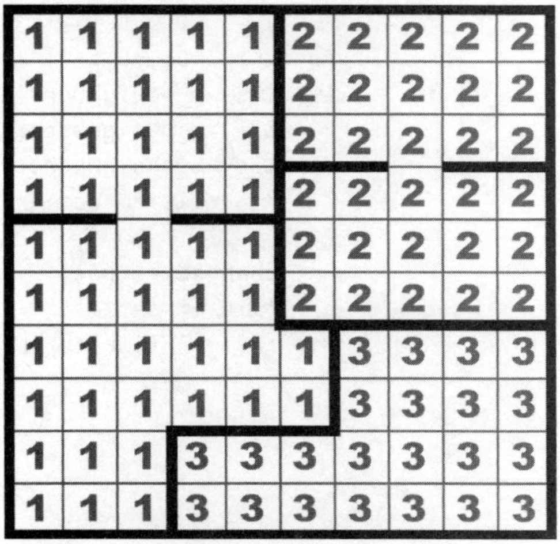

FIGURE 4.13 A map divided into three tile sets—1, 2, and 3.

```
void TERRAIN::CreateTileSets()
{
    int setNo = 0;

    //Set a unique set for each tile...
    for(int y=0;y<m_size.y;y++)
        for(int x=0;x<m_size.x;x++)
            m_pMapTiles[x + y * m_size.x].set = m_setNo++;

    bool changed = true;
    while(changed)
    {
        changed = false;

        for(int y=0;y<m_size.y;y++)
            for(int x=0;x<m_size.x;x++)
            {
                MAPTILE *tile = GetTile(x, y);

                //Find the lowest set of a neighbor
                if(tile != NULL && tile->m_walkable)
```

```
                {
                    for(int i=0;i<8;i++)
                    if(tile->m_pNeighbors[i] != NULL &&
                        tile->m_pNeighbors[i]->m_walkable &&
                        tile->m_pNeighbors[i]->m_set <
                            tile->m_set)
                    {
                        changed = true;
                        tile->m_set =
                                tile->m_pNeighbors[i]->m_set;
                    }
                }
            }
        }
    }
```

First we assign a unique set ID to each map tile. Then, we repeatedly check all the neighbors of each tile and always take the lowest set ID we find. We keep doing this until no changes are made. Then all tiles have a set ID that we can compare to the set ID of any other tile on the map. If two map tiles belong to the same set, a path between them is guaranteed, otherwise there's no need to look for one. Remember to run this function every time you change something on the terrain—for example, when buildings or walls are created or destroyed.

A Star Shall Guide Us

The most popular of all true pathfinding algorithms is the A* algorithm (pronounced A-star). The A* algorithm finds the least-cost path between two points on a map, if such a path exists. There are many good articles about implementing an efficient A* pathfinding system, see for example [Matthews02], [Higgins02a], [Higgins02b], [Higgins02c], [Cain02]. In this book, we will concentrate on a pretty simple implementation of the algorithm, rather than any of the more-advanced approaches covered in these articles.

A* is a directed search algorithm, which means that it searches in the direction of the goal, rather than searching in all directions like a breadth-width-first search or Djikstra's search. There are three important components of an A*-pathfinding system, the open list, the closed list and the heuristic function. Each tile also needs a G value and an F value, as well as a parent pointer.

Open list: The open list contains tiles that are being considered for further search.

Closed list: The closed list contains those tiles that already have been searched.

Heuristic function: The heuristic function (distance function) calculates an approximate distance to the goal from any point on the map.

G value: A tile's G value is the actual cost of traveling to a tile from its starting position.

F value: A tile's F value is the approximate distance from the start to the goal if the path crosses this particular tile.

Parent pointer: A tile's parent pointer is used to keep track of what tile opened this tile (i.e., put it into the open list). In the end, the path will be created by back-tracking from the goal to the start, using the parent pointers.

Here's an overview of the A* algorithm in pseudocode. It's a bit tough, and it usually takes a couple of implementation attempts to fully understand the algorithm.

1. Clear the Open and Closed lists.
2. Set the start node's G value to 0 and its F value to Heuristic (start, goal), then add it to the Open list.
3. Set the active node **A**, to the tile in the Open list with the smallest F value.
4. Calculate the new G value of going to any of **A**'s neighbors as **A**'s G value plus **A**'s cost.
5. For each neighbor **B** of **A**, check if it exists in the Open or Closed list.
   a. If **B** is not in the Open or Closed list: then set **B**'s G value to the new G value and the F value as the new G value plus the Heuristic (**B**, goal), then add it to the Open list and set its parent pointer to point to **A**.
   b. If **B** is in the Open or Closed list: then check if **B**'s G value is higher than the new G value, if it is update it, and set the parent pointer to **A**.
6. Remove **A** from the Open list and add it to the Closed list.
7. Repeat steps 3 to 6 until:
   a. **A** is the goal node.
   b. The Open list is empty. In this case there is no valid path between the start and the goal. Exit the algorithm.
8. Build a path by traversing the tiles, using the parent pointers, starting from the goal node until the start node is reached.
9. Reverse the path.

Before we starting implementing this, there is one important optimization we need to consider first: the way we represent the open and closed list. The easiest representation would probably be to implement these lists using an `std::vector`, adding and removing nodes from it as we go along. However, a problem with this is that as the map dimensions grow larger, so do the number of tiles—exponentially. For a medium-size map, we might get thousands of nodes that need to be stored and moved between these two lists. A better way to represent whether a node is open or closed is to store two Boolean values (open, closed) at each tile. So when we first start a search, we set the open and closed variables of all the tiles to `false`, which equals clearing the open and closed list. Whenever we open or close a tile, we just set the corresponding variable in the map tile to `true`. Now let's add some pathfinding variables to our `MAPTILE` structure:

```
struct MAPTILE{
    MAPTILE();                  //Set everything to 0

    int m_type, m_set;          //type & tileset of this tile
    float m_height, m_cost;
    bool m_walkable;            //can this tile be crossed?
    MAPTILE* m_pNeighbors[8];   //neighbor pointers
    // Pathfinding variables
    INTPOINT m_mappos;          //so the tile knows where it is
    float f,g;                  //the F and G value
    bool open, closed;          //Open and Closed variable
    MAPTILE * m_pParent;        //Parent pointer, Used by A*
};
```

Remember how we connected the tiles using the `neighbors[8]` variable? All the tiles are now interconnected and form a map (graph) that we can search using our A* algorithm. As mentioned before, A* is a directed-search algorithm. In other words, during the search, it favors tiles that are lying closer to the goal to be visited first. A* does this with the help of the heuristic function:

```
//Distance Function:
float H(INTPOINT a, INTPOINT b)
{
    return sqrt((a.x - b.x)*(a.x - b.x) +
                (a.y - b.y)*(a.y - b.y));
}

//Manhattan Distance Function:
float H(INTPOINT a, INTPOINT b)
{
    return abs(a.x - b.x) + abs(a.y - b.y);
}
```

The actual distance function calculates the distance more accurately, which may result in fewer nodes needing to be searched. The Manhattan distance function just returns the sum of the differences in the *x*- and *y*-dimension. The Manhattan function is the cheaper of the pair and the one favored by most game programmers. We can now have a look at the A* algorithm, itself:

```
std::vector<INTPOINT> TERRAIN::GetPath(INTPOINT start,
                                       INTPOINT goal)
{
    //Check that the two points are within the
    //bounds of the terrain
    MAPTILE *startTile = GetTile(start);
    MAPTILE *goalTile = GetTile(goal);

    //Check that startTile and goalTile are valid tiles here

    //Init maptiles, set Open & Closed variables to false,
    //and f & g variables to INT_MAX
    long numTiles = m_size.x * m_size.y;
    for(long l=0;l<numTiles;l++)
    {
        m_pMapTiles[l].f = m_MapTiles[l].g = INT_MAX;
        m_pMapTiles[l].open = m_MapTiles[l].closed = false;
    }

    std::vector<MAPTILE*> open;        //Create Our Open list

    //Init our starting point (SP)
    startTile->g = 0;
                    startTile->f = H(start, goal);
    startTile->open = true;
    open.push_back(startTile);         //Add SP to Open list

    //Search until a valid path is found, or there is no
    //open tiles left to search
    bool found = false;
    while(!found && !open.empty())
    {
        //Find tile with the lowest F value
        MAPTILE * best = open[0];
        int bestPlace = 0;
        for(int i=1;i<open.size();i++)
            if(open[i]->f < best->f)
            {
```

```
            best = open[i];
            bestPlace = i;
    }

if(best == NULL)break;          //No path found

//Remove best node from Open list
open[bestPlace]->open = false;
open.erase(&open[bestPlace]);

//If goal has been found
if(best->m_mappos == goal)
{
    std::vector<INTPOINT> p, p2;
    MAPTILE *point = best;

    //Generate path
    while(point->m_mappos != start)
    {
        p.push_back(point->m_mappos);
        point = point->m_pParent;
    }

    //Reverse path
    for(int i=p.size()-1;i!=0;i-)
            p2.push_back(p[i]);
    p2.push_back(goal);
    return p2;
}
else                    // otherwise, check neighbors
{
    for(i=0;i<8;i++)
        if(best->m_pNeighbors[i] != NULL)
        {
            //Calc new G and F value
            bool inList = false;
            float d, newF, newG = best->g + 1.0f;
            d = H(best->m_mappos,
                    best->m_pNeighbors[i]->m_mappos);
            newF = newG +
                    H(best->m_pNeighbors[i]->m_mappos,
                      goal) +
                      best->m_pNeighbors[i]->m_cost
                      * 5.0f * d;
```

```
                    if(best->m_pNeighbors[i]->open ||
                       best->m_pNeighbors[i]->closed)
                    {
                        // If the new F value is lower
                        if(newF < best->m_pNeighbors[i]->f)
                        {
                            // update the values of this tile
                            best->m_pNeighbors[i]->g = newG;
                            best->m_pNeighbors[i]->f = newF;
                            best->m_pNeighbors[i]->m_pParent =
                                best;
                        }
                        inList = true;
                    }

                    //If neighbor tile isn't Open or Closed
                    if(!inList)
                    {
                        //Set the values
                        best->m_pNeighbors[i]->f = newF;
                        best->m_pNeighbors[i]->g = newG;
                        best->m_pNeighbors[i]->parent = best;
                        best->m_pNeighbors[i]->open = true;
                        //Add it to the open list
                        open.push_back(best->m_pNeighbors[i]);
                    }
                }

            //best tile has been searched,
            //add it to the Closed list
            best->closed = true;
        }
    }

    //No path found, return an empty path
    return std::vector<INTPOINT>();
}
```

The function TERRAIN::GetPath() returns an std::vector<INPOINT>, which is a list of our 2D coordinates that will take us from the starting point to the goal. It is a massive function that may not be easy to understand at first glance. A good place to start is to try and make sense of pseudocode first, and then have a second look at the actual implementation.

Rather than writing std::vector<INPOINT> *whenever you want a path, you could create a* typedef *like this:*

```
typedef std::vector<INTPOINT> PATH;
```

Now you can simply refer to an std::vector<INTPOINT> as a PATH.

This is a fairly simple implementation of the A* pathfinding algorithm, and it is just meant to get you started, but it will do the job well enough for our purposes. This code doesn't support things like multiple paths being queried at the same time or splitting searches across multiple frames. This means that if many units are told to move across a large map at the same time, the game will pause until all units have had their path calculated for them. For a better A* implementation, have a look at the articles by [Higgins02a], [Higgins02b], and [Higgins02c], where some more-advanced A* topics are covered. Also see [Lester05] for broader look at A* pathfinding.

If you are new to A* pathfinding, know that there are a lot of professionals out there who have written many articles about it. Read as many of these as you can, try to understand them, and then code your own A* implementation. If you are aiming to implement a top-notch pathfinding system, you will most likely need to look into some of the following subjects:

Hierarchical pathfinding (very large maps)

Group pathfinding (many units)

Precomputed paths (small maps, high speed)

Load-balancing between frames (maintaining frame rate)

Example 4.13

On the CD-ROM, you'll find Example 4.13, which implements A* pathfinding as explained in this section. The path is green at the starting position and fades to red at the goal position. The blue dots mark those map tiles that were visited by the pathfinding algorithm. This should help you get an idea of how the A* algorithm works. It can also be clearly seen how the algorithm searches in the direction of the goal.

Giving the Path a Facelift

Even though the A* algorithm gives you the fastest or least-costly path, it can make the units move "unnaturally." For instance, in a regular grid, the A* algorithm may favor paths that go diagonally because that actually covers more distance while traversing fewer tiles. To sort this out, we need to apply a small penalty for diagonal paths to make the algorithm favor the more-natural looking "straight" path, as shown in Figure 4.14. We therefore multiply the distance between two tiles by the cost of traversing that specific tile. The result is a better-looking path.

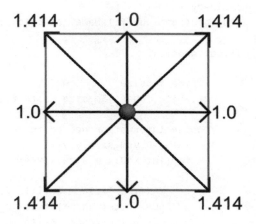

FIGURE 4.14   The penalty for diagonal paths.

SAVE AND LOAD THE TERRAIN

The time has come when you have a good-looking terrain that you want to save to a file—and be able load again, of course. As with everything else, there are a few different formats we can use to do this, such as the ASCII format or the binary format. The ASCII format has the advantage that you can use a text editor like Notepad to edit your maps—but then, so can anyone playing your game. However, when you store your maps in the ASCII format, you can't store advanced structures and objects directly; you have save each variable in your structures independently. All in all, it's a messy way of doing things. In this example, we'll save our maps using the binary file format because this allows us to easily store/retrieve our own data structures.

In the end, the approach you choose is totally up to what you are more comfortable with. The more important question is, what information do we store? As a rule of thumb, save all the information you need to recreate a map entirely; this includes information like the map tile height, type, path-finding restrictions, and so forth. Things like tile sets and costs are not necessary to store because they can be easily recalculated once the terrain has been loaded. We also store all the objects of the map in this file. Later on, we'll store information about players, units, buildings, and resources all in this map file, as well.

The `SaveTerrain()` and `LoadTerrain()` functions have been added to the TERRAIN class to handle saving and loading of the terrain:

```
void TERRAIN::SaveTerrain(char fileName[])
{
    //Binary format
    std::ofstream out(fileName, std::ios::binary);

    if(out.good())
    {
        //Write mapsize
        out.write((char*)&m_size, sizeof(INTPOINT));

        //Write information needed to recreate the map
        for(int y=0;y<m_size.y;y++)
            for(int x=0;x<m_size.x;x++)
            {
                MAPTILE *tile = GetTile(x, y);
                out.write((char*)&tile->m_type, sizeof(int));
                out.write((char*)&tile->m_height,
                        sizeof(float));
            }

        //Write all the objects
        int numObjects = m_objects.size();
        out.write((char*)&numObjects, sizeof(int));
        for(int i=0;i<m_objects.size();i++)
        {
        //Object variables
        out.write((char*)&m_objects[i].type, sizeof(int));
        out.write((char*)&m_objects[i]. m_mappos,
                sizeof(INTPOINT));

        out.write((char*)&m_objects[i].m_meshInstance.m_pos,
                sizeof(D3DXVECTOR3));
        out.write((char*)&m_objects[i].meshInstance.m_rot,
                sizeof(D3DXVECTOR3));
        out.write((char*)&m_objects[i].meshInstance.m_sca,
                sizeof(D3DXVECTOR3));
```

```
        }
    }

    out.close();
}
```

First we open an `ofstream` (output-file stream) and start dumping terrain information into it. We start by saving the size of the terrain. Note in this piece of code how we can save structures like `INTPOINT` or `D3DXVECTOR3` without having to save each of its individual variables one by one (as we would have had to do if we were using the ASCII file format). Next, we save all the objects, starting with the number of objects to save. When all the information has been stored, we close the output file, and that's it. Next up is the function that loads a terrain file stored using the `TERRAIN::SaveTerrain()` function:

```
void TERRAIN::LoadTerrain(char fileName[])
{
    //Binary format
    std::ifstream in(fileName, std::ios::binary);

    if(in.good())
    {
        Release();   //Release all terrain resources

        //read map size
        in.read((char*)&m_size, sizeof(INTPOINT));

        if(m_pMapTiles != NULL)   //Clear old maptiles
            delete [] m_pMapTiles;

        //Create new maptiles
        m_pMapTiles = new MAPTILE[m_size.x * m_size.y];
        memset(m_pMapTiles, 0,
                sizeof(MAPTILE)* m_size.x * m_size.y);

        //Read the maptile information
        for(int y=0;y<m_size.y;y++)
            for(int x=0;x<m_size.x;x++)
            {
                MAPTILE *tile = GetTile(x, y);
                in.read((char*)&tile->m_type, sizeof(int));
                in.read((char*)&tile->m_height,
                        sizeof(float));
            }
```

```
//Read number of objects
int numObjects = 0;
in.read((char*)&numObjects, sizeof(int));

for(int i=0;i<numObjects;i++)
{
    int type = 0;
    INTPOINT mp;
    D3DXVECTOR3 p, r, s;

    in.read((char*)&type, sizeof(int));
    in.read((char*)&mp, sizeof(INTPOINT));
    in.read((char*)&p, sizeof(D3DXVECTOR3));
    in.read((char*)&r, sizeof(D3DXVECTOR3));
    in.read((char*)&s, sizeof(D3DXVECTOR3));

    m_objects.push_back(OBJECT(type, mp, p, r, s));
}

//Recreate Terrain with the loaded information here...
}

in.close();
}
```

The TERRAIN::LoadTerrain() function reads the information in from a terrain file in the exact same order as it was stored in the TERRAIN::SaveTerrain() function. This time we create a binary ifstream object (input-file stream) to read our terrain file.

ON THE CD

Example 4.14

See Example 4.14, where these functions have been implemented.

SUMMARY

In this chapter, we had a look at how to create and render a terrain. We started by looking at different ways to create heightmaps and then saw how to create multiple mesh patches from a heightmap. The reason we don't create a large mesh for the entire terrain will be more apparent in the next chapter when we take a look at object culling.

We also made the terrain look a little bit better by using a couple of different methods to texture a terrain. We also added some random mesh objects to break the monotony. In the next chapter, we will have a look at how to light the terrain and the terrain objects by using a vertex shader. Also, we will implement a camera and a mouse class to handle player input, and cover subjects like picking, object culling, and level-of-detail rendering.

EXERCISES

- Create a couple of different terrains, like desert, jungle, snowy tundra, or canyons. Experiment with different noise functions, textures, and terrain objects.
- Allow objects to have a map size larger than 1×1. Take this into account when you do your pathfinding.
- Create the cost of a tile as a function of the slope and tile type.
- Write a function that flattens the terrain for a specific map rectangle, and then performs a local smoothing on this rectangle and its surroundings. This can be used to prepare the terrain for a building in this location.

REFERENCES

[Cain02] Cain, Timothy, "Practical Optimizations for A* Path Generation." *AI Game Programming Wisdom,* Charles River Media, 2002.

[Higgins02a] Higgins, Dan, "Generic A* Pathfinding." *AI Game Programming Wisdom,* Charles River Media, 2002.

[Higgins02b] Higgins, Dan, "Pathfinding Design Architecture." *AI Game Programming Wisdom,* Charles River Media, 2002.

[Higgins02c] Higgins, Dan, "How to Achieve Lightning-Fast A*." *AI Game Programming Wisdom,* Charles River Media, 2002.

[Lester05] Lester, Patrick, "A* Pathfinding for Beginners." Available online at: *http://www.policyalmanac.org/games/aStarTutorial.htm,* 2005.

[Matthews02] Matthews, James, "Basic A* Pathfinding Made Simple." *AI Game Programming Wisdom,* Charles River Media, 2002.

[Olsen04] Olsen, Jacob, "Realtime Procedural Terrain Generation." Available online at: *http://oddlabs.com/download/terrain_generation.pdf,* 2004.

[Perlin99] Perlin, Ken, "Making Noise." Available online at: *http://www.noisemachine. com/talk1/index.html,* 1999.

[Shoemaker04] Shoemaker, Shawn, "Random Map Generation for Strategy Games." *AI Game Programming Wisdom 2,* Charles River Media, 2004.

FURTHER READING

Elias, Hugo, "Perlin Noise." Available online at: *http://freespace.virgin.net/hugo. elias/models/m_perlin.htm,* 2000.

Wagner, Daniel, "Terrain Geomorphing in the Vertex Shader." Available online at: *http://www.ims.tuwien.ac.at/media/documents/publications/Terrain_ Geomorphing_in_the_Vertex_Shader.pdf,* 2003.

5 | Camera and Mouse

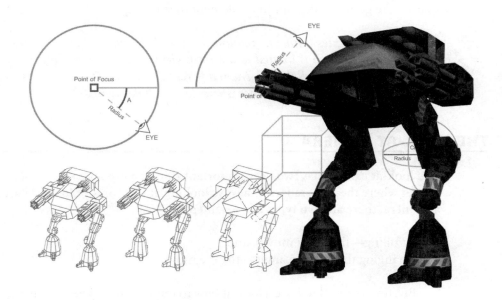

I n this chapter, we will look into how to create a functional camera and mouse
class for real-time strategy games. If you have completed an introductory book
about Direct3D, you have probably implemented some form of camera class, so
some of the things in this chapter shouldn't be altogether unfamiliar.

The camera is a very important object when making any game. It is from the
lens of a virtual camera that we see everything that happens in a game. There are a
few different types of cameras:

First person: The player sees the world through the character being controlled.
This camera type is common in First Person Shooter (FPS) games.

Third Person: The player is looking over the shoulder of the character being controlled. The camera follows the character as he moves around in the game. This
camera type is common in action games, such as Role Playing Games (RPG).

Look-at: The look-at camera is not bound like the other two perspectives to a particular character in the game. Instead, the camera is controlled independently by the player.

In traditional RTS games, the look-at camera style is generally the most commonly used. This allows you a bird's-eye view of all the action on the battlefield or from the safety of a mother ship, whichever the scenario. This is the camera type that we are going to attempt to implement in this chapter.

Most RTS games limit the amount of control the player have over the camera. Often, the camera is limited to a certain view angle (or view range), and all the player can do is scroll the camera in different directions. This is perhaps a remnant from the days when RTS games where done completely in 2D.

THE LOOK-AT CAMERA

The look-at camera has two very important things: a eye and a point of focus. No matter where the camera is, it is always looking at the point of focus. With a look-at camera, there are two types of movement:

- Scrolling—the focus moves, and
- Changing the viewing angle—the eye moves.

But first we need to have a look at how to implement a general camera. To render a 3D scene from a specific Point of View (POV), we need to set these three transformation matrices:

D3DTS_WORLD: This transformation matrix moves the object you want to render around in the world.

D3DTS_VIEW: This transformation matrix sets the camera viewpoint (i.e., the point in space the camera is looking from). It also sets where the camera is looking.

D3DTS_PROJECTION: This matrix sets the "zoom" of the camera and/or the projection. It enables you to do things like orthogonal rendering and more.

The D3DTS_WORLD Matrix

The D3DTS_WORLD matrix controls the position of the object being rendered. With this matrix, we control the translation, rotation, and scale of an object (see Chapter 4: Terrain Objects).

```
D3DXMATRIX p, r, s;
D3DXMatrixTranslation(&p, m_pos.x, m_pos.y, m_pos.z);
D3DXMatrixRotationYawPitchRoll(&r, m_rot.y, m_rot.x, m_rot.z);
D3DXMatrixScaling(&s, m_sca.x, m_sca.y, m_sca.z);

D3DXMATRIX world = s * r * p;
Device->SetTransform(D3DTS_WORLD, &world);
```

Here's the code from the MESHINSTANCE class again, which shows how we set up the D3DTS_WORLD matrix. The important thing to notice is that we create the world matrix by multiplying the p, r, and s matrix in the order of scale, rotation, and translation.

The D3DTS_VIEW Matrix

The D3DTS_VIEW matrix determines where the camera is looking from and what it is looking at. We create this matrix very simply with this D3DX library function:

```
D3DXMATRIX *D3DXMatrixLookAtLH(
    D3DXMATRIX *pOut,
    CONST D3DXVECTOR3 *pEye,
    CONST D3DXVECTOR3 *pAt,
    CONST D3DXVECTOR3 *pUp
);
```

The pOut matrix will hold the result of this function once it is complete. The pEye vector describes where the eye (or camera) is. The pAt vector tells the function where the camera is looking (i.e., our focus), and the pUp tells the function what direction is straight up. A typical call to this function might look like this:

```
D3DXMATRIX  matView;
D3DXVECTOR3 Eye    = D3DXVECTOR3(5.0f, 5.0f, 5.0f);
D3DXVECTOR3 Lookat = D3DXVECTOR3(0.0f, 0.0f, 0.0f);

D3DXMatrixLookAtLH(&matView, &Eye, &Lookat,
                   &D3DXVECTOR3(0.0f, 1.0f, 0.0f));

Device->SetTransform(D3DTS_VIEW, &matView);
```

Easy. The D3DXMatrixLookAtLH() function does all the complex behind-the-scenes calculations for us. This piece of code sets up a camera viewpoint from (5.0f, 5.0f, 5.0f) looking at (0.0f, 0.0f, 0.0f).

Sometimes it can be very handy to extract information from a view matrix. The following shows the different components of a view matrix:

$$viewMatrix = \begin{bmatrix} right.x & up.x & look.x & 0.0 \\ right.y & up.y & look.y & 0.0 \\ right.z & up.z & look.z & 0.0 \\ pos.x & pos.y & pos.z & 1.0 \end{bmatrix}$$

The vectors *right, up,* and *look* are all perpendicular to each other. The *look* vector describes the direction that the camera is looking. The *up* vector describes the camera's up vector. The four vectors right, up, look, and pos can easily be extracted like this:

```
D3DXMATRIX   matView;        //Contains our view matrix

D3DXVECTOR3 right = D3DXVECTOR3(matView(0,0),
                               matView(1,0),
                               matView(2,0));

D3DXVec3Normalize(&right, &right);
```

In this piece of code, the right vector is extracted from the matrix matView. In the same way, the up, look, or pos vector can be extracted.

The D3DTS_PROJECTION Matrix

The D3DTS_PROJECTION matrix is the most special one of the lot. There are two different projection types that we need to cover. One is perspective projection, and the other is orthogonal projection, as shown in Figure 5.1. The perspective projection is the most common projection matrix used in 3D computer games because this projection matrix gives you a sense of depth (i.e., objects appear smaller the further from the camera they are). You can use this projection matrix to do effects like a sniper scope, and so forth. The orthogonal projection matrix, on the other hand, removes all depth from the scene so two similar objects will have the same size no matter how far from the camera they are. We will use this type of projection matrix when we render the terrain minimap in Chapter 11.

Here's one D3DX library function to help you set up a perspective projection matrix:

```
D3DXMATRIX *D3DXMatrixPerspectiveFovLH(
    D3DXMATRIX *pOut,
```

```
        FLOAT fovY,
        FLOAT Aspect,
        FLOAT zn,
        FLOAT zf
    );
```

pOut: Will contain the resulting matrix.

fovY: This is the Field of View (FOV) in the *y*-directions (in radians).

Aspect: The target rendering aspect (i.e., image height/image width).

zn/zf: Z-near and Z-far (i.e., the near and far view planes).

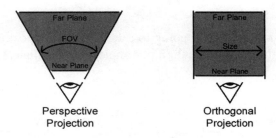

FIGURE 5.1   Perspective and orthogonal projection.

With the D3DXMatrixPerspectiveFovLH() function, we can create a perspective projection matrix like this:

```
D3DXMATRIX matProj;

float aspect = (float)_width / (float)_height;
float fov = degrees * (D3DX_PI / 180.0f);
D3DXMatrixPerspectiveFovLH(&matProj, fov, aspect,
                           1.0f, 1000.0f );

Device->SetTransform(D3DTS_PROJECTION, &matProj);
```

Just change the degrees variable to alter the "zoom" of your sniper scope. A small FOV value will result in a large zoom factor. Next, let's see how we can set up an orthogonal projection matrix.

```
D3DXMATRIX *D3DXMatrixOrthoLH(
    D3DXMATRIX *pOut,
    FLOAT w,
    FLOAT h,
    FLOAT zn,
    FLOAT zf
);
```

The w and h are the width and height of your view volume, and as in the previous function, zn and zf are your near and far planes. We'll cover this type of projection matrix in more detail later on when we render our minimap (and also in Chapter 10).

The CAMERA Class

In the CAMERA class, we are going to calculate the eye position relative to the focus point using three variables: the alpha angle, the beta angle, and the radius, as shown in Figure 5.2.

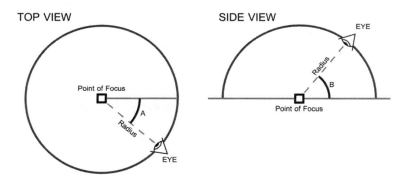

FIGURE 5.2   Our CAMERA class.

The alpha angle (A) determines the top rotation of the camera around the *y*-axis. The beta angle (B) determines the eye's position from the side view and the elevation from the ground. The eye's position can then be calculated with this simple equation:

```
height = radius * sin(B)
sideRadius = radius * cos(B)

eye.x = focus.x + sideRadius * cos(A)
eye.y = focus.y + height
eye.z = focus.z + sideRadius * sin(A)
```

To rotate the camera in any way, we simply change the A or B angle, and to move the camera closer or further away from the focus, we simply change the radius. Our CAMERA class looks like this:

```
class CAMERA{
    public:
        //Init Camera
        CAMERA();
        void Init(IDirect3DDevice9* Dev);

        //Movement
        void Scroll(D3DXVECTOR3 vec);//Move Focus
        void Pitch(float f);        //Change B-angle
        void Yaw(float f);          //Change A-angle
        void Zoom(float f);         //Change FOV
        void ChangeRadius(float f); //Change Radius

        //Calculate Eye position etc
        void Update(float timeDelta);

        //Calculate Matrices
        D3DXMATRIX GetViewMatrix();
        D3DXMATRIX GetProjectionMatrix();

    private:

        IDirect3DDevice9* m_pDevice;
        float m_alpha, m_beta, m_radius, m_fov;
        D3DXVECTOR3 m_eye, m_focus, m_right, m_look;
};
```

The Init() function sets up the camera variables; a good idea might be to send the initial focus point and angles to the Init() function if you are using more than one camera. The movement functions simply add to angles, FOV, or radius, and at the same time perform a test to make sure that these variables are within a desired range. The GetViewMatrix() and GetProjectionMatrix() functions calculate the two transformation matrices, as explained earlier. But let's have a quick look at what happens in the Update() function:

```
//KEYDOWN macro
#define KEYDOWN(vk_code) ((GetAsyncKeyState(vk_code)
                          & 0x8000) ? 1 : 0)

void CAMERA::Update(float timeDelta)
{
    //Move Focus (i.e. Scroll)
    if(KEYDOWN(VK_LEFT))  Scroll(-right * timeDelta * 20.0f);
    if(KEYDOWN(VK_RIGHT)) Scroll(right * timeDelta * 20.0f);
    if(KEYDOWN(VK_UP))    Scroll(look * timeDelta * 20.0f);
    if(KEYDOWN(VK_DOWN))  Scroll(-look * timeDelta * 20.0f);

    //Move Camera (i.e. Change Angle)
    if(KEYDOWN('A'))Yaw(-timeDelta);
    if(KEYDOWN('D'))Yaw(timeDelta);
    if(KEYDOWN('W'))Pitch(timeDelta);
    if(KEYDOWN('S'))Pitch(-timeDelta);

    //connect input to Zoom and FOV in a similar manner here.

    //Calculate Eye Position
    float sideRadius = m_radius * cos(m_beta);
    float height = m_radius * sin(m_beta);

    eye = D3DXVECTOR3(m_focus.x + sideRadius * cos(m_alpha),
                      m_focus.y + height,
                      m_focus.z + sideRadius * sin(m_alpha));

    //Set transformation matrices...
    m_pDevice->SetTransform(D3DTS_VIEW, &GetViewMatrix());
    m_pDevice->SetTransform(D3DTS_PROJECTION,
                            &GetProjectionMatrix());
}
```

The look and right vectors in this code are extracted in the GetViewMatrix() function. Other than that, this function maps keyboard input to the different movements Scroll(), Yaw(), Pitch(), Zoom(), and ChangeRadius().

Example 5.1

See Example 5.1 on the CD-ROM. Here, the CAMERA class is implemented and used. Try to get some feel for how the radius and FOV affect the final image.

THE MOUSE

Now we have a working camera class to handle all our camera movements. So far we have been using the keyboard as our main input device. It is now time to look at the mouse. The mouse is the main user input device in any real-time strategy game. In most RTS games, the mouse is used both to control the camera and the units.

The mouse operates in screen space and not 3D space (even though we need to bridge that gap later on). The MOUSE class we will implement in this chapter will handle all input from the mouse and paint the cursor on the screen. We'll also handle events like the mouse wheel, mouse buttons, and so forth with this class. So let's look at how we receive input from the mouse by using the DirectInput library. (Remember that you must link dinput8.lib to your project in order for this to work.) The first thing we need to do is create an LPDIRECTINPUT8 object. This is done very easily with the DirectInput8Create() function.

```
HRESULT WINAPI DirectInput8Create(
    HINSTANCE hinst,
    DWORD dwVersion,
    REFIID riidltf,
    LPVOID *ppvOut,
    LPUNKNOWN punkOuter
);
```

A call to this function might look like this (see the DirectX documentation for more details):

```
DirectInput8Create(GetModuleHandle(NULL), //App handle
                   0x0800,                 //v.8.0
                   IID_IDirectInput8,      //Interface ID
                   (VOID**)&directInput,   //DirectInput Object
                   NULL);
```

Acquiring the Mouse Device

The next step is to acquire the mouse device and use it to extract information from our physical device:

```
//Acquire Default System mouse
directInput->CreateDevice(GUID_SysMouse, &mouseDevice, NULL);
mouseDevice->SetDataFormat(&c_dfDIMouse);
mouseDevice->SetCooperativeLevel(wnd, DISCL_EXCLUSIVE |
                                      DISCL_FOREGROUND);
mouseDevice->Acquire();
```

GUID_SysMouse means that we acquire the default system mouse. Next we set the data format to the c_dfDIMouse value. This means that we will retrieve information from the mouse using the DIMOUSESTATE structure—position, mouse wheel, and four buttons. If you have a mouse with more than four buttons, you can use the DIMOUSESTATE2 structure instead. DIMOUSESTATE2 supports mice with up to eight buttons, but then you need to set the data format to c_dfDIMouse2. The DIMOUSESTATE structure looks like this:

```
struct DIMOUSESTATE {
    LONG lX;
    LONG lY;
    LONG lZ;
    BYTE rgbButtons[4];
}
```

The lX, lY values are the mouse cursors' relative values. This means that the DIMOUSESTATE structure only records changes in the mouse position and not the actual screen position itself. The lZ variable is our mouse wheel, and the rgbButtons[4] contains the state of our different mouse buttons.

So once we have set the data format, we set the cooperative level of the mouse device. This can be done using a couple of different flags:

DISCL_EXCLUSIVE: No other application may get the mouse exclusively.

DISCL_NONEXCLUSIVE: Other applications may use the mouse as they wish.

DISCL_BACKGROUND: The application window does not need to be in the foreground.

DISCL_FOREGROUND: Once the application window is no longer in the foreground, the mouse is unacquired.

For a full-screen RTS application, we set the mouse cooperation level to exclusive and in the foreground. The Acquire() function returns a HRESULT with the value DI_OK if acquiring the mouse worked. There we go. We now have a mouse device directly connected to our physical mouse. All we need to do now is to extract the information from the mouse once every frame.

```
DIMOUSESTATE mouseState;

//Retrieve mouse state
ZeroMemory(&mouseState, sizeof(DIMOUSESTATE));
mouseDevice->GetDeviceState(sizeof(DIMOUSESTATE),
                            &mouseState);
```

The mouse information is now stored in the mouseState structure. With this information, we can move our cursor and check buttons, the mouse wheel, and so on. The next thing we need is to draw a cursor to the screen.

Drawing Sprites

Sprites are simple 2D textures drawn in screen space. The simplest way to draw these is by using the ID3DXSprite interface. Again, we don't have to worry about creating quads using vertex buffers, then mapping textures onto them and render them. All we need to do is load a texture and then use an ID3DXSprite interface to render it directly in screen space. We create a texture and a sprite object like this:

```
IDirect3DTexture9* mouseTexture = NULL;
LPD3DXSPRITE Sprite = NULL;

//Load texture and init sprite
D3DXCreateTextureFromFile(Device, "cursor.dds",
                          &mouseTexture);
D3DXCreateSprite(Device, &Sprite);
```

Then we need to draw the texture in screen space, like this:

```
RECT srcRectangle = {0, 0, 20, 20};

Sprite->Begin(D3DXSPRITE_ALPHABLEND);

Sprite->Draw(mouseTexture,              //Source texture
             &srcRectangle,             //Source RECT
             NULL,                          //Center
             &D3DXVECTOR2(x, y, 0.0f),   //Position
             0xffffffff);               //Modulation Color

Sprite->End();
```

This piece of code extracts the srcRectangle (0, 0, 20, 20) and draws it at position (x, y). The sprite's Begin() function prepares the necessary rendering states for drawing 2D sprites (check the DirectX documentation for possible flags). The End() function restores all the settings to their original values, as they were before the Begin() function was called. With the Draw() function, you can control the rotation, scale, and color modulation of how a sprite should be drawn. Leaving the color modulation to 0xffffffff (pure white) means that the original colors of the texture will be used.

Creating a Cursor Texture

We now know how to acquire the mouse device and how to draw textures to 2D screen space. All we need to do now is create the cursor texture that we are going to use. Throughout this book, we are going to be using the DDS (DirectDraw Surface) format to store textures—things like alpha maps and normal maps. If you want to make the most out of editing DDS files, you might want to download some of the DDS plug-ins from the NVIDIA Web page at *http://developer.nvidia.com/object/ nv_texture_tools.html.*

Here are a few tools we can use to create a DDS texture.

The DirectX Texture Tool

The simplest way to create a DDS texture is to use the DirectX texture tool that comes with the DirectX SDK. Have a look at the Cursor1 example on the companion CD-ROM, where a DDS cursor is created using this tool.

1. Create a mouse pointer picture in, for example, Microsoft Paint, and save it as a bitmap.
2. Create another bitmap file from the first one. Paint black the areas where you want complete transparency. Paint areas where you want complete opacity, white. (Gray areas will be semi-transparent.) There shouldn't be

any color in this picture, just black, white, and shades of gray. This is your alpha channel. Save it to a new bitmap file.

3. Open up the DirectX Texture tool (see Figure 5.3). Select File, New Texture.
4. Select Standard Texture with the dimensions of the bitmaps you just created. Then set the surface format to: A8R8G8B8 (32-bit color, with 8 bits for each channel). Click Ok.
5. Go to File->Open Onto This Surface, and select the first mouse bitmap you created.
6. Go to File->Open Onto Alpha Channel Of This Surface, and select the black-and-white alpha bitmap you created.
7. Now save this image in the DDS format, and you're done.

FIGURE 5.3   The DirectX texture tool.

DDS Images in Photoshop

To create and edit DDS files in Photoshop, you have to install the NVIDIA Adobe Photoshop plug-in. See the Cursor2 example on the CD-ROM.

1. Create a new image in the RGB color mode and paint something that looks like a mouse cursor.
2. In the Channels window (Window->Channels), click the Create New Channel Button. This will create an alpha channel. Select this channel and paint your alpha channel here. Most of the time, you can just copy the information you have in the RGB channel, paste it into the alpha channel, and then edit it.
3. Save the image in the DDS format (A8R8G8B8). Done.

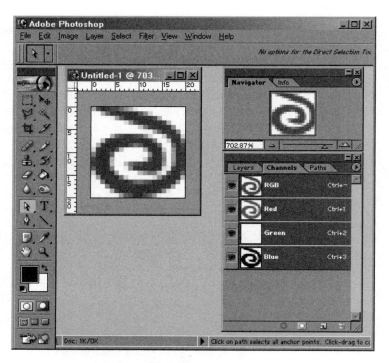

FIGURE 5.4   Adobe Photoshop.

DDS Images in 3ds Max

If you are lucky enough to have 3ds Max and know how to use it, creating a mouse cursor is a trivial project. Just like before, you will need the NVIDIA 3ds Max plug-in to read/write DDS files with 3ds Max. See the Cursor3 example on the compan-ion CD-ROM.

ON THE CD

Start 3ds Max and create your cursor mesh, lights, cameras, and so forth. If you are new to modeling in 3ds Max, see Chapter 6: "Creating 3D Models," or search the Internet for some tutorials.

1. Render an image.
2. Hit the Save button in the rendering window that appears.
3. Save the image using the DDS format (select A8R8G8B8), and you're done.

Creating DDS files using 3ds Max is much simpler than using Microsoft Paint or Photoshop, because you don't have to draw the alpha map separately; but it takes some know-how. Now, all we have to do is put the pieces together and implement our MOUSE class.

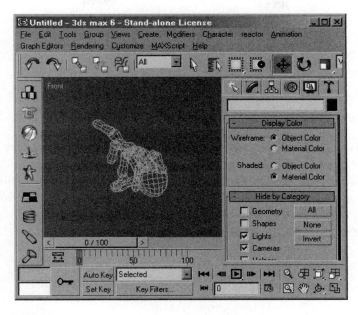

FIGURE 5.5   Creating an image using 3ds Max.

The MOUSE Class

The MOUSE class will, among other things, encapsulate the processes of acquiring the mouse, loading cursor textures, and rendering the cursor.

```
class MOUSE : public INTPOINT{
    public:
        MOUSE();
        ~MOUSE();
        void InitMouse(IDirect3DDevice9* Device, HWND wnd);
        bool ClickLeft();
        bool ClickRight();
        bool WheelUp();
        bool WheelDown();
        bool Over(RECT dest);
        bool PressInRect(RECT dest);
        void Update();
        void Paint();

        float m_speed;
        int m_type;
```

```
                private:
                    LPDIRECTINPUTDEVICE8 m_pMouseDevice;
                    DIMOUSESTATE m_mouseState;
                    IDirect3DTexture9* m_pMouseTexture;
                    LPD3DXSPRITE m_pSprite;
                    RECT m_viewport;
            };
```

First, the MOUSE class inherits from the INTPOINT class, which is nothing more than an *x* and *y* value. The InitMouse() function acquires the mouse device and stores it in the mouseDevice variable. It also loads the cursor image into the mouseTexture variable and creates our sprite object, just like we did in previous sections. At the initialization, we set the *x* and *y* value of the MOUSE class to the center of the viewport. Each call of the Update() function reads in the mouse state and updates the cursor position, like this:

```
        void MOUSE::Update()
        {
            //Retrieve mouse state
            ZeroMemory(&m_mouseState, sizeof(DIMOUSESTATE));
            m_pMouseDevice->GetDeviceState(sizeof(DIMOUSESTATE),
                                           &m_mouseState);

            //Update pointer
            x += m_mouseState.lX * m_speed;
            y += m_mouseState.lY * m_speed;

            //Keep mouse pointer within window
            if(x < m_viewport.left)   x = m_viewport.left;
            if(y < m_viewport.top)    y = m_viewport.top;
            if(x > m_viewport.right)  x = m_viewport.right;
            if(y > m_viewport.bottom) y = m_viewport.bottom;
        }
```

The relative position of the m_mouseState is added to the *x* and *y* value of our MOUSE class, which then contains the absolute position of the cursor. Also, note how we have a speed variable to scale the mouse input (i.e., the mouse sensitivity). We also make sure that the cursor stays within the bounds of the viewport. Here are some other functions we implement in the MOUSE class:

```
        bool MOUSE::ClickLeft()
        {
```

```
        return m_mouseState.rgbButtons[0];
    }

    bool MOUSE::WheelUp()
    {
        return m_mouseState.lZ > 0.0f;
    }

    bool MOUSE::Over(RECT dest)
    {
        if(x < dest.left || x > dest.right)return false;
        if(y < dest.top || y > dest.bottom)return false;
        return true;
    }
```

The Over() function performs a simple "cursor-within-rectangle" test.

Example 5.2

Have a look at Example 5.2 on the CD-ROM. In it, the MOUSE class is implemented.

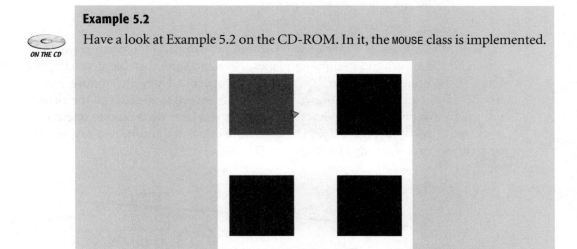

PICKING OBJECTS

In Example 5.2, we used the MOUSE class to click in a couple of colored rectangles that all reside in screen space. As our 3D world gets populated by units and buildings, we will want to use our mouse to give orders and do other tasks, won't we? However, our units exist in 3D space, so somehow we need to bridge the gap between the 2D screen space and our 3D world. This is done using a method known as "picking," as shown in Figure 5.6.

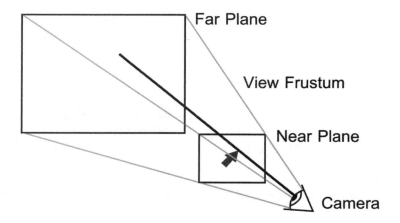

FIGURE 5.6 The concept of picking.

From the camera, we have a view frustum determined by the camera field of view, and the near and far clipping planes. Now, imagine that the near clipping plane is the computer screen (i.e., the screen space), where the mouse moves around. If you imagine a line drawn from the camera eye to the edge of the cursor, and which continues into the view frustum, then you have what is often referred to as a mouse "ray" (see Figure 5.7). Once we have calculated this mouse ray, we can see if it intersects with any objects in our 3D space.

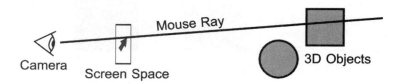

FIGURE 5.7 Mouse ray intersections.

Sound easy? Unfortunately, some of the math involved can be quite complex. But don't let that deter you. There are two steps to picking: First, calculate the mouse ray; and second, see if it intersects something.

Calculating the Mouse Ray

First we need to define what a ray is. The D3DX library uses rays that have a starting position and a direction. Because we are going to be using a lot of D3DX library functions for intersection tests, we'd better accommodate them and define our RAY structure like this:

```
struct RAY{
    RAY();
    RAY(D3DXVECTOR3 o, D3DXVECTOR3 d);

    //Our different intersection tests
    float Intersect(MESHINSTANCE iMesh);
    float Intersect(BBOX bBox);
    float Intersect(BSPHERE bSphere);

    D3DXVECTOR3 org, dir;
};
```

Our RAY structure has two vectors: org and dir (origin and direction). It also has three different intersection tests to see if our ray intersects with a mesh, box, or a sphere (more on this later). The problem we face now is how to calculate this ray from the cursor position in screen space and the camera view frustum. To do this, we need to work the view transformations backward. Sound confusing? Normally, we transform an object from 3D space to screen space like this:

Model Space→ World Space → View Space→ Screen Space

First the model is transformed into world space using the world transformation matrix, and then we transform the result into view space using the view transformation matrix. Last, we use the projection matrix to transform the result into screen space. Well, now we want to do the exact opposite; we want to transform a point in screen space to model space:

Model Space ← World Space ← View Space ← Screen Space

The code to do these backward (inverse) transformations is quite short, but also quite involved. The following function has been added to our MOUSE class to calculate the mouse ray:

```
RAY MOUSE::GetRay()
{
```

```
    float px = 0.0f, py = 0.0f;
    D3DXMATRIX projectionMatrix, viewMatrix;
    D3DXMATRIX worldViewInverse, worldMatrix;

    m_pDevice->GetTransform(D3DTS_PROJECTION,
                            &projectionMatrix);
    m_pDevice->GetTransform(D3DTS_VIEW, &viewMatrix);
    m_pDevice->GetTransform(D3DTS_WORLD, &worldMatrix);

    float width = m_viewport.right - m_viewport.left;
    float height = m_viewport.bottom - m_viewport.top;

    angle_x = (((2.0f * x) / width) - 1.0f) /
              projectionMatrix(0,0);
    angle_y = (((-2.0f * y) / height) + 1.0f) /
              projectionMatrix(1,1);

    RAY ray;
    ray.org = D3DXVECTOR3(0.0f, 0.0f, 0.0f);
    ray.dir = D3DXVECTOR3(angle_x, angle_y, 1.0f);

    D3DXMATRIX m = worldMatrix * viewMatrix;
    D3DXMatrixInverse(&worldViewInverse, 0, &m);
    D3DXVec3TransformCoord(&ray.org, &ray.org,
                           &worldViewInverse);
    D3DXVec3TransformNormal(&ray.dir, &ray.dir,
                            &worldViewInverse);
    D3DXVec3Normalize(&ray.dir, &ray.dir);

    return ray;
  }
```

Let's take this piece of code step by step. First we load our three transformation matrices—world, view, and projection—and store them. Next we get the width and height of our viewport. Then we scale the x and y values of our mouse cursor position to the range of [-1.0f, 1.0f], as well as divide it by the field of view for each dimension, as shown in Figure 5.8.

```
// This scales our x position the range of -1 to 1
angle_x = ((2.0f * x) / width) - 1.0f)

projectionMatrix(0,0)  //Field-of-View in the X-dimension
projectionMatrix(1,1)  //Field-of-View in the Y-dimension
```

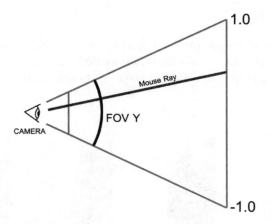

FIGURE 5.8   Mouse ray intersections.

The FOV values extracted from the projection matrix are both in radians. So we scale the cursor to the range of `-1.0f` to `1.0f` and then divide it by the FOV angle. The result is an inverse angle; and what do we do with an inverse angle? Well, first we create a ray using position `(0, 0, 0)` and direction `(angle_x, angle_y, 1.0f)`. Now, all we need to do is invert this ray using the inverse of our `world` and `view` matrix.

```
D3DXMATRIX m = worldMatrix * viewMatrix;
D3DXMatrixInverse(&worldViewInverse, 0, &m);
```

The `worldViewInverse` now holds the inverse of our transformation matrices.

```
D3DXVec3TransformCoord(&ray.org, &ray.org,
                        &worldViewInverse);
D3DXVec3TransformNormal(&ray.dir, &ray.dir,
                        &worldViewInverse);
D3DXVec3Normalize(&ray.dir, &ray.dir);
```

The `D3DXVec3TransformCoord()` function transforms a 3D coordinate using a specific matrix. Remember how we stored `(0, 0, 0)` as our ray origin? Well, this means that `(0, 0, 0)` in view space is the position of the camera, but when we invert it using the `worldViewInverse` matrix, we get the position of the camera in model space. In the same way, we transform the direction of the ray with the same `worldViewInverse` matrix and then normalize it. Remember how the direction `(angle_x, angle_y)` used to be the inverse of an angle? Well after this little inversion transformation, we now have a regular angle again. A lot of heavy math and backward thinking has finally given us our mouse ray, so what do we do with it?

Ray Intersection Tests

Now that our mouse ray is all figured out, we need to see if this ray intersects with any objects in our 3D world. When we do these intersection tests, we can represent objects in a couple of different ways, as shown in Figure 5.9.

| Actual Mesh | Proxy Mesh | Bounding Box | Bounding Sphere | Bounding Cylinder |

FIGURE 5.9   Object representations.

The most accurate (but costly) method is, of course, to test the ray against the actual object (i.e., the actual mesh). The next most accurate method would be to have an approximate mesh to test against (i.e., proxy mesh), but that means that for each mesh you have, you would have to create another mesh with fewer polygons. Then we have the most common bounding volumes—the box, the sphere, and the cylinder (though there are others, as well). For square objects like buildings, it can be accurate enough just to stick with a bounding box, for instance. Using bounding volumes is, of course, a lot less accurate than using the actual mesh. Therefore, some developers first test the ray against a bounding volume and then with a proxy mesh or actual mesh. How you decide to set up your picking procedures varies a lot from application to application. For real-time strategy games in general, though, we have a lot of units and buildings to run intersection tests on, so the cheaper the method, the better.

When choosing a bounding volume for your object, select the one with the closest fit. In Figure 5.9, both the bounding box and bounding cylinder are a lot better than the bounding sphere.

We will talk about low-polygon meshes a bit more later on (see Level-of-Detail Rendering). But for now, let's define the two most common bounding volumes—the box and the sphere:

```
struct BBOX{
    BBOX();
    BBOX(D3DXVECTOR3 _max, D3DXVECTOR3 _min);

    D3DXVECTOR3 max, min;
};

struct BSPHERE{
    BSPHERE();
    BSPHERE(D3DXVECTOR3 _center, float _radius);

    D3DXVECTOR3 center;
    float radius;
};
```

The bounding box is defined by a max and a min corner. The bounding sphere is defined by its center position and its radius, as shown in Figure 5.10.

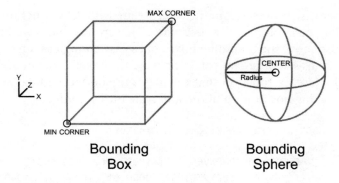

FIGURE 5.10   The box and sphere bounding volumes.

Box-Ray Intersection

Before we can test if the ray and box intersect, we must calculate the bounding box around the object we want to test. This can be done in many different ways. For argument's sake, let's say you want a bounding box around an ID3DXMesh object. In that case, there's an easy D3DX library function to do the work for you:

```
HRESULT D3DXComputeBoundingBox(
    LPD3DXVECTOR3 pFirstPosition,
    DWORD NumVertices,
```

```
        DWORD dwStride,
        D3DXVECTOR3 *pMin,
        D3DXVECTOR3 *pMax
);
```

The D3DXComputeBoundingBox() function is used like this:

```
BBOX bBox;

ObjectVertex* vertexBuffer = NULL;
mesh->LockVertexBuffer(0,(void**)&vertexBuffer);

D3DXComputeBoundingBox((D3DXVECTOR3*)&vertexBuffer[0],
                       mesh->GetNumVertices(),
                       sizeof(ObjectVertex),
                       &bBox.min, &bBox.max);


mesh->UnlockVertexBuffer();
```

There is, however, one little problem with this function. It calculates the bounding box volume in model space. That means that if we move the object, we must also move the bounding box. That's easy enough as long as we just move the object, but as soon as we rotate or scale the object, our bounding box becomes invalid. Here's a function that calculates the bounding box from a MESHINSTANCE object, taking position, rotation, and scale into account.

```
BBOX MESHINSTANCE::GetBoundingBox()
{
    BBOX bBox(D3DXVECTOR3(-10000.0f, -10000.0f, -10000.0f),
              D3DXVECTOR3(10000.0f, 10000.0f, 10000.0f));

    //Get this object's transformation matrix
    D3DXMATRIX World = GetWorldMatrix();

    //Lock vertex buffer of the object
    ObjectVertex* vertexBuffer = NULL;
    m_pMesh->m_pMesh->LockVertexBuffer(0,
                              (void**)&vertexBuffer);

    //For each vertex in the mesh
    for(int i=0;i<m_pMesh->m_pMesh->GetNumVertices();i++)
    {
```

```
        //Transform vertex to world space using the
        //MESHINSTANCE's world matrix
        D3DXVECTOR3 pos;
        D3DXVec3TransformCoord(&pos,
                               &vertexBuffer[i]._pos,
                               &World);

        // Check if the vertex is outside the bounds
        // if so, then update the bounding volume
        if(pos.x < bBox.min.x)bBox.min.x = pos.x;
        if(pos.x > bBox.max.x)bBox.max.x = pos.x;
        if(pos.y < bBox.min.y)bBox.min.y = pos.y;
        if(pos.y > bBox.max.y)bBox.max.y = pos.y;
        if(pos.z < bBox.min.z)bBox.min.z = pos.z;
        if(pos.z > bBox.max.z)bBox.max.z = pos.z;
    }

    m_pMesh->m_pMesh->UnlockVertexBuffer();

    return bBox;
}
```

This function opens up the vertex buffer of the underlying mesh and transforms each vertex with the world matrix of the MESHINSTANCE object, and creates a new bounding box. Another way to create the bounding box of an object is to simply create it manually by specifying the max and min vectors.

Now we have a ray and a bounding box. The next thing we need to do is check to see if they intersect. For this we use the D3DXBoxBoundProbe() function.

```
BOOL D3DXBoxBoundProbe(
    CONST D3DXVECTOR3 *pMin,
    CONST D3DXVECTOR3 *pMax,
    D3DXVECTOR3 *pRayPosition,
    D3DXVECTOR3 *pRayDirection
);
```

The D3DXBoxBoundProbe() function takes the min and max vector of our bounding box, as well as the origin and direction vectors of our mouse ray. The function returns true if they intersect and false if they don't. However, we want to get the distance from an intersection. This way, we can compare two objects that both intersect with the ray and pick the closest one. Our RAY::Intersect() function, therefore, looks like this:

```
float RAY::Intersect(BBOX bBox)
{
    if(D3DXBoxBoundProbe(&bBox.min, &bBox.max, &org, &dir))
        return D3DXVec3Length(
                    &(((bBox.min + bBox.max) / 2.0f) - org));
    else return -1.0f;
}
```

If the bounding box and the ray intersect, this function returns the distance from the ray's origin to the center of the bounding box, otherwise it returns -1.0f.

Sphere-Ray Intersection

The next intersection test is the sphere-ray intersection test. This test is done very much like the bounding box intersection test. First, the bounding sphere is calculated with the D3DX library function D3DXComputeBoundingSphere() in the exact manner as the D3DXComputeBoundingBox() function.

```
HRESULT D3DXComputeBoundingSphere(
    LPD3DXVECTOR3 pFirstPosition,
    DWORD NumVertices,
    DWORD dwStride,
    D3DXVECTOR3 *pCenter,
    FLOAT *pRadius
);
```

Also, the bounding sphere can be created from a MESHINSTANCE object just like the bounding box was in the previous section (see Example 5.3 on the companion CD-ROM). When we have our bounding sphere, we can check if the ray intersects it, like this:

```
float RAY::Intersect(BSPHERE bSphere)
{
    if(D3DXSphereBoundProbe(&bSphere.center,
                            bSphere.radius,
                            &org,&dir))
        return D3DXVec3Length(&(bSphere.center - org));
    else return -1.0f;
}
```

This time, the D3DXSphereBoundProbe() takes the center and radius of the bounding sphere, as well as the origin and direction of the ray. If these intersect, this function returns true. In that case, we return the distance from the mouse ray's origin to the center of the bounding sphere.

Mesh-Ray Intersection

The last type of ray intersection test that will be covered here is the mesh-ray intersection test. This time we don't create a bounding volume from the mesh, but we use the mesh itself (or a proxy mesh). Again, we can let the D3DX library do the work for us, since the other option would be to access each face of the mesh manually and see if the ray intersects it.

```
HRESULT D3DXIntersect(
    LPD3DXBASEMESH pMesh,
    CONST D3DXVECTOR3 *pRayPos,
    CONST D3DXVECTOR3 *pRayDir,
    BOOL *pHit,
    DWORD *pFaceIndex,
    FLOAT *pU,
    FLOAT *pV,
    FLOAT *pDist,
    LPD3DXBUFFER *ppAllHits,
    DWORD *pCountOfHits
);
```

To this function, we send a pointer to our mesh, and our mouse ray's origin and direction. From this function we get: if there was a hit, what face was hit, the UV coordinates of the hit (useful later), the distance to the hit, and a buffer containing all the hits. In 9 cases out of 10, we are just interested in the closest face of the object that was hit; if this is the case, then just leave the ppAllHits and pCountOfHits to NULL. Here is the D3DXIntersect() function in action:

```
float RAY::Intersect(MESHINSTANCE iMesh)
{
    // Collect only the closest intersection
    BOOL hit;
    DWORD dwFace;
    float hitU, hitV, dist;
    D3DXIntersect(iMesh.m_pMesh->m_pMesh, &org, &dir, &hit,
                &dwFace, &hitU, &hitV, &dist, NULL, NULL);

    if(hit)return dist;
    else return -1.0f;
}
```

This function assumes that the ray is in the model space of the mesh being tested. If it isn't, then it won't work. One way you can have these intersection tests work is to have each object keep track of their own intersection method as well as their own bounding volume.

Example 5.3

Check out Example 5.3 on the CD-ROM, where Brave Bob battles the dragon. In this example, the camera is controlled partially by the mouse as well, which is worth checking out.

FROM THE WORLD TO THE SCREEN

We know how to go from a cursor on the screen to a ray in 3D space. Now we are going to do the exact opposite . . . well, almost. Sometimes it can be good to know where a unit or object is in screen space—for example, when we want to select multiple units within a certain rectangle in screen space. To do this, we need to transform a 3D position into view space and then project it into screen space. Sound hard? Not really. Again, there's a perfect D3DX function for just this purpose.

```
D3DXVECTOR3 *WINAPI D3DXVec3Project(
    D3DXVECTOR3 *pOut,
    CONST D3DXVECTOR3 *pV,
    CONST D3DVIEWPORT9 *pViewport,
    CONST D3DXMATRIX *pProjection,
    CONST D3DXMATRIX *pView,
    CONST D3DXMATRIX *pWorld
);
```

This function takes a 3D position and all the transformation matrices, and returns a 3D vector with the screen position. Here's a little function created to encapsulate this D3DX function:

```
INTPOINT GetScreenPos(D3DXVECTOR3 pos,
                      IDirect3DDevice9* Device)
{
    D3DXVECTOR3 screenPos;
    D3DVIEWPORT9 Viewport;
    D3DXMATRIX Projection, View, World;

    Device->GetViewport(&Viewport);
    Device->GetTransform(D3DTS_VIEW, &View);
    Device->GetTransform(D3DTS_PROJECTION, &Projection);
    D3DXMatrixIdentity(&World);
    D3DXVec3Project(&screenPos, &pos, &Viewport,
                    &Projection, &View, &World);

    return INTPOINT(screenPos.x, screenPos.y);
}
```

As you can see, this function takes a 3D position and a pointer to our Direct3D device. First we use the device to acquire all the transformation matrices. Then we send it all to our D3DXVec3Project() function and return the result as an INTPOINT.

Selecting Units

We are now going to use this to build this chapter's first "RTS-ish" application—a unit-selection system. First, we want to be able to select units by clicking on them individually. But we also want to be able to select multiple units by marking a rectangle on the screen and selecting all units within it. We also need a way of marking a unit as selected or not. As with everything else, there are a few ways to do this; we could have the unit change color or have it glow. A preferred, old-fashion method has a 2D rectangle in screen space to show what units are selected, and luckily this also gives us another opportunity to test our GetScreenPos() function.

First we need to devise a function we can use to select/deselect units. At the moment, we don't really have units to select, so we'll select gnomes instead (a simple mesh object). Later on we'll use the same mechanism to select our units and buildings. For this example we have added a Boolean variable to our objects, called m_selected. If this variable is true, our object is selected; if it is false, then our object is not selected. Here's a function that deals with the mouse input and selects our units:

```
bool areaSelect = false;
INTPOINT startSel;                  // Area select starting point
std::vector<OBJECT> gnomes;         // all our little gnomes...
```

```
void Select()
{
    if(mouse.ClickLeft())     // If the mouse button is pressed
    {
        //Deselect all gnomes
        for(int i=0;i<gnomes.size();i++)
            gnomes[i].m_selected = false;

        //If no area selection is in progress
        if(!areaSelect)
        {
            //GetGnome() returns a Gnome using the mouse ray.
            //If no gnome is found this function returns -1
            int gnome = GetGnome();

            if(gnome >= 0)
                gnomes[gnome].m_selected = true;
            else
            {
                areaSelect = true;    // if no gnome is found,
                startSel = mouse;     // start area selection
            }
        }
        else    //Area Selection in progress
        {
            // Create area rectangle from startSel and mouse
            INTPOINT p1 = startSel, p2 = mouse;
            if(p1.x > p2.x)
            {int temp = p2.x;p2.x = p1.x;p1.x = temp;}
            if(p1.y > p2.y)
            {int temp = p2.y;p2.y = p1.y;p1.y = temp;}
            RECT selRect = {p1.x, p1.y, p2.x, p2.y};

            // Draw selection rectangle here!

            //Select any gnomes inside our rectangle
            for(int i=0;i<gnomes.size();i++)
            {
                INTPOINT p = GetScreenPos(
                                gnomes[i].GetPosition(),
                                Device);
                if(p.inRect(selRect))
                    gnomes[i].m_selected = true;
            }
```

```
            }
        }
        else if(areaSelect)              //Stop area selection
            areaSelect = false;
    }
```

Our little `GetGnome()` function returns the index of that `gnome` (if any) that intersect with our mouse ray. This is a simple mesh-ray intersection test that tests all our `gnomes` and returns the intersecting `gnome` closest to the camera. If no `gnome` is found, then `GetGnome()` returns `-1`. Our `Select()` function is called once every frame from, for example, our `Render()` function. Whenever the mouse button is pressed, we first see if the mouse ray intersects with a unit; in that case we select that unit. Otherwise, we start the area select. The area select continues as long as the mouse button stays pressed. Any units within the rectangle defined by the starting position and the mouse cursor are selected.

Drawing Lines in Screen Space

The next little thing we need to worry about is how to draw lines in screen space. Luckily, there's a D3DX interface for doing just this.

By now you've realized that there's D3DX functions and interfaces for most general tasks you can think of. If you are ever faced with a new problem, it's always a good idea to check the D3DX functions and see what's there to help you implement a solution.

For drawing lines in screen space, we can use the `ID3DXLine` interface. It works just like the `ID3DXSprite` interface when it comes to how they are created and used. This is how we create a line interface:

```
ID3DXLine *line = NULL;
D3DXCreateLine(Device, &line);
```

The `ID3DXLine::Draw()` function takes a list of 2D vertices, a vertex count, and a color:

```
HRESULT Draw(
    CONST D3DXVECTOR2* pVertexList,
    DWORD dwVertexListCount,
    D3DCOLOR Color
);
```

When we want to draw a line in screen space using the ID3DXLine interface, we use it like this:

```
D3DXVECTOR2 lineList[] = {D3DXVECTOR2(A.x, A.y),
                          D3DXVECTOR2(B.x, B.y),
                          D3DXVECTOR2(C.x, C.y)};

line->SetWidth(2.0f);
line->Begin();
line->Draw(lineList, 3, 0xffffffff);
line->End();
```

This code will draw two lines from point A to point B and from point B to point C. Here's the function that draws the "selection rectangle" around our gnomes:

```
void OBJECT::PaintSelected()
{
    if(!m_selected)return;

    float radius = 0.6f;
    float height = 2.2f;

    // Create 8 offset points according to the
    // height, radius of a unit
    D3DXVECTOR3 offsets[] = { ... };

    // Find the max and min points of these
    // 8 offset points in screen space
    INTPOINT pmax(-10000, -10000), pmin(10000,10000);

    for(int i=0;i<8;i++)
    {
        D3DXVECTOR3 pos = mInst.pos + offsets[i];
        INTPOINT screenPos = GetScreenPos(
                                pos, mInst.mesh->Device);

        if(screenPos.x > pmax.x)pmax.x = screenPos.x;
        if(screenPos.y > pmax.y)pmax.y = screenPos.y;
        if(screenPos.x < pmin.x)pmin.x = screenPos.x;
        if(screenPos.y < pmin.y)pmin.y = screenPos.y;
    }

    RECT scr = {-20, -20, 820, 620};
```

```
// Check that the max & min point is within our viewport
if(pmax.inRect(scr) || pmin.inRect(scr))
{
    float s = (pmax.x - pmin.x) / 3.0f;
    if((pmax.y - pmin.y) < (pmax.x - pmin.x))
        s = (pmax.y - pmin.y) / 3.0f;

    D3DXVECTOR2 corner1[] = {
                D3DXVECTOR2(pmin.x, pmin.y + s),
                D3DXVECTOR2(pmin.x, pmin.y),
                D3DXVECTOR2(pmin.x + s, pmin.y)};

    D3DXVECTOR2 corner2[] = { ... };
    D3DXVECTOR2 corner3[] = { ... };
    D3DXVECTOR2 corner4[] = { ... };

    //Draw the 4 corners
    line->SetWidth(2.0f);
    line->Begin();
    line->Draw(corner1, 3, 0xffffffff);
    line->Draw(corner2, 3, 0xffffffff);
    line->Draw(corner3, 3, 0xffffffff);
    line->Draw(corner4, 3, 0xffffffff);
    line->End();
}
}
```

ON THE CD

Example 5.4

In Example 5.4 on the CD-ROM, these techniques are used to select and deselect our little warrior gnomes.

VIEWPORT RENDERING

And now for something completely different! If you ever plan on implementing a game in which two players use the same computer at the same time, then you need to know how to render your game to different viewports. A viewport is a rectangle in screen space where our final rendered image will be drawn. All the examples until now have had the viewport set to cover the entire screen. Now we will have a look on how to target our rendered images to a specific area of the screen. To do this, we use the D3DVIEWPORT9 structure:

```
struct D3DVIEWPORT9
{
    DWORD X;
    DWORD Y;
    DWORD Width;
    DWORD Height;
    float MinZ;
    float MaxZ;
}
```

The X and Y values determine the upper-left corner of our rectangle. The Width and Height determine the width and height of our rectangle. The MinZ and MaxZ values determine the range of depth values [0.0f, 1.0f] that our scene will be written to. With these values, you can force objects to be rendered to a certain depth range. For most normal applications, just set these values to MinZ = 0.0f and MaxZ = 1.0f. We can acquire and set the active viewport like this:

```
D3DVIEWPORT9 v;
Device->GetViewport(&v);    // Gets the viewport
Device->SetViewport(&v);    // Sets the viewport
```

Often, we need to clear a viewport. Then we use the following function:

```
HRESULT Clear(
    DWORD Count,            // No of rectangles to clear
    const D3DRECT *pRects,  // List of rectangles to clear
    DWORD Flags,            // What buffer to clear
    D3DCOLOR Color,         // What color to clear to
    float Z,                // New Z value
    DWORD Stencil           // New Stencil value to store
);
```

The flags of this function can be any combination of the following three tags: D3DCLEAR_STENCIL, D3DCLEAR_TARGET, or D3DCLEAR_ZBUFFER. D3DCLEAR_STENCIL clears the stencil buffer to the stencil value, D3DCLEAR_TARGET clears our actual screen to the color we specified. D3DCLEAR_ZBUFFER clears our z-buffer to the specified z value. Set the z value to 1.0f for normal applications; this sets all the values in the z-buffer to be as far away from the camera as possible. To clear the entire viewport, we use the Clear() function, like this:

```
Device->Clear(0, NULL, D3DCLEAR_TARGET | D3DCLEAR_ZBUFFER,
              0x00000000, 1.0f, 0);
```

This clears the entire active viewport to black and sets the z-buffer to zero. So let's have a look at how we can use this to render to multiple viewports. For each viewport, we must do the following:

- Set the bounds of the active viewport.
- Set the transformation matrices for this viewport.
- Render all objects.

Yes, all objects must be rendered once for each viewport. This means that for complex scenes with a great many vertices, we are going to increase the rendering time for every viewport rendering we perform. So use this wisely; there are other ways to get similar results, as you'll see later on when we render our minimap.

Example 5.5

In Example 5.5 on the CD-ROM, this technique is used to build the split-screen racecar scene.

FRUSTUM CULLING

Up until now, we have rendered all the objects in a scene whether they are in the final image or not. This is, of course, not the most efficient way to do things, especially in an RTS game where hundreds of units might be out of sight. It would be best if objects that we know won't be in the final image are disregarded during the rendering phase. The process of figuring out what objects will appear in the screen or not is called frustum culling. This technique works best in scenes that have a lot of objects, and you only see a few of them at a time. Before we get into the actual culling, we need to have a look at planes in 3D space.

The mathematical definition of a plane is the following: a surface containing all straight lines that connect any two points on it. There are two common ways we can create a plane. Either we create it from a point on the plane and the plane normal, or we create it from three points on the plane. The two D3DX library functions that do this for us are shown in Figure 5.11.

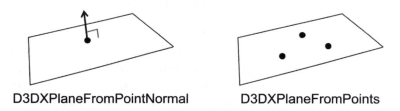

D3DXPlaneFromPointNormal   D3DXPlaneFromPoints

FIGURE 5.11   D3DXPlaneFromPointNormal() **and** D3DXPlaneFromPoints().

We use the D3DXPLANE structure to store our planes.

```
struct D3DXPLANE
{
    FLOAT a;
    FLOAT b;
    FLOAT c;
    FLOAT d;
}
```

The a, b, c, and d values in this structure are the coefficients in the well-known plane equation:

$$ax + by + cz + d = 0.$$

Take any point in 3D space with an *x*, *y*, and *z* value, and insert it into the plane equation. If the result is zero, then the point lies on the plane. Otherwise, if the result is less than zero, then the point is on the negative side of the plane, and vice versa if the result is positive. Now we have established that a plane has a positive side and a negative side, and how to test on what side of a plane a 3D point is. So how can we use this to determine if objects are within the viewing frustum or not? Well, if we define our viewing frustum as a series of planes, as shown in Figure 5.12, then we can easily test whether a point is within our viewing volume or not.

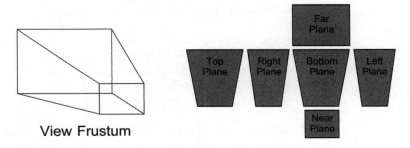

FIGURE 5.12   Breaking the view frustum into planes.

By extracting the six planes that define our view frustum, we can perform a simple check to see whether an object is within it or not. All six planes have their normals pointing into the viewing volume. This means that for an object to be outside the viewing volume, it has to be completely on the negative side of any of the six planes. So let's first take a look at how we extract the six planes from a camera.

```
//6-planes to store our view frustum added to our camera class
D3DXPLANE m_frustum[6];

void CAMERA::CalculateFrustum(D3DXMATRIX view,
                              D3DXMATRIX projection)
{
    // Get combined matrix
    D3DXMATRIX matComb;
    D3DXMatrixMultiply(&matComb, &view, &projection);

    // Left clipping plane
    m_frustum[0].a = matComb._14 + matComb._11;
    m_frustum[0].b = matComb._24 + matComb._21;
    m_frustum[0].c = matComb._34 + matComb._31;
    m_frustum[0].d = matComb._44 + matComb._41;
```

```
// Right clipping plane
m_frustum[1].a = matComb._14 - matComb._11;
m_frustum[1].b = matComb._24 - matComb._21;
m_frustum[1].c = matComb._34 - matComb._31;
m_frustum[1].d = matComb._44 - matComb._41;

// Top clipping plane
m_frustum[2].a = matComb._14 - matComb._12;
m_frustum[2].b = matComb._24 - matComb._22;
m_frustum[2].c = matComb._34 - matComb._32;
m_frustum[2].d = matComb._44 - matComb._42;

// Bottom clipping plane
m_frustum[3].a = matComb._14 + matComb._12;
m_frustum[3].b = matComb._24 + matComb._22;
m_frustum[3].c = matComb._34 + matComb._32;
m_frustum[3].d = matComb._44 + matComb._42;

// Near clipping plane
m_frustum[4].a = matComb._13;
m_frustum[4].b = matComb._23;
m_frustum[4].c = matComb._33;
m_frustum[4].d = matComb._43;

// Far clipping plane
m_frustum[5].a = matComb._14 - matComb._13;
m_frustum[5].b = matComb._24 - matComb._23;
m_frustum[5].c = matComb._34 - matComb._33;
m_frustum[5].d = matComb._44 - matComb._43;

//Normalize planes
for(int i=0;i<6;i++)
    D3DXPlaneNormalize(&m_frustum[i], &m_frustum[i]);
}
```

The six frustum planes are stored in our CAMERA class, and they are updated once every frame. First we multiply the view transformation matrix with the projection matrix, and then we extract the six planes from this combined matrix. For a more detailed explanation of the math behind this function, see [Gribb01] and [Celes04]. Also check out [Picco03] for a good tutorial on frustum culling. All we need to do now is test whether a bounding box or bounding sphere is outside the view frustum, and in that case cull it.

Sphere Culling

Remember our BSPHERE structure? Now we are going to check whether it is inside our viewing volume or not. We do this by calculating the distance from each of the six planes in the view frustum, like this:

distanceFromPlane = DotProduct(bSphere.center, plane.normal) + plane.distance

The plane distance is given by the d-value in the D3DXPLANE structure. Here's the code for culling bounding spheres:

```
bool CAMERA::Cull(BSPHERE bSphere)
{
    //For each plane in the view frustum
    for(int f=0;f<6;f++)
    {
        float distance = D3DXVec3Dot(&bSphere.center,

                                     &D3DXVECTOR3(m_frustum[f].a,
                                                  m_frustum[f].b,
                                                  m_frustum[f].c))
                                     + m_frustum[f].d;

        //Object is outside the volume
        if(distance < -bSphere.radius)
            return true;
    }

    //Object is inside the volume
    return false;
}
```

If the CAMERA::Cull() function returns true, it means that we should cull the object (i.e., not render it). Before rendering the objects in a scene, test their bounding volume with the CAMERA::Cull() function to determine whether they are inside the view frustum or not.

Box Culling

Another method is box culling. It works in the same way as sphere culling, only this time we use the BBOX structure. The BBOX structure describes an Axis-Aligned Bounding Box (AABB). Each box has eight corners, but since the box is axis-aligned, we only need to find the farthest and the closest corners of the box, and test these. It is easy to determine what corners are closest and farthest from a plane using only the plane normal. Table 5.1 shows what corners to use, depending on the plane normal

TABLE 5.1   Extracting Box Corners for Frustum Culling

Nx	Ny	Nz	Corner 1	Corner 2
+	+	+	[x-max, y-max, z-max]	[x-min, y-min, z-min]
+	+	−	[x-max, y-max, z-min]	[x-min, y-min, z-max]
+	−	+	[x-max, y-min, z-max]	[x-min, y-max, z-min]
+	−	−	[x-max, y-min, z-min]	[x-min, y-max, z-max]
−	+	+	[x-min, y-max, z-max]	[x-max, y-min, z-min]
−	+	−	[x-min, y-max, z-min]	[x-max, y-min, z-max]
−	−	+	[x-min, y-min, z-max]	[x-max, y-max, z-min]
−	−	−	[x-min, y-min, z-min]	[x-max, y-max, z-max]

Once we've located the corners on the bounding box to test, we simply run them through the plane equation for the six frustum planes. If both corners are on the negative side of any plane, we cull the object.

```
bool CAMERA::Cull(BBOX bBox)
{
    //For each plane in the view frustum
    for(int f=0;f<6;f++)
    {
        D3DXVECTOR3 c1, c2;

        //Find furthest & nearest point to the plane
        if(m_frustum[f].a > 0.0f)
        {c1.x= bBox.max.x; c2.x= bBox.min.x;}
        else {c1.x= bBox.min.x; c2.x= bBox.max.x;}
        if(m_frustum[f].b > 0.0f)
        {c1.y= bBox.max.y; c2.y= bBox.min.y;}
        else {c1.y= bBox.min.y; c2.y= bBox.max.y;}
        if(m_frustum[f].c > 0.0f)
        {c1.z= bBox.max.z; c2.z= bBox.min.z;}
        else {c1.z= bBox.min.z; c2.z= bBox.max.z;}
```

```
    //Run the 2 corners through the plane equation
    float distance1 = m_frustum[f].a * c1.x +
                      m_frustum[f].b * c1.y +
                      m_frustum[f].c * c1.z +
                      m_frustum[f].d;

    float distance2 = m_frustum[f].a * c2.x +
                      m_frustum[f].b * c2.y +
                      m_frustum[f].c * c2.z +
                      m_frustum[f].d;

    //If both points are on the negative
    //side of the plane, Cull!
    if(distance1 < 0.0f && distance2 < 0.0f)
        return true;
    }

    //Object is inside the volume
    return false;
}
```

First we find the two corners that are closest to and farthest from the plane we are checking. Then we put both of them into the plane equation to get their distances. If both are negative, then they are outside the viewing volume and can therefore be culled.

Example 5.6

On the CD-ROM, you can find Example 5.6 that implements viewing volume culling, like the one we've covered here. There's also a little "minimap" that shows what parts of the scene are being rendered, using orthogonal projection and viewport rendering.

LEVEL-OF-DETAIL RENDERING

In the previous section, we had a look at how to increase rendering speed by not rendering objects outside the viewing volume. Doing this can go a long way toward helping reduce the cost of rendering, especially for very complex scenes. Now let's take a look at a technique that helps reduce the rendering cost for those objects that are in the viewing volume and have to be rendered. Have a look at the three meshes shown in Figure 5.13.

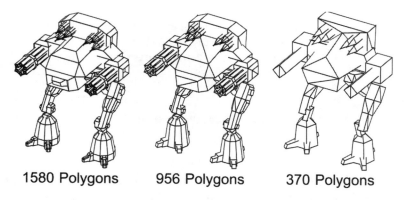

1580 Polygons   956 Polygons   370 Polygons

FIGURE 5.13 Three meshes at different levels of detail.

All three meshes in Figure 5.13 represent that same mech, but at different resolutions. Obviously, the fewer polygons we use to model an object, the faster it will render. Having an object in different resolutions allows us to render it at different levels of detail (see Figure 5.14).

See how we use the highest resolution mesh when the object is close to the camera and the lowest resolution mesh when it's far away from the camera. In this image, we rendered about 2,900 polygons, compared to 4,700 if we had rendered all three mechs using the high-resolution mesh. But anyone seeing this image wouldn't know the difference, would they? That's what Level-of-Detail (LOD) rendering is all about. Use your polygons where the player is more likely to notice them.

There are a few different ways to do this. You can build your meshes manually for each level of detail; this way gives you more control and better results at the cost of hard work. The other way is to use progressive meshes and simplify a high-resolution mesh with a simplification algorithm to create the lower levels of detail. This way is much faster to implement, but you lose some control over how your mesh is simplified.

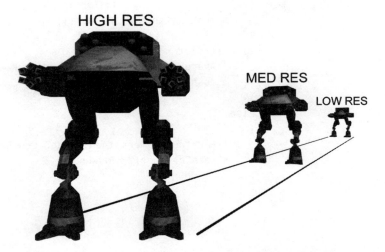

FIGURE 5.14 The concept of rendering objects at different levels of detail.

Creating the LOD Objects Manually

This the preferred approach when rendering objects at different LODs, because it gives you a better visual result and uses less memory than progressive meshes. The downside is that you have to create more than one mesh for each object you want in your game. But the extra effort is well worth it. The following function renders an object in different resolutions, depending on its distance from the camera:

```
void OBJECT::Render(CAMERA *camera)
{
    //If camera == NULL, Render High Res Mesh
    if(camera == NULL)
        m_meshInstance[0].Render();
    else
    {
        if(!camera->Cull(m_BBox))            //Cull objects
        {
            //Distance from objects to camera
            float dist;
            dist = D3DXVec3Length(&(meshInstance[0].m_pos -
                                    camera->m_eye));

            if(dist < 50.0f)                                  {
                //Close to the Camera then render High Res
```

```
                    m_meshInstance[0].Render();
                }
                else if(dist < 100.0f)                {
                    //Average distance render Medium Res Mesh
                    m_meshInstance[1].Render();
                }
                else
                {
                    //Far from camera then render Low Res Mesh
                    m_meshInstance[2].Render();
                }
            }
        }
    }
```

Example 5.7

In Example 5.7 on the CD-ROM, three meshes are used together with object culling to render a lot of mechs at different levels of detail. This example allows you to turn the LOD rendering and object culling on or off. Do this, and keep an eye on the frames-per-second counter, and see what happens.

The idea of having a mesh at different levels of detail also goes very well with picking, since the low-resolution mesh can be used as a proxy mesh during the picking.

Creating a Progressive Mesh

A progressive mesh allows you to change the number of polygons used during runtime. Creating a progressive mesh for each object that you want to render at different LODs is a lot faster than creating multiple meshes manually. This also allows you to render the mesh using any number of polygons between the minimum and maximum number of polygons of the progressive mesh. The largest downside of using progressive meshes is that it is very hard to control how the simplification affects the mesh. You can always achieve a better looking mesh using the same number of polygons as the progressive mesh by creating it yourself. Here's how you create a progressive mesh:

```
HRESULT D3DXGeneratePMesh(
    LPD3DXMESH pMesh,
    CONST DWORD *pAdjacency,
    CONST LPD3DXATTRIBUTEWEIGHTS pVertexAttributeWeights,
    CONST FLOAT * pVertexWeights,
    DWORD MinValue,
    DWORD Options,
    LPD3DXPMESH *ppPMesh
);
```

The pMesh variable is a pointer to our source mesh; the pAdjancency is a DWORD buffer with the adjacency table of the source mesh. The pVertexAttributeWeights and the pVertexWeights variables are used to define how important each single vertex in the mesh is. The more important a vertex is, the less likely it is to be removed during the simplification. This can, for example, be used to increase the weight values of silhouette vertices of an object to conserve its shape. However, this is a bit over the top for what we need; so we just set those two variables to NULL. The MinValue variable is the face or vertex count to aim for when creating the progressive mesh. Set this variable to 1 to simplify the source mesh as much as possible. The Options flag can be set to one of the following two values: D3DXMESHSIMP_VERTEX or D3DXMESHSIMP_FACE, depending on whether to simplify the vertices or faces. If all goes well, then our progressive mesh will be stored to the ppPMesh variable. Here's how we would create a progressive mesh using this function:

```
ID3DXMesh *mesh = NULL;      //Source Mesh
ID3DXPMesh *pmesh = NULL;    //Progressive Mesh

// Load mesh and textures from file here to the mesh object

//Create progressive mesh
DWORD *adj = new DWORD[mesh->GetNumFaces() * 3];

//get Adjacency Table
mesh->GenerateAdjacency(0.0f, adj);
```

```
D3DXGeneratePMesh(mesh, adj, NULL, NULL, 1,
                  D3DXMESHSIMP_FACE, &pmesh);

delete [] adj;
```

After you've created the progressive mesh from the source mesh, you can set the number of faces you want to render the object with by calling the following member function:

```
pmesh->SetNumFaces(numFaces);        //Set LOD
```

The function caps the numFaces variable so it isn't greater than the number of faces of the original or less than the minimum amount of faces of the progressive mesh. All you have to do now is create the numFaces variable as a function of the object's distance to the camera—and you have yourself an LOD system.

ON THE CD

Example 5.8

See Example 5.8 on the CD-ROM. A progressive mesh is created, and you can control the LOD of the mesh with the up and down arrows of your keyboard.

A SECOND LOOK AT THE TERRAIN CLASS

It's time we dust off our terrain implementation from the last chapter and integrate it with what we've learned in this chapter. First, we will create bounding boxes around all our patches and terrain objects, and cull them if they are outside the viewing volume. Second, we are going to extract the node on the map that is closest to our mouse cursor. We use this when we, for instance, tell units to move to a certain map node. Third, we will have the focus of our camera follow the mesh of the terrain.

Culling the Terrain Patches

Culling terrain patches not in the viewing volume is a great way to save CPU power. All we need to do is calculate the bounding boxes around each individual patch, and then run it through our CAMERA::Cull() function to find out if we need to render it or not.

```
//Excerpt from our PATCH::CreateMesh() function...

m_BBox.max = D3DXVECTOR3(-10000.0f, -10000.0f, -10000.0f);
m_BBox.min = D3DXVECTOR3(10000.0f, 10000.0f, 10000.0f);

//Create vertices
for(int z=source.top, z0 = 0;z<=source.bottom;z++, z0++)
    for(int x=source.left, x0 = 0;x<=source.right;x++, x0++)
    {
        MAPTILE *tile = ter.GetTile(x, z);
        D3DXVECTOR3 pos = D3DXVECTOR3(x, tile->height, -z);

        //Color Calculate UV's here as well...
        //Create the new vertex here...

        //Calculate bounding box bounds...
        if(pos.x < m_BBox.min.x)m_BBox.min.x = pos.x;
        if(pos.x > m_BBox.max.x)m_BBox.max.x = pos.x;
        if(pos.y < m_BBox.min.y)m_BBox.min.y = pos.y;
        if(pos.y > m_BBox.max.y)m_BBox.max.y = pos.y;
        if(pos.z < m_BBox.min.z)m_BBox.min.z = pos.z;
        if(pos.z > m_BBox.max.z)m_BBox.max.z = pos.z;
    }

//and so on...
```

We've added a BBOX to each patch, which we calculate during the PATCH::CreateMesh() function. In order to use the camera's culling function, you need to send a camera reference to the TERRAIN::Render() function. Then you can cull both the terrain patches and any terrain objects outside the view frustum.

```
void TERRAIN::Render(CAMERA &camera)
{
    //Set render states etc here...
```

```
for(int p=0;p<m_patches.size();p++)
    if(!camera.Cull(m_patches[p]->m_BBox))
        m_patches[p]->Render();

//Render Objects
for(int i=0;i<m_objects.size();i++)
    if(!camera.Cull(m_objects[i].m_BBox))
        m_objects[i].Render();
}
```

Retrieving the Mouse Cursor's Terrain Position

Next we want to figure out what map node is closest to our mouse ray. This is important to know further on when we want to be able to order units around to different terrain locations.

First we see which (if any) patch our mouse ray intersects with. We perform a cheap ray-box intersection with each patch to find possible candidates for an intersection. We then use the D3DXIntersect() function to check whether there's an actual ray-mesh intersection. If there is, then the D3DXIntersect() function will return the following information:

- What face was hit
- Distance to intersection
- The UV coordinates of the hit

Have a look at the terrain patch in Figure 5.15.

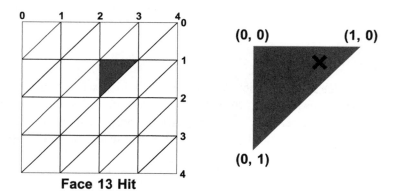

FIGURE 5.15   The information returned by D3DXIntersect().

In this case, the D3DXIntersect() function returned Face 13 as the face that was hit. However, this face has three possible map nodes connected to it—(2, 1), (3, 1), and (2, 2). We must then use the UV coordinates of the hit to calculate which one of these map nodes our mouse ray is closest to. In Figure 5.15, the UV hit is marked by the "X", and from this we can draw the conclusion that the closest map node is (3, 1). In theory this is pretty easy; in reality we also have to take into account where the patches are on the terrain, as well as the fact that the UV coordinates are different for the two faces in a quad. The CalculateMappos() function has been added to our MOUSE class to handle this:

```
void MOUSE::CalculateMappos(TERRAIN &terrain)
{
    //Get Mouse Ray
    D3DXMATRIX world;
    D3DXMatrixIdentity(&world);
    m_pDevice->SetTransform(D3DTS_WORLD, &world);
    RAY mRay = GetRay();

    float minDistance = 10000.0f;
    for(int i=0;i<terrain.m_patches.size();i++)
    {
        //Cheap Ray-Box intersection test
        if(mRay.Intersect(m_terrain.patches[i]->m_BBox) > 0)
        {
            // Collect only the closest intersection
            BOOL hit;
            DWORD dwFace;
            float hitU, hitV, dist;

            //More expensive Ray-Mesh intersection test
            D3DXIntersect(terrain.m_patches[i]->m_pMesh,
                        &mRay.org,
                        &mRay.dir,
                        &hit,
                        &dwFace,
                        &hitU, &hitV,
                        &dist, NULL, NULL);

            //Use the patch closest to the ray origin
            if(hit && dist < minDistance)
            {
                minDistance = dist;
                //Two faces to each map tile
                int tiles = dwFace / 2;
```

```
                    int tilesPerRow =
                            terrain.m_patches[i]->m_mapRect.right
                            —terrain.m_patches[i]->m_mapRect.left;
                    int y = tiles / tilesPerRow;
                    int x = tiles - y * tilesPerRow;

                    if(dwFace % 2 == 0)      //Hit upper left face
                    {
                        if(hitU > 0.5f)x++;
                        else if(hitV > 0.5f)y++;
                    }
                    else                     //Hit lower right face
                    {
                        if(hitU + hitV < 0.5f)y++;
                        else if(hitU > 0.5f)x++;
                        else {x++;y++;}
                    }

                    //Set mouse map location
                    mappos.Set(
                        terrain.m_patches[i]->m_mapRect.left + x,
                        terrain.m_patches[i]->m_mapRect.top + y);
                }
            }
        }
    }
```

Have the Camera Focus Follow the Terrain

In this example, we want the camera focus to follow the height of the terrain as we move it around. Again, we use the D3DXIntersect() function for this. First we check what terrain patch our camera focus is over, and then we perform an intersection test using this patch. But instead of using a mouse ray, we create a ray with the origin (m_focus.x, 10000.0f, m_focus.z) and direction (0.0f, -1.0f, 0.0f). The distance returned from the D3DXIntersect() function, minus 10000.0f, will then be the new *y*-value of our camera focus:

```
//Excerpt from the CAMERA::Update() function

//Have the focus follow the terrain heights
//Find patch that the focus is over
for(int p=0;p<terrain.m_patches.size();p++)
{
    RECT mr = terrain.m_patches[p]->m_mapRect;
```

```
//Focus within patch maprect or not?
if(m_focus.x >= mr.left && m_focus.x < mr.right &&
   -m_focus.z >= mr.top && -m_focus.z < mr.bottom)
{
    // Collect only the closest intersection
    BOOL hit;
    DWORD dwFace;
    float hitU, hitV, dist;
    D3DXIntersect(terrain.m_patches[p]->m_pMesh,
            &D3DXVECTOR3(m_focus.x, 10000.0f, m_focus.z),
            &D3DXVECTOR3(0.0f, -1.0f, 0.0f), &hit,
            &dwFace, &hitU, &hitV, &dist, NULL, NULL);

    //Set new y-value of the camera focus
    if(hit)m_focus.y = 10000.0f - dist;
}
}
```

Example 5.9

ON THE CD

Example 5.9 implements these new additions to the TERRAIN, MOUSE, and CAMERA classes.

LIGHTING THE TERRAIN

Until now, we haven't done any advanced lighting of the terrain. We've used the fixed function pipeline together with D3DLIGHT9 lights. Now we will take a look at lighting the terrain using a vertexshader. From now on, we won't use the fixed function pipeline to transform our vertices. This will all be done using vertexshaders. In this section, we will cover the following:

- Calculate terrain normals manually.
- Perform vertex transformations and directional lighting using a vertexshader.
- Calculate a terrain lightmap.
- Modify our terrain pixelshader to incorporate a lightmap and vertex lighting.

Calculating Terrain Normals

Before, we used the D3DXComputeNormals() function to calculate the normals of our terrain mesh automatically. This works fine if we only have one patch that covers the entire terrain, but as soon as we have multiple patches, this creates visual artifacts around the edges of the patches. The only way around this is to calculate the normals of our terrain vertices manually from our map tiles. The D3DXComputeNormals() function works by averaging the normals of all polygons connected to a certain vertex. We need to do the exact same thing. The only difference is that we work with the height information stored in the map tiles rather than an actual mesh. Consider Figure 5.16. In order to calculate the normal of vertex E, we need to consider all faces connected to this vertex—that is, the following six faces: DBE, BCE, CFE, FHE, GEH, and DEG.

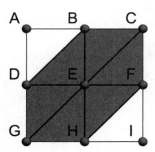

FIGURE 5.16 Faces to consider when calculating a vertex normal.

The following function has been added to our TERRAIN class to help calculate our normals:

```
D3DXVECTOR3 TERRAIN::GetNormal(int x, int y)
{
    //Neighboring map nodes (D, B, C, F, H, G)
    INTPOINT mp[] = {INTPOINT(x-1, y),   INTPOINT(x, y-1),
                     INTPOINT(x+1, y-1), INTPOINT(x+1, y),
                     INTPOINT(x, y+1),   INTPOINT(x-1, y+1)};
```

```
//if there's an invalid map node return (0, 1, 0)
if(!Within(mp[0]) || !Within(mp[1]) || !Within(mp[2]) ||
   !Within(mp[3]) || !Within(mp[4]) || !Within(mp[5]))
    return D3DXVECTOR3(0.0f, 1.0f, 0.0f);

//Calculate the normals of the 6 neighboring planes
D3DXVECTOR3 normal = D3DXVECTOR3(0.0f, 0.0f, 0.0f);

for(int i=0;i<6;i++)
{
    D3DXPLANE plane;
    D3DXPlaneFromPoints(&plane,
                        &GetWorldPos(INTPOINT(x, y)),
                        &GetWorldPos(mp[i]),
                        &GetWorldPos(mp[(i + 1) % 6]));

    normal +=  D3DXVECTOR3(plane.a, plane.b, plane.c);
}

D3DXVec3Normalize(&normal, &normal);
return normal;
}
```

This function calculates the normals of the six gray faces in Figure 5.16 and returns the average of these. To allow a normal to be assigned to a vertex, we've changed the constructor of the TERRAINVertex structure to accept a normal, as well as position and two UV coordinates.

Directional Light Using a Vertexshader

When lighting our terrain, we want to simulate daylight as closely as possible. The best type of light for this purpose is the directional light (i.e., parallel light rays). Have a look at Figure 5.17.

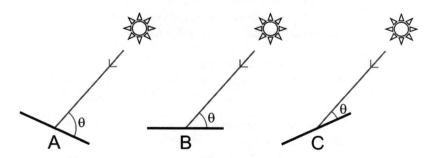

FIGURE 5.17   Directional lighting.

As you can see, the three faces A, B, and C all have a different angles to the rays of light. The idea is simple—the greater the angle, the brighter we want the polygon to be lit. In this case, polygon A would be the brightest lit.

Also, since we will be using a vertexshader to transform our vertices, from now on we set the world, view, and projection matrices in the vertexshader, rather than use the IDirect3DDevice9::SetTransformation() function. Here's the vertexshader that does the terrain lighting:

```
uniform extern float4x4 matW;        //World matrix
uniform extern float4x4 matVP;       //View-Projection matrix
uniform extern float3 DirToSun;      //The direction to the sun

struct VS_INPUT
{
    float4 position : POSITION0;
    float3 normal : NORMAL0;
    float2 uv : TEXCOORD0;           //alpha UV
    float2 uv2 : TEXCOORD1;          //diffuse UV
};

struct VS_OUTPUT
{
    float4 position : POSITION0;
    float2 uv : TEXCOORD0;
    float2 uv2 : TEXCOORD1;
    float  shade : TEXCOORD2;
};

VS_OUTPUT Main(VS_INPUT input)
{
    VS_OUTPUT output = (VS_OUTPUT)0;

    //transform World, View and Projection
    float4 temp = mul(input.position, matW);
    output.position = mul(temp, matVP);

    //Directional Lighting
    output.shade = max(0.0f, dot(normalize(input.normal),
                                 DirToSun));

    //Copy UV coordinates
    output.uv = input.uv;
    output.uv2 = input.uv2;
```

```
        return output;
    }
```

There are three things we need to set in order for this vertexshader to work: matW, matVP, and DirToSun. matW is our world transformation matrix; for the terrain, we just set this to the identity matrix. matVP is the view transformation matrix multiplied by the projection matrix, and DirToSun is the normalized direction to the sun. (See Chapter 3 for how to set shader variables.) Note that the VS_INPUT structure has the same contents as our TERRAINVertex. We've added a 1D texture coordinate to the VS_OUTPUT structure, called shade, which determines how lit a polygon will be. We calculate shade as the dot product of the vertex normal and the direction to the sun. (Make sure that the DirToSun is a normalized vector to get the correct lighting.)

Calculating a Terrain Lightmap

A lightmap is a precomputed texture containing the shadows of our terrain. Just like with the alpha texture used in texture splatting, the lightmap is stretched once over the entire terrain. Figure 5.18 shows how a 1D lightmap is created for a 2D terrain. For each pixel in the lightmap, a ray is first cast straight down onto the terrain. From the intersection point, another ray is cast in the direction of the light source. If this second ray hits the terrain, then this pixel is shadowed.

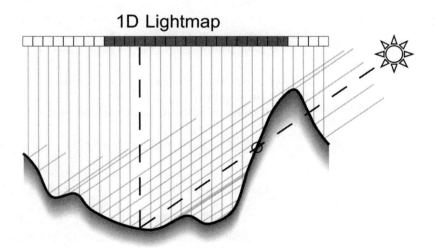

FIGURE 5.18 Creating a lightmap.

The following function has been added to our TERRAIN class to create a lightmap texture:

```
void TERRAIN::CalculateLightMap()
{
    //Clear old light map

    //Create new light map
    D3DXCreateTexture(m_pDevice, 256, 256, 1,
                      D3DUSAGE_DYNAMIC,
                      D3DFMT_L8, D3DPOOL_DEFAULT,
                      &m_pLightMap);

    //Lock the texture
    D3DLOCKED_RECT sRect;
    m_pLightMap->LockRect(0, &sRect, NULL, NULL);
    BYTE *bytes = (BYTE*)sRect.pBits;

    //Clear lightmap to white (i.e. no shadow)
    memset(bytes, 255, 256*sRect.Pitch);

    for(int y=0;y<sRect.Pitch;y++)
    for(int x=0;x<sRect.Pitch;x++)
    {
        float terrain_x = (float)m_size.x *
                          (x / (float)(sRect.Pitch));
        float terrain_z = (float)m_size.y *
                          (y / (float)(sRect.Pitch));

        //Find patch that the terrain_x, terrain_z is over
        bool done = false;
        for(int p=0;p<m_patches.size() && !done;p++)
        {
            RECT mr = m_patches[p]->m_mapRect;

            //Focus within patch maprect or not?
            if(terrain_x >= mr.left && terrain_x < mr.right &&
               terrain_z >= mr.top && terrain_z < mr.bottom)
            {
                // Collect only the closest intersection
                RAY rayTop(D3DXVECTOR3(terrain_x,
                                       10000.0f,-terrain_z),
                           D3DXVECTOR3(0.0f, -1.0f, 0.0f));
```

```
                 float dist =
                     rayTop.Intersect(m_patches[p]->m_pMesh);

                 if(dist >= 0.0f)
                 {
                     RAY ray(D3DXVECTOR3(terrain_x,
                                         10000.0f - dist+0.01f,
                                         -terrain_z),
                             dirToSun);

                     for(int p2=0;p2<m_patches.size() &&
                         !done;p2++)
                         if(ray.Intersect(
                             m_patches[p2]->m_BBox) >= 0)
                         {
                             //In shadow
                             if(ray.Intersect(
                                 m_patches[p2]->m_pMesh) >= 0)
                             {
                                 done = true;
                                 bytes[y * sRect.Pitch + x] = 128;
                             }
                         }
                     done = true;
                 }
             }
         }
     }

     //Unlock the texture
     m_pLightMap->UnlockRect(0);
}
```

Now we have a 2D texture containing the terrain shadow information. What do we do with it?

The Terrain Pixelshader

We need to take a second look at the pixelshader we created to do the texture splatting. The directional lighting must be incorporated, as well as the precomputed shadows stored in the lightmap.

```
        sampler alpha;
        sampler texture1;
```

```
sampler texture2;
sampler texture3;
sampler light;

float4 Main(float2 alphaUV : TEXCOORD0,
            float2 colorUV : TEXCOORD1,
            float shade : TEXCOORD2) : COLOR
{
    //Sample the textures
    float4 a  = tex2D(alpha,    alphaUV);
    float4 c1 = tex2D(texture1, colorUV);
    float4 c2 = tex2D(texture2, colorUV);
    float4 c3 = tex2D(texture3, colorUV);
    float4 l  = tex2D(light,    alphaUV);

    //Calculate the inverse
    float inverse = 1.0f / (a.r + a.g + a.b);

    //Multiply with alpha texture
    c1 *= a.b * inverse;
    c2 *= a.g * inverse;
    c3 *= a.r * inverse;

    //Return result
    return (c1 + c2 + c3) * shade * l;
}
```

We've added a new sampler that samples the lightmap (at texture stage four) and the new shade texture coordinate (TEXCOORD2). We perform the texture splatting just as explained in the previous chapter, but as we return the result, we multiply it by the shade and the lightmap. Both the shade and the lightmap are in the range 0.0f – 1.0f. Figure 5.19 shows a comparison of the lighting methods implemented.

The directional lighting is done in the vertexshader, and for this one it is easy to change the direction of the light, since the shade calculation is done once per frame. The lightmap, on the other hand, needs a lot of time to calculate, and if you decide to use this type of lighting, you won't able to change the direction of the light during runtime.

Visit the following Web page, Landscapes and Terrain: http://www.gamedev.net/reference/list.asp?categoryid=188. *You'll find some good articles about terrain generation, texturing, and other topics.*

| No Lighting | Directional Lighting | Directional + Lightmap |

FIGURE 5.19   Lighting the terrain.

ON THE CD

Example 5.10

Example 5.10 contains the methods covered in these past few sections concerning lighting the terrain. Also note that a second vertex and pixelshader pair have been implemented in this example to handle our terrain objects because these don't have the same vertex declaration as our terrain vertex. (Calculating the second UV coordinate on-the-fly will be covered in greater detail in Chapter 10.)

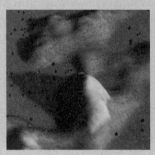

SUMMARY

In this chapter, we have created the CAMERA and MOUSE classes. As you can see, there are a lot of issues to consider regarding the camera and the mouse. We've covered things like picking, bounding volumes, frustum culling, level-of-detail rendering, and much more. Hopefully, now you are more comfortable with most of these topics and know how to integrate these techniques into your own games.

EXERCISES

- Implement a first-person camera that moves around on the terrain. Have the camera follow the terrain, and use the mouse to change viewing angles.
- Include terrain objects when creating the terrain lightmap.
- Create a split-screen application with a separate camera for each viewport, in which the camera moves independently across the terrain.
- Instead of moving the focus when bringing the cursor to the edge of the screen, create a camera movement system where you click-and-drag. When you click on a map location, dragging the mouse toward you moves the focus in this direction, and vice versa.

REFERENCES

[Celes04] Celes, Waldemar, "Extracting Frustum and Camera Information." *Game Programming Gems 4*, Charles River Media, 2004.

[Gribb01] Gribb, Gil, and Klaus Hartmann, "Fast Extraction of Viewing Frustum Planes from The World-View-Projection Matrix." Ravensoft. Available online at: *http://www2.ravensoft.com/users/ggribb/plane%20extraction.pdf*, 2001.

[Picco03] Picco, Dion, "Frustum Culling." FlipCode. Available online at: *http://www.flipcode.com/articles/article_frustumculling.shtml*, 2003.

FURTHER READING

Hook, Brian, "Mouse Picking Demystified." Available online at: *http://trac.bookofhook.com/bookofhook/trac.cgi/wiki/MousePicking*, 2005.

6 | Creating 3D Models

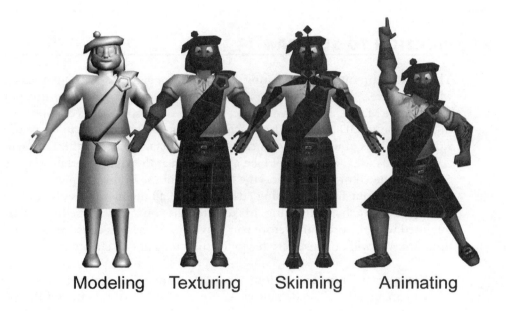

Modeling   Texturing   Skinning   Animating

This chapter might seem a little oddly hidden away between so many programming chapters. It's true that most programmers aren't great artists, maybe because art and logic are a little bit like oil and water. Who knows? Nevertheless, these days even programmers need to know a little bit about art, just as game artists need to know a little bit about logic and programming. A computer game, one could say, incidentally happens to be a perfect compromise between logic and art. In this chapter, we will take a look at how to model, texture, animate, and export a 3D model. Then, in Chapter 7, we will look at how to incorporate any "works of art" we create into our game. If you are really interested about this subject and want to learn more, you should look at some of the myriad of tutorials available online or buy a book specifically on the subject.

This chapter will only cover the absolute bare bones of what you need to know in order to create a 3D model using 3ds Max. There's a lot of content to cover in this chapter, which means that the pace will be quite fast. If you are new to these techniques and at some point feel lost, you should try some of the simpler tutorials available online. Then come back to the examples in this chapter and see if they make more sense.

If you feel that 3D modeling is generally not for you, or if you perhaps someone to help you with modeling, then you can just skip ahead to Chapter 7.

INTRODUCTION TO 3DS MAX

The most common tool for creating 3D content for games is, without question, 3ds Max. However, there are, of course, many other good programs for this purpose, for example Maya®, Lightwave®, Bryce™, to mention some. This chapter will focus on developing a 3D character from scratch using 3ds Max. You can find a trial version of 3ds Max at *www.autodesk.com* (see Products, Media & Entertainment).

Start 3ds Max, and we will take a brief look at the User Interface (UI). Figure 6.1 shows the UI of 3ds Max and the tools we will use in this chapter.

If this is your first time using 3ds Max, then all the menus, tools, and buttons may seem a little overwhelming. Make sure that you spend some time getting acquainted with the program before you move on. 3ds Max is an extremely powerful program. We will only use very few of its functions in this chapter:

Viewports: These are the four viewports from which you can view the model you are creating. The default viewports are Top, Front, Left, and Perspective. You can change the number of viewports, and their layout and type by selecting Viewport Configuration in the Customize menu.

Create Menu: In this menu you can create new objects, anything from standard primitives to advanced custom objects.

Modify Menu: Here you can modify existing objects in various ways. You do this by adding a modifier to the object. This can be, for example, Bend, Noise, Extrude, and many more options. The active modifiers for a certain object are shown in the Modifier list.

Hierarchy Menu: The most useful tool (for us) in the Hierarchy menu is the Affect Pivot tool. When selected, you can modify the pivot point of an object. (Rotations and so forth are done around the pivot point of an object.)

Display Menu: With this menu, you hide and unhide objects. This is very useful if you are working on a complex scene and want to reduce the clutter. Simply hide any object you are not working on and concentrate on a small portion of the scene; once done, simply unhide the other objects again before rendering.

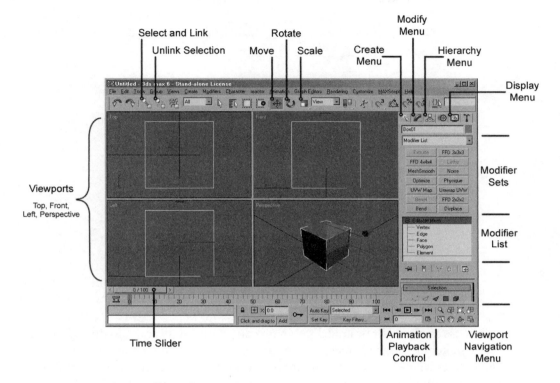

FIGURE 6.1   The user interface of 3ds Max.

MODELING A 3D MODEL

There are as many different methods to model a 3D model as there are tools to do it with. Luckily, we are at the moment only interested in modeling a low-polygon model, which limits us a little bit in which tools to use. Things like nurbs or patches are a bit overkill, since they generally produce models with far too-high polygon counts than are useful for computer games.

Sketch the Model

What may appear to be a skirt on the man in Figure 6.2 is, in fact, a kilt—the manliest garment on the planet. The absolute easiest way of modeling a 3D character is to first make a sketch on a piece of paper. Start by drawing your character from the front. Remember that there's no point in adding lots of small details, like freckles, eye lashes, and so on. This sketch will only be used to get the shape of our object, and therefore it doesn't need to be detailed at all. Once you've finished the front

FIGURE 6.2 A sketch of a Scottish person, hereafter referred to as "Scot."

view, use a ruler to draw guidelines in one direction (in this case, to the right). Then start sketching your character from the side with the help of the guidelines. The guidelines will help you to maintain the proportions of the character. Your finished sketch should look something like Figure 6.2 when it's complete.

Getting this sketch into your computer is best done with a scanner, but it can also be done with a digital camera. If you don't have access to either of these devices, you can also try to recreate your sketch in 3ds Max using splines. Once you have the sketch in your computer, divide the sketch into two images, front and side. You could also spend some time cleaning them up—removing the guidelines and so on in Photoshop or a similar program. Manipulate the images so that the background is gray; this makes it easier for us to see what's going on in 3ds Max. The easiest way to do this is by changing the Brightness/Contrast of the image.

The next step is to use these two images as background images in 3ds Max, as shown in Figure 6.3.

To set the background of a viewport, select Views, then Viewport Background. The Viewport Background window will appear, and you can select what image to use and how to use it. Select (checkmark) the Lock Zoom/Pan and Match Bitmap check boxes. Now all we have to do is model our character according to our sketch.

NOTE

Instead of using the viewport background to show your sketch, you can create two planes that are perpendicular to each other and map the images to these.

FIGURE 6.3   Using sketches as viewport backgrounds.

Creating Vertices and Faces

1. Create a new box in the facial area of the character. (Create Menu, Box).
2. Now select the Modify menu. Select the text in the modifier list that says Box, and right-click it.
3. Convert to Editable Mesh.
4. In the Editable Mesh menu, select the Vertex mode. (Other useful modes that we will access from this drop-down menu are the Edge and the Face editing modes.) See Figure 6.4.

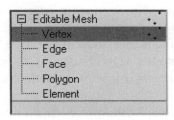

FIGURE 6.4   Mesh editing modes—Vertex, Edge, Face, Polygon, and Element.

5. Select all the corners of the box and hit the Delete key. This removes all vertices in the mesh and their associated faces. We will now create new vertices in the places we want.
6. Move down to the Edit Geometry drop-down list and select Create.
7. Make sure you place vertices along the lines drawn in your sketch, as shown in Figure 6.5. Place more vertices in detailed areas, like the nose. Also make sure you only work on one half of the character at a time if both sides are similar to each other.

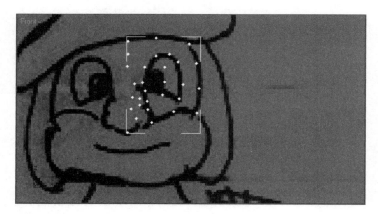

FIGURE 6.5   Placing vertices.

8. When you have placed all the vertices you need for a specific area (the fewer the better), select the Face editing mode in the Editable Mesh menu. This will make all your vertices disappear—but don't worry, they are still there.
9. In the Edit Geometry menu, select Create—and there are your vertices again.
10. Start creating faces by selecting vertices three at a time in clockwise order. This will create one face each time you do this. Create faces for all the vertices you are working with at the moment, as shown in Figure 6.6.

You should have something that looks a little bit like whatever you are modeling, at least from the front. From the side, it will still be flat. To change this, select to edit the mesh in Vertex mode. Move all the vertices in the x-direction only until they fit with the side view as well as the front view. You can manipulate selected vertices and faces using the Move, Rotate, or Scale tool.

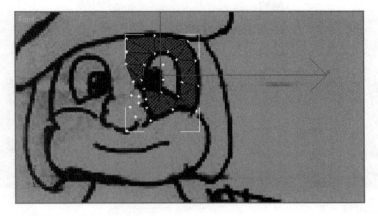

FIGURE 6.6   Creating faces.

Okay, that's one way of creating new vertices and faces. It might feel a little frustrating, trying to get things right, especially if you're new to 3ds Max. If that's the case, don't start with a 3D character (one of the hardest things to model). Start with something simpler that uses only a few faces.

Check out the beginner's tutorials at www.tutorialoutpost.com *for a quick start in 3ds Max. Or simply do a search for 3ds Max tutorials using your favorite search engine.*

TIP

Welding Vertices

The next modeling tool we will take a look at is welding. With the welding tool, we fuse two or more vertices together to make one. This is a great way to decrease the vertex and face count in a selected area (along with some detail as well, of course). See Figure 6.7 for an example of welding.

1. Select the Vertex editing mode.
2. Select two vertices you wish to weld together.
3. In the Edit Geometry menu, find the Weld box and press the Selected button. (Should a message box appear saying that no vertices are within range, you must increase the range value found next to the Selected button.)

Before moving on to the texturing step, you should always go over the model and see if there are any vertices you could weld together without losing any significant details. With each weld we perform, there is one less vertex the graphic card

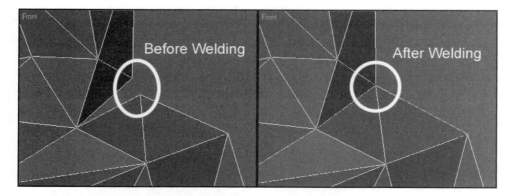

FIGURE 6.7 Before and after welding two vertices.

needs to transform and project in our game. The face and vertex count of a model is absolutely essential, especially in an RTS game where there may be many copies of the same unit running around.

Extruding Edges and Faces

Another very useful tool in low-polygon modeling is extrusion. This operation can be performed both on edges and faces, as shown in Figure 6.8.

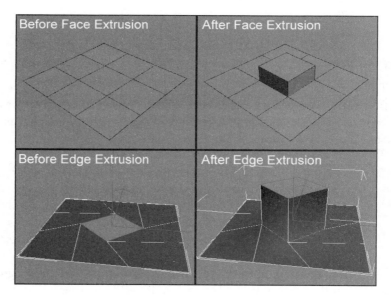

FIGURE 6.8 Face and edge extrusion.

1. Select the Face, Polygon, or Edge editing mode, depending on whether you want to extrude an face, polygon, or an edge.
2. Select the faces/edges you want to extrude.
3. Find the Extrude button in the Edit Geometry menu. Either enter the specific value you want to extrude the faces/edges with in the text box next to the Extrude button, or click the Extrude button and click-and-drag the selection to increase/decrease the extrusion.

Extrusion is a powerful modeling tool that is often used to create extremities, like arms, legs, fingers, and so on.

Don't Do the Same Work Twice: Mirror

Let's say you've just finished one side of Scot's face. If the other side of the face happens to be symmetrical (or close to it), then this little trick will save you a lot of time. Instead of creating the other side from scratch, we just copy the face, mirror it, and weld the two halves together, as shown in Figure 6.9.

1. Select the mesh you want to mirror. (Make sure you aren't in Mesh editing mode.)
2. Select the Move tool and move the mesh you want to mirror while holding down the Shift key. This will create a clone of the mesh. In the clone pop-up window that appears, select Ok.
3. Find the Mirror Selected Objects button and press it.
4. Move the mirrored mesh so the edge is aligned with the original half (see Figure 6.9, C).
5. In the Edit Geometry menu, find the Attach button and press it, then press the other half of the mesh. This joins the two meshes.
6. Now enter the Vertex editing mode and weld together all vertices along the edges of the two halves, as explained earlier.

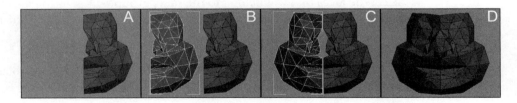

FIGURE 6.9   Mirroring a mesh.

Smoothing Groups

The final tool we will cover is smoothing groups. This doesn't affect how a mesh is built, only how it looks. Figure 6.10 shows a comparison of a mesh rendered using different smoothing group settings.

FIGURE 6.10 Different smoothing group results.

In the left image in Figure 6.10, all faces belong to individual smoothing groups—that is, no smoothing is done between faces. In the middle image, all faces belong to the same smoothing group. In this image, details that should stand out get blurred together. For example, it's impossible to see Scot's eyes in the middle image. The right image is what we want achieve. Here, faces belong to one or more smoothing groups. For example, the eyes belong to one smoothing group, the skin to another, and the beard to another still, and so on. The edge between two faces that belongs to the same group gets smoothed out, while an edge between two faces from different groups remains distinct.

1. Select the mesh in which you wish to edit the smoothing groups.
2. Enter the Face or Polygon editing mode.
3. Scroll down to the Surface Properties menu.
4. Select the faces that will belong to the same group.
5. In the Smoothing Groups menu, click one of the buttons numbered 1–32. These faces now belong to this group.

You can clear all groups with the Clear All button. It is also possible to assign faces to more than one group.

Final Modeling Checklist

Before we move on to the texturing of the model, there are some final things you need to check.

1. Remove any unseen or hidden faces and vertices. If they won't contribute to the final shape or image in the game, then they are just extra baggage. Things to check are the bottoms of houses, and so forth.

2. Check that there are no duplicate vertices that can be removed. An easy way to check this is to perform a weld operation on all vertices in the model with a weld range of 0.01. If there are any duplicate vertices, they will now be welded into one.

3. Make one last check that you don't have unnecessary details in your model. Remember, in an RTS game, the units are often seen from afar. Will a detail like an ear that costs a lot in terms of vertices and faces really affect the final quality of the game? In an RPG game it certainly would, but in an RTS it probably won't, and so details like ears should be removed.

The fewer faces and vertices you have, the easier the following steps in this chapter are going to be. There's always a balance, of course, between the amount of detail you want and the amount of vertices you need (or are allowed to use). To find out how many polygons you have in a scene or an object, go to the Utilities menu. Here you have a list of utilities, among which is a Polygon Counter utility. (If you can't find the Polygon Counter, press the More button and select it from the list.)

Figure 6.11 show a rendering of our Scot character. He's been completely modeled with the techniques covered in this section.

FIGURE 6.11   The finished Scot model.

Example 6.1

You can find the finished model of Scot on the CD-ROM.

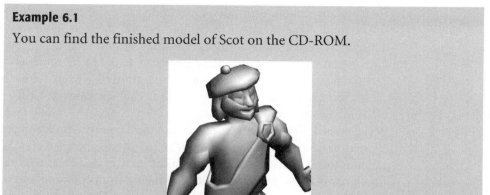

Texturing a 3D Model

In the previous section, we had a look at some common techniques that can be used to model a 3D character. In this section we will apply a texture to the model we created. The first thing we need to make is UV map the model. This may be one of the most tedious tasks you have to do to create a character for a game, but it also one of the more rewarding ones.

Creating the UV mapping for something as complicated as a 3D character is quite tricky. The method presented here is divided into several complex steps, all which must be performed correctly or it will fail. We first divide the character into several smaller pieces that can easily be flattened. A copy is made of the resulting collection of pieces (while the character is still in its original shape). We merge and hide the original, and can now start flattening the pieces of the remaining character. These pieces are flattened and placed so that they all form a square with as little space in between the pieces as possible. We assign a wireframe material to the pieces and render the pieces to an image file that we save. Next we use the UVW Map and the Unwrap UVW tool to fit the actual UV coordinates of the mesh to the image we created. Once done, we merge the pieces together and unhide the original character (still in its original shape). Using the Morph tool we morph the flat UV-mapped character back to its original shape, using the original character as a target. It's important that when morphing the flat character, it has the same number of vertices and faces as the target or the whole process will fail.

Step 1: Remove Duplicate Parts. First of all, make a copy of your mesh for safekeeping (and do so regularly). If this is one of your first attempts, you will surely need those backups before the end. Start by cutting away all the duplicate parts of the mesh—that is, parts that will have the same UV-mapping coordinates, such as similar body parts like arms, legs, hands, or feet that you want to look exactly the same. Only UV-map one of them. For our Scot, we'll want him to have exactly the same-looking legs and hands, so we'll take away one of each, as shown in Figure 6.12. The arms, however, we will give different looks, so we'll keep both arms for now. If you are making machinery like tanks or cars, there will be many parts that you'll only have to UV-map one of, like the wheel of a car, for instance. Just enter the Vertex or Polygon editing mode and simply delete any duplicate parts.

FIGURE 6.12   Scot after removing duplicate parts

TIP

In the future, you can move directly to this step by not modeling any duplicate limbs during the modeling of the character.

Step 2: Divide the Mesh.   No duplicate parts left? Well then, it's time to divide the mesh into smaller, manageable parts that belong together and can be flattened well. Go into the Polygon editing mode. Now start selecting parts of the mesh that fit together and that you can make flat as a pancake without too much trouble. Once selected, go to the Edit Geometry menu and Detach them into whatever object 3ds Max suggests. Do this until there is only one small part left, and leave that one as it is. Do not detach it. In our case, our mesh was called "Box01." You should now have your mesh exploded as a lot of different Objects and one piece called Box01 (or whatever your original mesh was called). After this stage, our Scot looks something like Figure 6.13 (the different parts are highlighted in different shades).

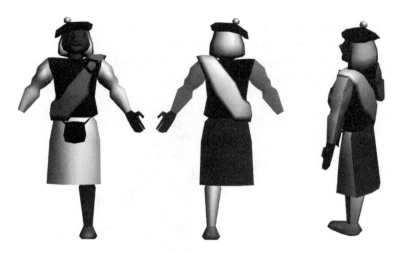

FIGURE 6.13 The mesh divided into smaller parts.

Step 3: Create Copies. Select all the small parts (CTRL+A) and copy them by holding down the Shift key and just moving/dragging them to the side. Make sure there is space between the two copies. Hide the copy you just made (Utilities, Hide Selected).

Step 4: Attach All. Select the part Box01 (or again, whatever was the original name of your mesh). Go to Modify, and then click the button Attach List under Edit Geometry. Attach all available objects. Also, make sure that you don't have anything else than the character visible in the scene when you do this. Go to Utilities and click the Unhide all button. You should now have one character made up of one mesh and one character made up of several smaller pieces. Now hide the character made up of one mesh so that only the exploded mesh is visible. From this point onward, it is very important that the number of vertices or faces of the model doesn't change at all.

Do not choose another part other than the original Box01 to attach all to or this entire process will fail.

Step 5: Flatten the Mesh. Now you should have one character made up of several small pieces with no duplicate pieces in front of you. First, move and rotate all of the pieces so that they are all separated and facing in the same direction (see Figure 6.14).

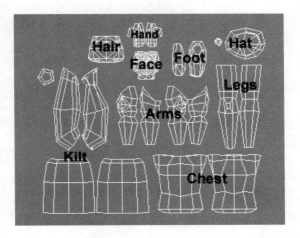

FIGURE 6.14   Separating the different parts of the mesh.

Now edit the vertices of each single piece, stretching them out, making the piece as flat as possible. This is a whole lot like laying a puzzle. If your target texture is going to be square, then try to make the pieces form a square as closely as you can. This is the most tedious part of the whole operation, and for a really detailed mesh, you can spend hours laying this puzzle. Again, remember not to delete any vertices or faces while you do this or it will be all for nothing. Learn to use the keys W, R, and T—the move, rotate, and scale fast keys; they really are your friends during this process. The finished result should look something like Figure 6.15.

Try to keep the flat faces in roughly the same proportions as in the original mesh.

TIP

Step 6: Lay the Puzzle. Create a box or a plane roughly the same size as the mesh you have, but make sure that the width by height proportions are the same as that of your target texture. For our Scot we want to create a 512×512 square texture, so we simply create a square box to use as an outline for our puzzle. Now the objective is to fit all the different pieces into the square, using up as much of the space inside it as possible.

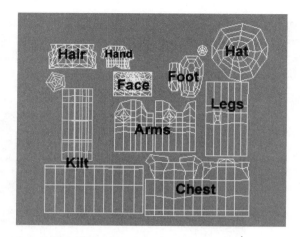

FIGURE 6.15 Scot after the flattening process.

- Leave a little bit space between the different pieces.
- Scale more-important parts, like the head, to take a little bit more space than in the original.
- Start with the large, square parts, and save the smaller parts to do last.
- Expend little texture area on small parts that are not visible or important, like the sole of a foot.

The finished puzzle should something look like Figure 6.16.

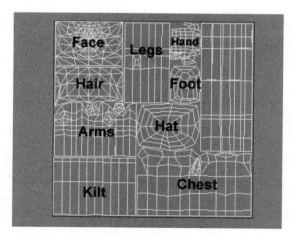

FIGURE 6.16 The finished puzzle.

Step 7: Render the Texture Outline. Okay, the puzzle is now finished. Create a new camera with Orthographic Projection, and align it so that it exactly covers the whole mesh. Remove the box/plane you used as an outline. Now open up the Material Editor (shortcut key "M") and create a black, wireframe material, and assign it to all the pieces. Also, go to the Rendering menu and select Environment. Set the background color to white. Now render the image with the dimensions you want for the final texture and save it as "outline.bmp" (see Figure 6.17). When creating textures for games, it is always a good idea to save it as dimensions that are the power of two (e.g., 128×128, 256×256, 512×512, or 1024×1024).

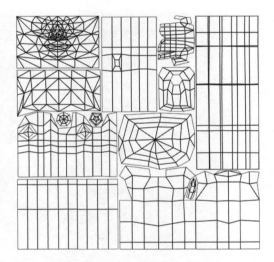

FIGURE 6.17   The outline bitmap.

Step 8: Set Up the UV Coordinates. Before we start painting away and creating a texture, we need to set up the texture coordinates of the mesh. Delete the camera now and select the mesh piece Box02 (or whatever you called your first mesh). We are going to merge all the flat pieces into one big mesh. We do this as before, by going to Modify, Edit Geometry, Attach List. Make sure that you do this with the object Box02 and no other piece. Once all the pieces are again just one mesh, open up the Material Editor again. Create a solid material with the image outline.bmp as a diffuse map and assign it to the mesh. Click in the Show in Viewport check box. Then go to Modify and add the UVW Map to the mesh. If it isn't in the list, simply select Configure the Modifier Sets, and find it in the long list that appears. Look at the mesh and make sure that the image roughly fits the mesh. Make sure the UVW map is a planar map. You also might have to flip the U or V coordinate to make it fit. You should now see the outline.bmp image overlaid on the mesh. Don't worry if the image doesn't follow the mesh perfectly; this is where our next modifier comes into the picture. First, however, right-click the UVW Mapping modifier and select Collapse All. Now add the Unwrap UVW modifier to the mesh. (As before, if you don't find it, select Configure the Modifier Sets and pick it out of the list.) Once the modifier has been added, press Edit in the Parameters drop-down menu. This will open up the Edit UVW window (see Figure 6.18).

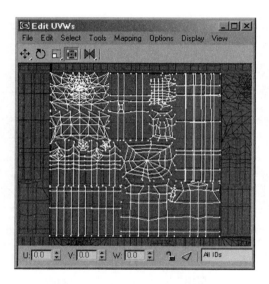

FIGURE 6.18 The Unwrap UVW modifier.

Select the Freeform mode (shown as active in Figure 6.18) and select all the points. Now zoom in to the upper-left corner and make sure that the left-upper vertex is aligned with the image. Zoom in to the bottom-right and do the same with the bottom-right-most vertex. The beauty of aligning only these two vertices using the Freeform mode is that all other vertices fall into place, as well. Close the Edit UVW window and Collapse the Unwrap UVW modifier like before. You should now have a mesh with the outline.bmp texture mapped perfectly onto it.

Step 9: Restore the Shape. It is now time to get our character back in shape. First Unhide all in the Display menu. This should unhide the first character we had back in Step 2. On your screen, you should now have the original mesh (maybe without some limbs) spread out flat. Both images should have the exact number of vertices, faces, and edges, otherwise this won't work. Now select the flat mesh and go to the Create menu, and select Geometry, then Compound Objects from the drop-down box. Select Morph (while having the flat character selected). Press the Pick Target button and select the original character. Your character should now look just like it did in Step 2, only now it should have the wireframe texture mapped onto it perfectly. If after you pressed Pick Target you ended up with something other than your original character, well this is when you go back to a backup file and do it all again. But if you are successful, you end up with something like Figure 6.19. Don't worry if it's rotated, moved, or scaled in some way. Just rotate/scale/move it back to where you want it.

FIGURE 6.19   The UV-mapped character.

Step 10: Fixing the Mesh.   It's now time to fix the mesh and put it back into the original shape. First, let's get rid of all unnecessary vertices. Where did they come from, you may wonder? Well, when you divided the mesh in Step 2, you create new vertices along the seams. Select the mesh and open the Modify menu, and Convert to Editable Mesh. Edit the mesh in the Vertex mode. Select all vertices (CTRL+A). Scroll down to the Edit Geometry menu, and next to the Weld button, enter "0.01." Then hit Weld. This will weld all duplicate vertices. Next it is time to restore any missing limbs. Do this for all missing limbs, as explained earlier (see "Don't Do the Same Work Twice: Mirror")—in Scot's case, the leg and the hand. Remember to weld the hand and the wrist together after mirroring it, as well.

Step 11: Create the Texture. Okay, now comes the time when we actually paint the texture for the character. Start Photoshop and open the outline.bmp file you saved. Now create a new layer on top of the background layer and start painting away. Every once in a while you can save your texture to another file. Go into 3ds Max, create a material with your texture in progress, and assign it to the mesh to see what it looks like on your character. Once you are finished, save the texture in your favorite file format, and load it onto your character in 3ds Max, as shown in Figure 6.20. And you're done!

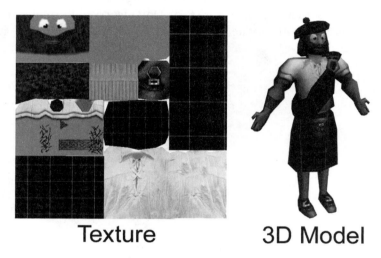

Texture   **3D Model**

FIGURE 6.20 The finished texture mapped to the 3D model.

ON THE CD

Example 6.2

Have a look on the CD-ROM where you'll find the textured model of Scot.

Skinning a 3D Model

In this section, we will take a look at how to create bones, and skin the mesh to these using 3ds Max and its Physique plug-in. This is a necessary step we need to do before we can animate the character. To skin the model, we will first create underlying bones that follow the shape of the character. Then we will "skin" the mesh to these bones so that when the bones are moved, rotated, or scaled, the mesh will be affected in a similar way. When we skin the mesh, we assign each vertex to one or more bones. If a vertex is assigned to more than two bones, then the position of that vertex is calculated as a blend of the bones' transformation matrices. This will all become clearer in Chapter 7 when we import the character into our game.

Step 1: Put the character in the center. A very important thing to do before we start is to place the mesh at the origin. Select your mesh and press for the Hierarchy menu; from there highlight Affect Pivot Only and move the pivot point to the center, between the character's feet, as shown in Figure 6.21. Now deselect Affect Pivot Only and left-click the Move icon (shortcut key "W"). When the Move icon is selected, right-click it. This will bring up the Move Transform Type-In window. Set the Absolute World coordinates, X, Y, and Z values to zero. This will move your character so its feet are firmly planted at the very center of the scene.

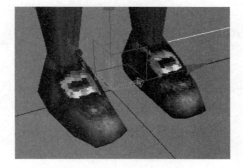

FIGURE 6.21   Placing the pivot point.

Step 2: Give your character some backbone. Now it is time to give some bones to our character. Go into the Create menu and select Helpers, and create a fair-size Dummy helper in the belly-button area of your character (or rough center if you are creating some form of nonhumanoid). Next, go to Systems in the Create menu and select Bones. Create the bones, as done in Figure 6.22.

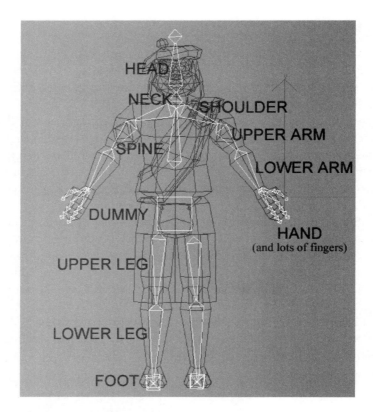

FIGURE 6.22   Bone placement.

Make sure that you keep the little end bone that 3ds Max creates for you at the end of each bone. This bone is your friend. If this is your first time skinning a mesh, you'll have better success by starting with an easy character. Start off with one that doesn't have fingers and other small extremities—one with a very simple mesh. Note how you can change the size of the bones by altering the Width and Height parameters. Make sure your bones aren't too big or small; for example, see how the finger bones are smaller than the rest of the bones. At the moment, all the legs and the spine aren't really connected to each other. We fix this by selecting the Select and Link tool. Now select the Spine bone and both Upper Leg bones, and click-and-drag them to the green Dummy01 object at the belly-button. This will link all the bones to the dummy, and you now have an attached skeleton. You can test this by selecting the Move tool and moving the Dummy around. The whole skeleton should follow the Dummy's movements.

Step 3: Skin them bones! Select the character and open up the Modify menu, and select the Physique modifier. (If it isn't visible, you'll have to press Configure Modifier Sets and pick it out of the list.) Then press the Link to Node button that appears, and press the Dummy01 object. A pop-up window appears; don't worry about that now, just hit the Initialize button. If everything went as it should, you should have a lot of orange lines following the bones of your character. What follows is the second-most tedious job of creating a 3D character—that is to assign each vertex of the mesh to one or more bones.

Select the active Physique modifier of the mesh, and in the drop-down menu, edit the modifier in Vertex mode. (Do not confuse this with editing the mesh in Vertex mode.) Select all vertices and hit the Assign to Link button, select No Blending in the blending drop-down box, and then the Blue Cross. Assign all these vertices to any bone. All this does is set all the vertices to be nondeformable vertices. Now we have a blank sheet and can start assigning specific vertices to specific bones.

Press the Select button again and make sure that the Red Cross isn't highlighted. Start by selecting vertices that clearly belong to one bone—like the head, for instance. Once you've selected all the vertices you think belong only to the head bone, hit the Assign to Link button again. This time, highlight the Red Cross (deformable vertices) and make sure the drop-down box says "No Blending," then click the head bone (or link). The vertices should now be highlighted in a bright red color, together with the bone you selected, as shown in Figure 6.23. Do this for all vertices that belong only to one bone. Note that once assigned as deformable vertices, you can't select them again as long as the Red Cross isn't highlighted.

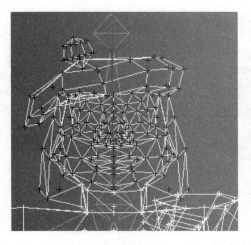

FIGURE 6.23   Assigning vertices to a bone.

Next we focus on vertices that belong to two bones. Once again, hit the Select button and select those vertices that belong to two specific bones; these vertices are the foremost ones in joints like elbows, knees, neck, and so forth. When the vertices are selected, change the drop-down box to "2 Links," and using CTRL or click-and-drag, select the two bones to which the vertices are to be assigned. See Figure 6.24; all vertices belonging both to the left-upper and lower arm have been assigned to these bones. The vertices become dark red when assigned to more than one bone. In the case where a vertex is assigned to more than two bones, simply pick the right number of links in the drop-down list and assign the vertices to the right number of bones. The art of assigning the vertices to the right bones takes a long time to learn, but hopefully you have the gist of it now.

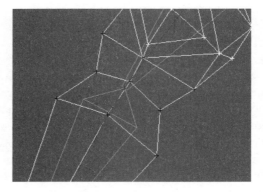

FIGURE 6.24   Assigning vertices to more than one bone.

FIGURE 6.25   Scot placed in different poses using the underlying bones.

Once all vertices have been assigned to at least one bone, you're finished, and you can exit the Physique modifier's Vertex mode. You can test the quality of the skinning by rotating the different bones and seeing how the vertices blend. If you get weird results with some of the joints, then just enter the Vertex mode again and change how the vertices are assigned to try and get better results. Now you can place your character mesh in any pose you want by rotating the bones, as shown in Figure 6.25.

ON THE CD

Example 6.3

Here's our finished Scot character. All that's left to do is to animate him and then finally export him.

EXPORTING A 3D MODEL

We have now had a look at how to create, texture, and skin a model. In this section, we will have a very brief look at how to create animations, and finally how to export our character to the .x file format. In the Chapter 7, we will load these animated .x files and render them in our game.

Animating a 3D Model

An animation is built up by several key frames describing the position, rotation, and scale of an object at a certain times. The smooth animation is then created by interpolating between the different key frames. To create a simple animation, simply do the following:

1. Click the Auto Key button.
2. Move the Time Slider to the desired frame you want the animation to end.
3. Select the object and move, rotate, or scale it as you want.
4. Repeat from Step 2 to create a series of animations.
5. When done, deactivate the Auto Key button.

6. You can now move the Time Slider and see how your object is animated (alternatively, you can use the Play button).

Creating key frames is very easy; creating a good animation, on the other hand, is very hard. In an RTS game, we will need several different animations. At the very least, we will need the following animations:

- Standing still
- Moving
- Attacking
- Dying

Animate your character with the different animations you want in consecutive order. In other words, let the standing still animation have the range of 0–5 frames, the moving animation a range of 6–35 frames, and so on.

Walk Cycle

Of the different animations, the moving animation is the hardest one to get correctly. If this is your first attempt at animation, then don't try to animate a walk cycle on your own. Get a reference walk cycle. To help you along with this, check out the following Web site: *http://www.idleworm.com/how/anm/02w/walk1.shtml*.

Installing the Exporter Plug-Ins

There are a couple of different plug-ins you can use to export a 3D character to the .x file format. Microsoft has an exporter plug-in called "XSkinExp.dle" that you can use. However, there's another plug-in, the Panda DirectX Exporter, available at the Pandasoft Web site at *http://www.andytather.co.uk/Panda/directxmax.aspx*.

ON THE CD

You can also find a copy of Panda DirectX Exporter on the companion CD-ROM. Whichever exporter you decide to use, copy the plug-in file (usually a .dle file) to the "plugins" folder of your 3ds Max folder. Restart 3ds Max, and the plug-in will be automatically loaded into the program.

Exporting to the .x File Format

Once you have created the desired animations for your character, it is time to finally export it. Before you export it, however, make sure of the following:

- Delete all objects that you don't wish to export, such as helper objects, cameras, and so forth.
- Make sure the pivot point of your character is placed at the center of its feet.

■   Make sure that the character is placed in the origin of the world (i.e., the pivot point should be at the absolute world coordinates 0, 0, 0).

Select Export in the File menu. From the Save as Type drop-down box, select the Panda DirectX (*.X) format. This will open up the exporter plug-in shown in Figure 6.26.

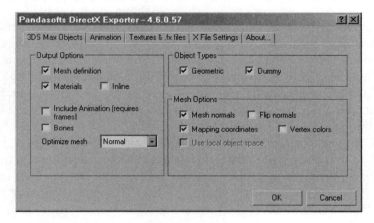

FIGURE 6.26   The Pandasoft DirectX Exporter.

Select the settings you want and hit OK. This will now export the character to the .x format. Make sure you set the ranges of the different animations you want, as well, in the Animation window.

ON THE CD

Example 6.4

In Example 6.4 on the CD-ROM, you'll find the models of our three units—the worker, the soldier, and the magician. These models are animated and ready to be exported. Export each of these three units and make sure you get the hang of how to use the exporter plug-in.

After you have successfully exported a character, make sure it was exported properly by viewing it in the Mesh Viewer program that accompanies the DirectX SDK. You can also view different animations, texturing, and normals in this program.

SUMMARY

In this fast-paced chapter, we have very briefly covered the different steps needed to create a low-polygon 3D character for a game. This is something that takes years to master fully, so don't be discouraged if your first attempt doesn't look that good. Hopefully, you will now have a deeper understanding of the specifics for creating 3D models for games. Remember to keep a low-polygon count; try instead to put extra details in textures. In an RTS game, we may have tens, if not hundreds of units running around. So you can probably imagine that the combined polygon count of all the units can quickly get out of hand. If you have the extra time, it's always a good idea to create a very low-polygon character to use when the character is far away from the camera, as explained in Chapter 5 (see Level-of-Detail Rendering).

As with anything else, the only way to get better at creating 3D art is by doing it—a lot. In the next chapter, we are going to look at how to load animated models like the one we've created here and render them in our game.

EXERCISES

Create your own character(s) using the techniques covered in this chapter. Create your own building(s), as well. You can, of course, skip the skinning and animation part when creating static objects.

7 Skinned Meshes

We have now arrived at one of the most technically advanced subjects covered in this book: skinned meshes. In games these days, skinned meshes (i.e., vertex blending) are a standard component used mainly for character animation. If you, as a beginner, tried to tackle the DirectX SDK SkinnedMesh example, you would know what a nightmare that can be. Hopefully, this chapter will prove somewhat easier to digest.

Skinned meshes are based on the idea that meshes are animated using an underlying bone structure ordered in a hierarchical fashion. When a bone is rotated, then the vertices in a mesh connected to this bone are deformed in the same way.

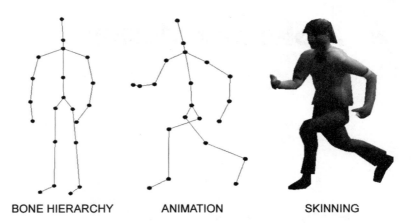

BONE HIERARCHY   ANIMATION   SKINNING

FIGURE 7.1   The three components of skinned meshes.

In this book, skinning has been divided into three parts, as shown in Figure 7.1. First, we load and try to understand the underlying bone hierarchy needed to create skinned meshes. Second, we animate this hierarchy and have a look at the ID3DXAnimationController interface. Third, we load the mesh and use the bone hierarchy to deform it.

LOADING THE HIERARCHY

In a hierarchy, objects are linked as parents, children, grandchildren, and so on. Any changes done to a parent object also affects its children objects and their children. The D3DX library uses the D3DXFRAME structure as the basic building block of a linked hierarchy.

```
struct D3DXFRAME
{
    LPTSTR Name;
    D3DXMATRIX TransformationMatrix;
    LPD3DXMESHCONTAINER pMeshContainer;
    struct _D3DXFRAME *pFrameSibling;
    struct _D3DXFRAME *pFrameFirstChild;
};
```

The frame has a name, contains a transformation matrix, a mesh, and two pointers. The pFrameFirstChild pointer points to the first child, and the pFrameSibling pointer points to a sibling. A hierarchy can be built as a linked list using these two pointers.

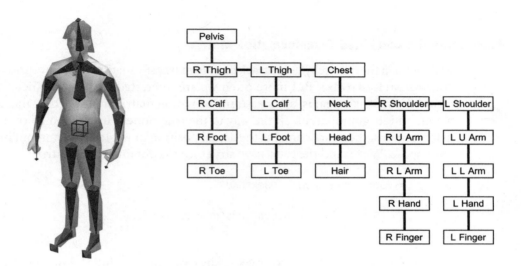

FIGURE 7.2   A bone hierarchy.

In Figure 7.2, siblings are marked with a horizontal connection, while children are marked with a vertical connection. If a change is done to any node in this hierarchy, then the change must also be applied to all of its children (and all of their children, and so on). Imagine for example that the bones in one of your arms belong to a hierarchy like this. Now stretch your fingers as far as you can in the direction that your nose is pointing. Without moving anything else, rotate your arm about your shoulder so that it points straight up. Did the your elbow, hand, and finger bones follow? They should have. They were affected by the change in your upper arm. The bone hierarchy we are going to implement in this section will work in the exact same way. The following function shows how to recursively traverse a linked bone hierarchy:

```
void TraverseHierarchy(D3DXFRAME* bone)
{
    //Do stuff with this bone...

    if(bone->pFrameSibling)
        TraverseHierarchy(bone->pFrameSibling);
```

```
        if(bone->pFrameFirstChild)
            TraverseHierarchy(bone->pFrameFirstChild);
    }
```

Calculating the Combined Transformation Matrix

Each node in the hierarchy keeps track of its own transformation matrix (D3DXFRAME::
TransformationMatrix). But more often we are interested in the combined transformation matrix—that is, a nodes-transformation matrix multiplied by that of its
parent and its grandparent, all the way to the root node. This combined transformation matrix therefore contains the actual position in world space and not just in
bone space. We extend the D3DXFRAME structure to contain such a matrix:

```
struct BONE: public D3DXFRAME
{
    D3DXMATRIX CombinedTransformationMatrix;
};
```

We also call this new structure BONE, since that makes a little bit more sense. We
can calculate this combined transformation matrix by traversing the hierarchy recursively, like this:

```
void UpdateMatrices(BONE* bone, D3DXMATRIX *parentMatrix)
{
    D3DXMatrixMultiply(&bone->CombinedTransformationMatrix,
                        &bone->TransformationMatrix,
                        parentMatrix);

    if(bone->pFrameSibling)
        UpdateMatrices((BONE*)bone->pFrameSibling,
                        parentMatrix);
    if(bone->pFrameFirstChild)
        UpdateMatrices((BONE*)bone->pFrameFirstChild,
                        &bone->CombinedTransformationMatrix);
}
```

We calculate the CombinedTransformationMatrix as the product of the bone's
transformation matrix and its parentMatrix (which is the CombinedTransformation
Matrix of its parent). The siblings get updated with the same parentMatrix, while a
bone's children get updated with the active bone's CombinedTransformationMatrix.
Note that we must cast the child and sibling pointers to BONE pointers because they

are stored as D3DXFRAME pointers. You should call this function every time the position/rotation of a bone changes, which in most cases means once per frame. We call this function on our root bone with the current world transformation matrix. This will then calculate the correct combined transformation matrix for all the bones in the hierarchy.

ID3DXAllocateHierarchy

So far we haven't talked about how we create this kind of hierarchy, only how to traverse it. Well, one way is to build the hierarchy manually by linking D3DXFRAME objects together using the child and sibling pointers, but this is in most cases not very useful. We will instead load meshes with their bone hierarchy, animations, and mesh, all from a single X-file (e.g., one of the characters created in Chapter 6, or similar). For this we use the D3DXLoadMeshHierarchyFromX() function:

```
HRESULT D3DXLoadMeshHierarchyFromX(
    LPCTSTR Filename,
    DWORD MeshOptions,
    LPDIRECT3DDEVICE9 pDevice,
    LPD3DXALLOCATEHIERARCHY pAlloc,
    LPD3DXLOADUSERDATA pUserDataLoader,
    LPD3DXFRAME* ppFrameHeirarchy,
    LPD3DXANIMATIONCONTROLLER* ppAnimController
);
```

MeshOptions: How you want the mesh to be loaded and into what pool to load the mesh. We use the D3DXMESH_MANAGED flag, for other options (see the DirectX documentation).

pAlloc: A pointer to a hierarchical frame-allocation object. We will cover this subject in more detail shortly.

pUserDataLoader: A pointer to a object that helps to read in user-defined data. We won't worry about this one, so just set it to NULL.

ppFrameHeirarchy: A pointer to the root frame in which our resulting hierarchy will be stored.

ppAnimController: An animation controller object. We will take a closer look at this parameter in the next section.

To this function, we supply the filename of the X-file that contains the skinned mesh that we would like to load. We also supply an ID3DXAllocateHierarchy object that will create the hierarchy for us. Later, when we discuss animation, we also supply an ID3DXAnimationController object to this function; but for now we just set the ppAnimController to NULL. As a result, from this function we get the whole loaded hierarchy (with mesh and animations) stored in the ppFrameHeirarchy variable.

The next important class to consider is the ID3DXAllocateHierarchy class. This is an abstract interface that we must inherit from and define in our subclass before we can use it. The BONE_HIERARCHY class in this chapter implements the abstract member functions of the ID3DXAllocateHierarchy class:

```
class BONE_HIERARCHY: public ID3DXAllocateHierarchy
{
    public:
        STDMETHOD(CreateFrame)(THIS_ LPCSTR Name,
                               LPD3DXFRAME *ppNewFrame);

        STDMETHOD(DestroyFrame)(THIS_ LPD3DXFRAME
                                pFrameToFree);

        STDMETHOD(CreateMeshContainer)( ... );
        STDMETHOD(DestroyMeshContainer)( ... );
};
```

CreateFrame: Creates a new frame (i.e., BONE).

CreateMeshContainer: Creates a new mesh, stored in the D3DXFRAME:: pMeshContainer variable.

DestroyFrame: Removes a frame and deallocates any memory used by the frame.

DestroyMeshContainer: Removes any mesh stored in the D3DXFRAME:: pMeshContainer variable.

At the moment, we won't worry about the functions concerning loading and destroying meshes, and instead concentrate on the CreateFrame and DestroyFrame functions. Here's how we create a new BONE:

```
HRESULT BONE_HIERARCHY::CreateFrame(LPCSTR Name,
                                    LPD3DXFRAME *ppNewFrame)
{
    BONE *newBone = new BONE;
    memset(newBone, 0, sizeof(BONE));
```

```
//Copy name
if(Name != NULL)
{
    newBone->Name = new char[strlen(Name)+1];
    strcpy(newBone->Name, Name);
}

//Set the transformation matrices
D3DXMatrixIdentity(&newBone->TransformationMatrix);
D3DXMatrixIdentity(&newBone->
                    CombinedTransformationMatrix);

//Return the new bone...
*ppNewFrame = (D3DXFRAME*)newBone;

return S_OK;
}
```

First we create a newBone and set all its members to 0 or NULL, including the child
and sibling pointers. Then we copy the name provided to the newBone and set its
transformation matrices to the identity matrix. Later when we search for a specific
bone, we will use the name of the bone to locate it. Last, we return the newBone using
the ppNewFrame pointer. Next let's see how to deallocate the memory used by our
bone hierarchy using the BONE_HIERARCHY::DestroyFrame function:

```
HRESULT BONE_HIERARCHY::DestroyFrame(LPD3DXFRAME pFrameToFree)
{
    if(pFrameToFree)
    {
        //Free name
        if(pFrameToFree->Name != NULL)
            delete [] pFrameToFree->Name;

        //Free bone
        delete pFrameToFree;
    }
    pFrameToFree = NULL;

    return S_OK;
}
```

There. That's how we implement the functions concerning creating and destroying frames in our BONE_HIERARCHY class. Next we need to create a wrapper class to hold our actual bone hierarchy and provide us with a nicer interface to skinned meshes. We call this class SKINNEDMESH:

```
class SKINNEDMESH
{
    public:
        SKINNEDMESH();
        ~SKINNEDMESH();
        void Load(char fileName[], IDirect3DDevice9 *Dev);
        void RenderSkeleton( ... );

    private:
        void UpdateMatrices(BONE* bone,
                            D3DXMATRIX parentMatrix);

        IDirect3DDevice9 *m_pDevice;
        D3DXFRAME *m_pRootBone;
};
```

The RenderSkeleton() is a temporary function that renders the bone hierarchy using lines and small spheres. This function is called from our APPLICATION::Render(). For the implementation of the RenderSkeleton() function, see Example 7.1. The Load() function simply takes our active device and the filename to the X-file that we want to load:

```
void SKINNEDMESH::Load(char fileName[], IDirect3DDevice9 *Dev)
{
    m_pDevice = Dev;

    BONE_HIERARCHY boneHierarchy;

    D3DXLoadMeshHierarchyFromX(fileName, D3DXMESH_MANAGED,
                              m_pDevice, &boneHierarchy,
                              NULL, &m_pRootBone, NULL);

    D3DXMATRIX i;
    D3DXMatrixIdentity(&i);
    UpdateMatrices((BONE*)m_pRootBone, &i);
}
```

Example 7.1

In Example 7.1, the bone hierarchy is loaded from an X-file using the D3DXLoad
MeshHierarchyFromX() function and the ID3DXAllocateHierarchy interface.

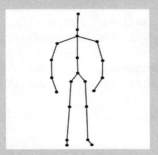

ANIMATING THE BONE HIERARCHY

So far it may seem like a lot of effort all for a few spheres and some lines, but
hang in there. It's about to get better. It is now time to take a look at how we can
animate this hierarchy. To control animations of hierarchies like these, we use the
ID3DXAnimationController interface. This interface allows us to select one of many
animations and run it, or even blend multiple animations together. We get this
interface by passing an ID3DXAnimationController object to the D3DXLoadMesh
HierarchyFromX() function:

```
ID3DXAnimationController *AnimControl = NULL;
BONE_HIERARCHY boneHierarchy;

D3DXLoadMeshHierarchyFromX(fileName, D3DXMESH_MANAGED,
                           m_pDevice, &boneHierarchy,
                           NULL, &m_pRootBone, &AnimControl);
```

Once the mesh hierarchy has been loaded, the ID3DXAnimationController contains all the animations (i.e., tracks) stored in the X-file. These animations are usually created in a 3D package and then exported to the X-file, as well. An animation
contains key frames for all the animated bones in the hierarchy. A key frame contains information about a bone's position, rotation, and scale at a specific time. The
animations are then created by interpolating between multiple key frames.

We can retrieve information about a specific animation from an ID3DXAnimation Controller object, like this:

```
for(int i=0;i<AnimControl->GetMaxNumAnimationSets();i++)
{
    ID3DXAnimationSet *anim = NULL;
    AnimControl->GetAnimationSet(i, &anim);

    anim->GetName();        //Get the name of the animation
    anim->GetPeriod();      //Get the period of the animation

    anim->Release();
}
```

This piece of code cycles through all available animation sets, and retrieves the name and period for each of them using the ID3DXAnimationSet interface. Here's a function that we use to activate a specific animation from the SKINNEDMESH class:

```
void SKINNEDMESH::SetAnimation(char name[])
{
    ID3DXAnimationSet *anim = NULL;

    for(int i=0;i < m_pAnimControl->GetMaxNumAnimationSets();
        i++)
    {
        anim = NULL;
        m_pAnimControl->GetAnimationSet(i, &anim);

        if(anim != NULL)
        {
            if(strcmp(name, anim->GetName()) == 0)
                m_pAnimControl->SetTrackAnimationSet(0, anim);

            anim->Release();
        }
    }
}
```

This function is used to set the animation of a skinned mesh using the name of the animation. We loop through the available animations until we find the one whose name matches and then active this animation with the SetTrackAnimation Set() function.

It would be more effective to store the index of each individual animation and use this to retrieve it directly with the `GetAnimationSet()` *function, rather than looking for it by comparing the name every time.*

We now know how to find information about the different animations and how to activate a specific animation. Let's now take a look at how we run the actual animation and update the bones:

```
void SKINNEDMESH::SetPose(D3DXMATRIX world,
                          ID3DXAnimationController* animControl,
                          float time)
{
    if(animControl != NULL)
        animControl->AdvanceTime(time, NULL);

    UpdateMatrices((BONE*)m_pRootBone, &world);
}
```

This function takes a world matrix, an animation controller, and an delta time. First, we advance the animation using the animation controller's `AdvanceTime()` function. Thereafter, we update all the bones using the supplied world matrix. The `SKINNEDMESH::SetPose()` function sets both the time of the animation, and the position/rotation and scale of our skinned mesh. Later, when we implement the UNIT class, the units will keep track of their own animation controller, animation time, and world matrix. This way we can use the same skinned mesh to draw multiple units, just like we did with the MESHINSTANCE structure. For each unit to have its own animation controller, we must take a look at how to clone these.

```
HRESULT CloneAnimationController(
    UINT MaxNumAnimationOutputs,
    UINT MaxNumAnimationSets,
    UINT MaxNumTracks,
    UINT MaxNumEvents,
    LPD3DXANIMATIONCONTROLLER * ppAnimController    // output
);
```

To clone the animation controller we retrieved when loading the mesh, we have the `SKINNEDMESH::GetAnimationControl()` function:

```
ID3DXAnimationController* SKINNEDMESH::GetAnimationControl()
{
    ID3DXAnimationController* newAnimController = NULL;
```

```
m_pAnimControl->CloneAnimationController(
    m_pAnimControl->GetMaxNumAnimationOutputs(),
    m_pAnimControl->GetMaxNumAnimationSets(),
    m_pAnimControl->GetMaxNumTracks(),
    m_pAnimControl->GetMaxNumEvents(),
    &newAnimController);

    return newAnimController;
}
```

This function creates and returns a clone of the animation controller of a skinned mesh. An animation controller clone will then be kept by each unit, and used with the SKINNEDMESH::SetPose() function to update and render a specific unit (more on this in Chapter 9). For other functions in the animation controller interface, see the DirectX documentation.

This marks the end of what you need to know about animating bone hierarchies for this book. However, if you want to look into advanced subjects, such as animation blending or animation callbacks, see [Luna04] or the DirectX documentation—for example, animation callbacks can generate events at a specific time in an animation, like playing footstep sounds and so on.

Example 7.2

ON THE CD

Example 7.2 on the CD-ROM implements an animated bone hierarchy using the ID3DXAnimationSet interface, as shown in this section.

SKINNING THE MESH

Unfortunately, this marks the end of the easy part concerning skinned meshes and the start of the slightly tougher section. We are now going to actually apply a mesh to our animated bone hierarchy and (hopefully) end up with something better looking than a bunch of spheres and lines dancing around. There are many ways we can do this. One common way is to do the vertex blending in hardware using a vertexshader. For an implementation of this, see [Luna04] or the DirectX SkinnedMesh sample. In this book we'll stick with the somewhat simpler software skinning method and do all the vertex blending in software, which gives us fewer things to worry about.

The following structure is used by the D3DX library to encapsulate a mesh in a bone hierarchy:

```
struct D3DXMESHCONTAINER
{
    LPTSTR Name;
    D3DXMESHDATA MeshData;
    LPD3DXMATERIAL pMaterials;
    LPD3DXEFFECTINSTANCE pEffects;
    DWORD NumMaterials;
    DWORD *pAdjacency;
    LPD3DXSKININFO pSkinInfo;
    struct D3DXMESHCONTAINER *pNextMeshContainer;
};
```

Name: Name of the mesh.

MeshData: The actual mesh is stored here.

pMaterials: A list of materials used.

pEffects: A list of effect filenames; not used.

NumMaterials: The number of materials.

pAdjacency: Mesh adjacency information; not used.

pSkinInfo: Contains information used to skin the mesh to the bones.

pNextMeshContainer: With this pointer, a linked list of mesh containers can be created.

However, we need more information than this to do efficient software skinning. Therefore, we extend the D3DXMESHCONTAINER and define our BONEMESH structure, as follows:

```
struct BONEMESH: public D3DXMESHCONTAINER
{
    ID3DXMesh* OriginalMesh;
    std::vector<D3DMATERIAL9> materials;
```

```
          std::vector<IDirect3DTexture9*> textures;

          DWORD NumAttributeGroups;
          D3DXATTRIBUTERANGE* attributeTable;
          D3DXMATRIX** boneMatrixPtrs;
          D3DXMATRIX* boneOffsetMatrices;
          D3DXMATRIX* currentBoneMatrices;
     };
```

OriginalMesh: Contains the original mesh.

materials: A vector containing the materials.

textures: A vector with the textures used by this mesh.

NumAttributeGroups: Number of attribute groups in the attributeTable.

attributeTable: Contains information about what parts of the mesh should be rendered with what material/texture.

boneMatrixPtrs: A list of pointers pointing to the combined transformation matrices of bones affecting this mesh.

boneOffsetMatrices: Contains the offset matrices for all the bones (more on this later).

currentBoneMatrices: This is the array of bone matrices that will be used to deform the mesh.

Remember how the D3DXFRAME had a pMeshContainer pointer pointing to a D3DXMESHCONTAINER object? When we call the D3DXLoadMeshHierarchyFromX() function, it automatically creates the bone hierarchy, but it also creates all mesh containers and connects them to the bones.

A bone offset matrix is used to transform the mesh from its bind pose to bone space. During rendering, we will first transform the mesh into bone space using the offset matrix, and then we use the bone's combined transformation matrix to transform the mesh back to world space. Luckily, we don't have to calculate this off-set matrix ourselves because it is supplied by the pSkinInfo object (which we get for free from the D3DXLoadMeshHierarchyFromX() function).

Once again, we take a look at our BONE_HIERARCHY that extends the abstract ID3DXAllocateHierarchy interface. This time we take a look at the CreateMesh Container() function:

```
HRESULT BONE_HIERARCHY::CreateMeshContainer(
                LPCSTR Name,
                CONST D3DXMESHDATA *pMeshData,
                CONST D3DXMATERIAL *pMaterials,
```

```
                         CONST D3DXEFFECTINSTANCE *pEffectInstances,
                         DWORD NumMaterials,
                         CONST DWORD *pAdjacency,
                         LPD3DXSKININFO pSkinInfo,
                         LPD3DXMESHCONTAINER *ppNewMeshContainer)
{
    //Create new Bone Mesh
    BONEMESH *boneMesh = new BONEMESH;
    memset(boneMesh, O, sizeof(BONEMESH));

    //Get mesh data
    boneMesh->OriginalMesh = pMeshData->pMesh;
    boneMesh->MeshData.pMesh = pMeshData->pMesh;
    boneMesh->MeshData.Type = pMeshData->Type;

    //Add Reference so that the mesh isn't deallocated
    pMeshData->pMesh->AddRef();

    //Get Device ptr from mesh
    IDirect3DDevice9 *Device = NULL;
    pMeshData->pMesh->GetDevice(&Device);

    //Copy materials and load textures here
    //(just like with a static mesh in the
    //MESHINSTANCE struct)

    if(pSkinInfo != NULL)
    {
        //Get Skin Info
        boneMesh->pSkinInfo = pSkinInfo;

        //Add reference so that the SkinInfo isn't deallocated
        pSkinInfo->AddRef();

        //Clone mesh and store in boneMesh->MeshData.pMesh
        pMeshData->pMesh->CloneMeshFVF(D3DXMESH_MANAGED,
                         pMeshData->pMesh->GetFVF(),
                         Device,
                         &boneMesh->MeshData.pMesh);

        //Get Attribute Table
        boneMesh->MeshData.pMesh->GetAttributeTable(NULL,
                         &boneMesh->NumAttributeGroups);
```

```
      boneMesh->attributeTable = new D3DXATTRIBUTERANGE[
                          boneMesh->NumAttributeGroups];
      boneMesh->MeshData.pMesh->GetAttributeTable(
                          boneMesh->attributeTable,NULL);

      //Create bone offset and current matrices
      int NumBones = pSkinInfo->GetNumBones();
      boneMesh->boneOffsetMatrices =
          new D3DXMATRIX[NumBones];
      boneMesh->currentBoneMatrices =
          new D3DXMATRIX[NumBones];

      //Get bone offset matrices
      for(int i=0;i < NumBones;i++)
          boneMesh->boneOffsetMatrices[i] =
          *(boneMesh->pSkinInfo->GetBoneOffsetMatrix(i));
   }

   //Set ppNewMeshContainer to the new boneMesh container
   *ppNewMeshContainer = boneMesh;

   return S_OK;
}
```

This is a massive function that takes all the parameters of the CreateMesh
Container() function, and creates and returns a new BONEMESH object from this
input. First, we create a new, empty BONEMESH object and copy the mesh data stored
in the pMeshData parameter to it. Note that we keep a pointer to the original mesh,
OriginalMesh. We need this later as a reference during the rendering of the skinned
mesh. Next, we clone the original mesh to the MeshData of the BONEMESH; this will be
our destination mesh. Then we retrieve the attribute table for the mesh. This table
contains information about what parts of the mesh should be drawn with what
material, what texture, and so forth. After that, we create the boneOffsetMatrices
and currentBoneMatrices arrays, and retrieve the bone offset matrices from the
pSkinInfo object. Finally we're done, and we return the new BONEMESH.

We've now seen how to create a new mesh container for our bone hierarchy,
but our BONE_HIERARCHY interface is also responsible for destroying the mesh containers. This is done with the BONE_HIERARCHY::DestroyMeshContainer() function:

```
HRESULT BONE_HIERARCHY::DestroyMeshContainer(
                    LPD3DXMESHCONTAINER pMeshContainerBase)
{
    BONEMESH *boneMesh = (BONEMESH*)pMeshContainerBase;
```

```
//Release textures
for(int i=0;i < boneMesh->textures.size();i++)
    if(boneMesh->textures[i] != NULL)
        boneMesh->textures[i]->Release();

//Release mesh data
if(boneMesh->MeshData.pMesh)
    boneMesh->MeshData.pMesh->Release();
if(boneMesh->pSkinInfo)
    boneMesh->pSkinInfo->Release();
if(boneMesh->OriginalMesh)
    boneMesh->OriginalMesh->Release();

delete boneMesh;

return S_OK;
}
```

Well, at least that was a bit simpler than creating a BONEMESH object. We simply release any loaded textures as well as the mesh objects.

You may recall that our BONEMESH structure contained the following three matrix arrays:

```
D3DXMATRIX** boneMatrixPtrs;

//Loaded by CreateMeshContainer
D3DXMATRIX* boneOffsetMatrices;
//Created by CreateMeshContainer
D3DXMATRIX* currentBoneMatrices;
```

We created and loaded the offset matrices in the CreateMeshContainer() function. The currentBoneMatrices was also created in the CreateMeshContainer() function; this array is updated each time the mesh is rendered. So what about the bone MatricPtrs array? This array was supposed to hold the pointers to the Combined TransformationMatrix variable of all the bones affecting this mesh. The problem with this is that we can't set the array when we are creating the BONEMESH objects because the D3DXLoadMeshHierarchyFromX() may actually not have finished loading the whole hierarchy yet. Therefore, we must have a function that creates the boneMatrixPtrs array after the whole hierarchy has been loaded. The SKINNEDMESH:: SetupBoneMatrixPointers() function does just this:

```
void SKINNEDMESH::SetupBoneMatrixPointers(BONE *bone)
{
    if(bone->pMeshContainer != NULL)
    {
        BONEMESH *boneMesh = (BONEMESH*)bone->pMeshContainer;

        if(boneMesh->pSkinInfo != NULL)
        {
            int NumBones = boneMesh->pSkinInfo->GetNumBones();
            boneMesh->boneMatrixPtrs =
                new D3DXMATRIX*[NumBones];

            for(int i=0;i < NumBones;i++)
            {
                BONE *b = (BONE*)D3DXFrameFind(rootBone,
                        boneMesh->pSkinInfo->GetBoneName(i));
                if(b != NULL)
                    boneMesh->boneMatrixPtrs[i] =
                    &b->CombinedTransformationMatrix;
                else boneMesh->boneMatrixPtrs[i] = NULL;
            }
        }
    }

    if(bone->pFrameSibling != NULL)
        SetupBoneMatrixPointers((BONE*)bone->pFrameSibling);
    if(bone->pFrameFirstChild != NULL)
        SetupBoneMatrixPointers(
                        (BONE*)bone->pFrameFirstChild);
}
```

This function traverses the bone hierarchy and finds the bones that have a
BONEMESH. It then creates a new boneMatrixPtrs array for this BONEMESH and fills it
with the pointers to each bone's CombinedTransformationMatrix. We call this function in our SKINNEDMESH::Load() function right after we've loaded the bone hierarchy. This function uses the following D3DXFrameFind() function:

```
LPD3DXFRAME D3DXFrameFind(
    LPD3DXFRAME pFrameRoot,          //Root bone...
    LPCSTR Name                      //Bone we are searching for
);
```

If there's a bone in the hierarchy with the name we are searching for, it will be returned by this function.

Okay, let's recap. We now have a bone hierarchy with bone meshes connected to some of the bones (usually we have just one mesh). Each bone keeps track of its own transformation matrix as well as its combined transformation matrix (i.e., where in the world map the bone is). We can animate this hierarchy easily with the animation controller. Each bone mesh keeps track of its own mesh data, materials, and textures. Bone meshes also have pointers to all combined transformation matrices that affect this mesh. Bonemesh also has all offset matrices for the bones so it can transform the mesh into their bone spaces. Well, it seems that there's nothing left but to render our skinned mesh.

The SKINNEDMESH::Render() function traverses the whole hierarchy and renders any BONEMESH objects it finds on the way:

```
void SKINNEDMESH::Render(BONE *bone)
{
    if(bone == NULL)bone = (BONE*)m_pRootBone;

    //If there is a mesh to render...
    if(bone->pMeshContainer != NULL)
    {
        BONEMESH *boneMesh = (BONEMESH*)bone->pMeshContainer;

        if(boneMesh->pSkinInfo != NULL)
        {
            //Update current bone transformations
            int numBones = boneMesh->pSkinInfo->GetNumBones();
            for(int i=0;i < numBones;i++)
                D3DXMatrixMultiply(
                        &boneMesh->currentBoneMatrices[i],
                        &boneMesh->boneOffsetMatrices[i],
                        boneMesh->boneMatrixPtrs[i]);

            //Update the skinned mesh
            BYTE *src = NULL, *dest = NULL;

            //Lock source and destination meshes
            boneMesh->OriginalMesh->LockVertexBuffer(
                            D3DLOCK_READONLY,
                            (VOID**)&src);
            boneMesh->MeshData.pMesh->LockVertexBuffer(
                            0, (VOID**)&dest);
```

```
                     boneMesh->pSkinInfo->UpdateSkinnedMesh(
                                    boneMesh->currentBoneMatrices,
                                    NULL, src, dest);

              //Unlock source and destination meshes
              boneMesh->MeshData.pMesh->UnlockVertexBuffer();
              boneMesh->OriginalMesh->UnlockVertexBuffer();

              //Render the skinned mesh
              for(int i=0;i < boneMesh->NumAttributeGroups;i++)
              {
                  int mtrlIndex =
                         boneMesh->attributeTable[i].AttribId;
                  m_pDevice->SetMaterial(&(boneMesh->
                                      materials[mtrlIndex]));
                  m_pDevice->SetTexture(0,boneMesh->
                                      textures[mtrlIndex]);
                  boneMesh->MeshData.pMesh->DrawSubset(mtrlIndex);
              }
          }
      }

      if(bone->pFrameSibling != NULL)
          Render((BONE*)bone->pFrameSibling);
      if(bone->pFrameFirstChild != NULL)
          Render((BONE*)bone->pFrameFirstChild);
  }
```

When a bone is found that has a valid BONEMESH object, one of the first things we
need to do is to calculate the array of current bone matrices. This is done by
multiplying the bone offset matrix by the combined transformation matrix of
each bone. The offset matrix stays the same over the whole time, but the combined
transformation matrix changes every frame as the hierarchy is animated. The results are stored in the currentBoneMatrices array. Next, we need to call the
ID3DXSkinInfo::UpdateSkinnedMesh() function to do the actual vertex blending
(skinning) in software for us:

```
HRESULT UpdateSkinnedMesh(
    CONST D3DXMATRIX *pBoneTransforms,
    CONST D3DXMATRIX *pBoneInvTransposeTransforms,
    PVOID pVerticesSrc,
    PVOID pVerticesDst
);
```

pBoneTransforms: We set this parameter to our `currentBoneMatrices` array.

pBoneInvTransposeTransforms: Only used when skinning bones with more than one position element. We just set this parameter to `NULL`.

pVerticesSrc: A pointer to the source vertex buffer (i.e., the original mesh).

pVerticesDst: A pointer to the destination vertex buffer (i.e., our resulting mesh).

Before calling this function, we lock the vertex buffer of the `OriginalMesh` and `MeshData.pMesh` of our `BONEMESH` object. Then we call the `UpdateSkinnedMesh()` function with our current bone matrices, the original mesh as the source mesh, and the `MeshData.pMesh` as our destination mesh. The destination mesh now contains our skinned mesh according to the animated bone hierarchy. We unlock the two vertex buffers and render the destination mesh using the settings stored in the attribute table.

ON THE CD

Example 7.3

In Example 7.3, the entire skinned mesh code is implemented. The resulting mesh is the lit using a vertexshader with directional lighting, similar to that one used in Example 5.10.

PLACING THE GUN IN THE HAND OF A SKINNED MESH

Sometimes it is necessary to locate a certain bone in the skinned mesh and use it to transform an external mesh. An example of this could be if we have a role-playing game where you want to be able to put different weapons in the hands of your character. The hard way to do this would be to create one skinned mesh for each type of weapon, but in reality this isn't really the smart way to go about it. Instead, we store the external meshes using our regular MESH class. Then during rendering, we just retrieve the combined transformation matrix of the specific bone we are interested in and use this matrix to transform the external mesh. To find a specific bone in the hierarchy, we again use the D3DXFrameFind() function from the D3DX library:

```
LPD3DXFRAME D3DXFrameFind(
    LPD3DXFRAME pFrameRoot,    //Root of the hierarchy
    LPCSTR Name                //Name of bone we are looking for
);
```

We have extended our SKINNEDMESH class with the FindBone() function, like this:

```
BONE* SKINNEDMESH::FindBone(char name[])
{
    return (BONE*)D3DXFrameFind(m_pRootBone, name);
}
```

This function takes a name as a parameter and then calls the D3DXFrameFind() function on the root bone of the hierarchy. The following code is an excerpt from Example 7.4, where we use this function to place a number of different items in the hands of our skinned mesh:

```
//Find specific bone
BONE* hand = skinnedMesh.FindBone("hand_Bone_Name");

//Offset mesh from bone
D3DXVECTOR3 hand_offset = D3DXVECTOR3(0.5f, 0.0f, -0.07f);

//Load weapon meshes here as well...

...

//Render weapon
if(hand != NULL)
{
    //Calculate weapon world matrix...
    D3DXMATRIX boneMatrix;
    boneMatrix = hand->CombinedTransformationMatrix;
    D3DXMATRIX offset, weaponTransform;
    D3DXMatrixTranslation(&offset, hand_offset.x,
                                   hand_offset.y,
                                   hand_offset.z);
```

```
            weaponTransform = offset * boneMatrix * world;

            Device->SetTransform(D3DTS_WORLD, &weaponTransform);
            weapons[activeWeapon].Render();
    }
```

First we use the SKINNEDMESH::FindBone() function to retrieve a pointer to the specific bone we want to attach the external mesh to. Using only the combine transformation matrix of this bone to transform the mesh will in most cases not produce an optimal result. Therefore, we also create an offset matrix that will be used to position the mesh in the exact location we want. To calculate the final transformation matrix of the external mesh, we simply multiply the offset matrix, the bone matrix, and the world matrix together, and use the result to transform the mesh.

NOTE

In this example, we offset the position of the mesh using an offset matrix. You can, of course, also add an offset rotation and/or scale to this matrix.

ON THE CD

Example 7.4

Example 7.4 demonstrates how to place an external mesh in the hands of a skinned mesh.

SUMMARY

In this chapter, we've covered the advanced subject of skinned meshes. We now know how to load a bone hierarchy from an X-file by implementing a class inheriting from the ID3DXAllocateHierarchy interface (our BONE_HIERARCHY class). We have also looked at how to animate the bone hierarchy using the ID3DXAnimation Controller interface. Finally, we learned how to apply a mesh to the bone hierarchy using software skinning. We also had a quick look at how to connect an external mesh to one of the bones in the hierarchy. If you are interested in other ways to implement skinned meshes, like hardware skinning, see any of the articles listed in the Further Reading section.

Now we have the necessary tools required to render animated units. Chapter 8 will cover how to tell apart units from different teams, using team colors.

EXERCISES

- Overload the SetAnimation() function to take an index (integer) of the animation you want to activate, rather than the name of the animation.
- Implement hardware skinning, which is faster but comes with some restrictions.

REFERENCES

[Luna04] Luna, Frank, "Skinned Mesh Character Animation with Direct3D 9.0c." Available online at: *http://www.moon-labs.com/resources/d3dx_skinnedmesh. pdf,* 2004.

FURTHER READING

Abdulla, Sarmad Kh, "Implementing Skin Meshes with DirectX8." Available online at: *http://www.gamedev.net/reference/programming/features/skinmesh/default. asp,* 2002.

Ditchburn, Keith, "X File Hierarchy Loading." Available online at: *http://www. toymaker.info/Games/html/load_x_hierarchy.html,* 2006.

Jurecka, Jason, "Working with the DirectX .X File Format and Animation in DirectX 9.0." Available online at: *http://www.gamedev.net/reference/articles/article2079. asp,* 2004.

Taylor, Phil, "Modular D3D SkinnedMesh." Available online at: *http://www. flipcode.com/articles/article_dx9skinmeshmod.shtml,* 2003.

8 Team Color

In this chapter, we will have a look at the concept of team color. Team color is different "patches" of color drawn on our units and buildings to help the player tell the different teams apart, as shown in Figure 8.1.

This technique can, of course, be used for more than just changing the team colors of your units. For example, if you create a car racing game, you can use this method to let the player pick a unique color for his car without your having to create extra textures for each possible color. To implement this technique, we need the following:

- A UV-mapped 3D model (as covered in Chapter 6)
- A texture with both color and alpha channels
- A pixelshader

Black Team   **White Team**

FIGURE 8.1 The same units rendered with different team colors.

In an RTS game, the 3D model will be either one of our animated units or one of our static buildings. The texture will have the color information of the unit (or building), as usual, but it will also contain an alpha channel describing what parts of the unit that should be painted in the team color.

Using the alpha channel like this prohibits the use of alpha blending, or any other methods that also make use of the texture's alpha channel. So if you want transparent units or buildings for some reason, you might have to use another method to do your team colors. See [Seegert04] for a couple of different team color implementations.

CREATING THE ALPHA CHANNEL

At this stage, you should have finished a 3D model with a corresponding texture (or textures), as shown in Figure 8.2. If not, then you can use the model found on the companion CD-ROM in Example 8.1. Start Photoshop and open up the texture file of your 3D model. (For example, you can use the `magician_original.psd` file in the Example 8.1 folder.)

We are now going to create an alpha map for this texture that can be used by our pixelshader to draw different team colors on this model. Note that originally the robe is intentionally quite colorless. This makes the team color stand out a little

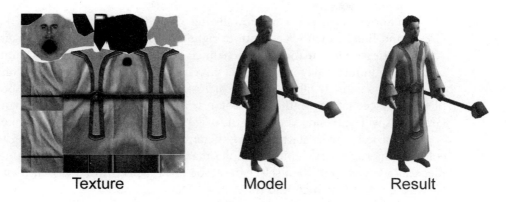

Texture   Model   Result

FIGURE 8.2   A texture applied to our magician mesh.

bit more. If you have a texture with too many different colors, it may be hard to pick out which color is the actual team color. Remember that it must be easy to pick out what units are friendly and what units are enemies in the heat of battle. The next step is to create an empty alpha channel. Go to the Window menu and select the Channels window (Figure 8.3).

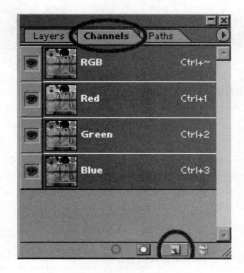

FIGURE 8.3   Adding an alpha channel in Photoshop.

You should now see a window listing your different channels—RGB, Red, Green, and Blue. Down to the bottom right of this window (circled in Figure 8.3) you have the icon for creating a new channel. Press this, and an Alpha 1 channel will be created automatically for you. Select this channel and start drawing. Anything you draw in this channel will be in grayscale. Areas that you draw white will be completely replaced later with the team color, while black areas will remain unaffected. Gray areas will be blended between the original texture color and the team color.

The easiest way to start creating the alpha map is to copy something from a color channel and paste it into the alpha channel. Using the `magician_original.psd` file, select Layers, and then select the Robe layer. Select All (Ctrl+A), then Copy (Ctrl+C). Select Channels and the Alpha 1 channel, and Paste (Ctrl+V) what you just copied from the color channel. Make sure that you move what you copied into alpha channel so that it is aligned with the information in the color channels.

Color Channels   Alpha Channel

FIGURE 8.4 Creating the alpha channel.

When you are done with creating your alpha channel, select File, Save As, and save the image using the DDS format (requires the NVIDIA Adobe Photoshop plug-in, which can be found at *http://developer.nvidia.com/object/nv_texture_tools.html*). Okay, all we need now to draw units in different team colors is a pixelshader.

THE TEAM COLOR PIXELSHADER

For this example, we will use the same vertexshader used to light our units in Chapter 7. It calculates the shade of a vertex depending on the vertex normal and the direction to the light source, just like we did in Chapter 5 when we lit the terrain using a vertexshader. The team color pixelshader extends the simple pixelshader used in Chapter 7 to also incorporate team colors.

```
sampler unitTexture;
uniform extern float4 tmCol;

float4 Main(float2 UV : TEXCOORD0,
            float shade : TEXCOORD1) : COLOR
{
    float4 c0 = tex2D(unitTexture, UV);

    //Calculate resulting pixel color by blending the pixel
    //from the unitTexture and the tmCol color, depending on
    //the value stored in the alpha channel
    float Inv = 1.0f - c0.a;
    float4 c1 = float4(c0.rgb * Inv + tmCol.rgb * c0.a, 1.0f);

    return c1 * shade;
}
```

unitTexture: The unit texture sampler.

tmCol: The team color we want to replace in any areas defined by the alpha channel of the unitTexture.

UV: The UV coordinates from our 3D model.

Shade: This is the per-vertex lighting value sent to the pixelshader by the lighting vertexshader (0.0 = dark, 1.0 = bright).

We first sample a pixel from the unitTexture using the UV coordinates of the 3D model and calculate the inverse of these pixels' alpha value. We calculate the alpha inverse in just the same way we did during the texture splatting of the terrain. This way, when we perform the following code, the result is always 1:

```
c0.rgb * Inv + tmCol.rgb * c0.a
```

The result is a blend controlled by the alpha value between the original color stored in the unitTexture and the team color. We return this blended pixel multiplied by the vertex shade value from the lighting vertexshader.

ON THE CD

Example 8.1

The result of the team color pixelshader can be found in Example 8.1 on the companion CD-ROM.

SUMMARY

Drawing units and buildings with different team colors is absolutely imperative in an RTS game. In this rather short chapter, we have had a go at implementing team colors using a texture with an alpha channel and a pixelshader. In the Chapter 9, we will use this concept to render both units and buildings as we implement the UNIT, BUILDING, and PLAYER classes.

REFERENCES

[Seegert04] Seegert, Greg, "Techniques to Apply Team Colors to 3D Models." *Game Programming Gems 4,* Charles River Media, 2004.

9 Players

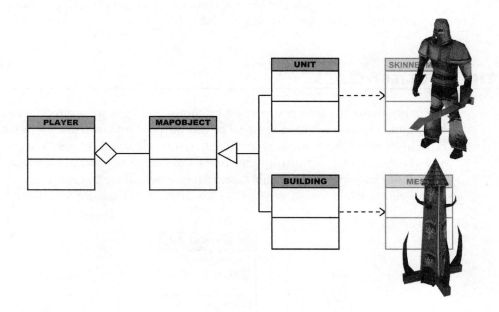

We've now reached a point in our journey were the preparations have been done, and we can actually start implementing our real-time strategy game. We know how to create a terrain, how to load static objects, and how to load and render skinned meshes for our units. We also know how to specify different teams by using different team colors.

In this chapter, we will concentrate on four classes: the MAPOBJECT, UNIT, BUILDING, and finally the PLAYER class. The MAPOBJECT class will be the base class that the UNIT and BUILDING class will inherit from. All things that units and buildings have in common will be implemented in this class. The UNIT class will cover all our unit-specific needs, such as speed, damage, mana, and so forth. The BUILDING class, on the other hand, will implement our buildings and handle things like unit production and weapon upgrades. Finally, the PLAYER class will contain all buildings and units owned by a specific player. The PLAYER class will also handle things like the placement of buildings, adding and removing map objects, and selecting units or buildings.

The code shown in this book is just one of many ways in which an RTS game can be implemented. Doubtless, you can come up with another structure that fits your own style better. Also, a lot of things will be different, depending on the specific game you are trying to implement. However, the example code presented in this chapter should be enough to get you started.

THE MAPOBJECT CLASS

There are many things our units and buildings will have in common, things like health, map location, and map size. For this purpose we create the MAPOBJECT base class from which both the UNIT and the BUILDING class will inherit. We try to put any variables and functionality that units and buildings have in common in the MAPOBJECT class; that way we only have to implement these once. Figure 9.1 shows a Unified Modeling Language (UML) class diagram of these three classes.

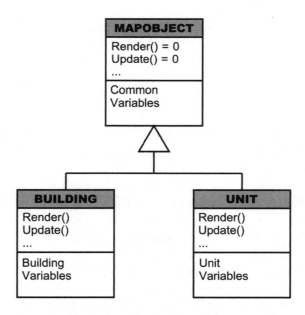

FIGURE 9.1 A UML class diagram of the MAPOBJECT, BUILDING, and UNIT class.

Here's a short list of things that units and buildings have in common:

Variables—Health, sight range, type, team, selected, name, and many more.

Functions—`Render()`, `Update()`, `TakeDamage()`, and so forth.

The benefit of having both the UNIT and the BUILDING class inherit from the same class is polymorphism. Polymorphism means that we can ask the same question of objects inheriting from the same base class, but they can respond in different ways. For instance, in our MAPOBJECT class, we will have a virtual function called `Render()`. Since both the UNIT and the BUILDING classes inherit from the MAPOBJECT class, they must implement this `Render()` function. However, they implement the function in different ways. The UNIT class renders a skinned mesh, while the BUILDING class just renders a static mesh. Later, when we implement the PLAYER class, it will keep a list of MAPOBJECT pointers, which will point to both units and buildings. When it's time to render all of a player's units and buildings, we simply need to loop through the list and call the `Render()` function for each MAPOBJECT. We don't care at all whether it's a unit or a building. Each object will know how to render itself. If you are new to concepts like inheritance and polymorphism, hopefully these topics will soon become a bit clearer.

As we progress and add things to our RTS game, we will need to add variables and functions to our three classes MAPOBJECT, UNIT, and BUILDING. The important lesson here is that anything the UNIT and the BUILDING classes have in common, we stick in the MAPOBJECT class. Some things will be implemented in exactly the same way for both the UNIT and the BUILDING classes, in which case we actually implement the function in the MAPOBJECT class. This saves us the trouble of implementing the same code in the two other classes. Other things, like the `Render()` function, will be done differently for units and buildings. In this case, we create a virtual function in the MAPOBJECT class and then do the different implementations of this function in any class that inherits the MAPOBJECT class. Again, other things may be unique to a unit or a building, and in this case we do the implementation of this function only in the UNIT or BUILDING class. An example of this could be the UNIT::`Goto()` function (unless you want moving buildings, as well).

So, let's take a look at the MAPOBJECT class. Remember that we will be adding a lot of functionality to these classes over the next few chapters:

```
class MAPOBJECT
{
    public:
    //Functions implemented in the MAPOBJECT class
```

```
        MAPOBJECT();                //Set all variables to 0
        RECT GetMapRect(int border);  //Get map rectangle + border
        void PaintSelected();       //Paint selection rectangle

        //Virtual Functions
        virtual void Render() = 0;
        virtual void Update(float deltaTime) = 0;
        virtual BBOX GetBoundingBox() = 0;
        virtual D3DXMATRIX GetWorldMatrix() = 0;

        //Variables
        TERRAIN *m_pTerrain;     //Used for unit pathfinding etc
        int m_hp, m_hpMax;       //Health and max health
        int m_range;             //Attack range
        int m_damage;
        INTPOINT m_mappos, m_mapsize;   //Location and mapsize
        float m_sightRadius;
        int m_team, m_type;
        bool m_selected, m_dead;
        std::string m_name;
        MAPOBJECT *m_pTarget;    //Used for targeting map objects
        D3DXVECTOR3 m_position;  //Actual world position
        IDirect3DDevice9* m_pDevice;

        bool m_isBuilding;       //Used when casting pointers etc...
    };
```

You can guess what most of the functions and variables in this class do by their names. The PaintSelected() function, for example, paints the selection rectangle around selected units, as explained in Chapter 5 (see Example 5.4), and this is done in the same way for both units and buildings. The GetWorldMatrix() function returns the world matrix of the map object. This function is used foremost to set the world matrix of whatever vertexshader we are running.

The virtual functions Render() and Update() in the MAPOBJECT class aren't implemented here, but instead they must be implemented in any class inheriting from the MAPOBJECT class. One function in the MAPOBJECT class worth mentioning is the GetMapRect() function:

```
        RECT MAPOBJECT::GetMapRect(int border)
        {
            RECT mr = {m_mappos.x - border,
                       m_mappos.y - border,
```

```
                    m_mappos.x + m_mapsize.x + border,
                    m_mappos.y + m_mapsize.y + border};

        return mr;
    }
```

This rather simple function returns a rectangle in terrain coordinates around the unit or building, as shown in Figure 9.2. The dark gray rectangle is our unit or building (most often, units will just have a map size of 1 × 1). The upper-left corner is the terrain location (m_mappos) of our map object, illustrated with a cross. The light-gray rectangle is the area that would be returned by calling GetMapRect(2).

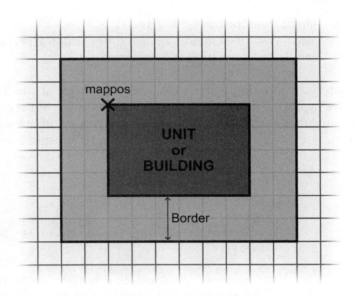

FIGURE 9.2 The MAPOBJECT::GetMapRect() function.

We will be using the GetMapRect() function to determine if a certain target is within range or whether a unit has reached its target destination, as well as during unit deployment. Well, that's our MAPOBJECT class. To sum up, you should implement anything that you will need in both your UNIT and your BUILDING class in your the MAPOBJECT class.

UNITS

As we covered in Chapter 2, the units are your chess pieces to move around the terrain as you see fit. Use them to conquer lands, guard resources, and vanquish the enemy. Simply put, in RTS games, your units can be people, tanks, flying saucers, or anything with the ability to move around the map, killing other units.

In this section, we will have a look at implementing the UNIT class to cover our units' needs. A lot of the "smarts" needed in the UNIT class will be covered in more detail in the Chapter 14, where we learn how to create a unit Artificial Intelligence (AI) using finite state machines. In this section, we are just going to implement the basic UNIT class, like this:

1. Inherit from the MAPOBJECT class.
2. Load any skinned meshes needed (one per unit type, not one per unit).
3. Handle unit animation and movement.

Advanced unit behavior like selecting what target to attack, patrolling, guarding, fleeing, and so forth will be covered in Chapter 14. At the moment, all we want from our units is that they walk around the terrain without bumping into buildings, trees, or each other. We define the UNIT class like this:

```
class UNIT : public MAPOBJECT
{
    public:
        UNIT(int _type, int _team, INTPOINT mp,
            TERRAIN *_terrain, IDirect3DDevice9* Dev);
        ~UNIT();

        //Implement the abstract functions declared
        //in the MAPOBJECT class
        void Render();
        void Update(float deltaTime);
        BBOX GetBoundingBox();
        D3DXMATRIX GetWorldMatrix();

        //Specific UNIT functions
        void Goto(INTPOINT mp);     //Order unit to mp
        void MoveUnit(INTPOINT to);  //Move the unit
        bool CheckCollision(INTPOINT mp);
        D3DXVECTOR3 GetDirection(INTPOINT p1, INTPOINT p2);
        void SetAnimation(char name[]);
        void SetAnimation(int index);
```

```
        private:

            //Animation variables
            float m_time;              //Animation delta time
            float m_speed;             //Movement & animation speed
            int m_animation;           //Current animation sequence
            D3DXVECTOR3 m_rotation, m_scale;
            ID3DXAnimationController* m_pAnimControl;

            //Movement variables
            std::vector<INTPOINT> m_path;      //The active path
            D3DXVECTOR3 m_lastWP, m_nextWP;    //waypoints
            int m_activeWP;                    //active waypoint
            bool m_moving;
            float m_movePrc;
    };
```

The constructor of the UNIT class takes a type and a map location, as well as a pointer to a TERRAIN object. The TERRAIN pointer is used to request paths, detect collisions, and so forth. The constructor initiates all the variables of the unit, such as health, range, damage, or acquires an animation controller clone.

As you can see from the UNIT class declaration, we don't keep any of the skinned meshes stored in this class. All we store is the m_pAnimControl, m_time, m_animation, and the unique world matrix of a unit. This information is all we need to update and render the skinned mesh of a unit. Let's take a look at how we load the skinned meshes so that they are accessible for all unit objects we create:

```
//Global array of skinned meshes
std::vector<SKINNEDMESH*> unitMeshes;

...

void LoadUnitResources(IDirect3DDevice9* Device)
{
    std::vector<std::string> fnames;

    fnames.push_back("unitMesh_1.x");
    fnames.push_back("unitMesh_2.x");
    ...
    fnames.push_back("unitMesh_N.x");
```

```
//Load all skinned meshes defined in the fnames vector
for(int i=0;i<fnames.size();i++)
{
    SKINNEDMESH *newMesh = new SKINNEDMESH();
    newMesh->Load((char*)fnames[i].c_str(), Device);
    unitMeshes.push_back(newMesh);
}
}
```

The global LoadUnitResources() function loads any skinned meshes you need and stores them in a global vector. In the same way, the UnloadUnitResources() function releases all the loaded meshes. Now, to render the mesh for a certain unit, all we need to do is use the type of the unit as an index in the unitMeshes vector:

```
void UNIT::Render()
{
    if(m_type < unitMeshes.size() &&
       unitMeshes[m_type] != NULL)
    {
        //Set active animation
        SetAnimation(m_animation);

        //Set pose of the skinned mesh
        unitMeshes[m_type]->SetPose(GetWorldMatrix(),
                                    m_pAnimControl,
                                    m_time);

        //Render the mesh
        unitMeshes[m_type]->Render(NULL);

        //reset delta time
        m_time = 0.0f;
    }
}
```

To render a specific unit, we first set the animation of the skinned mesh we want render. Then we set the time of the animation as well as the unit's world matrix (i.e., position, rotation, and scale). The UNIT::GetWorldMatrix() function calculates a world matrix in exactly the same way as the MESHINSTANCE class. Finally, we render the mesh. Storing the skinned meshes in a global array like this allows us to use the same mesh to render all units of the same type, no matter what position, rotation, or team color they have. Rendering the units is the easy part; next, we want our units to actually move across the terrain.

Moving the Units

We covered in Chapter 4 how to query the terrain for a path from one map node to another. Each map object has a pointer to the current terrain, and by using this pointer, each unit can query paths and so forth. In this section, we will take a look at how to make a unit smoothly follow a path described by terrain waypoints:

```
void UNIT::Goto(INTPOINT mp)
{
    if(terrain == NULL)return;

    //Clear old path
    m_path.clear();
    m_activeWP = 0;

    if(m_moving)          //If unit is currently moving
    {
        //Finish the active waypoint
        m_path.push_back(m_mappos);
        std::vector<INTPOINT> tmpPath;
        tmpPath = terrain->GetPath(m_mappos, mp);

        //then add new path
        for(int i=0;i<tmpPath.size();i++)
            m_path.push_back(tmpPath[i]);
    }
    else        //Create new path from scratch...
    {
        m_path = terrain->GetPath(m_mappos, mp);

        if(m_path.size() > 0)         //if a path was found
        {
            m_moving = true;

            //Check that the next tile is free
            if(!CheckCollision(m_path[m_activeWP]))
            {
                MoveUnit(m_path[m_activeWP]);
                SetAnimation("Run");
            }
        }
    }
}
```

The UNIT::Goto() function is a command that tells the unit to move to a certain map location. We first retrieve a path from the current map location (m_mappos) to the goal (mp). We store the resulting path (if any) in our path vector and use the following variables to have the unit follow the path to the goal:

m_activeWP: Current waypoint in the path vector.

m_lastWP: The actual world position of the last waypoint.

m_nextWP: The actual world position of the next waypoint.

m_movePrc: The progress from lastWP to nextWP, (0.0f – 1.0f).

m_rotation: The direction our unit is facing.

m_moving: Is the unit moving or not?

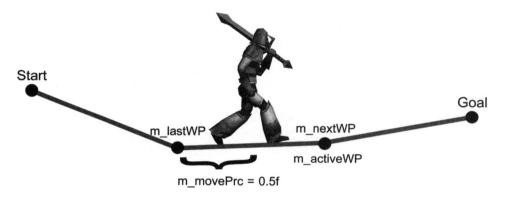

FIGURE 9.3 Moving a unit smoothly across the terrain.

Figure 9.3 shows how the previously listed variables are used to smoothly move a unit along a path. Every time the unit moves from one waypoint to another, we call the MoveUnit() function. This initializes all the movement variables:

```
void UNIT::MoveUnit(INTPOINT to)
{
    //Get World position of the current waypoint
    m_lastWP = terrain->GetWorldPos(m_mappos);

    //Rotate the unit in the direction it is going
    m_rotation = GetDirection(m_mappos, to);
```

```
        m_mappos = to;          //New mappos
        m_movePrc = 0.0f;

        //Get the world position of the next waypoint
        m_nextWP = terrain->GetWorldPos(m_mappos);
    }
```

The UNIT::GetDirection() function returns a rotation vector, depending on which direction the unit is moving. The m_activeWP variable keeps track of the current waypoint index, while m_lastWP and m_nextWP contain the actual 3D position of these waypoints. The m_movePrc variable is used to interpolate between m_lastWP and m_nextWP. The actual interpolation between to map nodes is done in the UNIT::Update() function:

```
void UNIT::Update(float deltaTime)
{
    //update unit animation time
    m_time += deltaTime * 0.8f * m_speed;

    //if the unit is moving...
    if(m_moving)
    {
        //Move the unit...
        if(m_movePrc < 1.0f)m_movePrc += deltaTime * m_speed;
        if(m_movePrc > 1.0f)m_movePrc = 1.0f;

        //waypoint reached
        if(m_movePrc == 1.0f)
        {
            //goal reached
            if(m_activeWP + 1 >= m_path.size())
            {
                m_moving = false;
                SetAnimation("Still");
            }
            //Next Waypoint
            else if(!CheckCollision(m_path[m_activeWP + 1]))
            {
                m_activeWP++;
                SetAnimation("Run");
                MoveUnit(m_path[m_activeWP]);
            }
        }
    }
```

```
                    //Interpolate position between lastWP and nextWP
                    m_position = m_lastWP * (1.0f - m_movePrc) +
                                 m_nextWP * m_movePrc;
            }
        }
```

Remember that the UNIT::Update() *function is called whether or not the unit is in the viewing volume, unlike, for example, the* UNIT::Render() *function. Therefore, we increase the unit's delta time during each update, and reset it only when the mesh is rendered.*

At the moment, we don't do any collision detection, so units will not consider the locations of other units when moving around on the terrain. Later in this chapter, we will implement the UNIT::CheckCollision() function to test that every map node is available before we start moving toward it. At the moment, the Check Collision() function returns false (i.e., no collision was detected). So in this implementation of our UNIT class, units simply move from point A to point B, regardless of whether another unit is standing there or not.

ON THE CD

Example 9.1

Example 9.1 on the CD-ROM implements the code we've been going through in this section. Try to select multiple units (left mouse button) and order them to move to the same map location (right mouse button). What happens?

BUILDINGS

Buildings in RTS games are usually houses or structures of some kind, used mainly to produce units. Traditionally, buildings are static objects without any movement capability (with a few exceptions, like in *Starcraft* or *Warcraft III*). Other buildings,

like turrets or guard towers, may have the capability of engaging the enemy—
but generally speaking, buildings are used for generating units and upgrading
technologies.

Implementing the BUILDING class is a whole lot simpler than implementing the
UNIT class, since we don't have to worry about things like skinned meshes, animation, and movement. The only tricky part is to determine what places on the map
are valid locations for buildings. Again, we load a global array of meshes instead of
loading a mesh for each building, just like we did with the skinned meshes for the
units. Here's our BUILDING class declaration:

```
class BUILDING : public MAPOBJECT
{
    public:
        BUILDING(int _type, INTPOINT mp, TERRAIN *_terrain,
                bool affectTerrain, IDirect3DDevice9* Dev);
        ~BUILDING();

        void Render();
        void Update(float deltaTime);
        BBOX GetBoundingBox();
        D3DXMATRIX GetWorldMatrix();

    private:

        BBOX m_BBox;
        MESHINSTANCE m_meshInstance;
        bool m_affectTerrain;
};
```

There are not many BUILDING class variables in addition to the ones inherited
from the MAPOBJECT. All we add is a bounding box and a mesh instance, and a
Boolean. The m_affectTerrain variable is used to determine whether the building
affects the pathfinding of the terrain or not. As you will see further on, we don't
want buildings to affect the terrain in all cases. With units, we have to calculate
bounding boxes for culling and picking on the fly because they move around, but
because buildings are static objects (at least in this game), it's enough to calculate a
bounding box when the building is created. The GetBoundingBox() function, therefore, just returns the bounding box of the building rather than calculates a new one
every frame. The Render() function is also very simple; it simply calls the Render()
function of the MESHINSTANCE object. The only function in the BUILDING class worth
taking a closer look at is the constructor:

```
BUILDING::BUILDING(int _type, INTPOINT mp, TERRAIN *_terrain,
                   bool _affectTerrain, IDirect3DDevice9* Dev)
{
    m_type = _type;
    m_mappos = mp;
    m_pTerrain = _terrain;
    m_affectTerrain = _affectTerrain;
    m_pDevice = Dev;
    m_meshInstance.SetMesh(buildingMeshes[m_type]);

    if(m_type == 0)            //Townhall
    {
        // Set Townhall values here
    }
    else if(m_type == 1)       //Barracks
    {
        // Set Barracks values here
    }
    else if(m_type == 2)       //Tower
    {
        // Set Tower values here
    }

    m_position = m_pTerrain->GetWorldPos(m_mappos) +
                 D3DXVECTOR3(m_mapsize.x / 2.0f, 0.0f,
                             -m_mapsize.y / 2.0f);

    m_meshInstance.SetPosition(m_position);
    m_BBox = m_meshInstance.GetBoundingBox();

    //Update the tiles of the terrain
    if(m_affectTerrain)
    {
        RECT mr = GetMapRect(0);

        for(int y=mr.top;y<=mr.bottom;y++)
            for(int x=mr.left;x<=mr.right;x++)
            {
                MAPTILE *tile = terrain->GetTile(x, y);
                if(tile != NULL)tile->m_walkable = false;
            }
```

```
                m_pTerrain->UpdatePathfinding(&GetMapRect(1));
            }
        }
```

In the constructor of the BUILDING class, we set up the mesh instance object to point to the right mesh. We also set all the variables of the BUILDING (e.g., health and sight range), depending on what type of building it is. However, the interesting thing here is that as we place (or remove) a building on the terrain, there are three things we must do:

1. Update the m_walkable variable of the affected map tiles.
2. Recalculate the neighbor pointers of these tiles.
3. Recalculate the map sets of all the map tiles.

If we fail to do these three things, then we will end up with faulty unit pathfinding. For example, units might walk through buildings or believe that paths exist when they don't. In the constructor of the BUILDING class, we just set the m_walkable variable of the map tiles affected if the m_affectTerrain variable is true. Then, we call the new TERRAIN::UpdatePathfinding() function:

```
void TERRAIN::UpdatePathfinding(RECT *r)
{
    if(r == NULL)
    {
        InitPathfinding();
        return;
    }

    //Connect m_pMapTiles using the m_pNeighbors pointers
    //Only check those tiles that are inside the rectangle r
    for(int y=r->top; y<=r->bottom; y++)
        for(int x=r->left; x<=r->right; x++)
        {
            MAPTILE *tile = GetTile(x, y);
            if(tile != NULL && tile->walkable)
            {
                //Clear old connections
                for(int i=0;i<8;i++)
                    tile->m_pNeighbors[i] = NULL;
```

```
                        //Possible neighbors
                        INTPOINT p[] = { ... };

                        //For each neighbor
                        for(int i=0;i<8;i++)
                            if(Within(p[i]))
                            {
                                MAPTILE *neighbor = GetTile(p[i]);
                                //Connect tiles if the neighbor
                                //is walkable
                                if(neighbor != NULL &&
                                   neighbor->m_walkable)
                                    tile->m_pNeighbors[i] = neighbor;
                            }
                    }
                }

        CreateTileSets();
    }
```

It's pretty unnecessary to recalculate the whole terrain when a building will just affect a very small part of the map. Therefore, the TERRAIN::UpdatePathfinding() function takes a pointer to a rectangle with map coordinates and updates these tiles only. Remember how we called this function with GetMapRect(1) in the constructor of the BUILDING class? This means that we update only those tiles that may be affected by a certain building.

When a building is destroyed or removed, remember to restore the m_walkable *variable of all map tiles affected by the building in the destructor of the* BUILDING *class. Then call the* UpdatePathfinding() *function of the active terrain object, other-wise units will act as if the building is still there.*

Determining Where a Building Can Be Placed

Of course, we can force a building to be located anywhere on the map, but in most cases this doesn't make much sense. In most cases we want to limit the placement of buildings in some way. Here's an example of general limitations you might want to implement:

■ Buildings can only be placed on a certain terrain type.
■ Buildings can only be placed on level terrain.

- Buildings can only be placed on explored map areas.
- Buildings cannot be placed too close or too far from other buildings.
- Buildings cannot be placed in areas occupied by enemy units.

In addition to these, you might want to implement game-specific limitations, as well. For example, we create the global PlaceOk() function, which is declared along with the BUILDING class. The idea of this function is simple. Send any information needed to determine whether a building can be placed at a certain location or not, and then return true if this location is okay, otherwise return false. Here's an example of what the PlaceOk() function might look like:

```
bool PlaceOk(int buildType, INTPOINT mp, TERRAIN *terrain)
{
    BUILDING b(buildType, mp, NULL, false, NULL);
    RECT r = b.GetMapRect(1);

    for(int y=r.top;y<=r.bottom;y++)
        for(int x=r.left;x<=r.right;x++)
        {
            //Building must be within map borders
            if(!terrain->Within(INTPOINT(x,y)))return false;
            MAPTILE *tile = terrain->GetTile(x, y);

            if(tile == NULL)return false;

            //The terrain must be level and walkable
            if(tile->m_height != 0.0f || !tile->m_walkable)
                return false;
        }

    return true;
}
```

With this function, we can now test any location and see if a certain building can be placed there or not. Later, during the game, the player will be able to select the location of his buildings. We can then use this function to visualize the building being placed in different ways and to indicate whether the location is okay or not. This implementation is rather strict, it requires that the ground is flat (zero). Other requirements can be that the ground is level, but can be at any height.

Example 9.2

See Example 9.2 where we place buildings on a terrain. The building being placed is rendered green if the location is okay, and red if it's not. We do this by supplying a vertex color to the lighting vertexshader (see the lighting.vs and teamCol.ps files).

PLAYERS

Okay, we've handled units and we've handled buildings. It's now time to take a stab at the PLAYER class. For each team in the game we will have one PLAYER object, whether that team is controlled by a human, a computer, or across the network. The APPLICATION class will hold a vector of players, and update and render these. In the PLAYER class, a lot of things will happen. This class will take responsibility for the creation, updating, and rendering of our units and buildings. It will also handle the selection of the units and buildings, unit orders, placing buildings, and much more. Here's the PLAYER class declaration:

```
class PLAYER
{
    public:
        PLAYER(int _teamNo, D3DXVECTOR4 _teamCol,
               INTPOINT startPos, TERRAIN* _terrain,
               IDirect3DDevice9* _Device);
        ~PLAYER();

        void AddMapObject(int type, INTPOINT mp,
                          bool isBuilding);
        void RenderMapObjects(CAMERA &camera);
        void PaintSelectedMapObjects(CAMERA &camera);
        void UpdateMapObjects(float deltaTime);
        INTPOINT FindClosestBuildingLocation(int buildType,
                                             INTPOINT mp);
```

```
        void Select(MOUSE &mouse);
        void UnitOrders(MOUSE &mouse);

    private:
        IDirect3DDevice9* m_pDevice;
        std::vector<MAPOBJECT*> m_mapObjects;
        D3DXVECTOR4 m_teamColor;
        TERRAIN *m_pTerrain;
        int m_teamNo;
        bool m_areaSelect;
        INTPOINT m_startSel;
};
```

AddMapObject(): Simply adds a unit or a building to the player.

RenderMapObjects(): Renders all the map objects of a player (and now controls the lighting and team color shaders that we previously had in the APPLICATION class).

PaintSelectedMapObjects(): Draws the selection rectangle around any selected mapObjects.

UpdateMapObjects(): Updates the units and the buildings.

FindClosestBuildingLocation(): This function will mostly be used by an AI player to find a valid building location close to the player's starting location.

Select(): Selects units and buildings. This function has been moved from the APPLICATION class to the PLAYER class because we will never need to select units from more than one player at a time. It has also now been changed to work with map objects, rather than unit or building objects.

UnitOrders(): This function is called for the active team to let a player order selected units around.

In this class, we can begin to see the beauty of polymorphism. Instead of having two separate arrays, one for our UNIT objects and one for our BUILDING objects, it is enough just to have one array of MAPOBJECT objects. Then we can use the common interface of our units and buildings defined in the MAPOBJECT class. Here's the AddMapObjectFunction(), where we add either a building or a unit to the array:

```
    void PLAYER::AddMapObject(int type, INTPOINT mp,
                              bool isBuilding)
    {
        if(isBuilding)
            m_mapObjects.push_back(new BUILDING(type, mp,
                                     m_pTerrain, true, m_pDevice));
```

```
        else m_mapObjects.push_back(new UNIT(type, mp,
                                    m_pTerrain, m_pDevice));
    }
```

See how we can push both BUILDING pointers as well as UNIT pointers into this vector? As far as the PLAYER class is concerned, it treats both buildings and units as map objects. For example, here's how we update our map objects:

```
void PLAYER::UpdateMapObjects(float deltaTime)
{
    for(int i=0;i<m_mapObjects.size();i++)
        if(m_mapObjects[i] != NULL)
            m_mapObjects[i]->Update(deltaTime);
}
```

We simply call the overloaded Update() function for all our map objects, and that's it. We do the exact same thing when we render the objects or when we paint the object selection rectangle. Other than this, the implementation of the PLAYER class is fairly straightforward. The constructor of the PLAYER class takes a map starting location and then places any initial buildings or units close to this location.

Creating a Playable Terrain

Because we now are going to play the game with multiple teams, it is important that each player gets the same starting conditions. For instance, each player must get roughly the same amount of available terrain to place buildings. The easiest way to do this is to load a heightmap from a file and multiply it by a random heightmap, as shown in Figure 9.4.

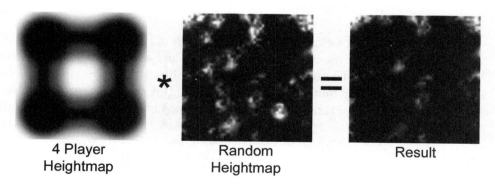

4 Player
Heightmap

Random
Heightmap

Result

FIGURE 9.4 Creating a fair RTS heightmap.

This four-player heightmap is created to ensure that each player gets an equal size of flat terrain (black areas). This heightmap also ensures that a path exists between the players. However, in itself, this heightmap would be pretty boring to play. Therefore, we multiply it by a random heightmap. The result is a random heightmap that has equal amounts of flat areas for all four players. From now on, we perform this operation in the `TERRAIN::GenerateRandomTerrain()` function whenever we want a fair multiplayer terrain.

MULTIPLE UNIT PATHFINDING

Remember how in Example 9.1 when you ordered multiple units to the same location they all ended up standing on the exact same map node? In this section, we will attempt to fix that problem by introducing a few new concepts. We can build a system that uses collision avoidance. This means that our units are so smart that they plan ahead and that way make sure that collisions never (or at least seldom) occur. Path planning and collision avoidance are very CPU expensive, and very hard topics. If you want to read more about these concepts, search for an example of "multi agent path planning" using your preferred search engine, or check out the "Cooperative Pathfinding" article by David Silver [Silver06].

Most RTS games use collision detection/resolution instead because it is computationally a lot less expensive. Collision detection means that the unit walks along as usual, and as soon as two (or more) units try to occupy the same space, a collision occurs. What happens next is that we use some form of collision resolution technique to resolve the problem. In the case of two units colliding, maybe both find a tile to the right of the other unit, move there, and then continue to their original goals. Another method could be to have the least-important unit move out of the way for the more-important one. For an example of a simple collision-resolution scheme, see Figure 9.5.

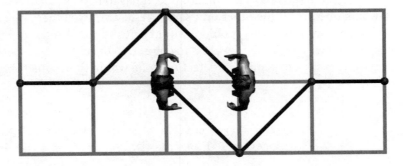

FIGURE 9.5 A simple right-rule collision-resolution scheme.

A simple scheme like the one presented in Figure 9.5 works well in open terrains with few units and a lot of available space. Unfortunately, in reality, this may not always be the case. Consider Figure 9.6.

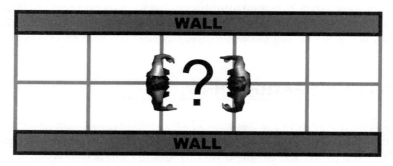

FIGURE 9.6 A collision resolution problem.

Figure 9.6 shows a little bit trickier collision-resolution problem. Here, the simple right-rule solutions can't be applied because there's no path other than through the occupied tile. This kind of situation results in a deadlock where neither unit can move anywhere. In an RTS game, we might have hundreds of units moving across the terrain, avoiding static objects and each other. The moral of the story is that it isn't easy to simply hard-code a set of rules for every situation that may occur. Therefore, we need to come up with a scheme or a set of rules that handles all (or close to all) possible collisions.

Unit Collision Detection

The first problem we need to solve is how to detect when a collision is about to occur. To do this, our units must be able to communicate with each other. As each unit is about to move to a new map node, it has to first ask all other units: "Are you standing on *x, y*?" If the other unit says, "Yes, I am," well then, we have a collision. The naive solution to this problem would be to supply a reference to the vector of players that we have in the APPLICATION object, to the UNIT::CheckCollision() function. In this case, the collision detection code would look something like this:

```
for each player
    for each unit
        if the active unit is standing on X_Next, Y_Next
            return Collision!

return No Collision
```

The problem with this approach is that as the number of players and units grow (and they will), this code gets increasingly more inefficient. Another downside of doing the collision detection this way is that we need to send references of the PLAYER objects all the way from the APPLICATION object down to the units. The units also need to be able to access the content of the PLAYER class, and so forth. The whole thing quickly gets very messy. But by using a little bit of memory, we can gain a lot in design and speed by letting the map tiles keep track of the units and buildings standing on them, as shown in Figure 9.7.

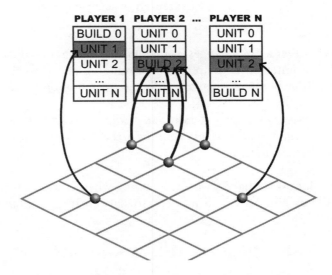

FIGURE 9.7   The MAPTILE m_pMapObject pointer.

Each MAPTILE object has a MAPOBJECT pointer, m_pMapObject, which may point to any unit or building in any team. Notice that multiple pointers can point to the same object, as well, if it takes up more than one map tile. This way the terrain keeps track of what units/buildings are standing on what map tiles. The units and buildings are, themselves, in charge of setting the m_pMapObject pointers of the map tiles. As the units move across the terrain, they also make sure they update the m_pMapObject pointer of the map tiles. We do this in the UNIT::MoveUnit() function:

```
void UNIT::MoveUnit(INTPOINT to)
{
    m_lastWP = m_pTerrain->GetWorldPos(m_mappos);
    m_rotation = GetDirection(m_mappos, to);
```

```
//Clear old MAPTILE unit pointer
MAPTILE *tile = m_pTerrain->GetTile(m_mappos);
if(tile != NULL)tile->m_pMapObject = NULL;

m_mappos = to;          //New mappos
m_movePrc = 0.0f;
m_nextWP = m_pTerrain->GetWorldPos(m_mappos);

//Set new MAPTILE unit pointer
tile = m_pTerrain->GetTile(m_mappos);
if(tile != NULL)tile->m_pMapObject = this;
}
```

Whenever a unit changes its map position from one tile to another, it also sets the unit pointer of the map tiles. The buildings, on the other hand, only need to change these pointers when a building is created or destroyed.

You need to set the m_pMapObject pointer of a MAPTILE object when you create a new unit. You also need to reset the m_pMapObject pointer when a unit is killed or otherwise removed.

Well, now we have a way of querying whether a unit is standing on a specific map tile or not. This is all we need to start creating our UNIT::CheckCollision() function:

```
bool UNIT::CheckCollision(INTPOINT mp)
{
    MAPTILE *tile = terrain->GetTile(mp);
    if(tile == NULL)return false;

    //Collision with another unit or building
    if(tile->m_pMapObject != NULL &&
       tile->m_pMapObject != this)
    {
        //more to come here later...

        return true;    //A Collision happened
    }

    return false;      //No Collision
}
```

We simply use the unit's terrain pointer to retrieve the tile of the next waypoint in our path. If the m_pMapObject pointer of this tile is empty, then we know for sure that there's no unit there, and we can safely start traveling toward this node. Should the m_pMapObject pointer, however, not be NULL, then we need to figure out a way to resolve the collision.

Unit Collision Resolution

Detecting the collision is the easy part; figuring out what to do next is not quite so easy. As we discussed before, a few hard-coded rules aren't enough because they won't cover all the possible cases. We need to recalculate the path, taking the location of other units into account. Our pathfinding could then be defined like this:

1. Calculate **path** from unit position to **goal.**
2. Store the **goal** as **finalGoal.**
3. Start moving the unit along the **path;** If a collision occurs:
    a. Find the next available node, **tempGoal,** in the **path.**
    b. Recalculate the **path** from the unit's position to **tempGoal,** taking other units into account.
6. Repeat from Step 3.
7. If the **goal** is reached: If the unit position is equal to **finalGoal,** exit loop.
8. If the unit position is not equal to **finalGoal,** repeat from Step 1.

This unit collision-resolution scheme gives us the behavior shown in Figure 9.8.

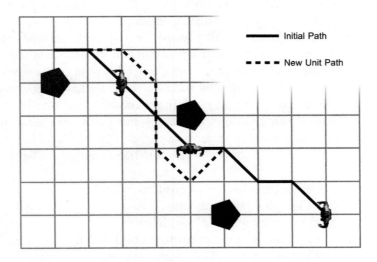

FIGURE 9.8   Unit collision resolution.

The strength of this scheme is that instead of relying on hard-coded rules to resolve collisions, we simply use the existing pathfinding system. This ensures that we cover (almost) all scenarios, and the only thing we need to do is tweak our pathfinder to ignore nodes that have a unit on them. You might wonder why we simply don't consider other units from the start and simply request a path that always avoids other units? Well, the problem is that all other units are (or might be) moving, as well. This means that a once-valid path can become blocked by other moving units as it is being executed. A unit might also seem to take the long way around invisible objects (i.e., places where other units once stood). Therefore, we calculate the original path without considering any other units and have a unit follow this path as closely as possible. Whenever a collision occurs, then we simply find a path around the blocking unit.

One way to get good-looking pathfinding is to calculate a new path taking other units into account every time a unit reaches a new map node. This is, of course, an expensive way to get good-looking pathfinding, but if you have a lot CPU cycles to spare (or few enough units), this could be one thing to try.

We need to consider the fact that other units are moving, as well. RTS games provide a very dynamic environment to find paths in. Dynamic content might not only be units—it can be anything that opens and closes, like gates, teleporters, or bridges. If you want any of these things in your game, then you need to consider the fact that a path passing through one of these objects might not be valid by the time the unit reaches it. These scenarios also result in collisions that need to be resolved. For our game, considering other units is work enough for now. Sometimes when a collision occurs between two units, the best action might not always be to recalculate the path around another unit. Consider Figure 9.9.

Unit A has started to walk toward the map node marked with a circle. At the same time, unit B tries to walk toward the same map node, when a collision occurs. With the scheme covered earlier, unit B would try to find a new path around unit A, but is this really the optimal solution? Unit B must cross the path of unit A at some point; doing this might result in yet another collision a little farther down the track. The best thing to do in a situation like this is, of course, for unit B to wait until unit A passes and then continue on as if nothing had happened. Let's therefore modify our pathfinding algorithm to handle collisions with moving units:

1. Calculate **path** from unit position to **goal.**
2. Store the **goal** as `finalGoal.`
3. Start moving the unit along the **path.**
4. If a collision occurs: If the other unit is not moving then:
    a. Find the next available node `tempGoal` in the **path.**

    b. Recalculate the **path** from the unit's position to `tempGoal`, taking other units into account.

7. Repeat from Step 3.
8. If the other unit is moving: Wait until the unit has passed.
9. Repeat from Step 3.
10. If the **goal** is reached and the unit's position is equal to `finalGoal`, exit the loop.
11. If the **goal** is reached and the unit's position is not equal to `finalGoal`, repeat from Step 1.

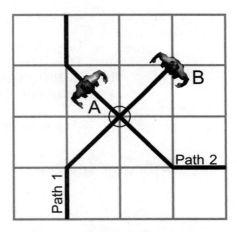

FIGURE 9.9 A simple collision between units A and B.

Okay, hopefully you have an idea now how this all fits together. To implement this, we need to extend our TERRAIN::GetPath() function to have as an option the ability to take units into account as well as static objects. This little addition is very easy because we now keep track of all the map objects using the m_pMapObject pointer in the MAPTILE class. The following is an excerpt of the modified TERRAIN:: GetPath() function:

```
std::vector<INTPOINT> TERRAIN::GetPath(INTPOINT start,
                                       INTPOINT goal,
                                       bool considerUnits)
{
    //Create Our Open list
    //Add start node to the Open list
```

```
        //... other initialization here...

    while(!found && !open.empty())
    {
        // Find the best node in the open list(lowest F value)

        if(best->m_mappos == goal) //If goal has been found
        {
            //return path
        }
        else
        {
            // otherwise, check the neighbors of the best node
            for(i=0;i<8;i++)
                if(best->m_pNeighbors[i] != NULL)
                    if(!considerUnits ||
                        best->m_pNeighbors[i]->
                        m_pMapObject == NULL)
                    {
                        //Search neighbor
                    }

            //Other stuff here as well...
        }
    }
}
```

First we take a Boolean considerUnits as a parameter to this function. If this parameter is true, then we also take units into consideration. The small addition to our GetPath() function is when we determine what neighbors of the best tiles to search. If we want to consider units, then we simply don't add any tiles to the open list that has a unit standing on them (i.e., a tile's m_pMapObject pointer that isn't NULL). Our pathfinding system will now ignore any tiles with units on them, therefore guaranteeing a "unit-free" path. The other thing we need to do is be able to pause our unit for a certain period of time. For this reason, we have added the UNIT::Pause() function:

```
    void UNIT::Pause(float time)
    {
        SetAnimation("Still");
        m_pauseTime = time;
    }
```

This function just sets the animation to "Still" and sets the m_pauseTime of the unit. Then we simply use the m_pauseTime in the UNIT::Update() function, like this:

```
void UNIT::Update(float deltaTime)
{
    //Pause the units...
    if(m_pauseTime > 0.0f)
    {
        m_pauseTime -= deltaTime;
        return;
    }

    //do other unit updating stuff here...
}
```

The UNIT::Update() function simply counts down the m_pauseTime, should the unit be "paused." We also need to store the original goal of the unit. Whenever we calculate a new path around a unit that is standing in the way, we erase the original path and replace it with the temporary one, and thus we loose the original goal. Therefore, when the unit has reached its temporary goal, it must know that it hasn't reached its final goal yet. We store the location of the final goal when we give a unit the order to move to a certain location. This location is then stored in the m_finalGoal variable in our UNIT class. Whenever a unit reaches the end of a path, it checks to see whether this location is the final goal that the user had in mind; if not, then the unit requests a new path to the final goal.

Now all we need to do is to implement the UNIT::CheckCollision() function properly, and we have ourselves a multiple-unit pathfinding system:

```
bool UNIT::CheckCollision(INTPOINT mp)
{
    MAPTILE *tile = m_pTerrain->GetTile(mp);
    if(tile == NULL)return false;

    //Collision with another unit
    if(tile->m_pMapObject != NULL && tile->m_pMapObject!=this)
    {
        UNIT *otherUnit = (UNIT*)tile->m_pMapObject;

        //The other unit is moving
        if(otherUnit->m_moving && otherUnit->m_pauseTime <= 0
            && m_speed <= otherUnit->m_speed)
        {
```

```
            //Pause the unit and wait for the other one to move
            Pause((100 + rand()%200) / 1000.0f);
            m_path.clear();
        }
        else    //Recalculate path
        {
            //Find next unoccupied walkable tile
            INTPOINT tempGoal = m_mappos;
            for(int i=m_activeWP+1;i<m_path.size();i++)
            {
                MAPTILE *tile = terrain->GetTile(path[i]);
                if(tile != NULL)
                    if(tile->m_walkable &&
                       tile->m_pMapObject == NULL)
                    {
                        tempGoal = m_path[i];
                        break;
                    }
            }

            //No available tile found
            if(tempGoal == m_mappos)
            {
                //Move to tile closest to the original goal
                INTPOINT newGoal = m_pTerrain->
                              GetClosestFreeTile(m_finalGoal,
                                                    m_mappos);

                //Close enough to the final goal or not?
                if(newGoal == m_mappos ||
                   m_mappos.Distance(m_finalGoal) < 2.0f)
                {
                    m_moving = false;
                    SetAnimation("Still");
                }
                else Goto(newGoal, false, true);
            }
            else
            {
                //Move to tempGoal to avoid blocking unit,
                //then continue onwards to the finalGoal
                Goto(tempGoal, true, false);
```

```
            }
        }

        return true;        //A Collision happened
    }

        return false;       //No Collision
    }
```

Again, we are faced with a pretty involved function. First we retrieve the tile in question that a unit is about to move toward. If this tile doesn't contain a map object, then all is well, and the unit in question can start moving. However, when there is a unit in the way, we first check to see what it is doing. If it is standing still, or if it is moving slower than the unit in question, then try to find another path around it. Otherwise, the unit can wait for the other unit to move out of the way.

This pathfinding system is still pretty far from the level of a commercial pathfinding system, but it should give you some insight into a couple of issues to be dealt with. Most professional games differentiate between short and long paths and use different pathfinding systems for these. If you want to take this pathfinding system a few steps further, you can look into topics like hierarchical pathfinding, unit formations, and group pathfinding.

ON THE CD

Example 9.3

On the CD-ROM, you'll find Example 9.3, where the PLAYER class has been implemented to contain both buildings and units. The multiple-unit pathfinding system covered in this section has also been implemented in this example. Make sure you play around with the code so that you completely understand this example, as we will build on this later on.

SUMMARY

This chapter has certainly been the one of the more code-intensive chapters so far. Hopefully you are still hanging in there. We now finally have something that actually looks a little bit like an RTS game. We have different players, units, and buildings that can be ordered around the terrain in a somewhat structured manner. Make sure to note that this multiple-unit pathfinding system is far from perfected. Making it perfect will be your job. Try to find scenarios in which the units in Example 9.3 could deal with the problem in a better way and then make those changes. Also, be sure to read the articles by Dave Pottinger ([Pottinger99a] and [Pottinger99b]) about coordinated unit movement. These articles require that you create a Gamasutra member account (this is free). Doing this is highly recommended because it allows you to access many articles and other game programming resources. There's also a very interesting article by David Silver [Silver06], which explores how units find paths in both space and time.

This chapter has taken us a big leap closer to our RTS game, but there is still much work to be done. At the moment, the other players don't really do anything, and in that way they are a bit boring. We won't correct this until later, when we cover computer opponents in Chapter 14. However, before we do that, we first need to complete our game engine. Over the next couple of chapters, we will add some standard RTS game features, like fog-of-war, a minimap, visual effects, and sound.

EXERCISES

- Check out the article "Toward More Realistic Pathfinding" by Marco Pinter [Pinter01] and see if you can implement some of the ideas presented there.
- Change the UNIT::GetDirection() function to return a smooth gradient turn as the unit changes direction.
- Create units of varying scale (e.g., tall units, chubby units, and so on).
- If a unit has been standing still for a random amount of time, then run the "idle" animation of the skinned meshes once (see Chapter 7).
- If a moving unit collides with a nonmoving unit from the same team, have the unit that's not moving move out of the way (then move back again to where it was standing).
- Try to optimize the MAPOBJECT::PaintSelected() method—because as is, this is done rather inefficiently.

REFERENCES

[Pinter01] Pinter, Marco, "Toward More Realistic Pathfinding." Available online at: *http://www.gamasutra.com/features/20010314/pinter_01.htm,* 2001.

[Pottinger99a] Pottinger, Dave, "Coordinated Unit Movement." Available online at: *http://www.gamasutra.com/features/19990122/movement_01.htm,* 1999.

[Pottinger99b] Pottinger, Dave, "Implementing Coordinated Movement." Available online at: *http://www.gamasutra.com/features/19990129/implementing_01.htm,* 1999.

[Silver06] Silver, David, "Cooperative Pathfinding." *AI Game Programming Wisdom 3,* Charles River Media, 2006.

10 | Fog-of-War

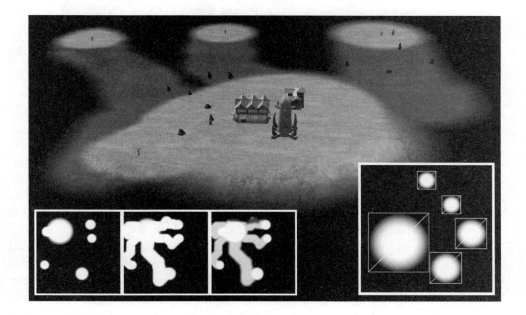

W e've now reached the very interesting topic of creating a fog-of-war effect
for our Real-Time Strategy game. So what is fog-of-war? Wikipedia defines fog-of-war like this:

> "The fog of war is the lack of knowledge that occurs during a war. Most impor-
> tantly, it refers to each side's uncertainty about the enemy's capabilities and
> plans."—Wikipedia, the free encyclopedia, "Fog of War," *www.wikipedia.org*

Well, that pretty much sums it up. In RTS games, fog-of-war is a shroud used
to hide places, buildings, and enemy units that a player hasn't yet seen. This means
that any areas that aren't within the sight range of a friendly unit are hidden from
the player's view by the fog-of-war. In a hidden area, the enemy might be gathering

a huge army to strike at your base, or there might be a whole lot of nothing going on there—who knows? Unlike in chess, for instance, where all the opponent's pieces are visible, the fog-of-war adds some uncertainty to your game that allows you to make (or be the victim of) a surprise attack.

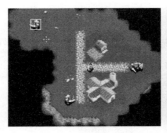

FIGURE 10.1   Fog-of-war in the games *Warcraft* and *Warcraft II*. (Warcraft® screenshots provided courtesy of Blizzard Entertainment, Inc.)

The concept of fog-of-war has been with us since the earliest real-time strategy games, like *Dune II* or *Warcraft* (see Figure 10.1). In all these years, the concept hasn't changed much. In the beginning, a one-layer fog-of-war was used to filter out any places that the player hasn't yet explored. However, once an area had been explored, the player could see what was going on in that area. *Warcraft II* solved this problem by adding a second layer to the fog-of-war. The second layer shows only those parts of the terrain that are currently within the sight range of a friendly unit or building. The second layer is usually rendered semi-transparent or grayed-out, showing the terrain, but not any enemy units. An example of this two-layer fog-of-war is shown in Figure 10.2. Most of today's games still use this two-layer fog-of-war style, and therefore, so shall we.

Here are a few definitions that we will use throughout this chapter:

Visible Tiles: These are the tiles that are fully visible by one or more friendly units. The player has full access to all information regarding these tiles, such as information about enemy units. In Figure 10.2, the visible tiles are the tiles within the sight radius of the unit.

Visited Tiles: These tiles have been visited (or at least seen) by a friendly unit in the past, but they are not visible at the moment. The player will get partial information about these tiles. Most games let the player see terrain and buildings residing in visited areas. In Figure 10.2, this is the semi-transparent Explored Area.

Hidden Tiles: These are the unexplored tiles of the terrain. The player will see neither terrain nor enemy units/buildings standing on hidden tiles. The hidden tiles are represented by the black Unexplored Area in Figure 10.2.

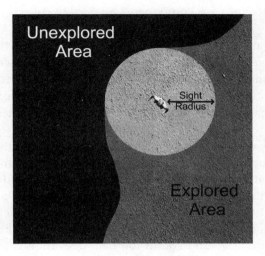

FIGURE 10.2   The concept of fog-of-war.

In many traditional 2D tile-based computer games, the fog-of-war is calculated and rendered on a tile basis. This is done by simply overlaying different types of "shadow" tiles, depending on whether the tile is visible, visited, or hidden. An example of 2D tile-based fog-of-war can be seen in Figure 10.3.

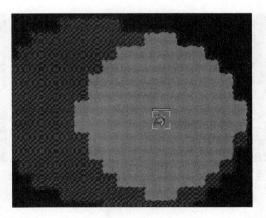

FIGURE 10.3   Traditional tile-based fog-of-war.

Note how the transition between visible, visited, and hidden tiles clearly follows the rectangular tile pattern. In this chapter, we will attempt a somewhat more-advanced implementation, where we get a smooth gradient circle around our units rather than a rectangular pattern. However, to create a more-advanced fog-of-war system, there are a few components we need to cover:

- Setting up the camera to render the terrain with orthogonal projection.
- Rendering to off-screen textures instead of to the screen.
- A few simple pixelshaders to blend textures together.
- Calculating a terrain-UV coordinate dynamically for units and buildings.
- Culling units with a logical representation (tile-based) of the fog-of-war.

If some of these steps don't make much sense at the moment, don't despair; they will hopefully become clearer as we go through this chapter. The fog-of-war implementation presented in this book builds on the idea of a lighting the terrain using a lightmap, like the one we covered in Chapter 5. In a nutshell, we simply create a 2D fog-of-war texture that describes what areas are visible, visited, and hidden. Then we overlay and multiply this 2D texture by the terrain (and units, buildings, etc.). Doesn't sound too bad, does it? Well, unfortunately we need to create the fog-of-war texture dynamically during runtime rather than during a pre-processing stage, like we did with the terrain lightmap.

First we separate the fog-of-war texture into two separate textures, one for each layer. We will have one texture for our visible tiles and call this texture the "visible texture." Then we'll have another texture for the visited tiles and call this texture the "visited texture." Figure 10.4 shows how the different textures will look and how they blend together to produce the final fog-of-war texture.

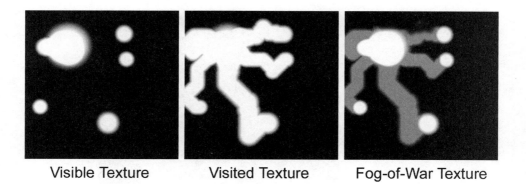

Visible Texture　　　Visited Texture　　　Fog-of-War Texture

FIGURE 10.4 The visible, visited, and fog-of-war textures.

As you can see, the visible texture paints a white circle around any unit or building with varying radius, depending on the sight radius of the unit (or building). The visited texture, on the other hand, is painted white in those areas that a friendly unit or building has seen at some point during the game, whether or not those areas are visible at the moment. Finally, we can create the complete fog-of-war texture by blending the visible and the visited texture. Note in the fog-of-war texture how visited areas are painted as gray, while visible areas are painted as bright white. Well, hopefully you now have an idea of how we are going to attack this problem.

CREATING THE VISIBLE TEXTURE

We'll have to start by first creating the visible texture. Once we have this texture, creating the other two is a fairly simple process. Also, since these three textures are going to be created dynamically for each frame, it needs to be a very fast process so the fog-of-war doesn't slow down the rest of the game. We now need a way of rendering the visible area of a map object as a white gradient circle whose size depends on the sight radius of the map object. We also need to make sure that the texture corresponds perfectly with the whole terrain, just like with the terrain lightmap. So later, when we stretch the fog-of-war texture over the terrain, it will fit perfectly and correspond with the location of our units.

We are going to create this texture by rendering to an off-screen texture (the visible texture) using an orthogonal view projection that covers the entire terrain. Then we will create a "sight" texture with a gradient white circle as well as a simple, four-vertex quad to hold it. We render this quad (with our sight texture) for each map object positioned at the center of the map object, scaled to the sight radius of the map object. The result will be our visible texture.

Remember that we only render the map objects of the active player to the visible texture and not the map objects of all the players. Otherwise, the whole idea of not being able to see what your opponents are doing is lost. For this reason, we have added the m_thisPlayer *variable in the* APPLICATION *class to keep track of which player in the array is the active player.*

Setting Up the Camera for Orthogonal Rendering

We are now going to set up the camera so that it covers the whole terrain, looking straight down on it. The texture we create is later going to be reapplied to the terrain, so it is important that the texture match the terrain exactly. We need to set up the projection matrix to precisely cover the size of the whole terrain. We also need to set the view matrix to position the camera eye and focus to the center of the terrain, as can be seen in Figure 10.5.

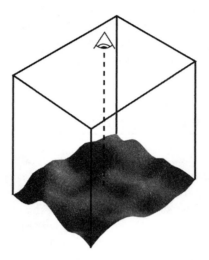

FIGURE 10.5   The desired camera setup for rendering the visible texture.

See how the viewing volume exactly matches the four corners of the terrain? This is a lot easier to do if you have orthogonal projection. If you don't remember how to create an orthogonal projection matrix, see "The D3DTS_PROJECTION Matrix" section in Chapter 5. Anyway, to help us set up our view and projection matrices to render the terrain in this fashion, the SetOrthogonalView() function has been added in the TERRAIN class, as follows:

```
void TERRAIN::SetOrthogonalView()
{
    D3DXMATRIX world, view, proj;

    //World matrix
    D3DXMatrixIdentity(&world);

    //View matrix (eye & focus in the center of the terrain)
    D3DXVECTOR2 center = D3DXVECTOR2((m_size.x - 1) / 2.0f,
                                     -(m_size.y - 1) / 2.0f);
```

```
D3DXMatrixLookAtLH(&view,
               &D3DXVECTOR3(center.x, 1000.0f, center.y),
               &D3DXVECTOR3(center.x, 0.0f, center.y),
               &D3DXVECTOR3(0.0f, 0.0f, 1.0f));

//Projection matrix
D3DXMatrixOrthoLH(&proj, m_size.x-1, m_size.y-1,
               0.1f, 2000.0f);

//Set transformation matrices
m_pDevice->SetTransform(D3DTS_WORLD, &world);
m_pDevice->SetTransform(D3DTS_VIEW, &view);
m_pDevice->SetTransform(D3DTS_PROJECTION, &proj);
}
```

You might wonder why we use `m_size.x − 1` instead of `m_size.x`. Remember, the amount of terrain nodes is measured with the `m_size` variable, but we are interested in the amount of terrain tiles, which is one less in each dimension. Note how we set the up vector of the view matrix to (0, 0, 1). This defines what part of the terrain will be "up" on the visible texture. Other than that, this function is pretty straightforward; we calculate and set the world, view, and projection matrices so that the camera is placed as shown in Figure 10.5. We will use this same function in Chapter 11, as well, when we render the minimap.

Textures as Render Targets

So far, the objects we've rendered have always been displayed directly on the screen. Now it's time for another method. Instead of rendering our scene to the screen, we want the result to end up in a texture. This is very useful for a large number of advanced effects, like blurring, glow, reflection, and many other post-processing filters. When we want to use a texture as a render target, we create it almost like we always do:

```
Device->CreateTexture(256, 256, 1, D3DUSAGE_RENDERTARGET,
               D3DFMT_A8R8G8B8, D3DPOOL_DEFAULT,
               &m_pVisibleTexture, NULL);
```

But instead of specifying the USAGE parameter as D3DUSAGE_DYNAMIC, we set it to D3DUSAGE_RENDERTARGET, indicating that we want to use this texture as a render target. In this example, we set the `m_pVisibleTexture`, `m_pVisitedTexture`, and the `m_pFogOfWarTexture` to 256 × 256 pixels, but you can play around with different texture resolutions as well. You can use the size of the fog-of-war textures as a tradeoff between memory, quality, and speed. The following code retrieves the surface of a texture and sets the render target to this surface:

```
//Surfaces
IDirect3DSurface9 *someSurface = NULL, *backSurface = NULL;

//Get original surface
Device->GetRenderTarget(0, &backSurface);

//Get texture surface
someTexture->GetSurfaceLevel(0, &someSurface);

//Set Render target
Device->SetRenderTarget(0, someSurface);

//Clear texture
Device->Clear(0, NULL, D3DCLEAR_TARGET | D3DCLEAR_ZBUFFER,
              0xff333333, 1.0f, 0);

Device->BeginScene();

//Render scene into the texture here...

Device->EndScene();

//Clean up, restore render target and release surfaces
Device->SetRenderTarget(0, backSurface);
backSurface->Release();
someSurface->Release();
```

First we create and retrieve the different surfaces we are going to need. We get the original back surface (i.e., the color buffer) so that we can restore it once we are done rendering to the texture. Then we get the surface of the render target texture (someSurface) and set it as a render target, using the IDirect3DDevice9::SetRenderTarget() function. We clear the render target and begin a scene as usual. After we've rendered everything we want, we restore the render target to the original back buffer and release all our surfaces. Well, now you know how to set up the camera so it covers the entire terrain, and you also know how to render a scene into a texture instead of onto the screen. The next question is, what do we render?

Rendering Map Objects to the Visible Texture

We now need to render all map objects of the active player to the visible texture. But instead of rendering the actual map objects, we are only interested in a representation of the objects' sight radius. As mentioned before, we represent this sight radius as a white gradient circle, like those shown in Figure 10.6.

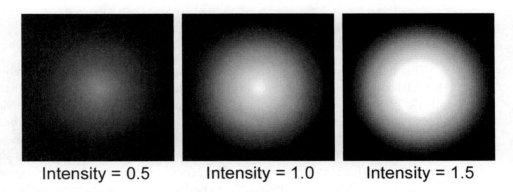

Intensity = 0.5   Intensity = 1.0   Intensity = 1.5

FIGURE 10.6   The sight texture of map objects.

The figure shows the sight texture we will use to represent areas within the sight range of a specific map object. This texture will be the same for all map objects; therefore, we create a global texture instead of many local ones. We create this texture in the LoadMapObjectResources() function, like this:

```
//Sight texture
Device->CreateTexture(64, 64, 1, D3DUSAGE_DYNAMIC, D3DFMT_L8,
                      D3DPOOL_DEFAULT, &sightTexture, NULL);

D3DLOCKED_RECT sRect;
sightTexture->LockRect(0, &sRect, NULL, NULL);
BYTE *bytes = (BYTE*)sRect.pBits;
memset(bytes, 0, sRect.Pitch*sRect.Pitch);

float intensity = 1.3f;
D3DXVECTOR2 center = D3DXVECTOR2(32.0f, 32.0f);

for(int y=0;y<64;y++)
    for(int x=0;x<64;x++)
    {
        float d;
        d = D3DXVec2Length(&(center - D3DXVECTOR2(x,y)));
        int value;
        value = ((32.0f - d) / 32.0f) * 255.0f * intensity;
```

```
            if(value < 0)value = 0;
            if(value > 255)value = 255;
            bytes[x + y * sRect.Pitch] = value;
        }

    sightTexture->UnlockRect(0);
```

This sight texture doesn't have to be that large—64×64 is more than enough. Also, observe that we only create a one-channel luminosity texture, rather than a full ARGB (Alpha, Red, Green, and Blue) texture, since this is all we need. The intensity value determines how visible the area around a map object will be. You can change the intensity value of this texture to simulate different conditions—like, for instance, night (low intensity) or day (high intensity). Next we need a simple mesh to apply this texture to before we can finally render it. We call this mesh the sightMesh, and it too is a global object created in the LoadMapObjectResources() function:

```
//Calculate sight mesh (a simple quad)
D3DXCreateMeshFVF(2, 4, D3DXMESH_MANAGED,
                SIGHTVertex::FVF, Device, &sightMesh);

//Create 4 vertices
SIGHTVertex* v = 0;
sightMesh->LockVertexBuffer(0,(void**)&v);
v[0] = SIGHTVertex(D3DXVECTOR3(-1, 0, 1),  D3DXVECTOR2(0, 0));
v[1] = SIGHTVertex(D3DXVECTOR3( 1, 0, 1),  D3DXVECTOR2(1, 0));
v[2] = SIGHTVertex(D3DXVECTOR3(-1, 0, -1), D3DXVECTOR2(0, 1));
v[3] = SIGHTVertex(D3DXVECTOR3( 1, 0, -1), D3DXVECTOR2(1, 1));
sightMesh->UnlockVertexBuffer();

//Create 2 faces
WORD* indices = 0;
sightMesh->LockIndexBuffer(0,(void**)&indices);
indices[0] = 0; indices[1] = 1; indices[2] = 2;
indices[3] = 1; indices[4] = 3; indices[5] = 2;
sightMesh->UnlockIndexBuffer();

//Set Attributes for the 2 faces
DWORD *att = 0;
sightMesh->LockAttributeBuffer(0,&att);
att[0] = 0; att[1] = 0;
sightMesh->UnlockAttributeBuffer();
```

We create the sight mesh with corners in the *xz*-plane; this makes the sight mesh completely perpendicular to the orthogonal camera we created before. We also create the mesh with the radius of 1.0f. This way, when we scale the sight mesh with a map object's sight radius, the mesh will cover the actual area that the unit can see. Okay, we now have a texture and a mesh to represent the sight radius of map objects. Now we need to render this sight mesh, mapped with the sight texture for each map object in the player's team, as shown in Figure 10.7.

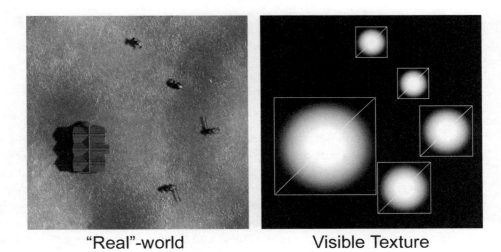

"Real"-world   Visible Texture

FIGURE 10.7   Rendering the visible texture.

As you can see, we render the same mesh and texture for both units and buildings. Therefore, we can implement a function in our MAPOBJECT class to handle the rendering of the sight mesh for us:

```
void MAPOBJECT::RenderSightMesh()
{
    //Set world transformation matrix
    D3DXMATRIX world, pos, sca;

    //Position the mesh at the center of the map object
    D3DXMatrixTranslation(&pos, m_position.x,
                                m_position.y,
                                m_position.z);
```

```
            //Scale mesh to the sight radius of the mapobject
            D3DXMatrixScaling(&sca,
                              m_sightRadius, 1.0f, m_sightRadius);

            //Create world matrix as Sca * Pos
            D3DXMatrixMultiply(&world, &sca, &pos);

            m_pDevice->SetTransform(D3DTS_WORLD, &world);

            //Set texture and material
            m_pDevice->SetTexture(0, sightTexture);
            m_pDevice->SetMaterial(&sightMtrl);    //White material

            //Draw the sight mesh
            sightMesh->DrawSubset(0);
        }
```

This function sets the world matrix to transform the sight mesh to the position/scale of a particular map object and render it. Now all we need to create is a function that loops through all the map objects of the active player and calls the RenderSightMesh() function. We have therefore added the FogOfWar() function to our APPLICATION class (which also holds the m_pVisibleTexture and the m_pVisited Texture). The FogOfWar() function can be divided into three parts, creating the m_pVisibleTexture, the m_VisitedTexture, and finally creating the m_pFogOfWarTexture:

```
        void APPLICATION::FogOfWar()
        {
            //Set orthogonal rendering view & projection
            m_terrain.SetOrthogonalView();

            //Retrieve the surface of the back buffer
            IDirect3DSurface9 *backSurface = NULL;
            m_pDevice->GetRenderTarget(0, &backSurface);

            //Set texture stages and Renderstates (Additive rendering)
            m_pDevice->SetTextureStageState(0, D3DTSS_ALPHAARG1,
                                            D3DTA_TEXTURE);
            m_pDevice->SetTextureStageState(0, D3DTSS_ALPHAARG2,
                                            D3DTA_TEXTURE);
            m_pDevice->SetTextureStageState(0, D3DTSS_ALPHAOP,
                                            D3DTOP_ADD);
            m_pDevice->SetTextureStageState(0, D3DTSS_COLORARG1,
                                            D3DTA_TEXTURE);
```

```cpp
m_pDevice->SetTextureStageState(0, D3DTSS_COLORARG2,
                                D3DTA_TEXTURE);
m_pDevice->SetTextureStageState(0, D3DTSS_COLOROP,
                                D3DTOP_ADD);

//Don't write to the Z-buffer
m_pDevice->SetRenderState(D3DRS_ZWRITEENABLE, false);
m_pDevice->SetRenderState(D3DRS_ALPHABLENDENABLE, true);
m_pDevice->SetRenderState(D3DRS_SRCBLEND,
                          D3DBLEND_SRCALPHA);
m_pDevice->SetRenderState(D3DRS_DESTBLEND,
                          D3DBLEND_DESTALPHA);

//Get the surface of the visibleTexture
IDirect3DSurface9 *visibleSurface = NULL;
m_pVisibleTexture->GetSurfaceLevel(0, &visibleSurface);

//Set render target to the visible surface
m_pDevice->SetRenderTarget(0, visibleSurface);

//Clear render target to black
m_pDevice->Clear(0, NULL,
                 D3DCLEAR_TARGET | D3DCLEAR_ZBUFFER,
                 0xff333333, 1.0f, 0);

m_pDevice->BeginScene();

//Render the sightTexture for all
//map objects of thisPlayer.
for(int u=0; u <
    m_players[m_thisPlayer]->m_mapObjects.size();u++)
    if(m_players[m_thisPlayer]->m_mapObjects[u] != NULL)
        m_players[m_thisPlayer]->
        m_mapObjects[u]->RenderSightMesh();

Device->EndScene();

//Restore renderstates etc.
m_pDevice->SetRenderState(D3DRS_ZWRITEENABLE, true);
m_pDevice->SetRenderState(D3DRS_ALPHABLENDENABLE, false);
m_pDevice->SetTextureStageState(0, D3DTSS_ALPHAOP,
                                D3DTOP_SELECTARG1);
m_pDevice->SetTextureStageState(0, D3DTSS_COLOROP,
                                D3DTOP_SELECTARG1);
```

```
//Release visible surface
visibleSurface->Release();

//To be continued...
```

We start this function by calling our `TERRAIN::SetOrthogonalView()` function. This sets up the camera view, as previously explained, to exactly cover the entire terrain. Then we set the texture stages and render states to allow for additive rendering. This means that when a pixel is rendered to the render target, it does not replace whatever pixel is already there. Instead, the two pixels are added together and the result is stored. This is important whenever the sight mesh of two (or more) map objects overlap because it would otherwise result in the visual artifact shown in Figure 10.8.

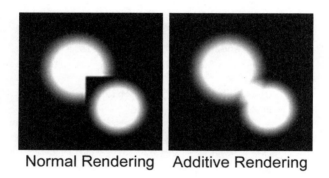

Normal Rendering   Additive Rendering

FIGURE 10.8 Normal rendering versus additive rendering.

See how the black corner of one of the sight textures is drawn on top of the other if we use normal rendering? This is the reason we use additive rendering to render our `sightMesh`. Okay, so after we've set up the texture stages and render states to perform additive rendering, we set the surface of the `m_pVisibleTexture`. Then we just loop through all map objects of our active player and draw the sight meshes using the `RenderSightMesh()` function. That's it. Finally, we do some clean up—reset some render states, release the visible surface, and so forth. The result of this operation should be something like the visible texture shown in Figure 10.4.

CREATING THE VISITED TEXTURE

Creating the visited texture is a pretty easy matter now that we have created the visible texture. We might render our visited texture it in the same manner as the visible texture, with the exception that we don't clear the texture between frames. This would work, but it would produce a low-quality visited texture. The reason for this is that because we use additive rendering, pixels would get added over time. So a pixel with the color value (1, 1, 1) would, after 255 frames, have the color value (255, 255, 255). This means that the visited texture would contain only extreme black and white colors, and not contain any gradient areas. A better solution is to create the visited texture directly from the visible texture. To do this, we create a simple pixelshader (`visited.ps`) to add the visible texture to the visited texture in each frame:

```
sampler visibleTexture;
sampler visitedTexture;

float4 Main(float2 UV : TEXCOORD0) : COLOR
{
    float4 c0 = tex2D(visibleTexture, UV);
    float4 c1 = tex2D(visitedTexture, UV);

    return max(c0, c1);
}
```

This extremely simple pixelshader just samples a pixel from both the visible texture and the visited texture. But instead of adding the two pixels together, we select the one with the highest intensity value and write it to the visible texture. This operation is also done in the `APPLICATION::FogOfWar()` function:

```
IDirect3DSurface9 *visitedSurface = NULL;
m_pVisitedTexture->GetSurfaceLevel(0, &visitedSurface);

//Render to the visited texture
m_pDevice->SetRenderTarget(0, visitedSurface);

//Clear the visited texture the first time
if(m_firstFogOfWar)
{
    m_pDevice->Clear(0, NULL,
                     D3DCLEAR_TARGET | D3DCLEAR_ZBUFFER,
                     0x00000000, 1.0f, 0);
    m_firstFogOfWar = false;
}

m_pDevice->BeginScene();
```

```
m_pDevice->SetTexture(0, m_pVisibleTexture);
m_pDevice->SetTexture(1, m_pVisitedTexture);

m_pSprite->Begin(0);       //Set Sprite renderstates
m_visitedShader.Begin();   //Set pixelshader

//Draw the result so it covers the destination surface
m_pSprite->Draw(m_pVisibleTexture, NULL, NULL,
            &D3DXVECTOR3(0.0f, 0.0f, 0.0f), 0xffffffff);

m_pSprite->End();          //Flush sprite

m_visitedShader.End();
m_pDevice->EndScene();

//Release visited surface
visitedSurface->Release();

//To be continued again...
```

As usual, when we have a texture as a render target, we first retrieve and set the surface of the m_pVisitedTexture as the active render target. If it is the first time we are rendering the visited texture, we first clear it to black. Then we start the pixelshader and set the textures. We draw the texture using a sprite interface and specify NULL as the source rectangle. This will draw the texture over the entire surface using the active pixelshader. Another way this can be done is to create a quad covering the entire terrain, and then draw this instead. But using a sprite to cover the entire surface is a little bit easier. Well, if all has gone well, the result should look something like the visited texture shown in Figure 10.4.

CREATING THE FOG-OF-WAR TEXTURE

We now have one texture with the visible areas of the terrain (i.e., the visible texture), and we also have a texture with all the areas that have been visited (i.e., the visited texture). Now we are going to blend these two textures together with the terrain lightmap to create the final fog-of-war texture. We will then use this texture as a lightmap for everything in our game. We have stored both the visible texture and visited texture in the APPLICATION class. The fog-of-war texture, however, needs to accessible to any object in the whole game. Therefore, it makes more sense to store this texture in the TERRAIN class, since from now on the fog-of-war texture will replace the terrain lightmap.

We create the fog-of-war texture in the same manner as we do the visited texture. The fog-of-war texture is also a render target texture with the same dimensions as the visible texture and the visited texture. To create the fog-of-war texture, we create the following pixelshader, FogOfWar.ps:

```
sampler visibleTexture;
sampler visitedTexture;
sampler lightMap;

float4 Main(float2 UV : TEXCOORD0) : COLOR
{
    float4 c0 = tex2D(visibleTexture, UV);
    float4 c1 = tex2D(visitedTexture, UV) * 0.5f;
    float4 c2 = tex2D(lightMap, UV);

    return float4(max(c0.rgb, c1.rgb), 1.0f) * c2.a;
}
```

We sample the visible texture, the visited texture, and the terrain lightmap. Note, however, that we multiply the visited texture by 0.5f. This is what makes the visited areas appear grayed out. You can play around with how transparent you want the visited areas to be by altering this factor. Then we return the max of the visible texture and the "dimmed" visited texture multiplied by the terrain lightmap. Now all we need to do is set the textures, activate this pixelshader, and draw the fog-of-war texture:

```
//Get and set surface of the FogOfWarTexture...
IDirect3DSurface9 *FogOfWarSurface = NULL;
m_terrain.m_pFogOfWarTexture->GetSurfaceLevel(0,
                                    &FogOfWarSurface);
m_pDevice->SetRenderTarget(0, FogOfWarSurface);

m_pDevice->Clear(0, NULL, D3DCLEAR_TARGET | D3DCLEAR_ZBUFFER,
            0x00000000, 1.0f, 0);

m_pDevice->BeginScene();

//Set Textures
m_pDevice->SetTexture(0, m_pVisibleTexture);
m_pDevice->SetTexture(1, m_pVisitedTexture);
m_pDevice->SetTexture(2, m_terrain.m_pLightMap);
```

```
//Draw to the Fog-of-War texture
m_pSprite->Begin(0);
m_FogOfWarShader.Begin();
m_pSprite->Draw(m_pVisibleTexture, NULL, NULL,
                &D3DXVECTOR3(0.0f, 0.0f, 0.0f), 0xffffffff);

m_pSprite->End();

m_FogOfWarShader.End();
m_pDevice->EndScene();

//Release Fog-of-War surface
FogOfWarSurface->Release();

//Reset render target to back buffer
m_pDevice->SetRenderTarget(0, backSurface);
backSurface->Release();
```

In this code section, we create the fog-of-war texture in much the same way we create the visited texture. Note also how in the end, we reset the render target to our original back surface (i.e., the color buffer). If you don't do this, then any scene you render won't appear on the screen because we still have the fog-of-war texture set as the active render target. This also marks the end of our APPLICATION::FogOfWar() function. We call this function once every frame from our APPLICATION::Update() function. You could experiment and only call this function every time a unit moves to a new tile. This would save some processing time, but it would also result in a less-smooth fog-of-war texture. Well, after all this work, you still won't see any difference in the actual game world. All we have so far is a texture in video memory filled with our fog-of-war information. The next step is to take this texture and apply it as a lightmap to our terrain, our units, and any other objects.

RENDERING TERRAIN, UNITS, AND OBJECTS WITH FOG-OF-WAR

As you may remember from Chapter 4, we covered the creation, texturing, and rendering of the terrain. We had two separate texture coordinates for the terrain and one UV coordinate that we used to tile the diffuse maps. The other UV coordinate was used to stretch the texture-splatting alpha map once over the entire terrain. We are going to need similar UV coordinates for all objects that we intend to shade with the fog-of-war texture. In Chapter 5, we covered how to light a terrain with a lightmap. The fog-of-war texture will be used in the same manner, stretched once over the entire terrain using the same UV coordinates as the texture-splatting alpha map. Okay, so rendering the terrain with the fog-of-war texture is pretty simple because the UV coordinates for this are already in place. From now on, we will refer to this UV coordinate system as the terrain-UV-space.

However, for other objects like units, buildings, trees and so on, we only have one set of texture coordinates that describe how to map the diffuse texture to the object. Now we need to calculate a second set of texture coordinates to describe the object's placement in the terrain-UV-space. What makes this problem even more difficult is that because units are moving around the terrain, we need to be able to calculate the terrain-UV-space coordinates on-the-fly each frame, and not just when we create the object, as shown in Figure 10.9.

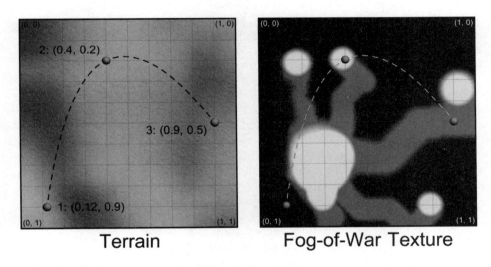

FIGURE 10.9   Calculating a UV coordinate dynamically.

In the figure, a single vertex belonging to a unit is moving across the terrain, starting in the bottom-left corner. As the vertex moves around on the terrain, we must update the terrain-UV-space coordinate of this vertex dynamically. We do this by dividing the vertex's world position in the xz-plane by the size of the terrain. Then we can use this calculated terrain-UV-space coordinate to sample the fog-of-war texture to determine if the vertex is in a visible area, a visited area, or an unexplored area. The following vertexshader (excerpt from lighting.vs) calculates the terrain-UV-space coordinate on-the-fly for our units and buildings:

```
uniform extern float4x4 matW;
uniform extern float4x4 matVP;
uniform extern float3   mapSize;

struct VS_INPUT
{
    float4 position : POSITION0;
    float3 normal   : NORMAL0;
    float2 uv       : TEXCOORD0;
};

struct VS_OUTPUT
{
    float4 position : POSITION0;
    float4 color    : COLOR;
    float2 uv       : TEXCOORD0;
    float2 uv2      : TEXCOORD1;
    float  shade    : TEXCOORD2;
};

VS_OUTPUT Main(VS_INPUT input)
{
    VS_OUTPUT output = (VS_OUTPUT)0;

    //Transform vertex to world space
    float4 worldPos = mul(input.position, matW);

    //Transform vertex to screen space
    output.position = mul(worldPos, matVP);

    //Transform normal...
    //Do the lighting calculation here etc...

    //Calculate the Terrain-UV-space coordinates
    output.uv2 = float2(worldPos.x / mapSize.x,
                       -worldPos.z / mapSize.y);

    return output;
}
```

This code is an excerpt from the vertexshader used to shade our units and buildings. We've now added an input variable to this vertexshader, called mapSize. We use this variable to calculate the second UV coordinate of a vertex, as shown. The output of the vertexshader is then sent to the following pixelshader that samples the fog-of-war texture, using the terrain-UV-space coordinate:

```
sampler unitTexture;
sampler fogOfWarTexture;
uniform extern float4 tmCol;

float4 Main(float4 vertCol : COLOR,
            float2 UV       : TEXCOORD0,
            float2 UV2      : TEXCOORD1,
            float  shade    : TEXCOORD2) : COLOR
{
    float4 c0 = tex2D(unitTexture, UV);
    float4 light = tex2D(fogOfWarTexture, UV2);

    //Calculate alpha inverse
    float Inv = 1.0f - c0.a;

    //Calculate team color
    float4 color = float4(c0.rgb * Inv + tmCol.rgb * c0.a,
                          1.0f);

    //Return resulting pixel
    return color * light * vertCol * shade;
}
```

We use the same method to use the fog-of-war texture as a lightmap for the terrain and all the terrain objects. The only difference is that we don't have to calculate the second UV coordinates of the terrain on-the-fly, since we do that at the creation of the terrain patches.

Okay, so we have now spent considerable time creating our three off-screen textures—the m_pVisibleTexture, the m_pVisitedTexture, and the m_pFogOfWar Texture. We have also learned how to calculate a second set of UV coordinates dynamically in "terrain space." Using these terrain-UV-space coordinates, objects, units, and buildings can sample the fog-of-war texture in a meaningful way and use it as a lightmap. If you render your game now, it should look something like Figure 10.10.

However, we aren't done yet. What we have now might look like a fog-of-war implementation. You would notice if you walked up to an enemy unit with one of your units and then walked away again. The enemy unit would still be visible, even if it is standing on a tile that no longer belongs to the visible area. This is because we haven't yet connected the fog-of-war concept to our game in any other way than our rendering process. There's another very important subject we must cover before our fog-of-war is completed.

FIGURE 10.10 The resulting fog-of-war.

FOG-OF-WAR CULLING

You might remember that in Chapter 5 we had a look at frustum culling, which means that we ignore rendering objects that are outside the camera's viewing volume. Now we will have a look at a similar concept—object culling using the fog-of-war. This means that we can simply ignore any objects, patches, units, or buildings that are in the unexplored areas of the terrain during the rendering phase. When it comes to the visited areas of the terrain, we render everything except units (which saves a lot of resources because we don't need to transform any skinned meshes, etc.). Rendering fog-of-war together with fog-of-war culling usually ends up saving a lot more CPU cycles that it costs to render the three off-screen textures, and so forth. It doesn't take culling that many skinned meshes before we actually start gaining on the whole operation.

How do we know if an enemy unit is standing on a visible tile or a visited tile? All we have at the moment is a fog-of-war texture describing the light intensity of certain areas. It wouldn't be very effective to query this texture to find out whether a unit is visible or not. Instead, we must build a logical representation of the fog-of-war. By a logical representation, we mean that we have a simple interface with which the state of a specific tile can be queried. For example, we could add two Booleans (Visible and Visited) to our MAPTILE class. But because we need to reset the visible variables each time we update the logical representation of the fog-of-war, it is cheaper to implement the visible and visited variables like an array of

Booleans. This way we can use the `memset()` function to reset the whole array without having to loop through all tiles. We create these arrays in the `Init()` function of the TERRAIN class, like this:

```
bool *m_pVisitedTiles, *m_pVisibleTiles;

...

m_pVisitedTiles = new bool[m_size.x * m_size.y];
m_pVisibleTiles = new bool[m_size.x * m_size.y];
memset(m_pVisitedTiles, false,
        sizeof(bool)* m_size.x * m_size.y);
memset(m_pVisibleTiles, false,
        sizeof(bool)* m_size.x * m_size.y);
```

This creates two arrays that contain one Boolean for each map tile in the terrain. We also set all the values in both arrays to `false` (i.e., every tile is invisible and unvisited). Now we need the units (and buildings) of the active player to set values in these arrays to `true`. Then we need all units, buildings, terrain objects, and patches to check these arrays, and determine whether they are visible or not before they are rendered. We update the graphical part of the fog-of-war every frame. However, it is enough to update the logical representation of the fog-of-war every time a unit changes map location from one map tile to another.

The objects need to access the visible and visited arrays to determine whether they are visible or not. For this purpose, we store a `visible` variable in the following classes: the MAPOBJECT, the OBJECT, and the PATCH class. Then we only need to render those objects whose visible variable is `true`. The TERRAIN::UpdateSight Matrices() updates the logical representation of the fog-of-war, and calculates the visible variable of all the patches and terrain objects, as follows:

```
void TERRAIN::UpdateSightMatrices(
                    std::vector<MAPOBJECT*> &mapObjects)
{
    //Reset the visible tiles to false
    memset(m_pVisibleTiles, false,
          sizeof(bool) * m_size.x * m_size.y);

    for(int i=0;i<m_mapObjects.size();i++)
        if(m_mapObjects[i] != NULL)
        {
            int sr = m_mapObjects[i]->m_sightRadius, a = 0;
            INTPOINT start = m_mapObjects[i]->m_mappos —
                            INTPOINT(sr, sr);
```

```
                    INTPOINT end = m_mapObjects[i]-> m_mappos +
                                   INTPOINT(sr, sr);

                    for(int y=start.y;y<=end.y;y++)
                    for(int x=start.x;x<=end.x;x++)
                        if(x >= 0 && y >= 0 &&
                           x < m_size.x && y < m_size.y)
                        {
                            int index = x + y * m_size.x;
                            m_pVisitedTiles[index] = true;
                            m_pVisibleTiles[index] = true;
                        }
                }

        //Calculate visibility variable of Patches
        for(int i=0;i<m_patches.size();i++)
            if(m_patches[i] != NULL)
            {
                m_patches[i]->m_visible = false;
                RECT r = m_patches[i]->m_mapRect;

                for(int y=r.top;y<=r.bottom &&
                    !m_patches[i]->m_visible;y++)
                for(int x=r.left;x<=r.right &&
                    !m_patches[i]->m_visible;x++)
                    if(m_pVisitedTiles[x + y * m_size.x])
                        m_patches[i]->m_visible = true;
            }

        //Calculate visibility of terrain objects
        for(int i=0;i<m_objects.size();i++)
            m_objects[i].m_visible = m_pVisitedTiles[
                                        m_objects[i].m_mappos.x +
                                        m_objects[i].m_mappos.y *
                                        m_size.x];
}
```

This function takes a vector of map objects as a parameter (this is, of course, the units and buildings of the active player). It loops through all of these map objects and creates a rectangle around the map object, which is the size of the sight radius. All values of the m_pVisibleTiles and m_pVisitedTiles arrays that are within this rectangle are set to true. Then we loop through all the terrain patches to see what patches contain a visited tile. Any patch with at least one visited tile must be rendered, and so it has its visible variable set to true. We also do the same thing for the terrain objects in this function.

In this implementation of the TERRAIN::UpdateSightMatrices() *function, we just test a rectangle around the supplied map objects. It would be more correct (if somewhat more expensive) to check a rough circle around a map object instead because the graphical representation of the sight radius is a gradient circle.*

Well, this function is called once only during those frames where one or more units have changed map location from one tile to another. We also have to check the buildings and units every time this happens to see if they are visible or not. We do this in the PLAYER::IsMapObjectsVisible() function:

```
void PLAYER::IsMapObjectsVisible()
{
    for(int i=0;i<m_mapObjects.size();i++)
    {
        if(m_mapObjects[i]->m_isBuilding)
        {
            RECT r = m_mapObjects[i]->GetMapRect(0);
            m_mapObjects[i]->m_visible = false;

            for(int y=r.top;y<=r.bottom &&
                !m_mapObjects[i]->m_visible;y++)
            for(int x=r.left;x<=r.right &&
                !m_mapObjects[i]->m_visible;x++)
                if(m_pTerrain->m_pVisitedTiles[x + y *
                                    m_pTerrain->m_size.x])
                    m_mapObjects[i]->m_visible = true;
        }
        else
        {
            INTPOINT mp = m_mapObjects[i]->m_mappos;
            m_mapObjects[i]->m_visible =
                m_pTerrain->m_pVisibleTiles[mp.x +
                                mp.y * m_pTerrain->m_size.x];
        }
    }
}
```

This function loops through all the map objects of a player and determines whether the map object is visible or not. Notice how we have different schemes to determine if a unit is visible or if a building is visible. All that is needed for a building to be visible is one visited tile in its map rectangle. The units, though, need to fulfill the somewhat stricter requirement of standing on a visible tile to be visible.

We have added the following code to the APPLICATION::Update() function to handle the logical update of the fog-of-war system:

```
...

//Update SightMatrices & visible variables
if(m_terrain.m_updateSight)
{
    m_terrain.m_updateSight = false;
    if(m_thisPlayer < m_players.size() &&
        m_players[m_thisPlayer] != NULL)
        m_terrain.UpdateSightMatrices(
                        m_players[m_thisPlayer]->
                        m_mapObjects);

    for(int i=0;i<m_players.size();i++)
        if(m_players[i] != NULL)
            m_players[i]->IsMapObjectsVisible();
}

...
```

The m_updateSight flag is set true by any unit moving from one map tile to another. Whenever the m_updateSight flag is true, we call the UpdateSightMatrices() function for our TERRAIN object as well as call the UpdateVisibleMapObjects() function for all PLAYER objects. Well, that's it. We now have another method of culling objects that doesn't contribute to the final image, and thus saves some valuable CPU resources.

ON THE CD

Example 10.1

After a pretty long run, it is now finally time to have a look at the actual project and the code, which is located on the CD-ROM.

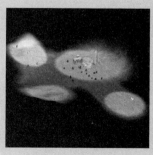

In this chapter, we rely heavily on using textures as render targets. These textures are stored in the D3DPOOL_DEFAULT *memory pool. Should the* Device *ever be lost due to a window resize event, minimize event, or similar occurrence, these textures will be lost. It would, therefore, be good to regularly store a copy of the* m_pVisited Texture *and* m_pVisibleTexture *in the* D3DPOOL_SYSTEMMEM *memory pool, for example. Should the* Device *ever be lost, we can recreate the visible, visited, and fog-of-war textures as soon as the* Device *is regained from these backup textures.*

SUMMARY

In this chapter, we have attempted to implement a fog-of-war system for real-time strategy games. Instead of just having fog-of-war on a tile basis, we implemented a system that allows gradient transitions using a fog-of-war texture as a lightmap. We created the visible texture by rendering a representation of the active player's units' sight radius off-screen. Then we created the visited texture and the fog-of-war texture using a couple of simple pixelshaders. We were then faced with the problem of generating terrain-UV-space coordinates on the fly for all units, buildings, and objects. We solved this problem by letting a vertexshader create the second UV coordinate as a function of the position of the vertex divided by the size of the terrain (in the *xz*-plane). Then we applied the fog-of-war texture as a lightmap to the terrain, the units, buildings, and terrain objects. We also implemented a logical representation of the fog-of-war that we could use to cull nonvisible patches, units, buildings, and so forth.

Make sure you take time to go through all the code in Example 10.1, and make sure that you grasp the whole concept. This particular fog-of-war implementation may seem hard to understand because many things are going on in a lot of different classes at the same time. In the next chapter, we will take a look at how to create minimaps. We will use the fog-of-war texture created in this chapter when rendering minimaps, as well.

EXERCISES

- Let the units affect the m_pVisibleTiles and m_pVisitedTiles arrays with a circular pattern rather than the rectangular pattern used in Example 10.1.
- Instead of having the unit visible variable as a Boolean, let it be a float value ranging from 0.0–1.0. Then rewrite the team color pixelshader to fade a unit in/out as they enter/exit visible areas.

11 Minimap

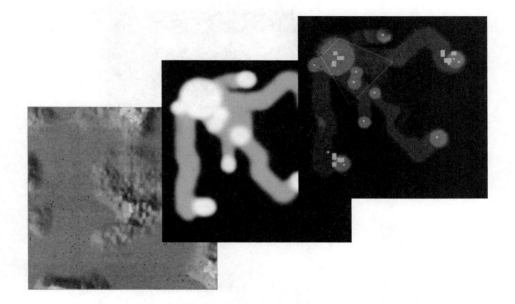

In this chapter, we are going to cover the subject of creating a minimap for our RTS game. A minimap is a small map that gives the player an overview of the entire terrain. In most RTS games, the minimap is located in one of the corners of the screen. The minimap is a great tool that provides a lot of information to the user at a quick glance. This can be information about the terrain, what areas are visible, troop movements, and more. Figure 11.1 shows the minimap we will attempt to implement in this chapter.

The minimap can also incorporate strategic locations, area ownership, area of influence, and other tools to help the player. The minimap can be used to give orders to the player's units—for example, to order units to a certain location on the map outside the current viewing frustum. All in all, it is a necessary part of any RTS game. The following is a list of the functionality we are going to implement in our minimap:

- Show the terrain landscape.
- Show the fog-of-war.
- Show units/buildings and what teams they belong to.
- Move the camera by clicking the minimap.
- Draw the camera viewing frustum in the minimap.

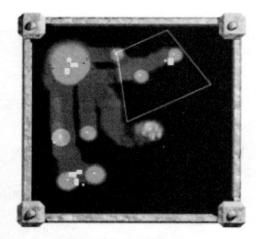

FIGURE 11.1 A minimap example.

Often, it can be quite good to see what the camera is looking at in the minimap. This helps the player get his bearing in the game. We do this by calculating where the viewing frustum intersects with the ground plane, and then extract the intersecting corners. Then we simply draw lines from corner to corner, and thus visualize the visible area in the minimap (see Figure 11.1). The minimap is comprised of a few different layers that are updated at different intervals, as shown in Figure 11.2.

Unit Layer: This layer shows the representation of the units and the buildings. These are represented as simple squares of various sizes, depending on their map size. These rectangles are filled with the team color of the player so units from different teams can be identified. This layer is only updated when a unit moves from one map tile to another.

Fog-of-War Layer: This layer consists of the fog-of-war texture we created in Chapter 10. The fog-of-war layer is updated each frame as the player's units move around.

Landscape Layer: The landscape layer is just an orthogonal rendering of the terrain that we do after it has been created. When this layer is created, things like the lightmap and the camera culling are ignored. We render the terrain into a landscape texture and only need to update this layer every time the terrain itself is changed (which only happens during initiation in most games).

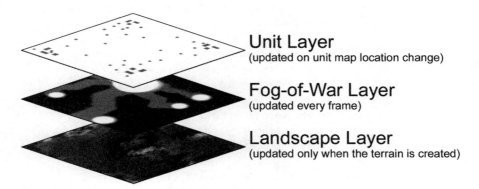

FIGURE 11.2   The layers of the minimap.

It is unnecessary to recreate the final minimap texture each frame in the game. Instead, we only update the minimap texture every time a unit changes map location. The fog-of-war layer was covered in the previous chapter, so that leaves the landscape and the unit layers. Let's start with the landscape layer.

RENDERING THE TERRAIN LANDSCAPE

Rendering the terrain landscape into a texture will be done in just the same way we rendered the visible texture in Chapter 10. First, we set up the camera to cover the terrain with an orthogonal projection using the TERRAIN::SetOrthogonalView() function. Then we simply render the whole terrain (all patches and all terrain objects); but instead of using the fog-of-war texture to light the terrain, we use a clean white texture. We do this because the lightmap of the terrain is already coded into our fog-of-war texture. If we rendered our terrain landscape texture using the lightmap, we would end up overexposing the lightmap later when we create the minimap texture. To render the terrain landscape texture, we add the RenderLandscape() function to our TERRAIN class:

```
//This variable has been added to our TERRAIN class...
IDirect3DTexture9* m_pLandScape;

...

void TERRAIN::RenderLandscape()
{
    //Set orthogonal rendering view & projection
    SetOrthogonalView();

    //Retrieve the surface of the back buffer
    IDirect3DSurface9 *backSurface = NULL;
    m_pDevice->GetRenderTarget(0, &backSurface);

    //Get the surface of the minimap texture
    IDirect3DSurface9 *landScapeSurface = NULL;
    m_pLandScape->GetSurfaceLevel(0, &landScapeSurface);

    //Set render target to the visible surface
    m_pDevice->SetRenderTarget(0, landScapeSurface);

    //Clear render target to black
    m_pDevice->Clear(0, NULL,
                    D3DCLEAR_TARGET | D3DCLEAR_ZBUFFER,
                    0x00000000, 1.0f, 0);

    //Create completely white lightmap
    IDirect3DTexture9* white = NULL;
    m_pDevice->CreateTexture(32, 32, 1,
                            D3DUSAGE_DYNAMIC, D3DFMT_L8,
                            D3DPOOL_DEFAULT, &white, NULL);
    D3DLOCKED_RECT sRect;
    white->LockRect(0, &sRect, NULL, NULL);
    memset((BYTE*)sRect.pBits, 255, 32 * 32);
    white->UnlockRect(0);

    m_pDevice->BeginScene();

    //Render terrain here!
    //Remember to not Cull patches and objects etc
    //Use the "white" texture we created to light the terrain
    //....
```

```
        m_pDevice->EndScene();

        //Release the white-lightmap
        white->Release();

        //Reset render target to back buffer
        m_pDevice->SetRenderTarget(0, backSurface);

        //Release surfaces
        landScapeSurface->Release();
        backSurface->Release();
    }
```

We create a completely white lightmap with 32×32 pixels instead of the fog-of-war texture we normally use when we render the terrain. If all went well, your m_pLandScape texture should now hold an image that looks like the one in Figure 11.3.

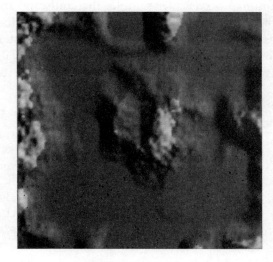

FIGURE 11.3 The finished landscape texture.

CREATING THE MINIMAP TEXTURE

Next we will combine the landscape texture, the fog-of-war texture, and the unit representation, all in one step to form the final minimap texture. The minimap texture is also a render target texture that we store in the APPLICATION class. We've also added the `UpdateMiniMap()` function to our `APPLICATION` class to update our minimap. Remember that this only needs to be done whenever a unit changes map location. The `UpdateMiniMap()` function first sets the minimap texture as the render target and then uses a simple pixelshader (`minimap.ps`) to combine the landscape and fog-of-war textures:

```
sampler landScape;
sampler FogOfWar;

float4 Main(float2 UV : TEXCOORD0) : COLOR
{
    float4 c0 = tex2D(landScape, UV);
    float4 c1 = tex2D(FogOfWar, UV);
    float4 c2 = c0 * c1;

    return float4(c2.rgb, 1.0f);
}
```

The minimap pixelshader samples the landscape and the fog-of-war texture and multiples them. Notice that we force the alpha value of the resulting pixel to 1.0f. This is important because we will use the sprite interface to draw the finished minimap to the screen. If we have pixels with an alpha value of less than 1.0f, these will become transparent. Here's the actual `APPLICATION::UpdateMiniMap()` function:

```
void APPLICATION::UpdateMiniMap()
{
    //Retrieve the surface of the back buffer
    IDirect3DSurface9 *backSurface = NULL;
    m_pDevice->GetRenderTarget(0, &backSurface);

    //Get and set surface of the FogOfWarTexture
    IDirect3DSurface9 *minimapSurface = NULL;
    m_pMiniMap->GetSurfaceLevel(0, &minimapSurface);
    m_pDevice->SetRenderTarget(0, minimapSurface);

    m_pDevice->Clear(0, NULL,
                    D3DCLEAR_TARGET | D3DCLEAR_ZBUFFER,
                    0x00000000, 1.0f, 0);

    m_pDevice->BeginScene();
```

```
//Set Textures
m_pDevice->SetTexture(0, m_terrain.m_pLandScape);
m_pDevice->SetTexture(1, m_terrain.m_pFogOfWarTexture);

//Draw to the minimap texture
m_pSprite->Begin(0);
m_miniMapShader.Begin();
m_pSprite->Draw(m_terrain.m_pLandScape, NULL, NULL,
                &D3DXVECTOR3(0.0f, 0.0f, 0.0f),
                0xffffffff);
m_pSprite->End();
m_miniMapShader.End();

m_pDevice->EndScene();

//To be continued...
```

Just like before, we use the sprite interface to cover the entire render target. This part of the UpdateMiniMap() function sets the minimap texture as the render target, starts the minimap pixelshader, and combines the landscape with the fog-of-war texture. We will now attempt to draw the representation of our units onto the same minimap texture, as well:

```
//Draw units and buildings in the player team color
for(int p=0;p<m_players.size();p++)
{
    std::vector<D3DRECT> rects;

    //Get rectangles in "Minimap Space"
    for(int m=0;m<m_players[p]->m_mapObjects.size();m++)
    if(!m_players[p]->m_mapObjects[m]->m_isBuilding)
    {
        INTPOINT mappos =
                   players[p]->m_mapObjects[m]->m_mappos;

        //Only add units standing on visible tiles
        if(m_terrain.m_pVisibleTiles[mappos.x +
                              mappos.y *
                              m_terrain.m_size.x])
        {
            INTPOINT pos(256.0f *
                     (mappos.x/(float)m_terrain.m_size.x),
                     256.0f *
                     (mappos.y/(float)m_terrain.m_size.y));
```

```
                    rects.push_back(SetRect(pos.x - 1, pos.y - 1,
                                            pos.x + 2, pos.y + 2));
                }
            }
            else
            {
                //Draw buildings in the same way
            }

            //Clear rectangles using the team color
            if(!rects.empty())
            {
                D3DXCOLOR c;
                c = D3DCOLOR_XRGB(
                        (int)(m_players[p]->m_teamColor.x * 255),
                        (int)(m_players[p]->m_teamColor.y * 255),
                        (int)(m_players[p]->m_teamColor.z * 255));

                Device->Clear(rects.size(), &rects[0],
                            D3DCLEAR_TARGET | D3DCLEAR_ZBUFFER,
                            c, 1.0f, 0);
            }
        }

    //Reset render target to back buffer
    m_pDevice->SetRenderTarget(0, backSurface);

    //Release surfaces
    backSurface->Release();
    minimapSurface->Release();
```

We draw the minimap unit representation by creating one or more rectangles for each unit and building. Then we use the Clear() function to clear the areas defined by these rectangles to a certain team color. We loop through all the players, and then loop through all the units of that player. We only consider those units that are standing on a visible tile to be represented in the minimap. Then we add that unit rectangle to the vector of rectangles, using the SetRect() helper function:

```
D3DRECT SetRect(long x1, long y1, long x2, long y2)
{
    D3DRECT r;
    r.x1 = x1;
    r.y1 = y1;
```

```
        r.x2 = x2;
        r.y2 = y2;
        return r;
}
```

Note that we do the buildings in a slightly different way. We add one rectangle for each visited tile in the building map rectangle, just like we did with the unit. When all is done in the `UpdateMiniMap()` function, we reset the render target and release the surfaces. Okay, we now have a function so that we can update the minimap every time a unit changes map location. Next we need to have a look at the function that will be used to render the minimap.

RENDERING THE MINIMAP

Unlike the `UpdateMiniMap()` function, we need to render the minimap to the screen every frame. For this we have created the `RenderMiniMap()` function in the `APPLICATION` class. In this function, we will also handle things like minimap camera movement and camera frustum representation. This function takes a destination rectangle as a parameter (where the minimap will be rendered), which makes it easy to move or animate the minimap during gameplay. The rendering part of this function is very easy; we simply use the sprite interface to scale and render the minimap to the destination rectangle, like this:

```
void APPLICATION::RenderMiniMap(RECT dest)
{
    float width = dest.right - dest.left;
    float height = dest.bottom - dest.top;

    D3DXVECTOR2 scale = D3DXVECTOR2(width / 256.0f,
                                    height / 256.0f);
    D3DXMATRIX sca;
    D3DXMatrixScaling(&sca, scale.x, scale.y, 1.0f);
    m_pSprite->SetTransform(&sca);

    m_pSprite->Begin(0);
    m_pSprite->Draw(m_pMiniMap, NULL, NULL,
                    &D3DXVECTOR3(dest.left / scale.x,
                                 dest.top / scale.y, 0.0f),
                    0xffffffff);

    m_pSprite->End();
```

```
D3DXMatrixIdentity(&sca);
m_pSprite->SetTransform(&sca);

//To be continued...
```

We calculate the width and height of the minimap destination rectangle and divide these values by 256 (i.e., the size of the minimap texture) to get the scale. Then we draw the minimap texture using the scale so that it fits the destination rectangle perfectly.

Giving Orders with the Minimap

The minimap can also be used to give orders to units or to move the camera to a certain location on the map. To do this, we need to convert a location on the minimap to a location in the "real" world—that is, the terrain. The following piece of code moves the camera to a certain location after the user has left-clicked somewhere in the minimap destination rectangle:

```
//Move camera using minimap
if(mouse.PressInRect(dest))
{
    float width = dest.right - dest.left;
    float height = dest.bottom - dest.top;

    int x = ((mouse.x - dest.left) / width) *
            m_terrain.m_size.x;
    int y = ((mouse.y - dest.top) / height) *
            m_terrain.m_size.y;

    m_camera.m_focus = m_terrain.GetWorldPos(INTPOINT(x, y));
}
```

Here we calculate the corresponding *x*- and *y*-coordinate after the user has clicked somewhere in the minimap destination rectangle, and move the camera focus to that location. Of course, this same method can also be used to order units to a certain location.

Drawing the View Frustum in the Minimap

The last thing we want to do in our minimap is to display what part of the terrain the camera is looking at. We do this calculation in the APPLICATION::RenderMiniMap() function each frame. We calculate four frustum rays—from the eye of the camera to each of the view frustum corners of in the far plane. After we have calculated these rays, we see where they intersect with the ground plane. Then we use these intersection points to draw the area the camera is looking at in the minimap, as shown in Figure 11.4:

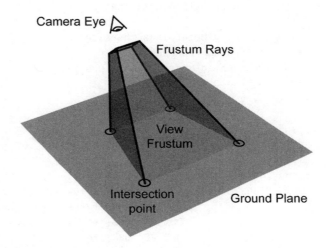

FIGURE 11.4   Calculating the visible area of the terrain.

We calculate the four frustum rays in exactly the same way we calculated the mouse ray (see Chapter 5). Then we use the D3DXPlaneIntersectLine() D3DX library function to extract the four intersection points with the ground plane (marked with a circle in Figure 11.4). These intersection points are all coordinates in world space that we need to convert to "minimap" space before we can use them. Then we simply draw lines between the four corners in minimap space to visualize the visible area. The D3DXPlaneIntersectLine() function is defined as follows:

```
D3DXVECTOR3 *D3DXPlaneIntersectLine(
    D3DXVECTOR3 *pOut,
    CONST D3DXPLANE *pP,
    CONST D3DXVECTOR3 *pV1,
    CONST D3DXVECTOR3 *pV2
);
```

This function takes a plane (pP) and two points that describe a line (pV1 and pV2). The result is returned using the pOut pointer. Should the line and the plane be parallel to each other, then the pOut variable will be NULL. The following code is an excerpt from the RenderMiniMap() function, showing how we render the view frustum representation in the minimap:

```
//Calculate camera frustum viewpoints
D3DXMATRIX view, proj, viewInverse;

view = m_camera.GetViewMatrix();
proj = m_camera.GetProjectionMatrix();

//fov_x & fov_y Determines the size
//of the frustum representation
float screenRatio = proj(0,0) / proj(1,1);
float fov_x = 0.4f;
float fov_y = fov_x * screenRatio;

//Initialize the four rays
D3DXVECTOR3 org = D3DXVECTOR3(0.0f, 0.0f, 0.0f);    //Origin

//Four different directions
D3DXVECTOR3 dir[4] = {D3DXVECTOR3(-fov_x,  fov_y, 1.0f),
                      D3DXVECTOR3( fov_x,  fov_y, 1.0f),
                      D3DXVECTOR3( fov_x, -fov_y, 1.0f),
                      D3DXVECTOR3(-fov_x, -fov_y, 1.0f)};

//Our resulting minimap coordinates
D3DXVECTOR2 points[5];

//View matrix inverse
D3DXMatrixInverse(&viewInverse, 0, &view);
D3DXVec3TransformCoord(&org, &org, &viewInverse);

//Ground plane
D3DXPLANE plane;
D3DXPlaneFromPointNormal(&plane,
                        &D3DXVECTOR3(0.0f, 0.0f, 0.0f),
                        &D3DXVECTOR3(0.0f, 1.0f, 0.0f));

bool ok = true;

//check where each ray intersects with the ground plane
for(int i=0;i<4 && ok;i++)
{
    //Transform ray direction
    D3DXVec3TransformNormal(&dir[i], &dir[i], &viewInverse);
    D3DXVec3Normalize(&dir[i], &dir[i]);
    dir[i] *= 1000.0f;
```

```
                //Find intersection point
                D3DXVECTOR3 hit;
                if(D3DXPlaneIntersectLine(&hit, &plane, &org, &dir[i])
                   == NULL)
                    ok = false;

                //Check that intersection point is on the positive
                //side of the near plane
                D3DXPLANE n = m_camera.m_frustum[4];
                float distance = n.a * hit.x +
                                 n.b * hit.y +
                                 n.c * hit.z + n.d;
                if(distance < 0.0f)ok = false;

                //Convert the intersection points to minimap coordinates
                if(ok)
                {
                    points[i].x = (hit.x / (float)m_terrain.m_size.x) *
                                  width;
                    points[i].y = (-hit.z / (float)m_terrain.m_size.y) *
                                  height;
                }
        }

        //Set the end point to equal the starting point
        points[4] = points[0];

        //Set viewport to destination rectangle only...
        D3DVIEWPORT9 v1, v2;

        v1.X = dest.left;
        v1.Y = dest.top;
        v1.Width = width;
        v1.Height = height;
        v1.MinZ = 0.0f;
        v1.MaxZ = 1.0f;

        m_pDevice->GetViewport(&v2);
        m_pDevice->SetViewport(&v1);

        //Draw camera frustum representation in the minimap
        if(ok)
        {
```

```
            m_pLine->SetWidth(1.0f);
            m_pLine->SetAntialias(true);
            m_pLine->Begin();
            m_pLine->Draw(&points[0], 5, 0x44ffffff);
            m_pLine->End();
        }

        //Reset viewport
        m_pDevice->SetViewport(&v2);
```

We create four rays describing our view frustum and transform them to world space just like we did when we calculated the mouse ray. Then we create the ground plane using the point (0, 0, 0) and the normal (0, 1, 0) and see where these four rays intersect with it using the D3DXPlaneIntersectLine() function. We also check that the lines aren't parallel with the ground plane or that the intersection points are behind the near plane (i.e., the camera is looking up and not down toward the ground). In either case, we don't render the frustum representation in the minimap. After that, we convert the intersection points from world coordinates to minimap coordinates. The intersection points can be outside the destination rectangle. So to make sure that we don't draw outside this rectangle, we set the active viewport to the minimap rectangle before drawing the lines. That's it. We clean up by resetting the viewport and so forth. Your minimap should now look something like the one in Figure 11.5.

FIGURE 11.5 A screenshot of the minimap view frustum representation.

Example 11.1

ON THE CD

Have good look at Example 11.1 on the CD-ROM for the minimap implementation.

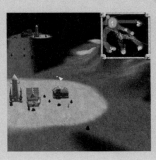

SUMMARY

In this chapter, we implemented the important minimap component for our real-time strategy game. First we created an overview texture of the terrain, which we called the landscape texture. Then we blended this with the existing fog-of-war texture to create our final minimap texture. On top of the minimap texture, we also drew a unit/building representation, as well as a view frustum representation. In Chapter 12, we will have a look at some special effects that can be very useful in a real-time strategy game.

EXERCISES

- Order units to a specific location on the terrain using the minimap.
- You could draw the unit representation using the sightMesh we created to render the m_pVisibleTexture with instead of using the Clear() function. Either fill the entire quad with the team color or map a gradient texture to it.

12 | Effects

This chapter is dedicated to making our real-time strategy game look prettier by implementing some common visual effects. Most of these effects can be used in any game type and not just real-time strategy games. We will have a look at creating billboards, particles systems, skyboxes, environment maps, lens flares, and finally a dynamic fire effect. But first we'll create a common interface for all these effects to make it simple to add, update, and remove different effects.

THE EFFECT CLASS

Different effects in games are usually hard-coded into a set of effect classes, so why do we need a common interface for all these effects? Well, imagine that you have implemented three effects in separate classes: EFFECT1, EFFECT2, and EFFECT3. To update and render these effects, you would have to write something like this:

```
//Create effect objects
EFFECT1 e1(...);
EFFECT2 e2(...);
EFFECT3 e3(...);

//Update effects
e1.Update();
e2.Update();
e3.Update();

//Render effects
e1.Render();
e2.Render();
e3.Render();

//And so on...
```

Now, imagine that you have 50 different effects hard-coded in your game. Without a common interface, you have to deal with each effect class separately. Therefore, we'll implement the EFFECT class to provide a common interface that all our specific effects will inherit from, as shown in Figure 12.1.

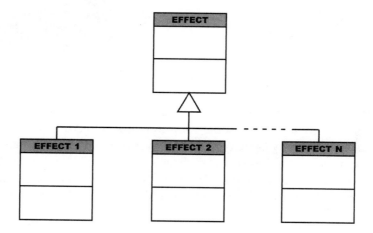

FIGURE 12.1   The EFFECT class interface.

In code, our EFFECT class is defined as follows:

```
class EFFECT
{
```

```
public:
    EFFECT(IDirect3DDevice9 *Dev);
    ~EFFECT();
    virtual void Update(float timeDelta) = 0;
    virtual void Render() = 0;
    virtual bool isDead() = 0;

    void PreRender();    //Set renderstates etc
    void PostRender();   //Restore renderstates etc

    //Common variables for all effects
    IDirect3DDevice9 *m_pDevice;
    float m_time;
    D3DXVECTOR4 m_color;
};
```

The effect class has three virtual functions: Update(), Render(), and isDead(). These must be implemented by any specific effect class inheriting from our EFFECT interface. We also have one function called PreRender() to set up render states, shaders, and so forth before rendering an effect, and one function called PostRender() to restore these states afterward. Generally, when we render effects, we want some form of alpha-blending done, but more on this later. Some effects have a limited life span, and after they are done, we want to remove them from our effect pool. The isDead() function tells the application whether a certain effect has finished and can be removed or not. Now we can add, update, and remove any type of effect, like this excerpt from the APPLICATION class:

```
//Effect pool
std::vector<EFFECT*> effects;

//Add Effects like this
effects.push_back(new SOME_EFFECT(Device, ...));
effects.push_back(new SOME_OTHER_EFFECT(Device, ...));


//Update all effects each frame like this
std::vector<EFFECT*>::iterator i;
for(i=effects.begin();i != effects.end();)
{
    if((*i)->isDead())
    {
        //Remove dead effects
        delete (*i);
```

```
                    effects.erase(i);
            }
            else
            {
                //Update effect
                (*i)->Update(deltaTime);
                i++;
            }
        }

        //Render all effects like this
        for(int i=0;i<effects.size();i++)
            if(effects[i] != NULL)
                effects[i]->Render();
```

This code is totally dynamic. You can implement a new effect that inherits from the EFFECT class and add it to the pool without changing anything else. The only thing you have to do is to implement the virtual functions declared in the EFFECT class. So now that we have our effect framework in place, let's take a look at one of the most common tools used for rendering effects.

BILLBOARDS

Billboards are one of the oldest ways to "fake" complex 3D objects. It works by having a texture-mapped quad that is always rotated to face the camera. Usually, some parts of the texture are transparent so that the player can't see the quad shape. Some of the early first-person shooter games, like *Wolfenstein 3D* or *Doom,* used this technique to draw animated sprites, like enemies. Figure 12.2 shows an example of a billboard texture.

This texture could then be used to draw skeletons in a 3D scene, as shown in Figure 12.3.

Notice in the top view of Figure 12.3 how all billboards are rotated to face the camera. So no matter how the player moves around in the 3D scene, he will never be able to see the back side of the skeletons.

As usual when we have shared resources, we create them globally to save memory. We create the billboard mesh and any effect textures we will need in the LoadEffectResources() function. We create the billboard mesh exactly like we created the sightMesh in Chapter 10. The only difference is that we also include normals in the vertex declaration. When created, the billboard mesh is a quad in the *xz*-plane with normals pointing straight up in the *y*-direction. We need the normals

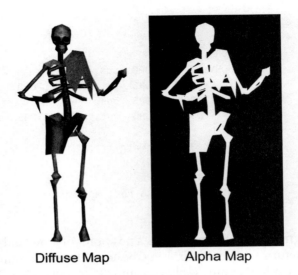

Diffuse Map   Alpha Map

FIGURE 12.2   An example of a billboard texture.

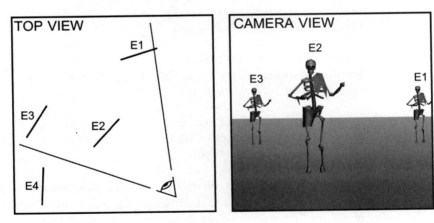

FIGURE 12.3   Drawing billboards.

later when we do some more-advanced shader effects. Obviously, we don't want to have the billboard in the *xz*-plane during rendering, so we need an easy way of creating a world matrix to transform the billboard mesh. For this we create the TRANSFORM structure, which works just like the MESHINSTANCE class, but without the mesh-pointer:

```
struct TRANSFORM
{
    TRANSFORM();
    TRANSFORM(D3DXVECTOR3 _pos,
              D3DXVECTOR3 _rot, D3DXVECTOR3 _sca);
    void Init(D3DXVECTOR3 _pos,
              D3DXVECTOR3 _rot, D3DXVECTOR3 _sca);

    D3DXMATRIX GetWorldMatrix();

    //Variables
    D3DXVECTOR3 m_pos, m_rot, m_sca;
};
```

The TRANSFORM structure keeps a position, rotation, and scale vector, and can be used to return a world matrix using the GetWorldMatrix() function. The WorldMatrix is calculated in the same way as in our MESHINSTANCE class. Now we can render the billboard mesh using different world transformations, like this:

```
//Create 2 different transformation objects
TRANSFORM t1(pos1, rot1, sca1);
TRANSFORM t2(pos2, rot2, sca2);

//Render the first billboard
Device->SetTransform(D3DTS_WORLD, &t1.GetWorldMatrix());
billboardMesh->DrawSubset(0);

//Render the second billboard
Device->SetTransform(D3DTS_WORLD, &t2.GetWorldMatrix());
billboardMesh->DrawSubset(0);
```

Okay, now we have a framework to store and maintain our effects, and we also have a billboard tool with which to draw something. So let us now take a look at implementing our first specific effect.

MAGIC SPELLS

Magic spells, explosions, novas, and many other effects can be created by using alpha-blended quads like the ones covered in the previous section. In this section, we will go through the implementation of a magic spell effect. This should hopefully provide enough groundwork for you to implement similar effects on your own. The purpose of the magic spell effect is to show to the user that something magical is indeed happening. For this specific effect, we will use the two alpha-blended textures shown in Figure 12.4.

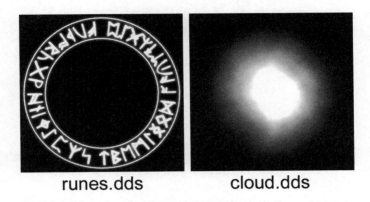

runes.dds   cloud.dds

FIGURE 12.4 The textures used in the magic spell effect.

Both textures are grayscale, alpha-blended DDS files. The reason we keep these images grayscale is that we will use a vertex (`effect.vs`) and pixelshader (`effect.ps`) to add our own color dynamically during runtime. Here's the effect vertexshader we will use for this:

```
uniform extern float4x4 matW;
uniform extern float4x4 matVP;
uniform extern float4 vertexColor;

struct VS_INPUT
{
    float4 position : POSITIONO;
    float2 uv : TEXCOORDO;
};

struct VS_OUTPUT
{
    float4 position : POSITIONO;
    float4 color : COLORO;
    float2 uv : TEXCOORDO;
};
```

```
VS_OUTPUT Main(VS_INPUT input)
{
    VS_OUTPUT output = (VS_OUTPUT)0;

    //Transform position
    float4 temp = mul(input.position, matW);
    output.position = mul(temp, matVP);

    //Set UV coordinates
    output.uv = input.uv;

    //Set vertex color
    output.color = vertexColor;

    return output;
}
```

As you can see, we supply an extern vertex color that we apply to all vertices in an object before we send the information on to the pixelshader. This vertexshader is used mainly for rendering our texture-mapped billboards. Next we have our rather short and simple effect pixelshader:

```
sampler effectTexture;

float4 Main(float4 color : COLOR0,
            float2 UV : TEXCOORD0) : COLOR
{
    float4 c0 = tex2D(effectTexture, UV);
    return c0 * color;
}
```

We sample a pixel from the active texture and multiply it by the interpolated vertex color before we return the result. We could also have done this in the fixed function pipeline, of course, but then we would first have had to add a vertex color in our billboard vertex declaration. Second, we would have to access the vertex buffer of the billboard mesh and change it manually every time we want to change the effect color. Therefore, it is much simpler to assign the vertex color using a vertexshader, instead.

Remember that starting in DirectX 10, the direct pipeline will be completely abolished, and this will all be done using shaders. So we might as well get used to it.

We want the spell effect to create a colored glow around the unit that is the target of the spell as well as a rotating set of runes emphasizing the fact that this is, in fact, a magic spell. The set of rotating runes is implemented as a simple texture-mapped billboard facing in the positive *y*-direction and rotates around the *y*-axis. The glow on the other hand is a little bit trickier, since it has to be able to be viewed from any direction. We could implement this as a billboard that is always facing the camera, but a nicer glow effect can be produced by placing several billboards, as shown in Figure 12.5.

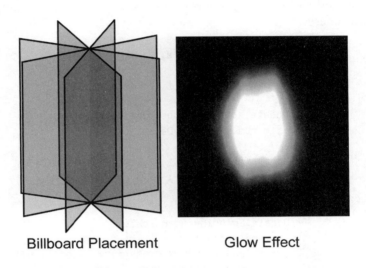

Billboard Placement   Glow Effect

FIGURE 12.5 Billboard placement and resulting glow effect.

By placing multiple billboards all facing in different directions and then rendering them with additive blending, we get the glow effect showed in Figure 12.5. Here is the EFFECT_SPELL class that implements the EFFECT interface, and that we can use to render a magic spell effect:

```
class EFFECT_SPELL : public EFFECT
{
    public:
        EFFECT_SPELL(IDirect3DDevice9 *Dev, D3DXVECTOR3 _pos);
        void Update(float timeDelta);
        void Render();
        bool isDead();
```

```
        private:
            TRANSFORM m_t1;            //Rune billboard transform
            TRANSFORM m_c[10];         //Glow billboard transforms
    };
```

No surprises here. As you can see, this class uses the EFFECT interface by implementing the Update(), Render(), and isDead() functions. We also store a number of different transforms that will be used to transform the billboard mesh during the rendering of the effect. These are set in the constructor along with the color of the effect and so forth. The Update() function can be used to animate the effect, as shown here:

```
void EFFECT_SPELL::Update(float timeDelta)
{
    m_time += timeDelta;

    //Update spinning runes...
    m_t1.m_rot.y += timeDelta;

    //Update glow
    for(int i=0;i<10;i++)
        m_c[i].m_rot.y -= timeDelta;

    //Update Spinning quad scale
    if(m_time < 1.5f)
        m_t1.sca += D3DXVECTOR3(1.0f, 1.0f, 1.0f) *
                    timeDelta * 4.0f;
    if(m_time > 4.5f)
        m_t1.sca -= D3DXVECTOR3(1.0f, 1.0f, 1.0f) *
                    timeDelta * 4.0f;

    //Calculate alpha
    m_color.w = m_t1.m_sca.x / 6.0f;
}
```

Then all we need to do is call the EFFECT_SPELL::Render() function to render the magic spell:

```
void EFFECT_SPELL::Render()
{
    PreRender();      //Sets up the blend modes etc...
```

```
//Spinning quad
m_pDevice->SetTexture(0, runesTexture);
effectVertexShader.SetMatrix(effectMatW,
                             t1.GetWorldMatrix());
billboardMesh->DrawSubset(0);

//Glow
m_pDevice->SetTexture(0, cloudTexture);
for(int i=0;i<10;i++)
{
    effectVertexShader.SetMatrix(effectMatW,
                                 c[i].GetWorldMatrix());
    billboardMesh->DrawSubset(0);
}

PostRender();
}
```

The EFFECT::PreRender() function sets up the blending modes, and the vertexshaders and pixelshaders before rendering the actual effect. Here's an excerpt from the PreRender() function that shows how to set the most important render states:

```
//Alpha blending On
m_pDevice->SetRenderState(D3DRS_ALPHABLENDENABLE, true);

//Additive Alpha Blending
m_pDevice->SetRenderState(D3DRS_SRCBLEND, D3DBLEND_SRCALPHA);
m_pDevice->SetRenderState(D3DRS_DESTBLEND, D3DBLEND_ONE );

//No culling
m_pDevice->SetRenderState(D3DRS_CULLMODE, D3DCULL_NONE);

//Don't write to the Z-buffer
m_pDevice->SetRenderState(D3DRS_ZWRITEENABLE, false);
```

ON THE CD

This function also sets the matrices and other variables of the effect vertexshader. For the full code, please refer to Example 12.1 on the companion CD-ROM. Finally, we set the isDead() function to return true when the runes billboard has disappeared (check the Update() function to see how the effect is animated):

```
bool EFFECT_SPELL::isDead()
{
```

```
        //return true if the spinning runes aren't visible
        return t1.sca.x < 0.0f;
    }
```

TIP

The meaning of a spell can easily be changed by simply changing the color of the effect. For instance, red usually indicates an evil spell, like a "curse," while a light blue color could be used to visualize a good spell, like "heal." Play around with colors, sizes, and animations, and you'll see that with just a few simple textures, you can produce hundreds of different spell effects.

Example 12.1

ON THE CD

Example 12.1 on the CD-ROM shows the result of the EFFECT_SPELL class. In this example, a random color is used each time you cast the spell. However in your game, you will most likely pick a certain color to represent whatever the spell does.

THE FIREBALL EFFECT

The effect we will cover now is not too different from the previous magic spell effect. Remember how in Chapter 2 we wanted our magician to be a medium-range unit? Well, the plan is to have the magician throw a fireball from his staff at his enemies. The rendering of the actual fireball will be done just as in the previous effect, with a couple of alpha-mapped billboards. However, the effect itself will be quite different. The effect has three phases, as shown in Figure 12.6.

Phase 1: The fireball is bound to the staff of the magician.

Phase 2: The fireball is flying in an arc through the air toward its target.

Phase 3: The fireball has hit the target, and the fireball explodes and fades out.

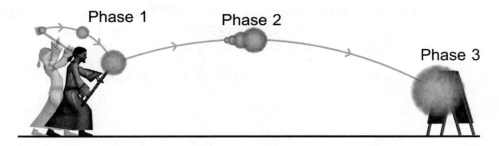

FIGURE 12.6   The different phases of the fireball effect.

To have the fireball follow staff we must first acquire the staff bone from the skinned mesh (see Chapter 7, Example 7.4). We then extract the combined transformation matrix of the staff bone at each frame. From this transformation matrix, we extract the staff position that we can use to transform the fireball during Phase 1. During Phase 2, we simply perform a linear interpolation between the origin of the staff and the target of the fireball. We also add an arc to make the fireball look more like it was being thrown. Note also how we have added a trail of smaller fireballs to the fireball to make it seem less like just a round ball. Finally, the fireball strikes the target, explodes, and then fades out. This also marks the end of the effect, and it is removed from the effect pool. We define the EFFECT_FIREBALL class as follows:

```
class EFFECT_FIREBALL : public EFFECT
{
    public:
        EFFECT_FIREBALL(IDirect3DDevice9 *Dev,
                        BONE * _src, D3DXVECTOR3 _dest);
        void Update(float timeDelta);
        void Render();
        bool isDead();
        D3DXVECTOR3 GetPosition(float p);

    private:
        BONE *m_pSrcBone;       //Bone to follow during Phase 1
        float m_speed;          //Speed of fireball
        float m_length;         //Distance to target
        float m_prc;            //Percentage of path complete
        TRANSFORM m_t1;         //fireball transformation

        D3DXVECTOR3 m_origin, m_dest;
};
```

The GetPosition() function is used to calculate the position of the fireball during Phase 2 (including the arc). During the rendering phase, we use this function to calculate the position of the actual fireball as well as the trail:

```
D3DXVECTOR3 EFFECT_FIREBALL::GetPosition(float p)
{
    if(p < 0.0f)p = 0.0f;
    if(p > 1.0f)p = 1.0f;

    //Linear Interpolation between origin and dest
    D3DXVECTOR3 pos = m_origin * (1.0f - p) + m_dest * p;

    //Add Arc
    pos.y += sin(p * D3DX_PI) * 3.0f;

    return pos;
}
```

Next let's have a look at the EFFECT_FIREBALL::Update() function, where all the animation is done:

```
void EFFECT_FIREBALL::Update(float timeDelta)
{
    m_t1.m_rot += D3DXVECTOR3(0.5f, 0.5f, 0.5f) * timeDelta;

    //Follow staff (Phase 1)
    if(m_time < 1.0f && m_pSrcBone != NULL)
    {
        m_time += timeDelta;
        D3DXMATRIX mat =
            m_pSrcBone->CombinedTransformationMatrix;

        //Extract position from staff bone
        m_t1.m_pos =
            D3DXVECTOR3(mat(3,0), mat(3, 1), mat(3, 2));

        //the fireball grows in size during Phase 1
        m_t1.m_sca = D3DXVECTOR3(1.5f, 1.5f, 1.5f) * m_time;

        //Fade in fireball (w = alpha)
        m_color.w = m_time;
```

```
            if(m_time > 1.0f)
            {
                m_color.w = m_time * 0.5f;
                m_origin = m_t1.m_pos;
                m_length = D3DXVec3Length(&(m_origin - m_dest));
            }
        }
        else if(m_prc < 1.0f)     //Fly towards target (Phase 2)
        {
            m_prc += (m_speed * timeDelta) / m_length;
            m_t1.m_pos = GetPosition(m_prc);
        }
        else        //Explode      (Phase 3)
        {
            m_prc += (m_speed * timeDelta) / m_length;
            m_t1.m_sca += D3DXVECTOR3(5.0f, 5.0f, 5.0f) *
                            timeDelta;
            m_color.w -= timeDelta * 0.5f;
        }
    }
```

Apart from the animation of this effect, it is otherwise quite similar to the previous effect. For the full rendering code, see Example 12.2.

The tricky thing with this sort of effect is, of course, to get the timing of the skinned mesh animation right, so that it matches the effect. It takes some tweaking to get the result to look good.

Example 12.2

Example 12.2 on the CD-ROM implements the EFFECT_FIREBALL class in full.

PARTICLE SYSTEMS

Now we will take a look at another tool often used to create special effects in games—particle systems. Particle systems can be used for many things. Some of the most common effects modeled with particle systems are smoke, fire, blood, sparks, rain, and snow. Whereas in the previous effects we used between 10 and 30 billboards, we now use hundreds or thousands of primitives. A particle system is a collection of billboards that follow a set of rules, such as gravity. We will make use of the point sprite functionality in DirectX, which allows us to define a particle using only one vertex. Older systems manually had to calculate the four corners of a particle and transform it to face the camera. But before we start talking about particle systems, let's first have a look at the smallest component: the particle.

A particle is rendered just like a rectangular billboard, always facing the camera; we can assign a texture to a particle, a vertex color, and so on. But more important, the particle has a number of attributes that control how it is animated. Here's a list of some common particle attributes:

Position: The current particle position.
Velocity: The velocity (and direction) of the particle.
Acceleration: The acceleration of the particle; this could be gravity, wind, etc.
Color: The color of the particle.
Size: The individual size of the particle.
Time to Live: How long the particle will live.
Dead: Is the particle dead or not?

These are just some of the most common attributes. Most likely you will need to add your own, as well. The position is updated each frame according to the velocity vector, which in turn is updated by the acceleration vector. We've created the PARTICLE structure to hold the necessary information for each particle, like this:

```
struct PARTICLE
{
    D3DXVECTOR3 position, velocity, acceleration;
    float time_to_live;
    D3DXCOLOR color;
    bool dead;
};
```

The particle structure will be used by our particle system class to hold any particles belonging to that system. However, when it's time to render the particles, it doesn't make sense to render things like velocity or time_to_live. When we render particles, we must declare a particle vertex type that we can fill a vertex buffer with. For that purpose, we have the PARTICLE_VERTEX structure:

```
struct PARTICLE_VERTEX
{
    D3DXVECTOR3 position;
    D3DCOLOR color;
    static const DWORD FVF;
};

const DWORD PARTICLE_VERTEX::FVF =
        D3DFVF_XYZ | D3DFVF_DIFFUSE;
```

For each frame, we have to copy the necessary information (position and color) from our PARTICLE objects to a vertex buffer containing PARTICLE_VERTEX objects, which we then can render.

All particles are usually controlled by a particle system class. The particle system controls how particles are spawned, updated, rendered, and killed. Because we will implement a couple different particle systems throughout this project, it makes sense once again to create a particle system base class. Then we will let all specific particle systems like rain, sparks, and smoke etc. inherit from this class. This base class should also implement the EFFECT interface so that we can maintain any particle systems just like we do with our other effects. We name our base particle system class PARTICLE_SYSTEM and let it inherit from the EFFECT class, like this:

```
class PARTICLE_SYSTEM : public EFFECT
{
    public:
        PARTICLE_SYSTEM(IDirect3DDevice9 *Dev);
        ~PARTICLE_SYSTEM();
        void Update(float timeDelta);
        void Render();
        bool isDead();

        void RenderBatch(int start, int batchSize);
        void PreRender();
        void PostRender();
```

```
//Particle variables
std::vector<PARTICLE*> m_particles;
IDirect3DTexture9* m_pTexture;
DWORD m_blendMode;
float m_particleSize;
};
```

We implement the virtual functions Update(), Render(), and isDead(), which the EFFECT interface requires. We also overload the PreRender() and PostRender() functions, since we will use quite different render states when rendering particles than when we render billboards. Later, when we cover the rendering of our particles, we will delve into the purpose and implementation of the RenderBatch() function in more detail. Our particle system also has a pointer to a texture that will be mapped on all particles in the particle system. The m_blendMode variable can be used to specify if we want additive or normal alpha-blending, and the m_particleSize variable controls the overall size of the particles. The class overview for our specific particle systems now looks something like Figure 12.7.

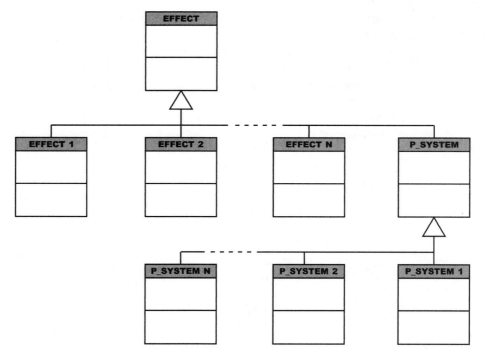

FIGURE 12.7 The effect structure overview.

As you can see, any specific particle system, like smoke or rain, inherits from the particle system base class, which in turn inherits from the EFFECT class. This means that it is okay to add a specific particle system into the effect pool, as well. The particle systems will then be maintained just like any other effect.

Most particle system classes encapsulate the vertex buffer used to render the actual particles. But because we want many different and usually small particle systems active at the same time, it is more efficient to store the particle vertex buffer as a shared resource, instead. The LoadParticleResources() function loads and creates all the resources needed by any particle system:

```
//Size of the buffer
int numParticles = 2048;

//The actual particle buffer
IDirect3DVertexBuffer9* particleBuffer = NULL;

//Render offset
DWORD bufferOffset = 0;

void LoadParticleResources(IDirect3DDevice9 *Dev)
{
    Dev->CreateVertexBuffer(numParticles *
                            sizeof(PARTICLE_VERTEX),
                            D3DUSAGE_DYNAMIC | D3DUSAGE_POINTS |
                            D3DUSAGE_WRITEONLY,
                            PARTICLE_VERTEX::FVF,
                            D3DPOOL_DEFAULT,
                            &particleBuffer, NULL);

    //Load all particle textures needed here as well...
}
```

The size of the particle vertex buffer is determined by the numParticles variable. This doesn't mean that we are limited to rendering only 2,048 particles per system, even if the vertex buffer can't hold more. This is because we will render the particles in batches. It is more efficient to render a large particle system in chunks rather than all at once (more on this later). This is because the CPU and the graphics card will then work in parallel, rather than one waiting for the other. Note also how we specify the usage parameter as D3DUSAGE_POINTS. This means that the vertex buffer will hold point sprites.

Since the rendering of particles is done in the same way in almost all particle systems, we implement the Render() function in the particle system base class rather than in all the specific particle system classes. Here's the implementation of the PARTICLE_SYSTEM::Render() function:

```
void PARTICLE_SYSTEM::Render()
{
    PreRender();

    //Set the texture of the particles
    m_pDevice->SetTexture(0, m_pTexture);

    //Set vertex format and source stream
    m_pDevice->SetFVF(PARTICLE_VERTEX::FVF);
    m_pDevice->SetStreamSource(0, particleBuffer, 0,
                        sizeof(PARTICLE_VERTEX));

    //Specify the batchSize and start rendering the batches
    int batchSize = 512;
    for(int i=0;i<m_particles.size();i+=batchSize)
        RenderBatch(i, batchSize);

    PostRender();
}
```

This function calls the PreRender() function that sets up all the render states for rendering particles. It also sets the texture, vertex format, and the source stream. Then we specify a batch size and call the RenderBatch() function for each batch. It is in the RenderBatch() function that all the heavy work is done:

```
void PARTICLE_SYSTEM::RenderBatch(int start, int batchSize)
{
    //If the end of the vertex buffer is reached, start over
    if(bufferOffset + batchSize >= numParticles)
        bufferOffset = 0;

    //Lock the vertex buffer
    PARTICLE_VERTEX *p = NULL;
    particleBuffer->Lock(
                    bufferOffset * sizeof(PARTICLE_VERTEX),
                    batchSize, (void**)&p,
                    bufferOffset ?
                    D3DLOCK_NOOVERWRITE : D3DLOCK_DISCARD);
```

```
int particlesRendered = 0;
for(int i=start;i<m_particles.size() &&
    i < start + batchSize;i++)
    if(!m_particles[i]->dead)
    {
        p->position = m_particles[i]->position;
        p->color = m_particles[i]->color;
        p++;
        particlesRendered++;
    }

particleBuffer->Unlock();

//Render batch
if(particlesRendered > 0)
    m_pDevice->DrawPrimitive(D3DPT_POINTLIST,
                             bufferOffset,
                             particlesRendered);

//Increase offset
bufferOffset += batchSize;
}
```

Because we only use a small part of the vertex buffer (whose start position is marked by the bufferOffset variable), should we risk writing outside the buffer, we start over from zero. Then we lock the particle vertex buffer so that we can begin to copy over our particle data. Notice that we use different flags for locking the vertex buffer, depending on whether we are at the start of the vertex buffer or not. The D3DLOCK_NOOVERWRITE flag means that the graphic card must finish drawing from the vertex buffer before we continue. The D3DLOCK_DISCARD flag, on the other hand, means that we overwrite any old data encountered in the vertex buffer. After we have locked the vertex buffer, we begin to copy any nondead particles into the vertex buffer (position and color only). After we have copied all particles across, we unlock the buffer and render the particles. Before exiting the function, we also increment the bufferOffset with the batchSize so that the next particle system (or batch) will use a different position in the vertex buffer. Now, before we start looking at implementing a specific particle system, we will take a quick look at some necessary render states (excerpt from the PARTICLE_SYSTEM::PreRender() function):

```
//Turn point sprites ON
m_pDevice->SetRenderState(D3DRS_POINTSPRITEENABLE, true);
```

```
//Scale particles depending on their distance from the camera
m_pDevice->SetRenderState(D3DRS_POINTSCALEENABLE, true);

//Overall particle size
m_pDevice->SetRenderState(D3DRS_POINTSIZE,
                          FtoDword(m_particleSize));

//Scale factors
m_pDevice->SetRenderState(D3DRS_POINTSCALE_A, FtoDword(0.0f));
m_pDevice->SetRenderState(D3DRS_POINTSCALE_B, FtoDword(0.0f));
m_pDevice->SetRenderState(D3DRS_POINTSCALE_C, FtoDword(1.0f));
```

The scale factors A, B, and C affect the size of the particles according to the distance D from the camera, using following formula:

$$S = \sqrt{\frac{1}{A + B * D + C * D^2}}$$

In other words, the factors A, B, and C determine how the size of the particles decreases as they move away from the camera. Refer to the DirectX SDK for a complete list of render states that affect point sprites. Also worth noting is that we need to convert a float value to a DWORD when we set these render states. For this we use the following function:

```
DWORD FtoDword(float f){return *((DWORD*)&f);}
```

The Magic Shower Particle System

We will now attempt to implement a specific particle system that will handle the creation and updating of many particles. The particle system base class doesn't handle anything else than the rendering of the particles; everything else must be implemented in its subclasses. The magic shower particle system we will implement doesn't really fill a specific RTS need for our game, but it nicely demonstrates a particle system effect.

```
class MAGIC_SHOWER : public PARTICLE_SYSTEM
{
    public:
        MAGIC_SHOWER(IDirect3DDevice9 *Dev,
                     int noParticles, D3DXVECTOR3 _origin);
        void Update(float timeDelta);
        bool isDead();
```

```
      private:
          D3DXVECTOR3 m_origin;
};
```

As you can see, we don't need much in this class to implement a particle system when we inherit the PARTICLE_SYSTEM base class. The constructor of the MAGIC_SHOWER class creates the initial particles, and the Update() function animates all the particles. Different systems will have different types of emitters (i.e., the source that emits new particles). This particular system just has a single point in space that all particles originate from.

```
MAGIC_SHOWER::MAGIC_SHOWER(IDirect3DDevice9 *Dev,
                           int noParticles,
                           D3DXVECTOR3 _origin) :
                           PARTICLE_SYSTEM(Dev)
{
    m_origin = _origin;

    //Add initial particles
    for(int i=0;i<noParticles;i++)
    {
        PARTICLE *p = new PARTICLE();
        memset(p, 0, sizeof(PARTICLE));
        p->time_to_live = rand()%5000 / 1000.0f;
        p->dead = true;
        p->acceleration = D3DXVECTOR3(0.0f, -0.75f, 0.0f);
        m_particles.push_back(p);
    }

    //Set texture
    m_pTexture = starTexture;
}
```

This particular particle system maintains a predefined number of particles and just respawns dead particles. In the constructor, we set initial things, like acceleration, but the most important thing is that we add the specified amount of particles to the particle array. The Update() function will then take care of animating these particles as well as respawning them when they die.

```
void MAGIC_SHOWER::Update(float timeDelta)
{
    for(int i=0;i<m_particles.size();i++)
    {
```

```
//Update live particles
m_particles[i]->time_to_live -= timeDelta;
m_particles[i]->velocity += m_particles[i]->
                            acceleration * timeDelta;

m_particles[i]->position += m_particles[i]->
                            velocity * timeDelta;

m_particles[i]->color.a =
                m_particles[i]->time_to_live / 5.0f;

//Re-spawn dead particles
if(m_particles[i]->time_to_live <= 0.0f)
{
    m_particles[i]->position = m_origin;

    //Random direction
    m_particles[i]->velocity = D3DXVECTOR3(
                    (rand()%2000 / 1000.0f) - 1.0f,
                    (rand()%2000 / 1000.0f) - 1.0f,
                    (rand()%2000 / 1000.0f) - 1.0f);

    D3DXVec3Normalize(&m_particles[i]->velocity,
                    &m_particles[i]->velocity);
    m_particles[i]->velocity *= 2.0f;

    //Random color
    m_particles[i]->color = D3DXCOLOR(
                            rand()%1000 / 1000.0f,
                            rand()%1000 / 1000.0f,
                            rand()%1000 / 1000.0f,
                            1.0f);

    //Random life span
    m_particles[i]->time_to_live =
                    rand()%4000 / 1000.0f + 1.0f;
    m_particles[i]->dead = false;
}
    }
}
```

That's it. The `Update()` function simply updates the `position`, `velocity`, `color`, and `time_to_live` variables of all the particles. Then if a particle runs out of "life," it simply respawns the particle at the origin with a random `velocity` vector, `color`, and `time_to_live`. Check out [Burg00], [Lai03], and [Latta04] for some more-advanced particle systems.

ON THE CD

Example 12.3

Example 12.3 on the CD-ROM has the full source code for the particle system classes covered in this section. Try to write some code that animates the origin of the particle systems and see what happens.

SKYBOXES AND ENVIRONMENT MAPS

A skybox is an axis-aligned cube surrounding the camera. The six sides of the cube are mapped with textures that give the illusion that instead of a simple cube, there's a detailed world surrounding the camera. These textures are usually created in a 3D program like 3ds Max or a similar application. (We will look at how to create these textures in 3ds Max in the next section.) Skyboxes or environment maps can't really be considered an effect in themselves. But many shader effects use environment maps to calculate things like reflections and refractions. Figure 12.8 shows how the textures are mapped to the cube.

As you can see, each side of the cube is mapped with a corresponding texture. These textures seamlessly join together in every direction so that no edge between them can be seen. A skybox is centered on the camera position at each frame, so no matter how long a player moves in any direction, he will never reach the edge of the skybox. In this section, we will cover two ways to create these seamless environment

6 Environment Textures   Finished Skybox

FIGURE 12.8 The concept of skyboxes.

textures. One way is to use a 3D program to create these textures. The other is to create them in code and render a 3D scene into the six textures. But first let's look at the SKYBOX class that we use to load and render a skybox:

```
class SKYBOX
{
    public:
        SKYBOX(IDirect3DDevice9 *Dev,
                char fileName[], float size);
        ~SKYBOX();
        void Render(D3DXVECTOR3 cameraPos);

    private:
        IDirect3DDevice9 *m_pDevice;
        std::vector<IDirect3DTexture9*> m_textures;
        ID3DXMesh *m_pMesh;
        D3DMATERIAL9 m_white;
};
```

This SKYBOX class contains a vector with our six textures in the following order: up, front, back, right, left, and down. It also contains a mesh with the six sides of the cube and a completely white material used during rendering. The textures and the mesh are created in the constructor of the SKYBOX class:

```
SKYBOX::SKYBOX(IDirect3DDevice9 *Dev,
                char fileName[], float size)
```

```
{
    m_pDevice = Dev;

    //Load the 6 Skybox textures
    std::string endings[] = {"_UP.jpg", "_FR.jpg", "_BK.jpg",
                             "_RT.jpg", "_LF.jpg", "_DN.jpg"};

    for(int i=0;i<6;i++)
    {
        std::string fName = fileName;
        fName += endings[i];

        IDirect3DTexture9* newTexture = NULL;
        D3DXCreateTextureFromFile(m_pDevice, fName.c_str(),
                                  &newTexture);
        m_textures.push_back(newTexture);
    }

    //Create Mesh
    D3DXCreateMeshFVF(12, 24, D3DXMESH_MANAGED,
                      SKYBOX_VERTEX::FVF, m_pDevice, &m_pMesh);

    //Create vertices
    SKYBOX_VERTEX* v = 0;
    m_pMesh->LockVertexBuffer(0,(void**)&v);

    //Define the 8 corners of the skybox
    D3DXVECTOR3 corners[8] =
                    {D3DXVECTOR3(-size,  size,  size),
                       /*and the seven other corners*/};

    //Up Face
    v[0] = SKYBOX_VERTEX(corners[1], D3DXVECTOR2(0.0f, 0.0f));
    v[1] = SKYBOX_VERTEX(corners[0], D3DXVECTOR2(1.0f, 0.0f));
    v[2] = SKYBOX_VERTEX(corners[3], D3DXVECTOR2(0.0f, 1.0f));
    v[3] = SKYBOX_VERTEX(corners[2], D3DXVECTOR2(1.0f, 1.0f));

    //Similar with the Front, Back, Right, Left and Down Face

    m_pMesh->UnlockVertexBuffer();
```

```
//Calculate Indices
WORD* ind = 0;
m_pMesh->LockIndexBuffer(0,(void**)&ind);

int index = 0;
for(int quad=0;quad<6;quad++)
{
    //First face
    ind[index++] = quad * 4;
    ind[index++] = quad * 4 + 1;
    ind[index++] = quad * 4 + 2;

    //Second Face
    ind[index++] = quad * 4 + 1;
    ind[index++] = quad * 4 + 3;
    ind[index++] = quad * 4 + 2;
}

m_pMesh->UnlockIndexBuffer();

//Set Attributes
DWORD *att = 0;
m_pMesh->LockAttributeBuffer(0,&att);

//Set each quad to its own sub mesh
for(int i=0;i<12;i++)
    att[i] = i / 2;

m_pMesh->UnlockAttributeBuffer();

//Set material
memset(&m_white, 0, sizeof(D3DMATERIAL9));
m_white.Diffuse = D3DXCOLOR(1.0f, 1.0f, 1.0f, 1.0f);
}
```

We load the six environment textures and push them into the texture array, and then we create the six sides of the skybox mesh. Once the skybox has been created, it is a simple matter to render its six sides with the corresponding textures:

```
void SKYBOX::Render(D3DXVECTOR3 cameraPos)
{
```

```
//Set Renderstates
m_pDevice->SetRenderState(D3DRS_LIGHTING, false);
m_pDevice->SetRenderState(D3DRS_ZWRITEENABLE, false);
m_pDevice->SetRenderState(D3DRS_ZENABLE, false);
m_pDevice->SetSamplerState(0, D3DSAMP_ADDRESSU,
                              D3DTADDRESS_CLAMP);
m_pDevice->SetSamplerState(0, D3DSAMP_ADDRESSV,
                              D3DTADDRESS_CLAMP);


//Set material
m_pDevice->SetMaterial(&m_white);

//Move skybox to center on cameraPos
D3DXMATRIX position;
D3DXMatrixTranslation(&position, cameraPos.x,
                         cameraPos.y, cameraPos.z);
m_pDevice->SetTransform(D3DTS_WORLD, &position);

//Render the six sides of the skybox
for(int i=0;i<6;i++)
{
    m_pDevice->SetTexture(0, textures[i]);
    m_pMesh->DrawSubset(i);
}

// Restore render states.
m_pDevice->SetRenderState(D3DRS_LIGHTING, true);
m_pDevice->SetRenderState(D3DRS_ZWRITEENABLE, true);
m_pDevice->SetRenderState(D3DRS_ZENABLE, true);
m_pDevice->SetSamplerState(0, D3DSAMP_ADDRESSU,
                              D3DTADDRESS_WRAP);
m_pDevice->SetSamplerState(0, D3DSAMP_ADDRESSV,
                              D3DTADDRESS_WRAP);
}
```

The only thing worth noting is that we render the skybox with the U and V sampler clamped to the range 0.0 - 1.0. This is so that there won't be any artifacts along the edges of the skybox. When we are done rendering the skybox, we set the UV sampler back to allow texture wrapping.

Example 12.4

Example 12.4 renders a skybox created in 3ds Max. No matter what angle the player looks in, the edges of the cube cannot be spotted.

Create Environment Textures with 3ds Max

This section will cover how to create the six environment textures using 3ds Max.

Step 1: Start up 3ds Max, and create a complex scene with a lot of objects and details (see Chapter 6 for more on this). Once you have created your environment, it is time to render the environment textures.

Step 2: Create a box with equal width, height, and depth. Then place the box in the location want your camera or viewpoint to be.

Step 3: Open the Material Editor and select/create a new material. Open the Maps drop-down menu and select Diffuse Color.

Step 4: Select Reflect/Refract from the list.

Step 5: In the Reflect/Refract parameters menu, set the following (also shown in Figure 12.9):

Source: From File

Size: Target Texture Size (512 or 1024 recommended)

Render Cubic Map Files, To File: Target filename

Step 6: Click the Pick Object and Render Maps button, and then select the box you created. This will now render the six environment textures and store them with the filename you specified.

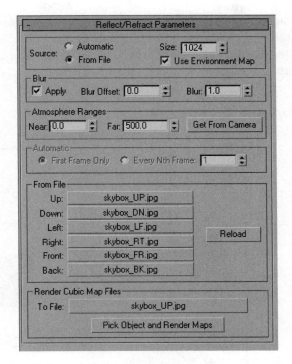

FIGURE 12.9   The Reflect/Refract Parameters settings.

That was easy enough. Remember that you can add as much detail, lights, and so forth to the scene as you like. The only thing that is going to matter in your game is the size of the textures you create. You can find the 3ds Max file that was used to create the environment textures in Example 12.4 on the CD-ROM.

The purpose of a skybox is to show far-away details, objects that the player never will get close to. Good examples of such objects are mountain ranges and far-off cities. If you place objects close to the camera, it will ruin the illusion that the scenery is a part of the game as soon as the player moves around.

Create Environment Textures in Code

The other way we can create these environment maps is by rendering them in code from a certain location in the world. By doing this, we lose the amount of detail we can have in the scene, compared to the previous method. However, we gain some other advantages. We can now render dynamic scenes and create skyboxes on the fly. This technique can also be very useful for other effects, like shader reflections.

This technique is very simple. We simply set one camera to render in each direction (up, front, back, right, left, and down). Figure 12.10 shows a 2D example of this:

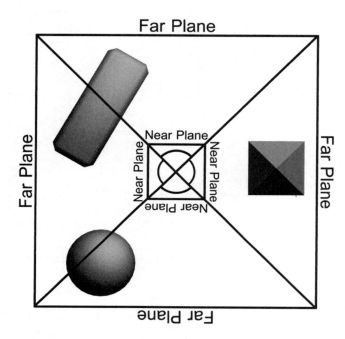

FIGURE 12.10   Setting up cameras to render environment maps.

The figure may seem a little bit cryptic; what you are looking at is four cameras from above. This is a 2D example of how to set the cameras up. See how the edge of the view frustum for each camera perfectly aligns with the boundaries of its neighbor? This will cause any images being rendered from two neighboring cameras to seamlessly join. To do this, each camera needs to have a field of view of 90 degrees as well as a rectangular render target. Of course, in the 3D case, we need two more cameras to get all six environment textures. We've added the GenerateEnvironMap() function to our SKYBOX class to render the six environment maps, as described here:

```
void SKYBOX::GenerateEnvironmentMap(D3DXVECTOR3 position)
{
    //Clear old textures here...

    //The Projection matrix
    D3DXMATRIX  proj;
    D3DXMatrixPerspectiveFovLH(&proj, D3DX_PI * 0.5f,
                        1.0f, 1.0f, 1000.0f );

    m_pDevice->SetTransform(D3DTS_PROJECTION, &proj);

    //The directions of the 6 cameras
    D3DXVECTOR3 directions[] = { ... };

    //The camera "UP" direction for the 6 cameras
    D3DXVECTOR3 up[] = { ... };

    LPDIRECT3DSURFACE9 backBuffer = NULL;
    m_pDevice->GetRenderTarget(0,&backBuffer);

    for(int i=0;i<6;i++)
    {
        //Set the view matrix
        D3DXMATRIX  view;
        D3DXMatrixLookAtLH(&view, &position,
                    &(position + directions[i]), &up[i]);

        m_pDevice->SetTransform(D3DTS_VIEW, &view);

        //Create the render target texture & surface
        LPDIRECT3DTEXTURE9 renderTexture = NULL;
        LPDIRECT3DSURFACE9 renderSurface = NULL;
        m_pDevice->CreateTexture(512, 512, 1,
                            D3DUSAGE_RENDERTARGET,
                            D3DFMT_A8R8G8B8,
                            D3DPOOL_DEFAULT,
                            &renderTexture, NULL);
        renderTexture->GetSurfaceLevel(0,&renderSurface);

        //render to the texture
        m_pDevice->SetRenderTarget(0, renderSurface);
        //clear texture
```

```
                    m_pDevice->Clear(0, NULL,
                                     D3DCLEAR_TARGET | D3DCLEAR_ZBUFFER,
                                     0x00ffffff, 1.0f, 0);
                    m_pDevice->BeginScene();

                    //Render the scene here...

                    m_pDevice->EndScene();

                    //Release variables
                    renderSurface->Release();
                    m_textures.push_back(renderTexture);
                }

                //Restore rendertargets
                m_pDevice->SetRenderTarget(0,backBuffer);
                backBuffer->Release();
            }
```

This function needs to have some kind of access to the scene that is to be rendered to the environment maps. In the example, a reference to a TERRAIN object is also passed as a parameter to this function.

ON THE CD

Example 12.5

Try Example 12.5 on the CD-ROM. Here, a TERRAIN object is rendered straight to six environment maps and then mapped onto a skybox, instead of being rendered the usual way. Again, you can see that it is impossible to find the seams or edges of the skybox (if everything was done right, that is).

LENS FLARES

In this section we will take a look at creating lens flares for games. A lens flare is a glare from a bright light passing through the lens of a camera. In fact, this is something photographers try to avoid. Game programmers, on the other hand, can use this natural-occurring defect to bring some more realism into their games, or maybe use them just because they look good. A lens flare is a simple 2D effect drawn completely in screen space as a series of different halos or flares, as shown in Figure 12.11.

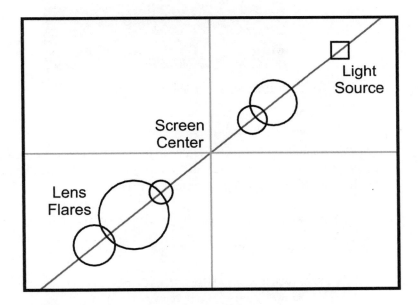

FIGURE 12.11   How lens flares are drawn in screen space.

First we need to convert the position of the light source creating the lens flare to screen coordinates (see Chapter 5, "From the World to the Screen"). Then we calculate the vector from the screen center to the light source (in screen space). It is along this ray that we will place all the lens flares. We get the lens flares from a texture like the one in Figure 12.12.

Note again how we use a black-and-white texture for this effect so we can assign our own color to each individual flare. This texture contains a couple of different flares of different shapes and sizes.

FIGURE 12.12 A lens flare texture.

TIP

The Photoshop Lens Flare filter is a good place to start for creating some lens flares. Remember to create a texture with an alpha channel like the one in Figure 12.12, but with RGB channels that are completely white.

In our code, we describe a single flare with the FLARE structure, like this:

```
struct FLARE
{
    FLARE(D3DXCOLOR _color, float _place,
        float _scale, int _sourceFlare);

    D3DXCOLOR color;     //Flare color
    float place;         //position along the ray
    float scale;         //Size of the flare
    int sourceFlare;     //Which flare from the texture to use
};
```

Now we need a class to hold and render all the flares of a specific lens flare effect. For this we have create the EFFECT_LENSFLARE class (which inherits from the EFFECT class, of course):

```
class EFFECT_LENSFLARE : public EFFECT
{
```

```
public:
    EFFECT_LENSFLARE(IDirect3DDevice9 *Dev,
                     int _type, D3DXVECTOR3 _position);
    void Update(float timeDelta);
    void Render();
    bool isDead();

private:
    float m_mainAlpha;          //Overall alpha
    bool m_inScreen;            //Inside screen bounds
    int m_type;                 //Flare type
    D3DXVECTOR3 m_position;      //Light source position
    std::vector<FLARE> m_flares; //Array of flares
};
```

We use the m_mainAlpha variable to fade the lens flare effect in and out, depending on whether it is inside the screen bounds or not. This makes the lens flare fade in and out smoothly, rather being turned on abruptly when, for example, the light source comes into view. The m_flares vector holds all our FLARE objects, describing how this effect should be rendered. These are set in the constructor of the effect like this:

```
EFFECT_LENSFLARE::EFFECT_LENSFLARE(IDirect3DDevice9 *Dev,
                                   int _type,
                                   D3DXVECTOR3 _position) :
                                   EFFECT(Dev)
{
    m_position = _position;
    m_type = _type;
    m_mainAlpha = 0.0f;
    m_inScreen = false;

    //Add Flares
    if(m_type == 0)      //Standard flare
    {
        //Add flares
        m_flares.push_back(FLARE( ... ));
        m_flares.push_back(FLARE( ... ));
        m_flares.push_back(FLARE( ... ));
        //and many more...
    }
    else if(m_type == 1)      //Some other flare...
    {
```

```
                        //set up your own flare here as a different type...
                }
        }
```

Depending on what type it is, we add different flares to the flares vector. The only thing the Update() function does is fade the effect in and out using the m_inScreen and m_mainAlpha variables. Whether the light source is within the bounds of the screen or not is calculated in the EFFECT_LENSFLARE::Render() function:

```
void EFFECT_LENSFLARE::Render()
{
    RECT sourceRectangles[7] = { ... };

    //Calculate screen position of light source
    D3DXVECTOR3 screenPos;
    D3DVIEWPORT9 Viewport;
    D3DXMATRIX Projection, View, World;
    m_pDevice->GetViewport(&Viewport);
    m_pDevice->GetTransform(D3DTS_VIEW, &View);
    m_pDevice->GetTransform(D3DTS_PROJECTION, &Projection);
    D3DXMatrixIdentity(&World);
    D3DXVec3Project(&screenPos, &m_position, &Viewport,
                    &Projection, &View, &World);

    //Get viewport
    D3DVIEWPORT9 v;
    m_pDevice->GetViewport(&v);

    //Check if light source is within the screen bounds
    if(screenPos.x < 0 || screenPos.x > v.Width ||
        screenPos.y < 0 || screenPos.y > v.Height ||
        screenPos.z > 1.0f)
        m_inScreen = false;
    else m_inScreen = true;

    //Calculate the ray from the screen center to light source
    D3DXVECTOR2 lightSource = D3DXVECTOR2(screenPos.x,
                                          screenPos.y);
    D3DXVECTOR2 screenCenter = D3DXVECTOR2(v.Width * 0.5f,
                                           v.Height * 0.5f);
    D3DXVECTOR2 ray = screenCenter - lightSource;
```

```
//Draw the different flares
sprite->Begin(D3DXSPRITE_ALPHABLEND);
for(int i=0;i<m_flares.size();i++)
{
    //Calculate Flare position in screen coordinates
    RECT r = sourceRectangles[m_flares[i].sourceFlare];
    D3DXVECTOR2 offset =
                    D3DXVECTOR2((r.right - r.left) / 2.0f,
                                (r.bottom - r.top) / 2.0f)
                    * m_flares[i].scale;

    D3DXVECTOR2 flarePos = lightSource + ray *
                            m_flares[i].place - offset;

    //Scale
    D3DXMatrixScaling(&sca, m_flares[i].scale,
                            m_flares[i].scale, 1.0f);

    //Calculate flare alpha
    D3DXCOLOR m_color = m_flares[i].m_color;

    float alpha;
    alpha = (D3DXVec2Length(&((flarePos + offset)
            - screenCenter)) + 150.0f) / (float)v.Height;

    if(alpha > 1.0f)alpha = 1.0f;
    m_color.a = alpha * m_mainAlpha * 1.5f;

    //Draw Flare
    sprite->SetTransform(&sca);
    sprite->Draw(lensflareTexture, &r, NULL,
            &D3DXVECTOR3(flarePos.x /m_flares[i].scale,
                        flarePos.y /m_flares[i].scale,
                        0.0f),
            m_color);
}
sprite->End();

D3DXMatrixIdentity(&sca);
sprite->SetTransform(&sca);
}
```

This function first calculates the screen position of the light source and then simply begins to draw each flare stored in the m_flares vector. Something worth noting is that we set the alpha of the individual flare as an inverse function of how close it is to the screen center. This means that if you are looking straight at the light source, the flares will be less visible than if the flare is near the edge of the screen. How you tweak these settings is of course up to you; it all depends on what effect you are looking for.

TIP

Remember to keep the lens flare effect fairly subtle. If you create a too-flashy and opaque lens flare, it will just distract the player. The trick is to have the lens flare add to the background ambience in a subtle way.

ON THE CD

Example 12.6

Example 12.6 demonstrates the lens flare effect. A standard lens flare has been added to the world position of the sun. Add multiple lens flares to the scene at different locations and see how it looks. You can also try to animate the world position of the lens flare.

CONSTRUCTING BUILDINGS

In real-time strategy games, buildings are a key concept. In many of these games, buildings are constructed gradually, step by step. In this section, we will take a look at how to create a mesh that gets rendered part by part in the game. This can of course be used for other things as well, such as simple mesh animations. Figure 12.13 show how a house can be built step by step with this method.

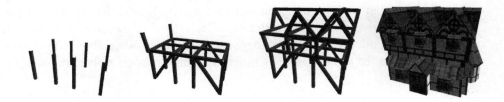

FIGURE 12.13   Constructing a building step by step.

To do this, we have to have two separate meshes—one "construction" mesh and then the finished building mesh. You already know how to create the finished meshes, so let us take a closer look at how to create the construction mesh.

Step 1: Start 3ds Max.

Step 2: Create the construction mesh as you want it to appear in the final stage before the building is complete. (Review Chapter 6 if necessary.)

Step 3: Select one primitive and click Modify Menu. Right-click the primitive name and Convert to Editable Mesh. Scroll down to the Edit Geometry menu that appears, and click the Attach List button.

Step 4: Click All, then the Attach button. Your scene should now contain only one mesh with the name of the original primitive that you selected.

Step 5: Now open up the Material Editor. Start creating as many materials—stages (frames)—as you want during the construction phase of your building. Name these materials 01, 02, 03, and so forth, and assign to these materials any textures or colors that you want.

Step 6: Click the Editable Mesh drop-down menu and start editing your mesh on a polygon level. Select the polygons that you want to appear in the first stage of your construction. Assign the 01 material to these, and then hide them using the Hide button. Continue with material 02 and so on, until all polygons have been assigned a material.

Step 7: Unhide all polygons and make sure the mesh is placed with its pivot point at (0, 0, 0).

Step 8: Export the mesh to an X-file.

You can find an example 3ds Max file in the Example 12.7 folder on the CD-ROM. Also, when you create your construction mesh, use your finished mesh as a guide.

NOTE

ON THE CD

Now that we have assigned different materials to different parts of the mesh; this separates the mesh into different subsets. Now all we have to do is create some code that renders only some of these subsets and not others. For this we have added the overloaded MESH::Render() function, which renders only some subsets of the mesh:

```
void MESH::Render(float prc)
{
    //Calculate the end subset to render
    int end = m_materials.size() * prc;

    for(int i=0;i<m_materials.size() && i < end;i++)
    {
        if(m_textures[i] != NULL)
            m_pDevice->SetMaterial(&m_white);
        else m_pDevice->SetMaterial(&m_materials[i]);

        m_pDevice->SetTexture(0, m_textures[i]);
        m_pMesh->DrawSubset(i);
    }
}
```

The prc parameter that is sent to this function will range from 0.0 to 1.0, which will be the construction percentage. Zero indicates that construction just started, and 1.0 indicates that construction is complete.

ON THE CD

Example 12.7

Example 12.7 shows you how to implement the code that constructs a building part by part.

FIRE AND SMOKE

Well, we know how to create buildings part by part. Now we'll take a look at how to destroy them, instead. Fire and smoke effects are a great way of telling the player that a building is damaged and/or under attack. The fire technique used in this section can also be used for magic spells, electricity, plasma, and many other effects. The most common ways of creating fire effects for 3D games is either to have animated textures or to use particle systems. If you use animated textures, it doesn't take that long for the fire effect to repeat itself, and it becomes clear that the fire is just looping a series of images. With particle systems, it is also very hard to create realistic-looking fire. We will instead use texture perturbation to create our fire effect as proposed by Isidoro and Guennadi [Isidoro02]. Texture perturbation means that we distort the UV coordinates sampling our diffuse texture by using a noise texture. With only two textures, a diffuse texture and a noise texture, we can create a good-looking, nonrepeating fire.

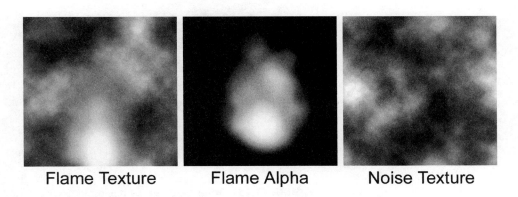

Flame Texture   Flame Alpha   Noise Texture

FIGURE 12.14   The textures needed for the fire effect.

Figure 12.14 shows the textures used for this fire effect in grayscale. The Flame Alpha is stored as the alpha channel in the Flame Texture. Very important to note is that the Noise Texture needs to be tileable in order for this effect to work.

For a simple way to create a tileable noise texture, check out the Photoshop Clouds filter (Filter, Render, Clouds).

TIP

This particular texture perturbation effect works by scrolling three noise textures on top of each other to make sure no cyclic pattern appears. We do this by creating three separate noise-UV coordinates in a vertexshader. These coordinates are animated as a time function with different coefficients. We then sample three pixels from the noise texture and add the results together. This result is then used to distort the UV coordinate used to sample the diffuse texture. We end up with a distorted sampling of the original flame texture. To make this flame appear as a volumetric effect rather than just a billboard, we apply this fire texture to multiple billboards rotated around the *y*-axis. However, this creates the visual artifact shown in Figure 12.15.

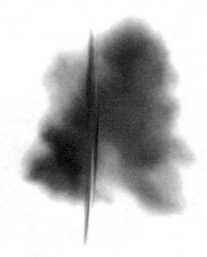

FIGURE 12.15 Artifact created by having nonperpendicular billboards to the camera.

As you can see in Figure 12.15, the plane that is perpendicular to the camera renders fine. However, it can clearly be seen from the other plane with a very small angle to the camera that this is indeed just a texture mapped to a flat billboard. We solve this by fading planes out the more nonperpendicular they become to the camera. We simply perform the same calculation we did with the dynamic lighting presented in Chapter 5. In a vertexshader, we compare the angle between the billboard normals and the direction to the camera. The greater the angle, the more visible the billboards are. Here's the vertexshader code (`fire.vs`) used for the fire effect:

```
uniform extern float4x4 matW;        //world matrix
uniform extern float4x4 matVP;       //view * projection matrix
uniform extern float3   DirToCam;    //Direction to camera
uniform extern float    time;        //time
uniform extern float    offset;      //Noise offset

struct VS_INPUT
{
    float4 position : POSITIONO;
    float3 normal   : NORMALO;
    float2 UV       : TEXCOORDO;
};

struct VS_OUTPUT
{
    float4 position  : POSITIONO;
    float2 UV        : TEXCOORDO;
    float2 UV_Noise1 : TEXCOORD1;
    float2 UV_Noise2 : TEXCOORD2;
    float2 UV_Noise3 : TEXCOORD3;
    float  mainAlpha : TEXCOORD4;
};

VS_OUTPUT Main(VS_INPUT input)
{
    VS_OUTPUT output = (VS_OUTPUT)0;

    // Project position
    float4 temp = mul(input.position, matW);
    output.position = mul(temp, matVP);

    //copy main UV coordinates across
    output.UV = input.UV;

    //Generate noise coordinates as a function of time
    output.UV_Noise1 = input.UV + float2(time * 0.7f + offset,
                                    time);

    output.UV_Noise2 = input.UV + float2(-time * 0.11f,
                                    time * 0.93f + offset);

    output.UV_Noise3 = input.UV + float2(time * 0.3f - offset,
                                    time * 0.71f);
```

```
//Transform normal
input.normal = mul(input.normal, matW);

//Calculate mainAlpha
output.mainAlpha = abs(dot(normalize(input.normal),
                          DirToCam));

return output;
}
```

This vertexshader takes a time to calculate the three different noise coordinates with. It also takes a noise offset from the application. This is so two flames next to each other won't look exactly the same. Other than that, we project the position of the vertex as usual and copy the main UV coordinates across. Something worth noting is that we animate the three noise coordinates mainly in the positive *y*-direction. This makes the flames appear to be lifting in an upward direction, much like real flames. You can play around with the way the noise coordinates are generated. Faster animation will make the fire appear more violent, for instance. Then we calculate the main alpha value of the vertex, depending on the normal and the direction to the camera. This is almost exactly the same calculation used as when we calculated the shade of the terrain mesh in Chapter 5. However, instead of clamping the dot product of the two vectors to the 0.0 – 1.0 range, we also accept a negative dot product. This means that if it is facing toward us, we treat the billboard the same way as if it is facing away. This information is then sent to the pixelshader (fire.ps):

```
sampler fireTexture;
sampler noiseTexture;

float4 Main(float2 UV        : TEXCOORD0,
            float2 UV_NOISE1 : TEXCOORD1,
            float2 UV_NOISE2 : TEXCOORD2,
            float2 UV_NOISE3 : TEXCOORD3,
            float  mainAlpha : TEXCOORD4) : COLOR
{
    //Sample noise pixels
    float n1 = tex2D(noiseTexture, UV_NOISE1);
    float n2 = tex2D(noiseTexture, UV_NOISE2);
    float n3 = tex2D(noiseTexture, UV_NOISE3);

    //Sum up noise and perturb the x coordinate of the main UV
    UV.x += (n1 + n2 + n3) * 0.1f - 0.05f;
```

```
    //Sample the diffuse texture
    float4 cO = tex2D(fireTexture, UV);

    //Multiply mainAlpha with this pixels alpha value
    cO.a *= mainAlpha;

    return cO;
}
```

We input five different UV coordinates to this pixelshader, the main UV coordinate of the billboard, three noise coordinates, and a single alpha value (passed as a single float UV coordinate). We start by sampling three noise pixels from the noise texture. Then we add these together and scale the result to the -0.05 – 0.05 range, and perturb the main UV x-coordinate with it. You can play around with this range for different effects. A larger range creates more violent flames, while a smaller range creates a more docile fire. Then we use the modified main UV coordinate to sample the fire texture, multiply the alpha value of this pixel with the main alpha value, and return the result. The EFFECT_FIRE class takes care of creating billboards, setting the vertexshader variables, and rendering the fire. (For the full code of the EFFECT_FIRE class, see Example 12.8.)

Texture perturbation can be used to create many different dynamic effects. See [Isidoro02] for a couple of different effects created using this technique.

Adding Smoke

There's no fire without smoke—or is it the other way around? What's certain is that our fire effect will need some smoke to be complete. For this we will implement a simple particle system class called SMOKE:

```
class SMOKE : public PARTICLE_SYSTEM
{
    public:
        SMOKE(IDirect3DDevice9 *Dev, int noParticles,
            D3DXVECTOR3 _origin);
        void Update(float timeDelta);
        bool isDead();
    private:
        D3DXVECTOR3 m_origin;
};
```

As you can see, this is a very simple class that inherits from the PARTICLE_SYSTEM base class. This particle system is very much like the magic shower particle system we covered in this chapter. The only differences are that we use another texture, the acceleration is pointing slightly upward, and we spawn particles from a random position near the origin instead of from the origin itself. Together with some billboards mapped with the dynamically created fire effect, the smoke completes the fire effect.

Example 12.8

Have a look at Example 12.8 on the CD-ROM, where the full source code of the SMOKE particle system and the EFFECT_FIRE class can be found. Play around with all the tweakable values in this example to get a feel for how to change the fire effect.

SUMMARY

In this chapter, we have covered a lot of ground and looked at many different topics. Most important in this chapter is the effect framework. This way we can code a new effect, and by using the EFFECT interface, all effects can be maintained, updated, and rendered as though they were the same. We also took a look at some effects that you may or may not need for your specific RTS game, such as lens flares and skyboxes. Then we covered things that you will more likely need, such as constructing buildings part by part and the dynamic fire effect. In Chapter 14, which covers AI techniques, we will put most of these effects to use. There we will implement some rudimentary "smarts" for the units, allowing them to build buildings, attack each other (and buildings), and so forth. But first we will cover how to load and play sound and music, something that all games need.

EXERCISES

- Extend the EFFECT class to contain a bounding box, and use this to cull the effect with frustum culling.
- Extend the EFFECT class to contain a map location and a map size, and use these variables to cull the effect using the logical representation of the fog-of-war.
- Make the fireball spell target move units or buildings (i.e., a MAPOBJECT) instead of a D3DXVECTOR3.
- Create a small yellow-red flare and attach it to the fireball and/or fire effect.
- If you want, you can calculate terrain UV-coordinates for all the effects and use the fog-of-war texture to light them, as well.

REFERENCES

[Burg00] van der Burg, John, "Building an Advanced Particle System." Available online at: *http://www.mysticgd.com/misc/AdvancedParticleSystems.pdf*, 2000.

[Isidoro02] Isidoro, John and Guennadi Riguer, "Texture Perturbation Effects." Available online at: *http://www.ati.com/developer/shaderx/ShaderX_Texture PerturbationEffects.pdf*, 2002.

[Lai03] Lai, Kent, "Designing an Extensible Particle System using C++ and Templates." Available online at: *http://www.gamedev.net/reference/articles/ article1982.asp*, 2003.

[Latta04] Latta, Lutz, "Building a Million Particle System." Available online at: *http://www.2ld.de/gdc2004/MegaParticlesPaper.pdf*, 2004.

FURTHER READING

ATI Technologies, "Procedural Fire." Available online at: *http://mirror.ati.com/developer/samples/ProceduralFire.html*, 2002.

Gordie, Alan, "Lens Flare Tutorial." Available online at: *http://www.gamedev.net/ reference/articles/article813.asp*, 1999.

Tanczos, Michael, "The Art of Modeling Lens Flares." Available online at: *http:// www.gamedev.net/reference/articles/article874.asp*, 1999.

13 The Sound of Music

Models in chapter provided courtesy of 3DCAFE.com.

In Chapter 12 we had a look at some useful visual special effects. Now we will take a look at playing sound effects and music. Today, sound is an obvious part of any game. Good sound drastically increases the realism. Try, for instance, to play a first-person shooter or any other fast-paced game without sound. Not quite the same experience, is it?

Sounds effects are usually synchronized with events in the game, such as explosions, gun shots, collisions, and so on. Music, on the other hand, is usually used to set the mood of a scene. For games, music is usually totally instrumental and in the background. In this chapter, we will cover how to load and play wave files (WAV, uncompressed sounds) and midi files (MID, Music Instrument Digital Interface). We will also take a look at how to load and play MP3 files (MPEG Audio Layer III, compressed sound) using a DirectShow filter.

A QUICK LOOK AT COM

COM stands for Component Object Model. COM objects are reusable objects that can be used across different applications (and programming languages). An example of this could be a spellchecker class. Many different programs would benefit from having a spellchecker class, but it would be unnecessary to implement the spellchecker individually in all these programs. Instead, we would create one single spellchecker class as a COM object, which then can be invoked from all applications that need it. Both DirectMusic and DirectShow build completely on COM objects. To create a COM object in a specific application, all we need to know is the identifier of the object. The identifier is stored as a GUID (Globally Unique Identifier), which is basically a 128-bit number. However, before we can create a COM object, we must first initiate the COM library. This is done with the following function:

```
HRESULT CoInitialize(
    LPVOID pvReserved
);
```

The pvReserved parameter is not used, and it must be set to NULL. In the same way, when we are done with the COM objects, we must call the following function to close the COM library and unload any loaded DLLs, and so forth:

```
void CoUninitialize(void);
```

To create a specific COM object, we use the CoCreateInstance() function:

```
STDAPI CoCreateInstance(
    REFCLSID rclsid,      //The Class GUID
    LPUNKNOWN pUnkOuter,  //Not used, set to NULL
    DWORD dwClsContext,   //Context in which the object will run
    REFIID riid,          //Interface to the object
    LPVOID *ppv           //The pointer to the resulting object
);
```

This function will then create an uninitiated copy of the requested object, which can then be used by the application. Luckily, the GUIDs and interface IDs for the DirectMusic and DirectShow objects are declared as constants in DirectX, as you will see later when we create the actual objects.

PLAYING WAV AND MID FILES

To load and play WAV and MID files, we will be using DirectMusic. You may wonder why we use DirectMusic and not DirectSound. The reason is that the DirectMusic API makes it much easier to load and play both WAV and MID files. DirectSound doesn't support midi file playback. There are some things in Direct-Sound, like capturing sound, reverb, and chorus effects, which may be of interest to some. However, for our application, DirectMusic is the better API to use.

We will build a wrapper class called SOUND to encapsulate the set up and initiation of DirectMusic. Then we will create one class called SOUNDFILE to store and deal with separate sound files (both WAV and MID files). There are three specific sound interfaces we need to create and initiate in order to play sounds with DirectMusic:

IDirectMusicPerformance8: The IDirectMusicPerformance8 interface manages all sound playbacks. With this interface, we set things like master volume, playback tempo, and more.

IDirectMusicLoader8: This interface is used to load a sound file. It can also be used to enumerate all sound files in a specific directory.

IDirectMusicSegment8: The IDirectMusicSegment8 interface stores actual sound data, whether it is WAV data or MID data.

To use the DirectMusic classes and interfaces covered in this section, you need to include the following files:

```
#include <dmusici.h>
#include <dsound.h>
```

You must also link the DirectSound library to your project (dsound.lib). We will encapsulate the IDirectMusicPerformance8 and the IDirectMusicLoader8 interfaces in our SOUND class, and the IDirectMusicSegment8 interface in our SOUNDFILE class. Our SOUND class is defined as follows:

```
class SOUND
{
    friend class SOUNDFILE;
    public:
        SOUND();
        ~SOUND();
```

```
        void Init(HWND windowHandle);
        void PlaySound(int soundID, bool loop);

        void SetMasterVolume(float volume);
        float GetMasterVolume(){return masterVolume;}

    private:
        IDirectMusicPerformance8 *m_pPerformance;
        IDirectMusicLoader8 *m_pLoader;

        float m_masterVolume;
        std::vector<SOUNDFILE*> m_sounds;
};
```

As you can see, this class encapsulates both the IDirectMusicPerformance8 and the IDirectMusicLoader8 interface. It also stores a vector of SOUNDFILE objects that can be played with the PlaySound() function. We also have the two functions SetMasterVolume() and GetMasterVolume() to control the volume. We will soon take a closer look at all these member functions, but first let's look at the declaration of the SOUNDFILE class:

```
class SOUNDFILE
{
    friend class SOUND;
    public:
        SOUNDFILE();
        ~SOUNDFILE();
        void Load(WCHAR fileName[], SOUND &sound);

    private:
        IDirectMusicSegment8 *m_pSegment;
};
```

This class is just a wrapper to make the usage of the IDirectMusicSegment8 interface a bit smoother. The only function of importance in this class is the Load() function, which loads a sound from a file. This function uses the IDirectMusicLoader8 interface that we have encapsulated in the SOUND class. Here's the code for the SOUND::Init() function, which initiates sound playback using DirectMusic:

```
void SOUND::Init(HWND windowHandle)
{
    CoInitialize(NULL);
```

```
CoCreateInstance(CLSID_DirectMusicPerformance, NULL,
                CLSCTX_INPROC,
                IID_IDirectMusicPerformance8,
                (void**)&m_pPerformance);

CoCreateInstance(CLSID_DirectMusicLoader, NULL,
                CLSCTX_INPROC, IID_IDirectMusicLoader8,
                (void**)&m_pLoader);

m_pPerformance->InitAudio(NULL, NULL, windowHandle,
                DMUS_APATH_SHARED_STEREOPLUSREVERB,
                64, DMUS_AUDIOF_ALL, NULL);
}
```

The components of DirectX audio are all COM objects, which means we have to create the objects using the `CoCreateInstance()` function. We use the `CoCreateInstance()` function to create both the `IDirectMusicPerformance8` and the `IDirectMusicLoader8` interfaces. Then we call the `InitAudio()` function of the `IDirectMusicPerformance8` interface, defined as follows:

```
HRESULT InitAudio(
    IDirectMusic** ppDirectMusic,
    IDirectSound** ppDirectSound,
    HWND hWnd,
    DWORD dwDefaultPathType,
    DWORD dwPChannelCount,
    DWORD dwFlags,
    DMUS_AUDIOPARAMS *pParams
);
```

ppDirectMusic and ppDirectSound: These pointers return a new DirectMusic and/or a DirectSound object from this function. We won't need either, so we set these to NULL.

hWnd: This function takes a handle to the window that created the IDirect MusicPerformance8 interface. You can set this handle to NULL; in that case the foreground window will be used.

dwDefaultPathType: This parameter sets the default audio path. An audio path defines how the sound is transported though a series of buffers and filters before it reaches the synthesizer. We set this parameter to the default value DMUS_APATH_SHARED_STEREOPLUSREVERB. Other audio paths are DMUS_APATH_ DYNAMIC_3D, DMUS_APATH_DYNAMIC_MONO, and DMUS_APATH_DYNAMIC_STEREO.

dwPChannelCount: This is number of performance channels to be created. Each channel can play a sound with a unique volume and balance.

dwFlags: Requested features of the performance object, we set this parameter to DMUS_AUDIOF_ALL, which means that we want all features. Check the DirectX documentation for a full list of the possible individual features.

pParams: Parameters of the synthesizer. Not used; set this parameter to NULL.

Well, that is how we create and initiate the DirectMusic interface. Next let's see how to load sounds.

Loading Sound Files

Loading sound files takes place in the SOUNDFILE::Load() function:

```
void SOUNDFILE::Load(WCHAR fileName[], SOUND &sound)
{
    //Create new segment
    CoCreateInstance(CLSID_DirectMusicSegment, NULL,
                     CLSCTX_INPROC, IID_IDirectMusicSegment8,
                     (void**)&m_pSegment);

    //Load from file using the loader
    sound.m_pLoader->LoadObjectFromFile(
                                CLSID_DirectMusicSegment,
                                IID_IDirectMusicSegment8,
                                fileName,
                                (void**)&m_pSegment);

    //Download sound to the performance interface
    m_pSegment->Download(sound.m_pPerformance);
}
```

We begin by creating a new IDirectMusicSegment8 segment. Then we use the loader of the SOUND object, sent as a parameter to this function to load a specific file. The LoadObjectFromFile() function specifies that we want to send the file described by the fileName parameter to our newly created IDirectMusicSegment8 object. Once the file is loaded, we must download the segment to the IDirectMusicPerformance8 interface in our SOUND object. This tells the performance object what settings to play the sound file with (e.g., things like music instruments, volume, and pan). Note also that the LoadObjectFromFile() function takes a wide character string (WCHAR[]) and not a normal character string. If you need to convert a char string to a WCHAR string,

use the `MultiByteToWideChar()` function. Otherwise, you can very easily create a
WCHAR string like this:

```
WCHAR wMusicFile[] = L"music.mid";
WCHAR wSoundFile[] = L"sound.wav";
```

We store all loaded SOUNDFILE objects in the m_sounds vector in the SOUND class.

Playing a SOUNDFILE Object

We play sounds using the SOUND::PlaySound() function. This function takes a
sound ID, which works like an index in the m_sounds vector.

```
void SOUND::PlaySound(int soundID, bool loop)
{
    //Faulty Sound ID
    if(soundID < 0 || soundID >= m_sounds.size())return;

    //Loop sound or not
    if(loop)
    {
        m_sounds[soundID]->m_pSegment->
                        SetRepeats(DMUS_SEG_REPEAT_INFINITE);
    }
    else
    {
        m_sounds[soundID]->m_pSegment->SetRepeats(0);
    }

    //Play Sound
    m_pPerformance->PlaySegment(m_sounds[soundID]->m_pSegment,
                        DMUS_SEGF_SECONDARY, 0, NULL);
}
```

This function also takes a Boolean value that tells whether or not we should
loop the sound. This is useful for things like background music; we don't need to
manually check to see if the song has finished and then restart it. We can just use the
`IDirectMusicSegment8::SetRepeats()` function to specify how many times we want
the sound to repeat. We can provide the DMUS_SEG_REPEAT_INFINITE constant to
make the sound loop an infinite amount of times. Next we call the `IDirectMusic`
`Performance8::PlaySegment()` function:

```
HRESULT PlaySegment(
    IDirectMusicSegment* pSegment,
    DWORD dwFlags,
    __int64 i64StartTime,
    IDirectMusicSegmentState** ppSegmentState
);
```

pSegment: Pointer to the segment we want to play.

dwFlags: We set this parameter to DMUS_SEGF_SECONDARY because this allows us to play multiple sounds at the same time. With this flag, you can do things like queue sounds and more. For the other flags, see the DirectX documentation.

i64StartTime: Time to delay the playback of the sound. If you want the sound to be played immediately, set this parameter to zero.

ppSegmentState: This parameter returns a pointer with a IDirectMusic SegmentState object that contains the state of the segment to be played. This parameter is not used, so just set it to NULL.

If you start a sound that is to be looped an infinite amount of times, you have to stop the sound manually. This is done with the IDirectMusicPerformance8:: Stop() function:

```
HRESULT Stop(
    IDirectMusicSegment* pSegment,
    IDirectMusicSegmentState* pSegmentState,
    MUSIC_TIME mtTime,
    DWORD dwFlags
);
```

The parameters to this function are very similar to the PlaySegment() function. See the DirectX documentation for full details. You can also use this function to stop all sounds currently played by an IDirectMusicPerformance8 interface, like this:

```
//Stop all sounds
m_pPerformance->Stop(NULL, NULL, 0, 0);
```

However, before you stop a sound, it can be a good idea to check whether it is actually still playing or not. This can be done with the IDirectMusicPerformance8:: IsPlaying() function. This function can be used like this:

```
if(m_pPerformance->IsPlaying(someSegment, NULL))
{
    //do something
}
```

You now know how to load and play a sound file. The `IDirectMusicSegment8` interface does not differentiate between WAV and MID files. They are both loaded and played the same way.

Set Master Volume

The next thing we'll have a look at is how to set the master volume. In most games, there's some form of setup screen where players can select what sound effects and music volume they want. Volume is usually measured in decibels (dB), which is a logarithmic scale.

TABLE 13.1   Direct Music Volume Constants

Direct Music Constant	Long Value	Sound Volume
DMUS_VOLUME_MIN	−20,000	−200 dB
DMUS_VOLUME_MAX	2,000	+20 dB

However, most of the ranges in Table 13.1 are useless. A good volume range is [0, -50] dB. We have created the `SOUND::SetMasterVolume()` function to set the volume. This function takes a float value between 0.0 and 1.0.

```
void SOUND::SetMasterVolume(float volume)
{
    //Cap volume to the range [0.0, 1.0]
    if(volume < 0.0f)volume = 0.0f;
    if(volume > 1.0f)volume = 1.0f;
    m_masterVolume = volume;

    //Translate to the decibel range [-500, -4000]
    long vol = -3500 * (1.0f - volume) - 500;

    //Set master volume
    if(m_pPerformance)
```

```
m_pPerformance->SetGlobalParam(GUID_PerfMasterVolume,
                               (void*)&vol,
                               sizeof(long));
}
```

We transform the `float` volume to a `long` variable in the right range. Then we set the master volume using the `SetGlobalParam()` function.

You can use the `SetGlobalParam()` function to set the playback tempo, as well. Then just use `GUID_PerfMasterTempo` as a reference.

NOTE

Cleaning Up

When you are done playing sounds, you should release the DirectMusic interfaces in the reverse order that you created them. It is also important that you call the `IDirectMusicPerformance8::CloseDown()` function on the performance object before you release it:

```
m_pLoader->Release();

m_pPerformance->CloseDown();
m_pPerformance->Release();
```

That marks the end of what you need to know in order to load and play WAV and MID files. For a deeper look into the DirectMusic API see [Hays98].

ON THE CD

Example 13.1

This example plays a couple of different sound effects using the techniques presented in this chapter.

PLAYING MP3 FILES

MP3 files are compressed, high-quality sounds usually used in games for music or character speech. Even though MP3 files are compressed, they can still be a couple of megabytes in size. So rather than loading a lot of them into memory, we take a different approach with these files. We will be streaming data using DirectShow, instead. DirectShow is an API used for streaming and capturing multimedia files. You can also do conversions using DirectShow—for instance, you can convert WAV files to MP3 files, and vice versa. DirectShow is a very powerful and complex API; we'll only scratch the surface of it in this book. For a more detailed look at Direct-Show see [Thompson00]. To use DirectShow to play MP3 files you need to do the following:

- Include the dshow.h header.
- Link the strmiids.lib library file to your project.

As mentioned before, DirectShow also uses mainly COM objects. There are a couple of different classes we will use to play MP3 files:

IGraphBuilder: This object builds a graph that describes how to render a specific file. This file can be any type of supported video or sound file. A graph is a series of filters describing how to read, manipulate, decode, and finally output a specific file type. We will use this object to "render" an MP3 file using the default graph. You can also build your own graphs manually for special effects, but this is outside the scope of this chapter.

IMediaControl: The media control object is the interface with which we can control the flow of a media file. This includes basic functions like playing, pausing, and stopping.

IMediaPosition: We can use this object to set playback rate, read the current position of the playback, and so on. We also use this object to tell whether a file has finished playing or not.

IBasicAudio: The IBasicAudio class is used to control the balance and volume of the playback.

For a complete list of member functions for these classes, see the DirectX documentation. In the meantime, we'll encapsulate all these interfaces in our own MP3 class, which we define as follows:

```
class MP3
{
```

```
public:
    MP3();
    ~MP3();
    void Release();
    void Init();
    void LoadSong(WCHAR fName[]);
    void Play();
    void Stop();
    bool IsPlaying();
    void SetVolume(float volume);
    void SetBalance(float balance);

private:
    IGraphBuilder *m_pGraphBuilder;
    IMediaControl *m_pMediaControl;
    IMediaPosition *m_pMediaPosition;
    IBasicAudio *m_pBasicAudio;
};
```

The MP3::Init() function creates the COM objects, as shown here:

```
void MP3::Init()
{
    Release();

    //Initialize COM Library
    CoInitialize(NULL);

    //Create the Filter Graph Manager
    CoCreateInstance(CLSID_FilterGraph, NULL, CLSCTX_INPROC,
                     IID_IGraphBuilder,
                     (void **)&m_pGraphBuilder);

    //Query MediaControl, MediaPosition and BasicAudio objects
    m_pGraphBuilder->QueryInterface(IID_IMediaControl,
                                    (void **)&m_pMediaControl);

    m_pGraphBuilder->QueryInterface(IID_IMediaPosition,
                                    (void**)&m_pMediaPosition);

    m_pGraphBuilder->QueryInterface(IID_IBasicAudio,
                                    (void **)&m_pBasicAudio);
}
```

From the `IGraphBuilder` interface, we query the `IMediaControl`, `IMediaPosi-`
tion, and `IBasicAudio` interfaces. After we have these objects initialized, playing an
MP3 file is a simple matter:

```
void MP3::LoadSong(WCHAR fName[])
{
    //Init the DirectShow objects
    Init();

    //Create standard graph
    m_pGraphBuilder->RenderFile(fName, NULL);
}

void MP3::Play()
{
    //rewind...
    m_pMediaPosition->put_CurrentPosition(0);

    //Play
    m_pMediaControl->Run();
}
```

The `LoadSong()` function initiates all the DirectShow objects and then calls the
`IGraphBuilder::RenderFile()` function with the provided filename. If you call this
function with an AVI file, for instance, it would open up a new window and render
the video to this window. In the `MP3::Play()` function, we set the current position
to zero (i.e., the beginning of the song or movie). Then we call the `IMediaCon-`
`trol::Run()` function to start the playback. You can use `IMediaControl::Stop()`
function or the `IMediaControl::Pause()` function to stop or pause the playback,
respectively. The `MP3::IsPlaying()` function uses the `IMediaPosition` interface to
determine if a song is playing or not:

```
bool MP3::IsPlaying()
{
    REFTIME currentPos;
    REFTIME duration;

    m_pMediaPosition->get_CurrentPosition(&currentPos);
    m_pMediaPosition->get_Duration(&duration);

    if(currentPos < duration)
        return true;
    else return false;
}
```

It does this by simply comparing the duration of the song with the current play-back position. Finally, we need to be able to set the volume of the MP3 playback, as well. This is done with the MP3::SetVolume() function. This function takes a float value in the range [0.0, 1.0], just as the SOUND::SetMasterVolume() function does:

```
void MP3::SetVolume(float volume)
{
    if(volume < 0.0f)volume = 0.0f;
    if(volume > 1.0f)volume = 1.0f;

    if(m_pBasicAudio)
    {
        long vol = -10000 * (1.0f - volume);
        m_pBasicAudio->put_Volume(vol);
    }
}
```

The only difference in the IBasicAudio::put_Volume() function is that it takes a long value in the range [-10000, 0], where zero is full volume. This is also trans-lated to the decibel range of [-100 db, 0 db].

Well, that concludes how to load and play an MP3 file. The important differ-ence between playing sounds using DirectMusic and DirectShow is that with DirectMusic, we load the sounds into memory, while with DirectShow, we stream the data from the hard drive. This, of course, allows us to play larger files without affecting the amount of available memory.

Example 13.2

This example loads two MP3 songs and allows you to fade in and out between them.

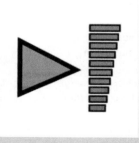

SUMMARY

In this chapter, we had a brief look at playing sounds using DirectMusic and DirectShow. We encapsulated both APIs in our own high-level SOUND, SOUNDFILE, and MP3 classes. This chapter is only meant to get you started with sound programming. There is still much in this area to learn, for example DirectSound, and 3D sounds. A good place to start is with the DirectX sample programs that hopefully will make a little bit more sense after reading this chapter. In Chapter 14, we will take a look at how to create an artificial opponent that is capable of playing an RTS game.

EXERCISES

- Implement 3D sound; check out [Murray03].
- Implement sound transitions using the IDirectMusicComposer8 interface.

REFERENCES

[Hays98] Hays, Tom, "DirectMusic for the Masses." Available online (free membership required) at: *http://www.gamasutra.com/features/19981106/hays_01. htm*, 1998.

[Murray03] Murray, Toby, "3D Sound with DirectX Audio." Available online at: *http://www.gamedev.net/reference/articles/article1881.asp*, 2003.

[Thompson00] Thompson, Chris, "DirectShow for Media Playback in Windows." Available online at: *http://www.flipcode.com/articles/article_directshow01.shtml*, 2000.

FURTHER READING

Smith, Mason, "Using DirectX Audio 8." Available online at: *http://www.gamedev. net/reference/articles/article1689.asp*, 2002.

14 AI

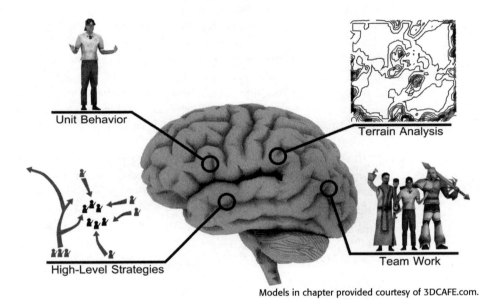

Unit Behavior

Terrain Analysis

High-Level Strategies

Team Work

Models in chapter provided courtesy of 3DCAFE.com.

enerally speaking, Artificial Intelligence (AI) is the art of simulating intelligence in a computer program. The single most famous AI program in history is without a doubt the chess program *Deep Blue*. In 1996, *Deep Blue* was the first program to ever win a round against a reigning chess champion. *Deep Blue* and most other chess programs like it rely on a brute force approach that "searches" for the best possible move. There is unfortunately no real intelligence in programs like this, though it does takes a lot of programming know-how make one. Programs like *Deep Blue* work by testing the possible moves from a certain game state, then testing the possible moves from those game states, and so on. This sort of AI is possible only in games like chess, checkers, and tic-tac-toe. These games have relatively few possible moves, they are all turn-based, and both players have full access to the current game state.

Real-time strategy games may, at the very core, share some similarities with chess, for instance, but unfortunately this is not enough. RTS games are not turn-based, which means as the AI is thinking about what to do, the situation (i.e., game state) may already have changed enough so that the AI must start over. The amount of game states possible in most RTS games is close to infinite, making the search space much larger than that of, for example, chess. To make matters even worse, the players do not have a complete picture of the current game state due to the fog-of-war. This alone makes it theoretically impossible to calculate "the best move" in an RTS game. We are therefore forced to rely on another type of solution. But then again, to find the best move is not necessary. The purpose of RTS AI is not to beat the player, it is merely to provide a good challenge. In this chapter, we aim to create an artificial opponent that is capable of playing our RTS game against us.

As a whole, artificial intelligence is a huge research field, too large to cover in a single book, let alone a single chapter. Artificial intelligence for computer games can be divided into a number of different topics, of which some are the following:

Script-Based AI: The opponent acts according to a predefined script. A script is nothing more than a series of simple actions. Just like when you go to a restaurant, each action has its place in time. For a real-time strategy game, an AI opponent could have a script like this:

1. Find a suitable base location.
2. Establish a base.
3. Build building A.
4. Build building B.
5. ...
6. Train units.
7. Train three footmen.
8. Train two archers.
9. ...
10. Attack player P.
11. Repeat from Step 6.

Finite State Machines: In a finite state machine, the AI opponent can be in one of several states. There's also a set of rules explaining how to move from one state to another. Examples of states for an RTS AI could be "Find base location," "Construct base," "Train army," and so on (very similar to the actions in the script). The difference between a state machine and a script is that scripts are much more sensitive. If something should go wrong—that is, a situation occurs that isn't in the script—then a scripted AI usually stops working as intended. We will take a much closer look at finite state machines further on in this chapter.

Fuzzy Logic: Fuzzy logic uses approximate reasoning to sort data into vaguely defined sets. With fuzzy logic, a specific state is given a membership probability to each of the existing sets. For instance, in Boolean logic, the question "are you hungry?" can only be answered with "Yes" or "No." With fuzzy logic, on the other hand, we have the two sets: "Hungry" and "Not Hungry." For example, a certain state could belong 30 percent to the "Hungry" set and 70 percent to the "Not Hungry" set. From this we could decide to eat different things according to how hungry we are. If peckish, have a salad. If somewhat hungry, have some spaghetti. But if starving, have the roast beef—and so on. More-impressive behaviors than this can be created when you base decisions on a number of different factors. For RTS games, this could be used to determine the current game state. We could, for instance, have the sets "Under Attack," "Peace," "Out of Resources," and so on.

Genetic Algorithms: Genetic algorithms (GAs) build on the concept of evolution. For a given problem, we start with a number of random solutions. Each solution is referred to as an individual, and all the solutions together are called the population. For each generation (i.e., iteration of the algorithm), we pick a number of good solutions (parents) and breed them together using a crossover operation (i.e., take some genetic material from each parent) to form new solutions (the children). The new individuals may also be mutated in some way before they are inserted into the population. For each generation, good solutions get to breed new solutions, while bad solutions are removed from the population. As you can see, genetic algorithms mimic all the components of evolution, such as natural selection, survival of the fittest, inheritance, and mutation. Genetic algorithms can be used to solve problems with a large search space—which an RTS game certainly has. However GAs tend to be very CPU demanding, which makes them hard to adapt to real-time strategy games. But if the attempt is made, GAs could potentially learn the strategy used by a player and figure out how to beat them. Perhaps in the future we will see more of these types of algorithms used in RTS games. If you are interested in this research area, look into a specific subset of genetic algorithms called Learner Classifier Systems (LCS). See for example [Bull04] for an introduction to Learner Classifier Systems.

Neural Networks: Just like genetic algorithms, neural networks (NN) has its roots in biology. Artificial neural networks tries to mimic the way interconnected neurons in a brain operate. A neuron can have many inputs but only one output. Each input value is multiplied with a single weight before being processed in the neuron. If the sum of the weighted inputs is above a certain threshold, the neuron's output is set to high (usually 1.0). This single output value may, however, be the input of several other neurons. Together, several interconnected neurons form a neural network. The neural network can be trained to perform specific tasks by adapting the weight values of all these neuron inputs. This training is usually done with a back propagation algorithm or similar, which "programs" the network using a set of training cases. A trained network can then be used to draw good conclusions from similar cases, even though it hasn't seen these exact cases before. The good news about neural networks is that they are extremely fast during runtime. Neural networks work like a black box, where you insert any data you have in one end, and out in the other end comes the answer. The bad news is that they are hard to train, tweak, and change. They are also trained to perform very specialized tasks. So if used in an RTS game, it is more likely that many small neural networks would be trained very for specific tasks, rather than one big mastermind network.

As you can see, there are many advanced AI research areas. Some other AI research areas include expert systems, artificial life, understanding language and phonetics, and robotics. In this chapter, we will take a closer look at finite state machines and use them to control our AI entities. However, you can of course use any of these more-advanced techniques instead. Keep in mind that very often you will have limited resources for your game AI—especially when creating an AI for an RTS game, where most of the resources are chewed up by pathfinding.

We have spent the previous 13 chapters creating something that looks like a real-time strategy game. We have our terrain, units, and buildings, and our visual and audio effects. But one of the most important components is still missing. Our games still don't *behave* as we expect an RTS game to behave, and behavior is a key word when creating a game AI. If an entity behaves intelligently in a situation, we draw the conclusion that this entity must indeed be intelligent. So in this chapter, our aim is not really to create intelligence, but rather to create (or simulate) intelligent behavior.

DIFFERENT LEVELS OF INTELLIGENCE

Imagine that an enemy unit starts attacking one of your idle units. First off, the unit under attack needs to respond with a counterattack automatically—otherwise, its behavior is not very intelligent. The same goes for a friendly unit that just stands there while its friend is getting a beating (i.e., not much of a friend). The player expects the idle unit to automatically also engage in the fight if it's not doing something more important. Otherwise, this too makes little sense. The examples go on and on. The important thing here is that we need to program our units to behave the way the player expects his units to behave. Otherwise, the player will become frustrated that he has to manually tell a nearby idle unit to engage in the battle. We will take a look at how we can implement this low-level unit intelligence using finite state machines. A finite state machine is a very reactive type of AI. The unit responds in a predefined manner to a specific scenario. We will implement low-level unit AI in the already existing UNIT class.

Next we will have a look at controlling groups of units. Have you ever played a game where enemy units seem to come at you one by one rather than as a strong, unified group? To unify computer-controlled units, we will take a look at how to group units together to form a group entity. Group members can talk to each other and support each other in battle, and so on. We will look at how we can implement communication between units in a group and make a computer opponent behave smarter. The group behavior will be created in a new class called GROUPAI.

Finally, we will implement a high-level AI capable of playing our RTS game at a strategic level. The high-level AI will control multiple groups, analyze the terrain, and so on. This AI will also control all high-level decisions, like what buildings to construct, what units to train, and what map location to conquer. We will implement this high-level AI in the MASTERAI class.

Dividing the AI into different distinct layers like this (unit AI, group AI, and master AI) is a well-known technique called "multi-tiered AI." In multi-tiered AI, all high-level (expensive) operations usually run only once per every couple of seconds, while low-level (cheap) operations can run several times during a second, or even once per frame. This approach is illustrated in Figure 14.1.

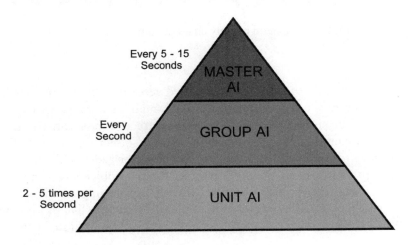

FIGURE 14.1 A Multi-tiered AI approach.

As you can see, the unit AI is controlled by the group AI, which in turn is controlled by the master AI. The reason we update the unit AI several times per second is because the units need to be responsive if they are attacked. Otherwise, when a situation changes, they would stand around deciding what to do until the unit AI is updated. The master AI, on the other hand, is only concerned with the high-level overall strategy, and therefore does not need to be updated as often. Updating the master AI also includes many expensive operations, like extracting strategic information from the terrain. Therefore, it is good that we don't do it to often. Compare Figure 14.1 to Figure 14.2, where a simplified military chain of command is shown.

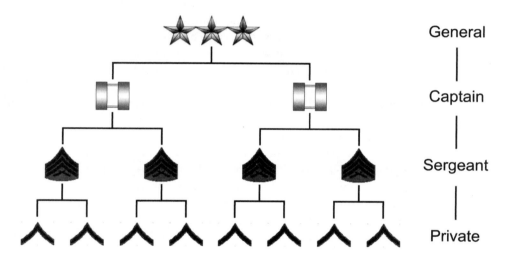

FIGURE 14.2   A simplified military chain of command.

Figure 14.2 shows a very simplified version of the normal chain of command found in most military organizations (though many ranks are omitted). Hopefully you see the similarity between this structure and the multi-tiered AI approach. A general can't concern himself with a single soldier on the battlefield. Instead, he works with abstract issues, like battalions and brigades. The further up in the chain of command you go, the more abstract are the problems you have to solve. We face the exact same problem when we will attempt to implement an AI opponent for our RTS game. The best way to build an AI structure like this is from the bottom-up. So let's start with our privates and see what kind of intelligence they will need.

FINITE STATE MACHINES

Low-level intelligence in RTS games is easiest to create using a Finite State Machine (FSM). A finite state machine has a predefined number of "states" as well as a set of rules describing how to move from one state to another. On our journey through this book, we have already created a number of simple finite state machines. For instance, Figure 14.3 shows a very simple state machine controlling the movement of our units.

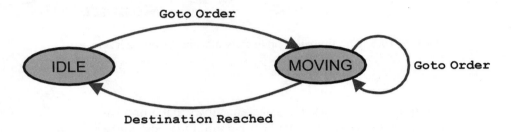

FIGURE 14.3   A simple finite state machine.

This state machine only has two states, IDLE and MOVING. The unit can only be in one of these states at a time. We have a set of rules that control how we can switch between states. In this case, we can change from the IDLE state if we get a Goto order. This would then change the unit's active state to MOVING. Note that if we get a Goto order in the MOVING state, we remain in the MOVING state, but the destination may have changed. Once the destination is reached, the state is again set to IDLE. As with most simple state machines, this one can be coded using just a couple of simple `if` statements or a `switch` statement. Visualizing behavior with a diagram like the one in Figure 14.3 is a great way of understanding a specific behavior. Try to think of all possible states you want to have, as well as what rules will apply. Remember, the more planning, designing, and thinking you do beforehand, the less actual code you will have to write. A simplified behavior diagram of a real-time strategy unit could be summarized as shown with Figure 14.4.

Remember that Figure 14.4 only shows the core of what our unit AI should be capable of. If a unit is given the Attack order, it first starts moving in the direction of its target (i.e., the SEARCH state). Whenever an enemy unit is within range of our unit (as long as our unit is in the IDLE or SEARCH state), we go into the ATTACK state. Also, notice that there is no way to return from the DEAD state (unless you have some

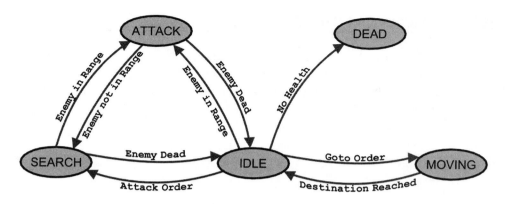

FIGURE 14.4 The simplified finite state machine of our unit AI.

kind of resurrect spell). This diagram shows that a unit can only go into the DEAD state from the IDLE state, but of course a unit may also die in any other state as well. The same applies to the Goto order; this order would also cancel the SEARCH or ATTACK state.

On top of all this, the unit AI must also be able to handle unit-specific things, like the worker constructing buildings, the magician casting spells, and so forth. The unit AI also takes care of unit animations and creating effects like the fireball effect. But before we cover the actual implementation of our unit AI, we need to have a look at a few related helper functions.

Find Targets Within Range of a Unit

In order to create our unit AI, we first need to create a couple of simple functions that will deal with common requests made by the AI. One such request is to find any enemies within a certain range from a specific unit. This search range can be either the sight range or the attack range of unit. This is a very simple function to implement because all units have access to the TERRAIN object. The terrain keeps tracks of all units and buildings using the m_pMapObject pointers in the MAPTILE structure. We implement this function in the MAPOBJECT class so it is accessible for both the UNIT and BUILDING class:

```
std::vector<MAPOBJECT*>
            MAPOBJECT::GetTargetsWithinRange(int theRange)
    {
    std::vector<MAPOBJECT*> enemies;
```

```
        RECT r = GetMapRect(theRange);

        for(int y=r.top;y<=r.bottom;y++)
            for(int x=r.left;x<=r.right;x++)
            {
                MAPTILE *tile = m_pTerrain->GetTile(x, y);

                if(tile != NULL && tile->m_pMapObject != NULL)
                if(tile->m_pMapObject->m_team != team &&
                    !tile->m_pMapObject->m_dead)
                    if(m_mappos.Distance(INTPOINT(x, y))
                        <= theRange || m_isBuilding)
                        enemies.push_back(tile->m_pMapObject);
            }

        return enemies;
    }
```

We get the map rectangle for a specific map object and scan this rectangle for any nondead, nonfriendly map objects. If the enemy map object is within range, we add it to a vector that we return once we've scanned the entire map rectangle. Now the AI has a tool to find what enemy units are within sight or attack range of a certain friendly unit. Sometimes during a game there will be more than one enemy within range. Then the next problem to solve is how to choose which one of these enemies to attack.

Picking the Best Target to Attack

In a couple of different situations, the AI will have to figure out which target in a list of enemies is the best to attack. Obviously, this may vary greatly from game to game, depending on which strategy you would like to use, as well as many game-specific details. This function will score all enemy units in the list from the perspective of a single friendly unit. Here are a couple different examples of strategies that could be used to score targets:

- The weakest target
- The most powerful target (i.e., the enemy that can do the most damage)
- The closest target (good for keeping formations)
- Supporting unit (i.e., units that can heal other enemy units)
- Target already under attack (i.e., help a friendly unit kill his target)
- Combination of the above

Other things you can take into account when scoring a target may be how much jeopardy you put a unit in when you decide to attack a target—for instance, if your unit is currently positioned in a secure location, high ground or similar, and has to move into an open space to attack a target. This function is therefore up to you to implement as you see fit. For our demo, we have the following scoring system for a target:

```
MAPOBJECT* MAPOBJECT::BestTargetToAttack(
                          std::vector<MAPOBJECT*> &enemies)
{
    if(enemies.empty())return NULL;

    int lowestCost = 10000;
    MAPOBJECT *bestTarget = NULL;

    for(int i=0;i<enemies.size();i++)
        if(enemies[i] != NULL && !enemies[i]->dead)
        {
            int cost = enemies[i]->hp +
                m_mappos.Distance(enemies[i]->m_mappos) * 30;

            if(score < lowestCost)
            {
                bestTarget = enemies[i];
                lowestCost = cost;
            }
        }

    return bestTarget;
}
```

We simply weigh together the health of a target with the distance to it. So in short, we use a "pick on the closest weakling" strategy to select which target to attack. Well, now we have a method of creating a list of possible targets within range as well as method of selecting a specific target from this list to attack. The next detail to figure out is from where to attack the target.

Determine the Attack Position

Next we need to create a function that retrieves the closest available position to attack a target from. Remember that during battle, the units are vulnerable when they are moving because then they cannot strike back at an enemy. Therefore, it is important that we minimize the number of tiles a unit needs to move in order to attack a target. It is also necessary to update the path every time the target moves or the intended map location becomes occupied. Figure 14.5 shows the result of the `MAPOBJECT::GetAttackPos()` function.

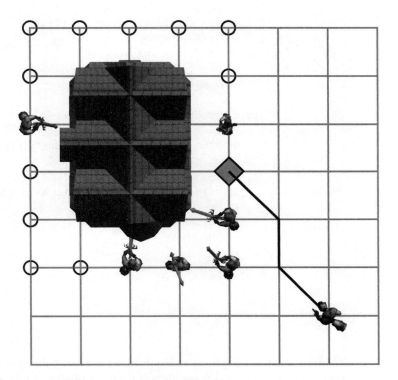

FIGURE 14.5   Finding the closest attack location.

In Figure 14.5, the town hall is under attack by six soldier units. A seventh soldier is about to attack the town hall, as well. It therefore requests from the town hall map object what map location to attack from, using the `GetAttackPos()` function. This function then finds any available attack positions around the town hall (marked with a circle). From these locations, it finds the closest position to the unit making the request and returns this position (marked with a square).

```
INTPOINT MAPOBJECT::GetAttackPos(INTPOINT from)
{
```

```
RECT r = GetMapRect(1);
RECT mr = GetMapRect(0);

INTPOINT bestDest(-1, -1);
float dist = 10000.0f;

//Find the closest available attacking position
for(int y=r.top;y<=r.bottom;y++)
    for(int x=r.left;x<=r.right;x++)
    {
        INTPOINT p(x, y);

        if(!p.inRect(mr))
        {
            MAPTILE *tile = m_pTerrain->GetTile(p);
            float d = from.Distance(p);

            if(tile->m_pMapObject == NULL && d < dist)
            {
                dist = d;
                bestDest = p;
            }
        }
    }

return bestDest;
}
```

With these three functions—GetTargetsWithinRange(), BestTargetToAttack(), and GetAttackPos()—we now have all the tools needed to implement the finite state machine outlined in Figure 14.4. But first let's take a look at some special cases that can occur when using these functions.

Calculating a Map Tile's Accessibility

What works for few units may not always work for many. As the number of units grows, special cases occur when simple state machines like the one presented here can create some unexpected bugs. For an example, consider Figure 14.6.

In this scenario, unit A is under attack and surrounded on all sides by enemy units. Unit B would like to join in the carnage and help his friends vanquish unit A. Unit B requests an available attack position from unit A, and as you can see, there is one available position (marked with a circle). Unit B will query a path from the

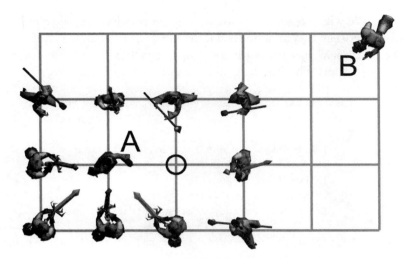

FIGURE 14.6   Multiple-unit pathfinding bug.

TERRAIN::GetPath() function to the attack position. This starts the A* search that first will check that both the start and end node belong to the same tile set (which they do), and therefore unit B will think that a valid path exists. However, there is no valid path from unit B to the attack position because it is blocked by other units. The A* function will therefore end up searching the entire map for all map nodes accessible from unit B. This will, of course, stall the game a lot, depending on the size of the map (especially if the same path is requested over and over again). For example, in the case of a 150 × 150 map, we might end up searching over 20,000 map nodes only to find that there is no valid path. There are a couple of different ways you can avoid a problem like this:

- Limit the number of open nodes during the pathfinding and return a partial path (i.e., a path to the node closest to the goal when the limit is reached).
- Have a small rectangle that encompasses the start and end nodes, plus a few tiles in each direction. Then make sure that the A* algorithm doesn't search outside this rectangle.
- Calculate dynamically whether the start and end nodes are connected before starting a search.

Check out [Cain02] for some optimizations of the A* pathfinding algorithm, including iterative deepening, which is useful for temporary blocked paths and such. We will take a closer look at how we can dynamically check whether a path exists between two map nodes, taking units into account, as well. For this purpose, the PositionAccessible() function has been added to the TERRAIN class. This allows a unit to query whether the goal is accessible before querying a path to it.

```
bool TERRAIN::PositionAccessible(MAPOBJECT *unit,
                                    INTPOINT position)
{
    //Set start and end location of the search
    INTPOINT start = unit->mappos;
    INTPOINT end = position;
    if(start.x > end.x)std::swap(start.x, end.x);
    if(start.y > end.y)std::swap(start.y, end.y);

    //Set the open variable of search area's mapTiles to false
    int searchBorder = 3;
    for(int y = start.y - searchBorder;
        y <= end.y + searchBorder; y++)
    for(int x = start.x - searchBorder;
        x <= end.x + searchBorder; x++)
        if(Within(INTPOINT(x, y)))
            m_pMapTiles[y * m_size.x + x].open = false;

    //Set the open variable of the start location to true
    m_pMapTiles[position.y * m_size.x + position.x].open=true;
    searchBorder-;

    //Iterate any open nodes to its neighbors if
    //they are unoccupied by units
    bool changed;

    do
    {
        changed = false;

        for(int y = start.y - searchBorder;
            y <= end.y + searchBorder; y++)
        for(int x = start.x - searchBorder;
            x <= end.x + searchBorder; x++)
            if(!m_pMapTiles[y * m_size.x + x].open)
                for(int i=0;i<8;i++)
                {
```

```
                 MAPTILE *t;
                 t = m_pMapTiles[y * m_size.x + x].
                                              neighbors[i];

                 if(t != NULL && Within(t->m_mappos) && t->open
                 &&
                     (t->m_pMapObject == NULL ||
                     t->m_pMapObject == unit))
                 {
                     m_pMapTiles[y * m_size.x + x].
                                              open = true;
                     changed = true;
                     i = 8;
                 }
             }

     //If the open variable of the end node
     //is true then a path exists
     if(m_pMapTiles[unit->m_mappos.y * m_size.x +
                 unit->m_mappos.x].open)
         return true;
 }
 while(changed);

 //No path exists
 return false;
}
```

The TERRAIN::PositionAccessible() function takes a pointer to the unit that made the request as well as the goal position as a parameter. Then we calculate a map rectangle that will limit our search to contain the map position of the unit and the goal location. We also extend this rectangle with a border size. Otherwise this search would be much too strict. We make use of the open variable stored in the MAPTILE structure and set all the open variables within the search rectangle to false. Then we set the open variable of the goal location to true. We check to see if the start and goal location are connected by iteratively propagating an open tile to its neighbors. The search ends if the open value of the unit's map location is true (i.e., the two tiles are connected), or if there is no change during a single iteration (i.e., no path exists). This is exactly the same way we calculated the tile sets in Chapter 4. Only now we consider a small subset of the entire terrain, as well as take units into account. As you can see, a big part of creating a real-time strategy game AI is creating a good pathfinding system and resolving all pathfinding issues that pop up. Unfortunately, the complexity of the pathfinding problem increases as the number of units increases.

THE UNIT AI

It is a comparatively simple matter to implement the unit AI. The low-level intelligence that we need to create is very concrete, and can be described with a couple of simple rules and states—for example, "if an enemy unit is within sight range, then attack it," and similar rules. You will soon see that the higher level of intelligence you attempt to implement, the more abstract and difficult it becomes. However, by implementing a good low-level AI for your units, your job will be much easier when it comes to implementing the more-abstract AI layers further along. Figure 14.4 outlines the basics of what we want to achieve with the unit AI. The implementation of the different AI layers is, of course, game-specific (and also tends to be quite involved). Therefore, we will look mainly at pseudocode for the remainder of this chapter. We implement the unit AI as a member function in the already-existing UNIT class in the UnitAI() function:

```
void UNIT::UnitAI( ... )
{
    switch(m_state)
    {
        case STATE_IDLE:
        {
            //Idle behavior here
            break;
        }
        case STATE_MOVING:
        {
            //Moving behavior here
            break;
        }
        case STATE_DEAD:
        {
            //Stay dead here...
            break;
        }
        case STATE_SEARCH:
        {
            //Get within attack range of selected target
            break;
        }
        case STATE_ATTACK:
```

```
        {
            //Attack selected target
            break;
        }

        //Add other states like retreat,
        //constructing buildings here etc. as well
    }
}
```

The individual units keep track of their own internal state using the m_state variable. The UnitAI() function then tells the unit to behave in a certain way depending on what state the unit is in. We will take a closer look at some of the more-complex states and cover the traditional RTS behavior associated with these states.

The Idle State

The idle state is the starting state of all units. If it hasn't been given any orders and if no enemies (or other external events) affect it, then this is the state the unit should be in. This is also important for the higher levels of the AI because this means that the unit is available to be given high-level tasks. Say, for instance, that the master AI has decided it wants to assign three units to scout out a certain area. This is a fairly low-priority task that would make sense to assign to idle units rather units currently involved in a battle or other more-important things.

The only thing an idle unit needs to worry about is scanning the area within its sight range, then attack any enemy that should happen to enter it. This can, of course, be done very easily with the helper function we create:

```
std::vector<MAPOBJECT*> enemies =
                  GetTargetsWithinRange(m_sightRadius);

if(enemies.size() > 0)
{
    m_pTarget = BestTargetToAttack(enemies);
    m_state = STATE_ATTACK;
}
```

We use the GetTargetsWithinRange() function to get a list of all the targets within a unit's sight range. Then we pick the best target to attack using the BestTarget ToAttack() function (remember that this function implements the target selection policy you want for your game). After that, we simply change the unit's state to the attack state.

The Search and Attack States

The search and attack states are closely linked together. A unit is in the search state when the selected target isn't within the unit's attack range. The unit will then move closer toward one of the free attack positions to its target. Once the target is within attack range, the unit's active state is changed to the attack state. In this state, the unit will attack its target until either of them dies (or it is given a retreat order). We will start with having a look at the search state, which in pseudocode looks something like this:

```
case STATE_SEARCH:
{
    if target is dead then
    {
        state = STATE_IDLE
    }
    else
    {
        if target is within attack range then
        {
            state = STATE_ATTACK
        }
        else
        {
            P = target->GetAttackPos()

            if unit is not moving or is P not
            equal to finalGoal then
                Goto(P)
        }
    }

    break;
}
```

We begin the search behavior by checking that the target is still alive; if not, then we set the active state to the idle state. Next we check to see if the target already is within attack range. In that case, we set the active state to the attack state. Should the target still be outside the attack range, we retrieve an available attack position from the target. Retrieving an attack position is a pretty cheap operation that we perform every time the search state behavior is run. Calculating a path, on the other hand, can be a pretty expensive operation, so we only do this if the attack location changes (i.e., the target is moving or another unit occupies the attack position), or if the unit is standing still. Here is the pseudocode of the attack state:

```
case STATE_ATTACK:
{
    if target is dead then
    {
        state = STATE_IDLE
    }
    else
    {
        if target is within attack range then
        {
            attack target
        }
        else
        {
            state = STATE_SEARCH;
        }
    }

    break;
}
```

The attack state is somewhat simpler than the search state. Here we also start by checking that the target is alive before continuing. Should the target be within attack range, we simply attack the target. Here's where you would implement details like attack animations, fireball effects, applying damage to the targets health points, and so on. Should the target flee outside the attack range, we set the active state back to the search state. This will make the unit pursue the target.

Other States

Many other states can be implemented in exactly the same way. For instance, some RTS games allow you to set the aggressiveness of your units. An aggressive unit would attack any enemy within its sight range no matter what its own status is. An evasive unit, on the other hand, would run away from an enemy at all times. A defensive unit might attempt to hold a map location with force if necessary, but it wouldn't pursue its enemy if it flees. This sort of behavior could easily be implemented using finite state machines by creating three different substates—IDLE_AGGRESSIVE, IDLE_EVASIVE, and IDLE_DEFENSIVE. The unit AI could also determine which of these states are best for a given situation, taking into account things like unit health, opposition, and distance to other friendly units. The possibilities are endless. Other common states you might want to implement are GUARD, PATROL, RETREAT, EXPLORE, or STEALTH_ATTACK. In addition to these states, you will also have unit-specific states, like the worker unit's GOTO_CONSTRUCTION_SITE or CONSTRUCT_BUILDING.

On its own, this type of unit AI is very predictive and not much of a challenge. Once a player realizes the rules that change the states of the enemy units, he can easily use this knowledge to best the AI opponent. An example of this is the "attack enemy units within sight range" rule. A smart person can use this rule to vanquish a large group of enemy units by luring them out one by one. This can be done by carefully entering the sight radius of only one enemy unit at a time. This unit will then enter its search state and pursue the player. The player can then retreat with his unit to a location where an ambush is waiting for the foe. This sort of behavior is a weakness you will find in some older games that use rule-based AI systems. So to fix this problem, we need to go beyond working with single units and take a look at grouping units together.

THE GROUP AI

The unit AI only controls the actions of a single unit, based on the input that unit receives from the game world. This means that if a friendly unit A is under attack but outside unit B's sight range, then unit B won't know about it, and therefore won't help unit A. This kind of cooperation doesn't exist in the lowest-level AI layer. We will now attempt to group units together by providing a higher level of intelligence. This layer will control groups of units instead of individual units, as shown in Figure 14.7.

As you can see, a group consists of one or more units. Each time the unit AI is updated, it relays some information to the group AI (i.e., a report). When the group AI is updated, it reads through all the reports filed by its units and then decides what the best course of action for the entire group is. It then sends orders to all the units, which it leaves to the unit AI to implement. An example of this is when a group is scattered over a large area, performing some form of scouting maneuver. Unit #2 spots an enemy building and reports this to its group AI. The group AI then determines whether to attack this building or not. Either it orders Unit #2 to back away, or it orders the other units in the group to join Unit #2 in an assault on the enemy building. It could also send a request to the master AI for backup (more on this later).

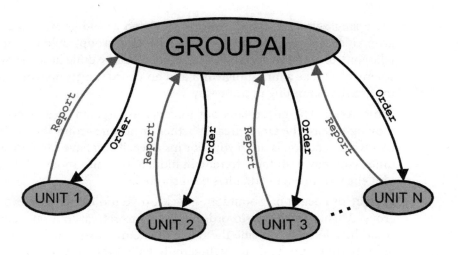

FIGURE 14.7   The relationship between the group AI and the units.

The group AI sits on top of the unit AI. If, for instance, the group AI wants to attack an enemy base, it doesn't need to worry about the low-level implementation of the attack. All it has to do is order the units in the group to move to the location of the enemy base. The unit AI will then take care of the low-level details of the attack—things like finding the best enemy to attack, pursuing enemies, and so forth. However, should the enemy base prove too much of a challenge for the group, it is up to the group AI to order the units to retreat because this isn't covered by the unit AI.

Group Maneuvers

In the GROUPAI class, we will implement a couple of high-level maneuvers that can later be used by the MASTERAI class to control the different groups. Here is an abbreviated list of maneuvers that could be implemented in the GROUPAI class:

Attack Location: The whole group moves in a gathered formation to the location, attacking any enemy unit or building that is in the way. It is important that the group stays together during this maneuver for maximum effect.

Defend/Hold Location: The whole group stays close to the location, attacking any enemy unit that approaches their position. However, should the enemy flee, the units in the group will not pursue, since this would allow an enemy to use a single unit to lead the whole group on a wild goose chase. While the group is chasing the enemy unit, another enemy group could then move in and take control of the location. This must, however, be done in such a way that the enemy can't take a long-range unit and bombard the group from afar without the group responding in some way.

Scout Area: The group fans out to cover as large an area as possible while moving toward the target area. Whether or not the group should engage hostiles while scouting is up to you. For instance, if you have some form of stealth units, you may wish these to remain hidden in stealth mode while an infantry unit engages an enemy that has been spotted.

Retreat to Location: Should an attack prove too difficult or expensive, the group AI should be able to order the units to retreat to a safe location. This could be a location outside the range of enemy missile towers, maybe to another friendly group, or it might simply tell all the units to run home to the base.

Patrol Area/Path: The patrol area (or path) maneuver is very similar to the defend location maneuver. The only difference is that you can set the group to patrol a large area. It would be best if the group moves in a tight formation, randomly, or in a predefined pattern across the area. This is better than scattering the units because the objective of the patrol maneuver is quite different from that of the scout maneuver.

Group Formations: To maximize the efficiency (i.e., attack power, defense value, etc.) of the group, it always make sense to put long-range units behind short-range units when engaging the enemy. Otherwise the weak, long-range units will take the first beating while the friendly short-range units are blocked by their fellow long-range units. Instead, the short-range and more heavily armored units should stand between the enemy and the weaker long-range units, which in turn can support the short-range units. The same goes for supporting spell-casting units, healing units, and miscellaneous units like workers and engineers. See [Dawson02] for a good article about unit formations in real-time strategy games.

These are just some of the most common maneuvers a group can perform. You can also implement other military maneuvers, like providing covering fire during a retreat, flanking, and ambushing. For some further reading about this, see the articles by William van der Sterren ([Sterren02a] and [Sterren02b]) about squad tactics and team AI. In this chapter, we will only implement the Attack Location, Defend Location, and Scout maneuvers. The rest will be up to you.

Unit Messages

The units talk to the group AI by sending some form of messages. These messages could contain information about who sent the message and the status of that unit. It should also contain a message of some sort. A few examples of unit messages could be the following:

- Enemy unit or building spotted
- Under attack by enemy unit
- Healing/Repair needed

A message like "Healing needed" could then be sent by a unit with low health to the group AI. The group AI would look through its units and see if there's an available unit with healing powers. If there is, the group AI could then simply order a healing unit to heal its wounded comrade. In order to send messages to and from the unit AI and the group AI, the units must store a pointer to the GROUPAI object controlling them. The group AI also has to maintain a list of pointers to the different units assigned to it.

The GROUPAI Class

We will now have a look at the actual implementation of the GROUPAI class. All groups will be maintained by the MASTERAI, which we will cover in more detail later. The MASTERAI class will be responsible for creating, maintaining, and destroying all groups. The MASTERAI will also be responsible for setting the active task of all groups.

```
class GROUPAI
{
    public:
        GROUPAI(MASTERAI *_master);
        ~GROUPAI();

        void AddMember(MAPOBJECT *newMember);
        void RemoveMember(MAPOBJECT *oldMember);
        void DisbandGroup();

        void EnemiesSpotted(
                    std::vector<MAPOBJECT*> &manyEnemies);
        GROUPAI* SplitGroup(std::vector<int> units);

        void GroupAI();
        bool isDead();
        INTPOINT GetCenter();
```

```
//Orders
void SetTask(int newTask, RECT *area);
void Goto(RECT mArea);
void Attack(std::vector<MAPOBJECT*> &enemies);
void RetreatTo(RECT ma);

private:
    MASTERAI *m_pMaster;
    std::vector<MAPOBJECT*> m_members, m_visibleEnemies;
    int m_task;
    int m_state;
    RECT m_mapArea;
};
```

The GROUPAI class also keeps a pointer to the MASTERAI object that created it. This is so it can send reports to the master AI. The group AI is also controlled by a very simple state machine, and therefore we keep a state variable to keep track of the internal state. Here is a list of the member functions in the GROUPAI class:

AddMember: The AddMember() function adds a member to the group. Note that we add a MAPOBJECT pointer, which means we can also add buildings to a group. Buildings may not be able to receive orders from a group AI, but they can still report sighted enemies and so forth. This function also sets the group pointer of the map object to point to this current group. This means that any reports this member makes will now be sent to the correct group.

RemoveMember: A member in the group is removed and the group pointer in the member is set to NULL. So from then on, this unit will not send any reports until it is added to another group.

DisbandGroup: This function calls the RemoveMember() function for all the members in the group. Effectively, this means that all members assigned to this group will be released. The group object, itself, will also be removed by the master AI after this operation.

EnemiesSpotted: Members of the group use this function to report sighted enemies to the group AI. Any spotted enemies are added to the m_visibleEnemies vector, which is cleared each time the group AI is updated.

SetTask: This function is used by the master AI to set the active task of the group. Tasks can be any of the maneuvers listed in the previous group maneuvers section. This function takes a pointer to a map area, as well. This map area is, for example, used in certain tasks, like defend area X or attack area Y.

SplitGroup: Used to split a group into two groups, a parameter of this function is a wish list of the amounts and types of the units that should be transferred to the new group, and returns the pointer to the newly created group. This function will be used by the master AI to split large groups—for instance, when it wants to assign a few units from a large group to another task, like scouting the terrain.

GroupAI: This is where the group AI state machine is implemented. This function is called on a regular basis by the MASTERAI class (recommended to be called with at least a one- to five-second interval). This function also deals with the reports sent by group members.

isDead: If all members of the group have been killed or the number of members is zero, this function returns true. The master AI class will use this function to determine whether it can remove the group or not.

GetCenter: This function returns the center location of the group. It can be used to move all members toward the center of the group for a tighter formation and can also be used to scatter all members by moving them farther away from the center.

Goto: All group members currently not involved in a battle are ordered to move to a certain map area.

Attack: This function orders all available units in the group to attack the best target in the list of enemies passed to this function.

RetreatTo: All units (even those involved in an attack) are ordered to retreat to the map area supplied to this function.

All the member functions listed here are very straightforward to implement, with perhaps the exception of the GroupAI() function. It is in this function that all the smarts of the GROUPAI class is located:

```
void GROUPAI::GroupAI()
{
    for each member m in group
    {
        if m is dead then
        {
            RemoveMember(m);
        }
        else
        {
            //Read state of m
        }
    }
```

```
                    //Set group state depending on the state of its members

                    switch(m_state)
                    {
                        case GROUP_STATE_IDLE:
                        {
                            //Group Idle behavior here
                            break;
                        }
                        case GROUP_STATE_MOVING:
                        {
                            //Group Moving behavior here
                            break;
                        }
                        case GROUP_STATE_BATTLE:
                        {
                            //Group Attack behavior here
                            break;
                        }
                    }

                    //Report enemies to Master AI
                }
```

The group AI state machine is slightly different from the unit AI state machine because we have different behaviors in the states, depending on what task the group is performing. For instance, if the group is currently in the attack state but performing the Defend Location task, the group AI must behave differently than if the task should be Attack Location. If the group task is to defend a location, then members are not allowed to pursue enemies outside this location. The most important thing with the GROUPAI class at this stage is that we now have a common interface for units. Units belonging to the same group will no longer act as single entities; they can work together. This alone will increase the illusion of intelligence in our AI opponents.

Group Pathfinding

Another way to decrease the amount of pathfinding calls is to do the pathfinding on a group basis. Instead of calculating one path for each unit, we calculate one path for the entire group. The units try to keep their relative position in the group as they all move along the group path. This is often done by having a "leader" unit that the others follow. Group pathfinding is closely linked to group formations; if you implement one, you might as well implement the other.

That concludes the GROUPAI class. However, despite the addition of the group AI, the AI opponent is still very reactive and boring. The AI opponent doesn't do anything unless provoked. Next, we will take a look at how to extract strategic information from the terrain.

TERRAIN ANALYSIS

We have now had a look at how to control individual units as well as control groups of units. Before we delve into creating the MASTERAI class, we will take a look at how to read strategic information from the terrain. There are a number of different ways to extract abstract information from the terrain that the AI opponent can use to base decisions on. The reason we need abstract information is because there's simply too many things happening and too much low-level information to sift through. We need to provide some easily digestible information for the AI. We will have a look at two powerful techniques for this: influence maps and area decomposition.

Influence Maps

An influence map is a strategic information layer that sits on top of the geographical representation (i.e., the terrain). Originally, the idea of influence maps comes from thermodynamics and is also known as "attractor-repulsor" systems. In its simplest form, this is a 2D array of values, the same size as the terrain. An influence map is very simple to create. Start by setting the entire array to zero, then for each friendly unit, assign a positive value at the unit's location. For all enemy units, assign a negative value. Propagate/smooth these values to neighboring cells. Figure 14.8 shows an example influence map.

In the figure, the heroic white triangles are battling the evil dark squares for total domination of the very large square. As you can see, the white triangles are surrounded by positive numbers. These numbers decrease the farther away from a white triangle they get. In the same way, the dark square is surrounded by negative numbers. Tiles with positive numbers are under friendly influence, while tiles with negative numbers are under enemy influence. Tiles with the number zero are neutral territory. The tile influence value is cumulative, which means that if you have a high number of friendly units in a small area, then the influence value for these tiles

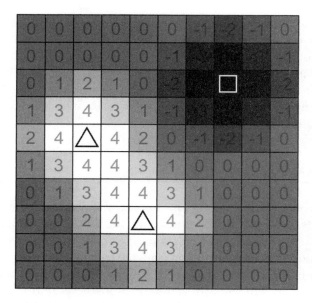

FIGURE 14.8   An influence map.

will be the sum of influences from each unit. To create an influence map like this, there are two things you need to determine:

Unit Value Function: Calculate a single value describing the combat fitness of a unit. When calculating this value, you could take into account unit health, damage, range, speed, mana, and so forth. How you weigh these values together to form the unit value is up to you.

Fall-Off/Smooth Function: The fall-off function determines how the unit value is propagated to neighboring cells. This can either be done by iteratively smoothing the entire influence map with a smoothing function a preset number of times, or each unit can add their influence to all affected cells with a fall-off value.

Now, every time you need to update your influence map, you reset all the tiles in the influence map to zero. Then you cycle through all friendly units and add positive values to the influence map according to the unit value and fall-off functions. You do the same with the enemy units, but this time you use a negative value. From influence maps some of the following basic information can be extracted by the AI:

Enemy Presence: These are the tiles with a negative influence value. The lower the value, the more enemy units affect this area.

The Front/Conflict Areas: These are positive tiles that have an immediate negative neighbor, or vice versa. This happens as two units of different teams approach each other and their influence areas overlap.

What Areas Are Still Neutral: These tiles are, of course, the tiles with an influence value of zero. There is, however, one more possibility for a tile's influence value to be zero. This is when the influence of two units from opposing teams cancel each other out.

With the information stored in the influence map, an AI opponent can determine strategic weak spots, choke points, and so on. It can even be used to create some interesting pathfinding behavior. Imagine that you have an assassin unit that you want to sneak past the enemy's defenses to kill some of the enemy high brass. This could be done by having the pathfinding system put a penalty on tiles under enemy influence.

Variants of Influence Maps

The idea of influence maps can be used for more than just describing what player controls which parts of the terrain. What if we create another influence map layer—but this time instead of mapping spotted units, we map only dead units. We call this layer the "killed units" layer. Why is this good, you might ask? Well, imagine that there are two ways to get to an enemy base, a short way and a long way. The AI will of course always choose the short path. However, the enemy has constructed fortified defenses along this path, and our attacks never even reach the enemy base. How will the AI know not to make the same mistake again? Figure 14.9 shows the idea of a killed units layer.

How will the AI know which approach has the most chance of success? Unfortunately, there's no easy way of calculating this before an attack is launched. But we can make sure that the AI doesn't repeat the same mistake over again. This certainly helps to make the AI more challenging as well as more interesting. In Figure 14.9, a unit has been ordered to attack the enemy base. It is faced with a decision of choosing one of two paths. Looking down the short path we see the tombstones of a lot of fallen comrades. This is a "field of death" marked in the killed-units influence map. The AI can then make the deduction that this area is heavily fortified by the enemy and should probably be avoided if possible. This layer only needs to be updated every time a unit dies, of course. The killed-units layer is just one example of information the AI can benefit from storing as an influence map. Check [Tozour01] and [Tozour04] for other suggestions of information that can be stored as

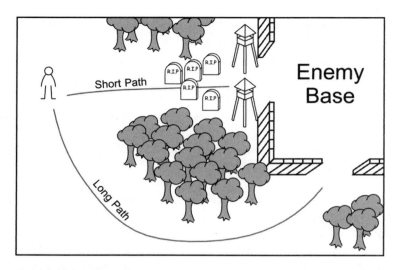

FIGURE 14.9 Storing the location of fallen units in the killed units layer.

influence maps. Also, you can make your AI smarter by giving it a memory of actions that failed in the past. For instance, if attacking the enemy base with three units fails every time, maybe something else should be tried. The more "memory" you can give an AI about past actions, the more it will seem to learn. This is something that a human opponent will greatly appreciate.

Another example of information that could be stored as an influence map layer is strategic terrain information. Say that your game gives units an attack or defense bonus depending on their map location. You could then store this information in an attack-bonus layer and a defense-bonus layer. These layers would only have to be computed when the terrain is created and then used at runtime by the AI opponents. Things that could contribute to these layers could include the following:

The elevation of a tile. Units could, for instance, receive an attack bonus if they are holding the high ground.

The openness of a tile. Some areas, like forests, may have a higher defense bonus than others. Retreating units could then favor these areas.

Tile type. Units may suffer an attack or movement penalty while moving through difficult terrain, like swamp, mud, or snow.

The influence map layer shown in Figure 14.10 illustrates an example terrain; the black lines are height curves and the black dots represent trees/forest. The attack bonus layer is calculated from the heightmap of the terrain, while the defense bonus layer is calculated from the forest areas. In some locations, the positive effects of these two bonus layers overlap. These positions are, of course, excellent positions to face enemy units from. Adding terrain bonuses like these adds another interesting game element to your game, especially if the AI plays accordingly. The player must then plan his attacks/defense a little bit more.

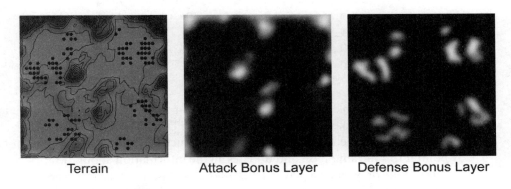

| Terrain | Attack Bonus Layer | Defense Bonus Layer |

FIGURE 14.10   The attack and defense bonus layers.

Area Decomposition

Area decomposition is another useful technique for extracting abstract information from the terrain. This works by dividing the terrain into a number of larger areas. Each area keeps track of what is happening within it, as well as many other area-specific details. By dividing the terrain into a smaller number of large areas, it becomes easier for the AI to assess what goes on where. For instance, an area can keep track of friendly and enemy presences within the area. It can also keep track of whether the AI has visited this area or not, or whether the area is visible at the moment or not. But most important, it can keep track of any resources or other valuable items/buildings residing in this area. The area can keep track of its own value to the AI. For example, if there's a gold mine in the area, the area value could be equal to the amount of gold available in the mine. When the gold runs out, there's no longer a reason for the AI to fight for this area. With only these few pieces of information, the AI can, for instance, calculate if fighting the existing enemy presence in a specific area is worth it or not. See [Pottinger00] for a more-detailed look at area decomposition. For the purpose of area decomposition, we add the AREA structure to the long list of classes and structures in this project:

```
struct AREA
{
    AREA(RECT mArea);
    void Update(TERRAIN *terrain, int teamNo);
    bool Connected(TERRAIN *terrain, INTPOINT from);
    INTPOINT GetCenter();

    RECT m_mapArea;              //Actual map area
    int m_status;                //Owner, visited, conflict etc
    int m_enemy_presence;
    int m_friendly_presence;
    int m_value;                 //Resources, strategic value etc
};
```

In this example, we use simple rectangular areas, but you can also use irregular-shape areas, like is done in [Pottinger00]. The actual map area is stored in the m_mapArea variable, which is set in the constructor. The Update() function takes a pointer to a terrain object and updates all the information about the area. Note that this is done only when a player's MASTERAI object is updated. The Connected() function checks if the area is physically connected with another tile on the terrain. This is used to make sure we don't try to send our units to a location that isn't accessible from where they are. The areas described here can also be used for high-level pathfinding. As the number of units increases you will be forced to implement a hierarchical pathfinding system where units use a rough representation of the terrain for long paths.

A Brief Look at AI Cheating

Sometimes the easiest (or only) way to raise the challenge of your AI opponent is to cheat, but try to do this as little and as unpredictably as possible. Cheating can be done by giving the AI opponent access to information it normally wouldn't possess, or perhaps make the AI opponents' units stronger than the player's. Yet another way to cheat is to give the AI opponent discount prices when purchasing units, buildings, or upgrades. Some of these cheats are totally invisible to the player if not exaggerated. If you are desperate to raise the challenge of your AI opponent, this sort of bias is easiest to implement as well most likely to go unnoticed by the player.

However, remember that the real challenge is to build an AI opponent that doesn't cheat at all. This means that the AI can't know an enemy unit exists until it has seen that unit with the eyes of one its own units; therefore, the AI can't let that enemy unit contribute to the influence map. Otherwise, it becomes impossible for the player to do things like launch surprise attacks, for instance. The person playing the game will then quickly become bored, and we will have failed our ultimate goal to build a *fun* AI opponent. It is important that the player can catch the AI opponent off-guard every once in a while; this makes the AI opponent seem more human.

The STRATEGY_MAP Class

The purpose of the STRATEGY_MAP class is to extract and provide strategic information from the terrain to the MASTERAI class. This can be done with whatever technique you find suitable for your game. In this example, we will look at how to create a noncheating influence map as well as how to divide the terrain into simple rectangular areas.

```
class STRATEGY_MAP
{
    public:
        STRATEGY_MAP(TERRAIN *_terrain, PLAYER *_player,
                     INTPOINT numAreas);
        ~STRATEGY_MAP();

        void Update(std::set<MAPOBJECT*> &enemies);

        AREA* GetScoutArea(INTPOINT from);
        AREA* GetAttackArea(INTPOINT from);
        AREA* GetRandomArea();

    private:
        TERRAIN *m_pTerrain;
        PLAYER *m_pPlayer;
        INTPOINT m_size;
        int *m_pInfluenceMap;
        std::vector<AREA> m_areas;
};
```

The constructor of this class takes a pointer to the terrain object as well as a pointer to the player that owns the strategy map. This is so the strategy map can know what units are friendly and what units are enemies. To the constructor, we also send the numAreas parameter. This tells the strategy map how many rectangular areas we should divide the terrain into. The influence map and subareas can then be created in the constructor. The Update() function takes a list of enemies that the strategy map is to take into consideration. This list is, of course, the list of enemies reported by the units, which makes sure that the AI doesn't know more than it should. The three functions GetScoutArea(), GetAttackArea(), and GetRandomArea() are used by the high-level AI layer to retrieve a suitable terrain area for a certain group maneuver.

GetScoutArea: To this function, we send the position of the group assigned to exploration. This function returns an unexplored area close to both the group and the base location of the player. This makes sure that we first scout areas close to the base before venturing farther away.

GetAttackArea: This function works in almost the exact same manner as GetScoutArea(). But instead of returning an area that hasn't been explored, this function returns that area where an enemy was last spotted. This is also weighted so that areas close to the group and to the base are prioritized. This is important because it will make the AI prioritize threats that are closer to the base.

GetRandomArea: In some cases there are no unexplored areas left to explore, or there may be no areas in which an enemy was last spotted. Then both of the previous functions will return a random area using this function, selected from the list of areas in the STRATEGY_MAP class.

It is up to you to implement any similar functions you may need for your game. Let's take a look at the Update() function where the influence map is calculated and the subareas update:

```
void STRATEGY_MAP::Update(std::set<MAPOBJECT*> &enemies)
{
    //Reset influence map
    memset(m_pInfluenceMap, 0,
           sizeof(int) * m_size.x * m_size.y);

    //Add positive influence from friendly units
    for(int m=0;m<m_pPlayer->m_mapObjects.size();m++)
        if(m_pPlayer->m_mapObjects[m] != NULL &&
           !m_pPlayer->m_mapObjects[m]->m_dead)
        {
            MAPOBJECT *mo = m_pPlayer->m_mapObjects[m];
            RECT r = mo->GetMapRect(mo->m_sightRadius);

            for(int y=r.top;y<=r.bottom;y++)
            for(int x=r.left;x<=r.right;x++)
            {
                INTPOINT p(x, y);
```

```
            if(m_pTerrain->Within(p))
            {
                float multiplier = (
                                mo->m_sightRadius —
                                mo->m_mappos.Distance(p)) /
                                mo->m_sightRadius;

                if(multiplier < 0.0f)
                    multiplier = 0.0f;

                m_pInfluenceMap[y * m_size.x + x] +=
                    mo->m_hp * mo->m_damage * multiplier;
            }
        }
    }

//Subtract negative influence from enemy units
std::set<MAPOBJECT*>::iterator i;
for(i=enemies.begin();i != enemies.end();i++)
{
    //same as above but use a negative multiplier
}

//Update Map Sub Areas
for(int i=0;i<m_areas.size();i++)
    m_areas[i].Update(m_pTerrain, m_pPlayer->m_teamNo);
}
```

We reset the influence map to zero and then add the influence of all friendly and all visible enemy units. We let the unit influence an area the size of their sight radius in the same way we created the sight texture in Chapter 10. Here we use the unit health multiplied with the damage of a unit as the unit fitness value. This means that a damaged unit won't contribute as much to the influence map as a healthy one. We have now had a look at a couple of different methods that can be used to extract strategic, high-level information from the terrain. It is time we put this information to use and tie all the parts in this chapter together with the master AI layer.

THE MASTER AI

The master AI is responsible for all high-level decisions an AI opponent makes and is divided into responsibility areas. Each area has a manager that takes care of that specific area. In this example we use two simple managers, the build and the strategy managers. The build manager is responsible for constructing buildings, training units, upgrading technologies, and so forth. The strategy manager, on the other hand, is the general that controls the units and the groups on the battlefield, using terrain analysis tools like influence maps or area decomposition.

In this example, the build and strategy managers are implemented as simple member functions of the MASTERAI class. But in larger and more-advanced RTS games, it may advantageous to implement the build and strategy managers as their own classes, instead. You may even need to divide the responsibilities into more than just these two classes. You might want to have managers for areas like diplomacy, research, or economy. Many times these managers need to talk and make requests of each other. For instance, the strategy manager should be able to request a specific unit it would need from the build manager, and so on. For some good articles about high-level RTS AI implementation, see [Kent04], [Scott02], and [Ramsey04]. Here's the definition of our MASTERAI class:

```cpp
class MASTERAI
{
    public:
        MASTERAI(PLAYER *_player, TERRAIN *_terrain);
        ~MASTERAI();

        void Update(float deltaTime);
        void HandleGroups();
        void MasterAI();

        void BuildManager();
        void StrategicManager();

        void EnemiesSpotted(
                std::vector<MAPOBJECT*> &manyEnemies);

    private:
        PLAYER *m_pPlayer;
        TERRAIN *m_pTerrain;
        STRATEGY_MAP *m_pStrategyMap;

        GROUPAI m_unitPool;
        std::vector<GROUPAI*> m_groups;
        std::set<MAPOBJECT*> m_visibleEnemies;
```

```
        float m_nextGroupUpdate, m_nextUpdate;
        RECT m_base;
    };
```

As you can see, we keep a pointer to the terrain and to the player we want to control with this master AI. We also create a unique STRATEGY_MAP object for each AI opponent we have. The EnemiesSpotted() function is used by the master AI's groups to report sighted enemies. These are then used to update the strategy map. Let's now take a look at the individual managers of the master AI.

Build Manager

As previously mentioned, the build manager is responsible for training units and constructing buildings. It is the build manager's responsibility to find and do its best to fill the needs of the player. The build manager should perform at least the following:

■ Assess current situation (count number of units and buildings).
■ Estimate needed units or buildings.
■ Deal with requests from other managers.
■ Train needed units.
■ Construct needed buildings.
■ Make requests to other managers (e.g., if a certain type of resource is needed, the build manager can request the strategy manager to acquire this resource).

Performing Actions

The AI opponent needs to perform certain game actions as it plays the game. Examples of these actions can be to train units, construct buildings, and so on. If you remember the technology tree in Chapter 2, some units and buildings have prerequisites before they can be trained or constructed. For example, you can't train a magician unless you have a tower, and you can't build a tower unless you have a barrack and a town hall. In addition to all of the prerequisites, you also need enough funding. The build manager of the master AI will make requests like "train me a soldier" or "train me a magician," and so on. But in some cases the prerequisites are not in place, so we must translate the build manager's wish to train a magician into a prerequisite action if necessary. For this purpose, we have created the virtual AI_ACTION interface that specific actions must inherit from:

```
        class AI_ACTION
        {
            public:
```

```
                virtual AI_ACTION* RequiresAction(PLAYER *player) = 0;
                virtual void PerformAction(PLAYER *player) = 0;
        };
```

The RequiresAction() function should return any necessary prerequisite action needed before a specific action can be performed. The PerformAction() gives the necessary orders needed to perform the action. In this chapter, we will take a look at two specific actions implemented in the TRAIN_UNIT and CONSTRUCT_BUILDING classes. The two classes are defined as follows:

```
class TRAIN_UNIT : public AI_ACTION
{
    public:
        TRAIN_UNIT(int unitType);
        AI_ACTION* RequiresAction(PLAYER *player);
        void PerformAction(PLAYER *player);

    private:
        int m_unitToTrain;
};

class CONSTRUCT_BUILDING : public AI_ACTION
{
    public:
        CONSTRUCT_BUILDING(int buildingType);
        AI_ACTION* RequiresAction(PLAYER *player);
        void PerformAction(PLAYER *player);

    private:
        int m_buildingToMake;
};
```

Both these classes take the type of unit or building that is to be trained or constructed. The master AI can then just create a TRAIN_UNIT object for the specific unit it would like to train. Call the RequiresAction() to find out if a prerequisite action is needed before it can start to train this unit or not. If all is okay, it can just call the PerformAction() function, and the specific action class will take care of the low-level details. Both the RequiresAction() and the PerformAction() functions take a pointer to the player object that the master AI wants to perform the action on. Here's the implementation of the CONSTRUCT_BUILDING class (the TRAIN_UNIT class is implemented in the same manner):

```
CONSTRUCT_BUILDING::CONSTRUCT_BUILDING(int buildingType)
{
    m_buildingToMake = buildingType;
}
```

The constructor just takes a parameter describing what building the master AI wants built and stores this.

```
AI_ACTION* CONSTRUCT_BUILDING::RequiresAction(PLAYER *player)
{
    //Check that we have a worker
    if(!player->HasMapObject(WORKER, false))
        return new TRAIN_UNIT(WORKER);

    //Check that we have all prerequisite buildings
    if(m_buildingToMake == BARRACKS ||
      m_buildingToMake == TOWER)
        if(!player->HasMapObject(TOWNHALL, true))
            return new CONSTRUCT_BUILDING(TOWNHALL);

    if(m_buildingToMake == TOWER)
        if(!player->HasMapObject(BARRACKS, true))
            return new CONSTRUCT_BUILDING(BARRACKS);

    //All is ok, no prerequisite action is required
    return NULL;
}
```

In the `RequiresAction()`, we check that the provided player object has all the necessary prerequisites for the action. In the CONSTRUCT_BUILDING class, we start by checking that the player has a worker; if not, we need to train one, and therefore return a TRAIN_UNIT object. Next we move on to check that the necessary buildings exist for the building we intend to construct. If they don't, then we return a CONSTRUCT_BUILDING object with the needed building. If all is well and there's nothing we need to do before we can perform this action, then we just return NULL. The PLAYER::HasMapObject() simply returns true or false whether the player has a map object or not that fits the description sent with the parameters of the function.

```
void CONSTRUCT_BUILDING::PerformAction(PLAYER *player)
{
    //Check that the player has cash to train the unit
    if(player->money < GetCost(m_buildingToMake, true))return;
```

```
                    //Get Building position
                    INTPOINT buildPos = player->FindClosestBuildingLocation(
                                             m_buildingToMake,
                                             player->m_teamStartLocation);

                    //Get Available worker
                    UNIT *worker = player->GetAvailableUnit(WORKER);
                    if(worker == NULL)return;

                    //Build building
                    worker->ConstructBuilding(m_buildingToMake, buildPos);
                }
```

In the PerformAction() function, we first make sure that the player has the necessary resources needed to construct the building. If the player doesn't, then we exit the function and will try again the next time the master AI build manager is updated. Next we query the player for a suitable building location and retrieve the pointer to an available worker unit. If all is well, we order the worker to start constructing the building at the player's preferred location. The PLAYER::Get AvailableUnit() function returns a pointer to an available unit that fits the description. This function returns NULL if all units with that description are busy, in which case the PerformAction() exits and waits until a unit is available. A similar function exists called PLAYER::GetAvailableBuilding(), which is used in the TRAIN_UNIT class. Okay, we've seen how to create actions that keep track of what prerequisite actions are needed as well as how to perform the action. This makes it very easy for the build manager to specify an action and perform it (excerpt from the MASTERAI::BuildManager() function):

```
        AI_ACTION *action = new TRAIN_UNIT(nextUnitToBuild);
        AI_ACTION *preAction = NULL;

        do
        {
            preAction = action->RequiresAction(player);

            if(preAction != NULL)
            {
                delete action;
                action = preAction;
            }
```

```
}
while(preAction != NULL);

//Perform action
if(action != NULL)
{
    action->PerformAction(player);
    delete action;
}
```

Here we define the action as a new `TRAIN_UNIT` object. Then we enter a loop where we extract any prerequisite action needed until the `RequiresAction()` function returns `NULL` (i.e., no further prerequisite actions needed). Then we simply perform this action using the `PerformAction()` function. A word of warning is in order here. Consider the case shown in Figure 14.11.

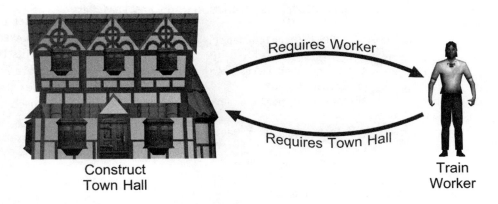

FIGURE 14.11   An infinite action loop.

Here's a common case of actions forming a loop. A town hall needs a worker to be constructed, but a worker needs a town hall to be trained. Of course, this is fine as long as we have at least one town hall or one worker, but what happens when we don't? We enter an infinite loop of actions requesting each other. This scenario is one that you need to take care to avoid. In this case it is simple enough to do, but as the number of actions grow, so does the complexity of the problem. Here we make sure that before the `TRAIN_UNIT::RequiresAction()` function returns a `CONSTRUCT_BUILDING(TOWNHALL)` object it first checks that the player has a worker.

That pretty much covers how to create and implement the build manager. How to assess what units are needed, as well as the communication between managers, is highly game-specific, so that will be left to you. The build manager is one of the easier managers to implement. Next up is the hardest one: the strategy manager.

Strategy Manager

The strategy manager is the master AI's general in charge of troop movement, conquest, defense, and exploration. We have already covered how to extract strategic information from the terrain using influence maps or area decomposition. Now it's time to figure out how to use this information. The strategy manager is also responsible for creating, maintaining, and destroying groups. When a build manager has trained a new unit, this unit is stored in a unit pool (a group AI). The unit pool's default task is to defend the base. Whenever the strategy manager needs a new group to perform a task, it picks available units from the unit pool, creates a new group with these, and assigns this new group to the specific task. For this purpose, we have the HandleGroups() function in the MASTERAI class:

```
void MASTERAI::HandleGroups()
{
    Add unassigned units to the unit pool
    Update unit Pool
    Set the unit pool to defend the base

    for each group G of MasterAI
    {
        if G is dead then
        {
            delete G
        }
        else
        {
            Update G
        }
    }
}
```

This function takes care of adding new units to the unit pool and updating all the groups (including removing dead groups). Next follows the core of the master AI's strategy manager, the StrategyManager() function. This manager, whether function or class, needs to deal with the following:

- Explore terrain.
- Determine areas of strategic importance—for example, enemy bases, resources, ambush locations, enemy strong/weak spots, and so on (which, of course, goes hand in hand with exploring the terrain).
- Assess current threat, distance to threat, magnitude, and priority.
- Deal with requests from other managers.
- Decide what actions to take.
- Create groups and assign tasks.
- Make requests to other managers—for example, the strategy manager could request the research manager to find better firearms, and so forth.

To create new a group and assign it to a specific task, all we need to do is the following:

```
//Retrieve scout area
AREA* area = m_pStrategyMap->GetScoutArea(
                        m_pPlayer->m_teamStartLocation);

if(area != NULL)
{
    //Create wish list
    std::vector<int> unit;
    unit.push_back(SOLDIER);
    unit.push_back(SOLDIER);
    unit.push_back(MAGICIAN);

    //Split group
    GROUPAI *newGroup = m_unitPool.SplitGroup(unit);

    //Set group task and add to groups
    if(newGroup != NULL)
    {
        newGroup->SetTask(TASK_SCOUT, &area->m_mapArea);
        m_groups.push_back(newGroup);
    }
}
```

We request an area from the strategy map that hasn't been explored yet. We make a wish list of units we would like to use in the scout group we are about to send and use this wish list to split the unit pool with. We then set the task of the group using the GROUPAI::SetTask() method and add the new group to the list of groups in the master AI. This is how groups are created and assigned tasks. For an example implementation of a simple strategy manager, see Example 14.1, where the entire code for the StrategyManager() function is listed.

Introducing Some Randomness

To make the AI less predictable, it can be a good idea to introduce some randomness into its thinking. However, making the AI more random does not mean that it should become more stupid. You could, for instance, have a couple of different methods for selecting the best target for your units. Sometimes they could all attack the weakest units they encounter, and at other times they could attack the enemy unit that inflicts the most damage. There are many examples of where you could introduce randomness in all three AI layers. In the group AI, you can play with different formations or different implementations of the same maneuver. In the master AI, you can use random numbers to affect decisions, like what units to produce. However, always keep a certain level of control. If you make decisions look too random, you will lower the overall "intelligence" of the AI. For instance, in one specific round, an AI might produce nothing but workers if this decision is fully random. You want the AI to behave in a somewhat unpredictable way; but at the same time, you must make sure that the random decisions that are made aren't stupid decisions.

AI Personality

Another topic closely linked to random actions, is biased actions. If you have ever played several times against the same human opponent, you often find that this player favors certain tactics, unit types, or game style. You can mimic this behavior in an AI opponent by giving it a personality. Things you can incorporate into an AI personality are:

- Aggressiveness
- Exploration rate
- Unit preferences (e.g., favors long-range units, etc.)
- Level of difficulty
- Allowed to cheat (yes, no, a little?)

You can probably think of many more attributes that can be used to describe an AI personality. As your game becomes more complex, it becomes more interesting to fight AI opponents with different personalities because these differences become more apparent.

ON THE CD

Example 14.1

In this example, four AI-controlled teams battle each other. The fog-of-war has been disabled so you can fully study the actions of the AI opponents. The game speed has also been increased to three times the normal speed. Try to see if you can spot what actions are governed by what AI layer (master, group or unit layer). With a little effort, you can change this example so that you can control one of the teams instead of an AI.

SUMMARY

If you are a seasoned real-time strategy game player, you won't find much of a challenge in beating the simple AI opponent presented in this chapter. This chapter is more meant to serve as an eye-opener and a brief introduction to the extremely complex problem of creating a virtual opponent operating in an environment such as an RTS game. We have covered a multi-tiered AI with three different layers: the unit AI, the group AI, and the master AI. Together, these three layers form a framework you can use to build your own (more advanced) real-time strategy opponents. There are many good articles and books available on this topic. Be sure to check out the *AI Game Programming Wisdom* series by Charles River Media. In it, there are a lot of useful articles about creating RTS AIs.

If you have run Example 14.1, you will have noticed how close we are to a finished game. We've incorporated the effects from Chapter 12, however there is one important RTS component we have yet to implement, and that is networking.

EXERCISES

- Implement a "Repair Building" behavior for the worker unit using a finite state machine.
- Implement some of the mentioned group maneuvers, like retreat, scout, and patrol.
- Implement the UNIT_MESSAGE structure that can be used to send messages from units to the GROUPAI class. Also, have the GROUPAI class handle all incoming messages.
- Implement the GROUP_MESSAGE structure that gets sent from the groups to the master AI. Let these two message types replace the simple EnemiesSpotted() functions in the MASTERAI class and the GROUPAI class.
- Implement group formations and group pathfinding.
- Implement a couple of technology upgrades—for example, better armor for the soldiers, longer range for the magicians, and so on. Implement a UPGRADE_TECHNOLOGY action that inherits from the AI_ACTION class.

REFERENCES

[Bull04] Bull, Larry, "Learner Classifier Systems: A Brief Introduction." Available online at: *http://www.cems.uwe.ac.uk/lcsg/introchap.pdf,* 2004.

[Cain02] Cain, Timothy, "Practical Optimizations for A* Path Generation." *AI Game Programming Wisdom,* Charles River Media, 2002.

[Dawson02] Dawson, Chad, "Formations." *AI Game Programming Wisdom,* Charles River Media, 2002.

[Kent04] Kent, Tom, "Multi-Tiered AI Layers and Terrain Analysis for RTS Games." *AI Game Programming Wisdom 2,* Charles River Media, 2004.

[Pottinger00] Pottinger, Dave, "Terrain Analysis in Realtime Strategy Games." Available online at: *http://www.gamasutra.com/features/gdcarchive/2000/pottinger.doc,* 2000.

[Ramsey04] Ramsey, Michael, "Designing a Multi-Tiered AI Framework." *AI Game Programming Wisdom 2,* Charles River Media, 2004.

[Scott02] Scott, Bob, "Architeching an RTS AI." *AI Game Programming Wisdom,* Charles River Media, 2002.

[Sterren02a] van der Sterren, William, "Squad Tactics: Team AI and Emergent Maneuvers." *AI Game Programming Wisdom,* Charles River Media, 2002.

[Sterren02b] van der Sterren, William, "Squad Tactics: Planned Maneuvers." *AI Game Programming Wisdom,* Charles River Media, 2002.

[Tozour01] Tozour, Paul, "Influence Mapping." *Game Programming Gems 2,* Charles River Media, 2001.

[Tozour04] Tozour, Paul, "Using a Spatial Database for Runtime Spatial Analysis." *AI Game Programming Wisdom 2,* Charles River Media, 2004.

FURTHER READING

Borovikov, Igor, "Orwellian State Machines." *AI Game Programming Wisdom 3,* Charles River Media, 2006.

Martin, John, "Strategy and Tactics." Available online at: *http://www-cs-students. stanford.edu/~amitp/Articles/StrategyAndTactics.html,* 1996.

15 | Networking

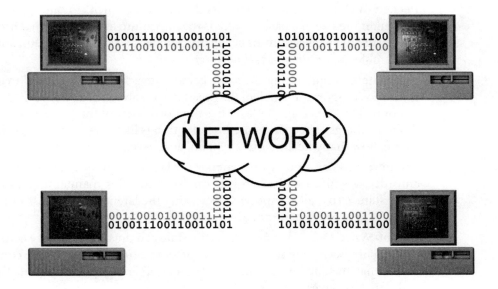

In Chapter 14, we had a look at how to create an artificial opponent to play our RTS game against us. However, most seasoned RTS players find artificial opponents rather boring. These players can only be challenged by other human opponents. To enable multiple humans to play an RTS game against each other, we need to make some form of network connection between them. For this we will use DirectPlay, which is incorporated in DirectX. DirectPlay is a networking API that sits on top of whatever network protocol is used (TCP/IP, IPX, modem, serial link, etc.). Before we delve deeper, let's first define a few common concepts:

Network: A physical connection between two or more computers. This can be over the Internet, a Local Area Network (LAN), a direct link (modem or null link cable), or various other types of networking links.

Session: An instance of a multiplayer application. The session is created by the host computer, and other computers can connect it. A session can be password-protected, allowing only clients with the correct password to join. It also has a maximum limit of clients.

Packet: A chunk of data sent across the network, which contains game information. If the size of a packet exceeds the maximum allowed length, DirectPlay will divide the packet automatically into smaller packets, send them, and then reassemble the original packet at the receiver.

Game State: Maintaining the same game state across all connected machines is the most important problem that needs to be solved for all networked games, not only RTS games. Each player has their own view of the game, which shows different things. The game state includes things like what units are positioned where, how many health points remain, and so on.

Latency: In a computer game, latency (or lag) is the time delay between when an order was given and when it is carried out. After maintaining a uniform game state across all computers, decreasing the latency is the most important task of a network programmer.

Out-of-Sync: Due to latency, the game state can drastically change across several machines, causing them to be out-of-sync. For instance, on one computer unit A may be killed by a bullet, while on another computer the bullet misses and unit A survives.

So to put the problem we are faced with in one sentence: We need to maintain a uniform game state across as many machines as possible with as little latency as possible. The complexity of the problem increases, of course, the more units and players we have. To make matters worse, a network programmer has to consider that different computers may have different connection speeds, hardware, and so on. This chapter is only meant to get you started with this very complex subject. Therefore, we will assume that our game will always be played over a fast and reliable LAN. Even so, making a networked RTS game is no picnic.

PEER-TO-PEER VERSUS CLIENT-SERVER

Generally speaking there are two network architectures used for real-time strategy games. One is the peer-to-peer model, which means that each computer maintains one connection to each of the other computers in the game. In the client-server model, on the other hand, the client computers just have one connection to the server, which keeps a connection to each of the connected clients. See Figure 15.1, where the two architectures are compared.

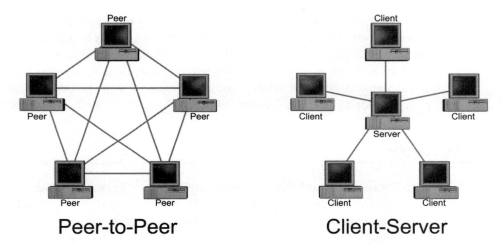

Peer-to-Peer

Client-Server

FIGURE 15.1   Comparison of the peer-to-peer and client-server models.

Peer-to-Peer: In the peer-to-peer model, each computer acts both as a server and as a client to each of the other computers. When a player changes the game state, he must send updates to all the other peers. The peer-to-peer model is often used in RTS games because of its low latency. However, as the number of connections (i.e., players) increases, so does the complexity. Most RTS games using the peer-to-peer model support up to eight players, but not more. (This architecture is also commonly used for file-sharing applications, etc.)

Client-Server: In the client-server model, there is one central computer (the server), to which all client computers are connected. The server computer should be the most powerful computer available, since it will need to perform several additional network-related tasks. When a player changes the game state, it sends an update to the server. The server processes the change and relays it to the other client computers. This means that for each update, all information has to be sent via the server, where (as in the peer-to-peer model) it is sent directly to the other computers.

With the peer-to-peer model, each computer maintains a copy of the global game state, while in the client-server model, the global game state is stored on the server computer. It's easier to maintain a uniform game state in the client-server model, since the current game state on the server is always the correct one. In the peer-to-peer model, it can be hard to figure out what is wrong and what needs to be done to correct it. Even though the peer-to-peer model results in lower latency for fewer players, we will take a look at implementing the server-client model in this chapter. We select the client-server model because it is easier to maintain a uniform game state with this model (which takes priority). Initiating DirectPlay to function according to the peer-to-peer model is fairly simple, even though the architecture is fundamentally different. After reading this chapter, you should have no trouble creating a peer-to-peer application with the help of the DirectX documentation.

DIRECTPLAY

DirectPlay is a Microsoft API for writing multiplayer games. All low-level tasks, like finding sessions, connecting to other computers, managing groups, and so on, is managed by DirectPlay. So are tedious tasks, like dividing large packets into many smaller ones and reassembling them on the other side. DirectPlay also contains advanced functions for in-game voice communication over the network. Just like DirectSound or DirectMusic, DirectPlay is implemented with a couple of COM objects.

In many cases you have two separate applications in the server-client model—the server application and the client application. The client application is usually a lightweight program that deals with user input and makes requests to the server. The server application, on the other hand, runs on the server machine and deals with maintaining clients, client requests, and so on. Usually, data storage and any heavy processing is done by the server. Our application (and games in general) is a bit different from this standard way of implementing the client-server architecture. We will contain both the server behavior and the client behavior in the same application. The application will simply be in a server-state or a client-state and behave differently according to what state it is in.

The initial set up of the client-server state, connections, and so on is usually done in a lobby. DirectPlay has a lobby interface that can be used for this purpose. The lobby interface is especially used for applications over the Internet. However, the lobby interface is a bit over the top for what we need, and so instead we will build our own simple lobby interface using only basic DirectPlay components. The interested reader can read more about the DirectPlay lobby components in the DirectX documentation. So let's now have a look at the basic DirectPlay components needed to build a multiplayer application:

IDirectPlay8Server: This class manages the server part of a client-server networked application. An IDirectPlay8Server object can be used to host sessions on the local machine, handle clients, and send data to one or more clients.

IDirectPlay8Client: This class handles the client side of a client-server application. With an IDirectPlay8Client object, we can find active sessions, connect to a session hosted by a server, and of course send data to the server.

IDirectPlay8Address: The IDirectPlay8Address class encapsulates a network address to which DirectPlay can connect. An address object can describe an IP address, a modem phone number, IPX network and node, or serial cable settings, depending on what connection type is used by the application.

In addition to these three classes, there is also a wide array of structures used by DirectPlay, which we will cover in more detail in the following sections. We will eventually encapsulate these three classes into our own NETWORK class that will handle both the server and the client side of the application. Figure 15.2 shows the two sides of a client-server application and an example flow of events:

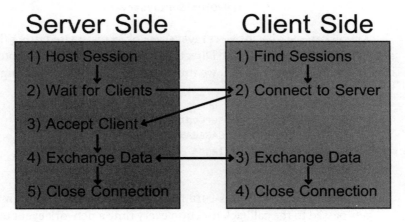

FIGURE 15.2   An example flow of events in a client-server application.

All the server (or the host in a peer-to-peer application) needs to do is host a session and wait for clients to connect. The clients, on the other hand, need to search for active sessions it can join and then try to connect to one. The server will then accept or reject the clients' requests to connect to the session. Once a client has been accepted into the session, the server and client can start exchanging data. This can go on until either of them disconnects. Let's now take a closer look at the IDirectPlay8Server and the IDirectPlay8Client classes.

THE SERVER SIDE

This section will look at initiating and setting up a server application. We will cover how to create a DirectPlay session and how to accept new connections from clients, and so on. We will also take a look at the necessary server callback function. This is the function that is called each time a network event takes place. These events can be anything, from new players joining the game to standard data packets being received. It is in this callback function that most of our communication structure is implemented. Here is how we would create a server object:

```
IDirectPlay8Server *dPlayServer = NULL;

//Initiate COM library
CoInitialize(NULL);

//Create new server object
CoCreateInstance(CLSID_DirectPlay8Server, NULL,
                 CLSCTX_INPROC_SERVER, IID_IDirectPlay8Server,
                 (LPVOID*)&dPlayServer);
```

As you can see, the `IDirectPlay8Server` object is created using the `CoCreateInstance()` function, just like the DirectMusic components (see Chapter 13). After we have created the server object, we must initiate it with the following function:

```
HRESULT Initialize(
    PVOID const pvUserContext,
    const PFNDPNMESSAGEHANDLER pfn,
    const DWORD dwFlags
);
```

pvUserContext: With this VOID pointer, you can set a user context value that gets passed to the callback function every time a network event takes place. This can be useful when you want to use the same callback function from more than one object. For instance, instead of having one callback function for the server and one for the client, we could create just one callback function. Then we would use the user context value to determine from what object the callback function was called.

pnf: This is a pointer to the callback function the object will use as a message handler.

dwFlags: Here you can specify that this object operates on a local area network, for instance. We use the default settings and set this parameter to zero. (For a full list of flags, see the DirectX documentation.)

A call to the initialize function looks something like this:

```
dPlayServer->Initialize(NULL,                //User context
                        ServerCallback,      //Callback function
                        0);                  //flags
```

That's all we need to do to create and initialize a DirectPlay server object. We will take a closer look at the `ServerCallback()` function later on. Next, the server needs to create a session that the clients can connect to.

Hosting Sessions

A session can be compared to a room. Once a client connects (i.e., enters the room) it can take part in any of the events going on in this room. During the course of a game, new players may come and go. It is the host's (i.e., the server's) job to update the other clients in the session of what is happening. In a game environment, the host must also send the global game state to any newcomers so that they know what's going on. Managing sessions, keeping track of clients, and so on requires quite a bit of code, but luckily it's all pretty easy.

We create a new session using the `IDirectPlay8Server::Host()` function. But before we look at this function, we need to check out the `DPN_APPLICATION_DESC` structure. This structure is used by DirectPlay to describe a multiplayer application:

```
typedef struct DPN_APPLICATION_DESC
{
    DWORD dwSize;
    DWORD dwFlags;
    GUID  guidInstance;
    GUID  guidApplication;
    DWORD dwMaxPlayers;
    DWORD dwCurrentPlayers;
    WCHAR *pwszSessionName;
    WCHAR *pwszPassword;
    PVOID pvReservedData;
    DWORD dwReservedDataSize;
    PVOID pvApplicationReservedData;
    DWORD dwApplicationReservedDataSize;
}
```

dwSize: This structure must know the size of itself before it can be used. So we simply set this member to sizeof(DPN_APPLICATION_DESC).

dwFlags: We set this member to DPNSESSION_CLIENT_SERVER, meaning that we want a client-server application. There are other flags used for peer-to-peer applications, password protected applications, and so on (again, see the DirectX documentation).

guidInstance: This is the GUID of the instance. You don't have to worry about this member because it is set automatically by DirectPlay.

guidApplication: You do need to worry about this one though, the GUID of the application. This member makes sure that DirectPlay games with different application GUID can't connect to the same session.

dwMaxPlayers: This member sets the maximum number of players allowed in the session (set by the server or host).

dwCurrentPlayers: The number of players currently connected to this session. If a player tries to connect to a session that is full, he will automatically get rejected.

pwszSessionName: This is the name of the session, which is used only to describe the session. Usually, when a client looks for open sessions in a game, there's a list with active sessions described by this member. The session name is set by the server and can be anything from "Pete's game" to "Kill the Bunny."

pwszPassword: This is the password of the session. If a client tries to connect to a password-protected session with a faulty password, the client will automatically get rejected. Most games use this feature to allow players to keep unwanted company out of their sessions.

The rest of the members are all either reserved or not used, and should be set to NULL. The following code shows a simple way to initialize the DPN_APPLICATION_ DESC structure:

```
//Create Wide Char Session name
char sessionName[] = "Someone's Game";
WCHAR strHost[128];
mbstowcs(strHost, sessionName, strlen(sessionName) + 1);

//Create an Application ID
GUID guidApp = { 0xd962eee5, 0x7783, 0x4018,
                {0x9c, 0xd, 0xc3, 0x26, 0x82,
                0x1f, 0x80, 0x8f} };
```

```
// Set up the Application Description.
DPN_APPLICATION_DESC desc;
ZeroMemory(&desc, sizeof(DPN_APPLICATION_DESC));
desc.dwSize = sizeof(DPN_APPLICATION_DESC);
desc.dwFlags = DPNSESSION_CLIENT_SERVER;      //App Description
desc.guidApplication = guidApp;               //GUID for the app
desc.pwszSessionName = strHost;               //Session name
```

We use the ZeroMemory() function to set the whole DPN_APPLICATION_DESC object to NULL. Then we set the few attributes of it that we use. As you can see, we set the GUID variable RTS_APP_ID to a long string of hexadecimal values. If we create a new game, we need to generate a new unique GUID value for it. This value is usually generated by a program, but you can also find a couple of different online Web sites that can generate a GUID for you. The Microsoft GUID generator might be easiest (see Figure 15.3). You'll find this program in the Visual Studio Tools folder.

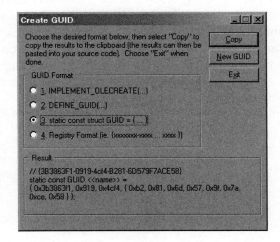

FIGURE 15.3   The Microsoft GUID generator.

Use this program to generate a guaranteed-unique GUID, then copy-and-paste the hexadecimal values into your code. Okay, so we now know how to describe the DirectPlay application we want to run with the DPN_APPLICATION_DESC structure. Before we can host a session, we need to cover the IDirectPlay8Address class, since this is needed by the IDirectPlay8Server::Host() function.

```
IDirectPlay8Address *myAddress = NULL;

CoInitialize(NULL);

CoCreateInstance(CLSID_DirectPlay8Address, NULL,
                 CLSCTX_ALL, IID_IDirectPlay8Address,
                 (LPVOID*)&myAddress);
```

As you can see, we create an `IDirectPlay8Address` object, just like for any other COM object. The only thing we need to do with the address object before we can use it to host a game is to set the service provider used. This is done with the `IDirectPlay8Address::SetSP()` method:

```
HRESULT SetSP(const GUID *const pguidSP);
```

The `pguidSP` parameter can be set to one of the following constants: `CLSID_DP8SP_TCPIP`, `CLSID_DP8SP_SERIAL`, `CLSID_DP8SP_MODEM`, `CLSID_DP8SP_IPX`, or `CLSID_DP8SP_BLUETOOTH`. Obviously, we will be using the most-common `CLSID_DP8SP_TCPIP`, which specifies the TCP/IP protocol. After setting up the application description and initiating an address object, we are good to go and can start hosting a session using the following member function of the `IDirectPlay8Server` class:

```
HRESULT Host(
    const DPN_APPLICATION_DESC *const pdnAppDesc,
    IDirectPlay8Address **const prgpDeviceInfo,
    const DWORD cDeviceInfo,
    const DPN_SECURITY_DESC *const pdpSecurity,
    const DPN_SECURITY_CREDENTIALS *const pdpCredentials,
    VOID *const pvPlayerContext,
    const DWORD dwFlags
);
```

pdnAppDesc: This is a pointer to a `DPN_APPLICATION_DESC` object containing the description of what kind of networked session we want to create.

prgpDeviceInfo: This parameter is an array of address objects from which we should host the session. You could, for instance, create two address objects with different service providers (e.g., TCP/IP and IPX) and then allow clients to connect using either network protocol.

cDeviceInfo: This parameter is a `DWORD` that contains the amount of address objects that were sent to the `prgpDeviceInfo` parameter.

pvPlayerContext: This is an optional parameter to which we can send a context value of a player. We will use this to determine if a new player is a local player or a remote player.

The rest of the parameters are reserved or not used, so we set them to NULL. A call to this function then looks something like this:

```
dPlayServer->Host(&desc, &myAddress, 1, NULL, NULL, NULL, 0);
```

With this, the server object now hosts a new session that other clients can search and connect to. Next we will look at how to deal with actual network messages and events.

Server Callback Function

The server callback function is one that we must implement completely on our own. In this function, you will indicate what your program should do in the case of certain network events. For instance, what if a new player joins in the middle of a game? Should he be rejected or allowed to connect? The server callback function also deals with the actual data sent between clients and the server. This callback function must have a certain format, as shown here:

```
typedef HRESULT (CALLBACK *PFNDPNMESSAGEHANDLER)(
    PVOID pvUserContext,
    DWORD dwMessageType,
    PVOID pMessage
);
```

pvUserContext: This is the same user context value that was set in the Initialize() function.

dwMessageType: This is the type of event/message that the callback function has to deal with.

pMessage: The actual message.

Our actual server callback function looks like this:

```
HRESULT WINAPI ServerCallback(PVOID pvUserContext,
                              DWORD dwMessageType,
                              PVOID pMessage)
```

```
    {
        switch(dwMessageType)
        {
            case DPN_MSGID_CREATE_PLAYER:
            {
                //New player has connected
                break;
            }
            case DPN_MSGID_DESTROY_PLAYER:
            {
                //Player has left the game
                break;
            }

            //Add all other cases here as well
        }

        return S_OK;
    }
```

This code shows that the callback function catches the CREATE_PLAYER and DESTROY_PLAYER events. Here is a short list of some of the most common message types used by a server:

DPN_MSGID_CREATE_PLAYER: A new player has joined the session. The message contains information about the new player. This should be stored in a list so that later on we know what players are connected. Note that this message type is also generated when the server hosts a new session.

DPN_MSGID_DESTROY_PLAYER: A player has left the session. This is where we would remove a player from the list and also relay this information on to any other clients still in the session.

DPN_MSGID_RECEIVE: This is actual data that the server has received from one of its clients. The server must read the message and act accordingly; in some cases the server may also need to relay the information to the other clients.

DPN_MSGID_TERMINATE_SESSION: This message type occurs when the session is terminated by the host.

This is just a short example of all available message types. There are other message types for clients, which we will cover later on. There are also some concerning the peer-to-peer model (see DirectX documentation for the full list). The actual message sent to the callback function is of course different depending on what type of message it is. The message types have the DPN_MSGID prefix, while the actual message structure has the same name but uses the DPNMSG prefix. So in the case of the DPN_MSGID_CREATE_PLAYER message type, the actual message structure is DPNMSG_CREATE_PLAYER. These message structures contain all the information you need in order to handle the message. For instance, in the CREATE_PLAYER message, you get the DirectPlay Id of the new player. This is stored using the DPNID type, and it is a unique value for each player in the session. The following code shows a callback function that handles the CREATE_PLAYER event:

```
HRESULT WINAPI ServerCallback(PVOID pvUserContext,
                              DWORD dwMessageType,
                              PVOID pMessage)
{
    switch(dwMessageType)
    {
        //New player has connected
        case DPN_MSGID_CREATE_PLAYER:
        {
            //Cast pMessage of the callback function
            PDPNMSG_CREATE_PLAYER msg =
                        (PDPNMSG_CREATE_PLAYER)pMessage;

            //Read DPNID of the new player
            DPNID newPlayerID = msg->dpnidPlayer;

            //store new player ID in a list...

            break;
        }
    }

    return S_OK;
}
```

Here we cast the incoming message to the correct message type—in this case, a DPNMSG_CREATE_PLAYER message. Then we can read any information stored in this structure. We will take a closer look at receiving application-defined data when we discuss sending messages. In the meantime, try to cover as many of the relevant message types as possible in your callback function. Just remember the simple prefix rule and how to map a message type to its actual data structure.

Server Cleanup

After we are done with our networked application and we want to clean up, there are some specific things we need to do. First we need to release any address objects we've used. This is done with the usual `Release()` method:

```
if(myAddress != NULL)
    myAddress->Release();

myAddress = NULL;
```

Next we need to call the `Close()` function of the `IDirectPlay8Server` object. This closes all network connections to any clients and destroys all players. After this function returns, it is safe to shut down the application. This function can be called with the `DPNCLOSE_IMMEDIATE` flag, which means that any outstanding calls won't be completed before the `IDirectPlay8Server` object is closed.

```
//Finish outstanding calls
dPlayServer->Close(0);
```

Or,

```
//Close immediately
dPlayServer->Close(DPNCLOSE_IMMEDIATE);
```

That's all we need to do to clean up after a server object. That concludes setting up the server side of an application using DirectPlay.

THE CLIENT SIDE

We've had a look at how to create a server object, host sessions, and deal with server events. Now we will look at creating the client side of a networked application. Most things are very similar in the way they work compared to the server side. As you might recall, a client differs mostly in that we search for active sessions to join, rather than host the session. The client side is also a bit more lightweight, since we don't need to worry about maintaining clients, relaying information, and so on. We implement the client behavior using the `IDirectPlay8Client` interface. An `IDirectPlay8Client` object is created in the exact same way as the server object. The only difference is, of course, that we have a client callback function instead:

```
IDirectPlay8Client *dPlayClient = NULL;

//Initialize COM library
CoInitialize(NULL);

//Create new COM object
CoCreateInstance(CLSID_DirectPlay8Client, NULL,
                CLSCTX_INPROC_SERVER, IID_IDirectPlay8Client,
                (LPVOID*)&dPlayClient);

//Initialize Client
dPlayClient->Initialize(NULL, ClientCallback, 0);
```

Enumerating Available Sessions

For a client to connect to a session, it first needs to find any available sessions. The client will first describe what kind of application it wishes to connect to, using the DPN_APPLICATION_DESC structure. The most important member in this structure is, of course, the guidApplication variable. This makes sure that only sessions from the correct application will be listed. The next thing we need to set is the address of the server we wish to connect to. After that, we call the IDirectPlay8Client:: EnumHosts() function:

```
HRESULT EnumHosts(
    PDPN_APPLICATION_DESC const pApplicationDesc,
    IDirectPlay8Address *const pdpaddrHost,
    IDirectPlay8Address *const pdpaddrDeviceInfo,
    PVOID const pvUserEnumData,
    const DWORD dwUserEnumDataSize,
    const DWORD dwEnumCount,
    const DWORD dwRetryInterval,
    const DWORD dwTimeOut,
    PVOID const pvUserContext,
    HANDLE *const pAsyncHandle,
    const DWORD dwFlags
);
```

pApplicationDesc: The description of the type of application you would like to connect to.

pdpaddrHost: The host address. If you haven't specified a specific address or host name, DirectPlay will broadcast the session enumeration request.

pdpaddrDeviceInfo: This is the device address. The only thing important to set in this parameter is the service provider you want to use (e.g., TCP/IP, IPX, etc.).

pvUserEnumData: A block of user-defined data that gets sent with the enumeration request. We won't use this, so we'll set this parameter to zero.

dwUserEnumDataSize: The size of the user-defined block of data.

dwEnumCount: This parameter specifies how many times the enumeration request should be sent.

dwRetryInterval: Amount of time in milliseconds between enumeration attempts.

dwTimeOut: Time to wait for answers.

pvUserContext: This value will be sent to the client callback function when the enumeration responses are received.

pAsyncHandle: A handle that you can use to cancel the enumeration process.

dwFlags: There are several possible flags to this function. DPNENUMHOSTS_SYNC means that the process runs synchronously. If the DPNENUMHOSTS_OKTOQUERY FORADDRESSING flag is set, a pop-up window will appear if additional address information is needed. The DPNENUMHOSTS_NOBROADCASTFALLBACK flag disables broadcasting.

A simple call to this function looks like this:

```
//Setup what kind of sessions you are looking for
DPN_APPLICATION_DESC desc;
ZeroMemory(&desc, sizeof(DPN_APPLICATION_DESC));
desc.dwSize = sizeof(DPN_APPLICATION_DESC);
desc.guidApplication = RTS_APP_ID;

//Setup the host address you would like to connect to
WCHAR addrIP[MAX_PATH] = L"123.47.10.255";
size_t addrSize;
StringCbLengthW(addrIP, MAX_PATH, &addrSize);

serverAddress->SetSP(&CLSID_DP8SP_TCPIP);

serverAddress->AddComponent(DPNA_KEY_HOSTNAME,
                            addrIP,
                            addrSize, DPNA_DATATYPE_STRING);
```

```
//Start the enumeration process
dPlayClient->EnumHosts(&desc,          //Application Desc
                serverAddress,         //Host Address
                myAddress,             //Device Address
                NULL,                  //User Enum data
                0,                     //User Enum data size
                1,                     //Enummeration attempts
                0,                     //Retry Interval
                0,                     //Time Out
                NULL,                  //User Context
                NULL,                  //Async Handle
                DPNENUMHOSTS_SYNC);//Flags
```

This will send an enumeration request to the address specified in the server
Address variable. You can leave the IDirectPlay8Address::AddComponent() call out,
which specifies a particular IP address. In that case, DirectPlay will broadcast the
enumeration request on the client's subnet. If an enumeration request is successful
and there are some available sessions, the client will receive responses from the
sessions in the form of a network message. This message (DPN_MSGID_ENUM_HOSTS_
RESPONSE) must be handled in the client's callback function. As explained before, we
use the PDPNMSG_ENUM_HOSTS_RESPONSE structure to receive the message. Here are
some useful components of this structure:

pAddressSender: Host address.

pApplicationDescription: The description of the session. This includes the
name of the session, number of players, and so on.

dwRoundTripLatencyMS: Latency measured in milliseconds; often used to measure how good the connection is between the server and the client.

For the full list of the members of the PDPNMSG_ENUM_HOSTS_RESPONSE structure,
see the DirectX documentation. The only real important ones are the address of the
host and the application description. These are the two components we need to
connect to a session. We therefore create a new structure to hold the information
necessary to connect to a session:

```
struct SESSION
{
    SESSION(char _name[],
            DPN_APPLICATION_DESC _desc,
            IDirectPlay8Address *_address)
```

```
    {
        name = _name;
        desc = _desc;
        if(_address != NULL)
            _address->Duplicate(&address);
    }

    std::string name;
    DPN_APPLICATION_DESC desc;
    IDirectPlay8Address *address;
};
```

This structure holds the name of the session, the description of the session, and the address of the host. We can now save the enumeration responses we receive in an array of SESSION objects and then create a list of these, and allow users to select which session they would like to connect to. The following code shows how to deal with an enumeration response and create a new SESSION object from it (excerpt from the client callback function):

```
switch(dwMessageType)
{
    case DPN_MSGID_ENUM_HOSTS_RESPONSE:
    {
        PDPNMSG_ENUM_HOSTS_RESPONSE msg =
                        (PDPNMSG_ENUM_HOSTS_RESPONSE)pMessage;

        const DPN_APPLICATION_DESC* desc =
                        msg->pApplicationDescription;

        //Extract session name from description
        char sessionName[128];
        wcstombs(sessionName, desc->pwszSessionName,
        wcslen(desc->pwszSessionName) + 1);

        //Create new SESSION object
        SESSION(sessionName, *desc, msg->pAddressSender);

        break;
    }
```

```
                //Also deal with all other messages here...
    }
```

You can easily add the latency time to the SESSION structure and also extract this from a host's enumeration response. In this section, we have covered how to send a session enumeration request from the client and how to deal with responses from available hosts. Now all we need to do is to connect to a certain session.

Connecting to a Session

As mentioned in the previous section, we need the address of the host and the application description to connect to a certain session. When we have this information, we can connect with the IDirectPlay8Client::Connect() function:

```
HRESULT Connect(
    const DPN_APPLICATION_DESC *const pdnAppDesc,
    IDirectPlay8Address *const pHostAddr,
    IDirectPlay8Address *const pDeviceInfo,
    const DPN_SECURITY_DESC *const pdnSecurity,
    const DPN_SECURITY_CREDENTIALS *const pdnCredentials,
    const void *const pvUserConnectData,
    const DWORD dwUserConnectDataSize,
    void *const pvAsyncContext,
    DPNHANDLE *const phAsyncHandle,
    const DWORD dwFlags
);
```

The parameters of this function are very similar to the IDirectPlay8Client:: EnumHosts() and the IDirectPlay8Server::Host() functions, and will therefore not be covered in detail here. A typical call to this function looks something like this:

```
dPlayClient->Connect(&session.desc,    //Application Desc
                     session.address,  //Host Address
                     myAddress,        //Device address
                     NULL,             //Security Desc
                     NULL,             //Security Credentials
                     NULL,             //User Connect Data
                     0,                //User Connect Data Size
                     NULL,             //Async Context
                     NULL,             //Async Handle
                     DPNCONNECT_SYNC); //Flags
```

This function usually returns one of the following values, depending on how the connection request went:

DPNERR_HOSTREJECTEDCONNECTION: The host rejected the connection.

DPNERR_INVALIDHOSTADDRESS: The host wasn't found.

DPNERR_INVALIDPASSWORD: The password was wrong (only used when a session is password-protected).

DPNERR_SESSIONFULL: The session is full.

S_OK: All went as it should, and the client is now connected to the session.

Assuming that the connection went okay, the client will now be connected to the server, and they can start exchanging information.

Client Callback Function

The client callback function works in the same way as the server callback function. Which callback function the client should use is specified in the IDirectPlay8 Client::Initialize() function. The only difference between the client and server callback functions is that they handle different messages; otherwise they look the same. Some important messages the client callback function must handle are:

DPN_MSGID_ENUM_HOSTS_RESPONSE: Session enumeration responses (see the Enumerating Available Sessions section).

DPN_MSGID_TERMINATE_SESSION: The connection was terminated, and the client was disconnected from the server.

DPN_MSGID_RECEIVE: Application-specific data received from the server. We will take a closer look at this message type in the next section.

APPLICATION MESSAGES

We have covered all the necessary preparations needed to connect clients with a server. Now we will look at the core of every network application: exchanging data. In this section, we will create many application-specific packages and send these across the network to other computers. As usual, when we have many structures that share similarities, we create a base structure from which the others can inherit. We put all common variables and functionality into the base structure. This type of message structure is shown in Figure 15.4.

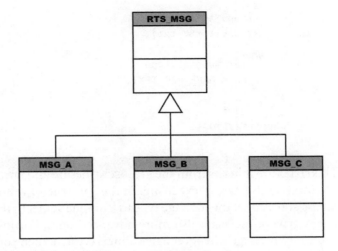

FIGURE 15.4   Application message structure.

The three specific structures MSG_A, MSG_B, and MSG_C all inherit from RTS_MSG, our base structure. Later, when we send and receive messages, we only have to worry about sending messages of the RTS_MSG type, and so we don't have to handle each specific message type individually. The base structure can look something like this:

```
struct RTS_MSG
{
    DWORD type;
};
```

As you can see, this structure does not contain any specific data, just a variable that keeps track of what type of message this is. The type variable is set by any sub-classes inheriting from the RTS_MSG structure, and it must be unique for each inheriting structure or class. For example, here's a text message we can use to send simple text strings:

```
struct MSG_TEXT : public RTS_MSG
{
    MSG_TEXT(char txt[])
    {
```

```
                    //copy text
                    strcpy(text, txt);

                    //Set message type
                    type = GAME_MSG_TEXT;
              }

        char text[100];
      };
```

This structure inherits from the RTS_MSG structure and encapsulates the data we want to send, in this case a text string. In the constructor of this class, we copy the text across and also set the message type to a unique value. In the same way, you can create any type of message, also more-advanced ones. For instance, if you would like to create a message whenever a new unit is created, then you would create a new structure inheriting from the message base structure and encapsulate the necessary information (e.g., what player, unit type, map position, and so on). Okay, we now have a way of encapsulating the application-specific information we want to send; then next thing is to look at how to send it.

Sending Messages

To send information over the network using DirectPlay, there are two specific functions we need to use: the IDirectPlay8Server::SendTo() function and the IDirectPlay8Client::Send() function (depending, of course, on whether the computer is a server or client). Both these methods send data encapsulated using the DPN_BUFFER_DESC structure:

```
        struct DPN_BUFFER_DESC
        {
            DWORD dwBufferSize;         //Size of data
            BYTE *pBufferData;          //pointer to the data
        };
```

To encapsulate a D3DXVECTOR3 object, we would just write:

```
        DPN_BUFFER_DESC desc;
        D3DXVECTOR3 aVector = D3DXVECTOR3(0.3f, 1.4f, -3.2f);

        desc.dwBufferSize = sizeof(D3DXVECTOR3);
        desc.pBufferData = (BYTE*)&aVector;
```

In the same way, we can encapsulate our own application-specific message structures in the DPN_BUFFER_DESC structure before we send them. The IDirect Play8Server::SendTo() function and the IDirectPlay8Client::Send() function are almost identical. The only difference is that the server's SendTo() function takes a DPID (DirectPlay Id) stating what client to send the data to, whereas the client can only send to the server. The IDirectPlay8Server::SendTo() function looks like this:

```
HRESULT SendTo(
    const DPNID dpnid,
    const DPN_BUFFER_DESC *const pBufferDesc,
    const DWORD cBufferDesc,
    const DWORD dwTimeOut,
    void *const pvAsyncContext,
    DPNHANDLE *const phAsyncHandle,
    const DWORD dwFlags
);
```

dpnid: The ID of the recipient. If you would like to broadcast a message (something which is very useful) you can specify the DPNID_ALL_PLAYERS_GROUP constant for this parameter. This will broadcast the message to all players in the session.

pBufferDesc: An array of DPN_BUFFER_DESC objects (up to eight objects) that should be sent.

cBufferDesc: The number of DPN_BUFFER_DESC objects pointed to by the pBufferDesc parameter.

dwTimeOut: The number of milliseconds to wait to send the message. If time runs out, the message is dropped from the send queue. Set this parameter to zero to guarantee that the message gets sent.

dwFlags: Again, there's a long list of flags that can be used to send messages in different ways. For the full list, see the DirectX documentation. Here is a short list of the most commonly used flags:

- DPNSEND_SYNC—The message is sent synchronously.
- DPNSEND_GUARANTEED—This flag guarantees that the message will be delivered; however, a guaranteed delivery also takes much longer to complete.
- DPNSEND_NOLOOPBACK—If the message is to be broadcasted, then this flag makes sure that the sender doesn't receive its own message.

The IDirectPlay8Client::Send() function has the same parameters as the server's SendTo() function, except for the DPNID parameter, since it always just sends data to the server. Sending a simple text message can look like this:

```
//Create new text message
MSG_TEXT textMessage("A text message!");

//Encapsulate using DPN_BUFFER_DESC structure
DPN_BUFFER_DESC desc;
desc.pBufferData = (BYTE*)&textMessage;
desc.dwBufferSize = sizeof(MSG_TEXT);

//Send message
dPlayServer->SendTo(
        DPNID_ALL_PLAYERS_GROUP,            //DirectPlay ID
        &desc,                              //Buffer Desc
        1,                                  //num desc
        0,                                  //Time Out
        NULL,                               //Async Context
        NULL,                               //Async Handle
        DPNSEND_SYNC | DPNSEND_NOLOOPBACK); //Flags
```

The message has now been sent, and there is nothing left to do but receive it.

Receiving Messages

Once a message has been sent, receiving it is pretty simple. An incoming message generates an event in the client or server callback function with the DPN_MSGID_RECEIVE Id. The corresponding DPNMSG_RECEIVE structure looks like this:

```
struct DPNMSG_RECEIVE
{
    DWORD dwSize;
    DPNID dpnidSender;
    PVOID pvPlayerContext;
    PBYTE pReceiveData;
    DWORD dwReceiveDataSize;
    DPNHANDLE hBufferHandle;
    DWORD dwReceiveFlags;
};
```

Extracting our application-specific data from this structure is easy and done like this:

```
//Cast pMessage to a PDPNMSG_RECEIVE object
PDPNMSG_RECEIVE data = (PDPNMSG_RECEIVE)pMessage;
```

```
//Cast the received data to our message base class
RTS_MSG *msg = (RTS_MSG*)data->pReceiveData;

//Handle specific message depending on the message type
switch(msg->type)
{
    case GAME_MSG_TEXT:         //Text message
    {
        MSG_TEXT *textMessage = (MSG_TEXT*)msg;
        //Deal with text message here...
        break;
    }
    case GAME_OTHER_MSG:        //Other message
    {
        MSG_OTHER *other = (MSG_OTHER*)msg;
        //Deal with other message here...
        break;
    }
}
```

Using the `type` member of the `RTS_MSG` structure, we can decode an incoming message and determine how to handle it by using a simple `switch` statement.

What Data to Send?

At this stage, we know how to create and connect server and clients, and how to send and receive data. Now we will take a look at general things you must consider when sending data across a network. In these days of a monstrous information flow, concepts like bandwidth or connection speed are common knowledge. It all boils down to how many bytes we can push across a certain connection. This number is always limited—for some connections more than others. On a dial-up connection you might be limited to a couple of hundred bytes per second, whereas on a broadband connection, you can transfer several thousand bytes per second. Then there's an LAN, where you can push across a couple of megabytes per second. No matter which connection you are running over, the less information we need to transfer the better. Have a look at the following table:

Table 15.1 lists some basic data types with their sizes in bytes and their ranges. The most commonly used data type in 3D programming is the float data type. Sometimes, however, it is unnecessary to have values with floating-point precision. Imagine a 200 × 200 heightmap comprised of 40,000 float values. We would reduce the precision and store this heightmap using simple byte values, instead, say from 156 KB to 39 KB. This means that it will only take one quarter of the time to send the heightmap across the network if we use bytes instead of floats. This is of course a pretty drastic decrease in precision. Consider using shorts instead. Short values would give you 65,535 different values, and only half the amount of byte float values would be used.

TABLE 15.1 Data Types and Their Ranges

Data Type	Size	Max Value	Min Value
Double	8	1.8e+308	2.2e-308
Float	4	3.4e+38F	1.2e-38F
Int	4	2147483647	−2147483648
Short	2	32767	−32768
Char	1	127	−128
Byte	1	255	0

The moral of the story is that you should make sure you need the extra range or precision before you use the larger data types in your network messages. For example, something that often gets sent across the network is terrain coordinates. If the map is smaller than 255×255 map tiles, why not use bytes to send the map coordinates across?

THE NETWORK CLASS

It is now time to introduce the NETWORK class. This class encapsulates all that we have covered so far in this chapter, including both the server side and the client side of our multiplayer game. The network class looks like this:

```
class NETWORK
{
    friend HRESULT WINAPI ServerCallback( ... );
    friend HRESULT WINAPI ClientCallback( ... );
```

```
public:
    NETWORK();
    ~NETWORK();

    void Init(bool _server, char _playerName[]);
    void Release();
    void HostNewSession(char sessionName[]);
    void FindSessions();
    HRESULT ConnectToSession(int index);
    DP_PLAYER *FindPlayer(DPNID id);
    void Send(RTS_MSG *msg);
    void SendTo(DPNID id, RTS_MSG *msg);

    //Public Variables
    bool server, connected;
    char playerName[64];         //Name of local player
    char activeSession[50];      //name of active session
    std::vector<SESSION> sessions;
    std::vector<DP_PLAYER> players;
    std::vector<std::string> chat;

private:
    IDirectPlay8Server *m_pServer;
    IDirectPlay8Client *m_pClient;
    IDirectPlay8Address *m_pMyAddress, *m_pServerAddress;
    DPNID m_localID;
};
```

As you can see, this class contains server functions, like HostNewSession(). It also contains client-specific functions, like FindSessions() and ConnectToSession(). The NETWORK class encapsulates both the IDirectPlay8Server and the IDirect Play8Client interfaces, of which it only uses one at a time. The idea is that we initiate the NETWORK class differently depending on whether the computer acts as a server or not. However, once the NETWORK class has been set up (with sessions hosted or clients connected), external objects can use the NETWORK class to send messages regardless if it functions as a server or a client. External objects just use either the Send() or the SendTo() function, and the NETWORK class knows which underlying DirectPlay interface to use. All the member functions of this class are implemented as shown in all the precious sections. The NETWORK class just binds all the tedious details into one class, giving us an easy interface that external objects can use. Setting up the NETWORK class is a process that requires a lot of user interaction. Next we will take a look at how to create a nice User Interface (UI) to do just this.

BUILDING A LOBBY

We have now covered all the practical details necessary to create both the server and client side of a multiplayer application. We've also bound the two sides together in the NETWORK class, making it easy for external objects to send messages without worrying about the underlying DirectPlay interfaces. The NETWORK object setup can easily be done in code, of course. However, almost all multiplayer games these days let the user control the setup of a network connection. This section will go through how to create a user interface (i.e., a lobby) that will allow the user to determine who's hosting the game, player names, and so on. Most multiplayer games use a similar user-interface flow to set up the game. Figure 15.5 shows an example of this simplified lobby UI flow.

Player Name (1): In this window, the user enters the name or nickname he would like to use in a session. In games such as role-playing games, the player might also select things such as appearance and so on in this screen.

Server or Client (2): Next follows a simple screen that queries the user if he would like to either host a game or join an existing game. In the server-client model, the server always hosts the game. Here the flow splits, and hosts move to (3a), while clients move on to (3b).

Session Info (3a): In its simplest form, all the user needs to input is the name of the session. (This could, of course, be generated using the player's name, as well.) Other things that can be set up in this screen are session-specific details, such as password, maximum number of players, map/scene/stage, resources, technology limits, and much more. These are options that the host decides upon. Another option is to have these settings done in the Chat Room (4). This allows the players to discuss what settings they want before the game starts. Once the host is satisfied with the session settings, he moves on to the Chat Room (4).

Join Session (3b): This window lists all sessions available to the client. The client can enter a specific host address here or simply broadcast an enumeration request to the local subnet. Usually, a list with the available sessions is shown in this screen. In the list, it's common to show information such as session name, number of players, maximum number of players, latency, map, and so on. The client can then select a session to join and attempt to connect to it. If successful, the client will move on to the Chat Room (4) of the selected session.

Chat Room (4): In this screen, the players can chat with each other before the game starts and while awaiting more players. It's common in RTS games that the players can select things like team color, race, teams, and starting location in this screen, as well. When everybody is ready, the host usually starts the game, and all the players in the session move on to the Loading (5) screen.

Loading (5) Game Data: This screen is shown while initial game data is transferred between the server and the clients. Initial game data can be things like the terrain, terrain objects (e.g., trees, rocks, etc.), units and buildings, and so on. Usually, a loading bar of some sort is shown; some games even allow the users to see the loading progress of the other players. Once all players have received the initial game data, the game starts.

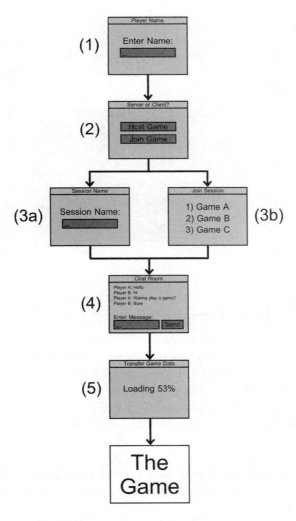

FIGURE 15.5 Example of a lobby UI flow.

As you've surely realized, the purpose of the lobby is to set up the NETWORK object. In the second screen (2), the user selects whether to initiate the NETWORK as a server or as a client. If it is set up as a server, then next screen (3a) collects the necessary information from the user to host a new session. Should the user be a client, the screen that follows (3b) enumerates the available sessions and allows the user to select which one he wishes to connect to. Creating the specific graphical details of a lobby like this is easy. Just use, for example, the sprite object to draw textures and create a button function or text box for user input.

ON THE CD

Example 15.1

This example implements a simple chat program using the UI flow presented in this section. Check out the LOBBY class that implements the user interface presented in this section.

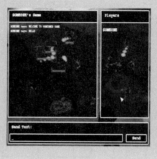

RTS NETWORKING

Up until now, this chapter has been looking at creating a general-purpose NETWORK class that can be used as a base to create any multiplayer application. We haven't yet looked at the specific RTS details we need to deal with before we can play our game over the network. In other words, we now have the structure in place to send information to and from remote computers, but what information should we send? To answer this, let's have a look at the different states a multiplayer game goes through:

1: Connecting Players. This is what we did in the previous sections of this chapter. Servers and clients are created and connected using, for example, a lobby.

2: Initiating the Game. Initial data is sent from the server to all the clients. This information includes large chunks of static data, like the terrain. We need to transfer the heightmap as well as the terrain objects so that all players are actually playing on the same terrain. We also must transfer all initial units and buildings for all players. This process can take some time, especially if the terrain is large and the connection is slow. So while this is being done, a loading-progress screen is usually shown. The idea is that once the game starts, all players will have exactly the same game state in front of them.

3: Playing the Game. During the game, many small packets will be transferred back and forth to update the other players of any changes being made to the game state. Examples of such messages are: "Unit #32 killed Unit #29" or "Building #5 created at Position (3, 2)," and so on. The difficulty during this phase of the game is to keep all players concurrent so that their game states still are the same.

4: Aftermath. The game is now over and we show some scores. Usually the player is transferred back to the chat room of the session, where they can talk about what happened or start another round.

Transferring Initial Game Data

Transferring the initial game data is quite easy. We just need to construct a series of network messages (all inheriting from the RTS_MSG base structure, of course) to carry our initial data across. These will be sent with a guaranteed-delivery method to make sure all clients get them. An example of this type of message could look like this:

```
struct MSG_OBJECT : public RTS_MSG
{
    MSG_OBJECT(OBJECT &obj);

    int objType;
    INTPOINT mp;
    D3DXVECTOR3 pos, rot, sca;
};
```

This structure is designed to carry an object description across the network and enable clients to recreate the terrain object in the same way as it is on the server. We only send the information that is absolutely necessary to recreate the object. For instance, we don't send the bounding box of a specific object across because this can easily be recalculated by the client. Same thing with the terrain—it is enough that we send the heightmap across (at least if the texturing is done using height ranges and not map tiles). Sending small object descriptions like this across is not a problem. However, it is a bit more problematic to send large chunks of data like the heightmap across in one package. To get a smooth progress bar, it is better to manually divide the terrain into packets of manageable size before sending them. The communication between the client and the server would then look something like this:

Client: Request Terrain Packet #1
Server: Send Terrain Packet #1
Client: Request Terrain Packet #2
Server: Send Terrain Packet #2

...

Client: Request Terrain Packet #200
Server: Terrain Transfer Done

Remember that during this initiating phase, the priority is to get the information across and rebuild it so that all the players have the same game state. Later, when the game is played, we also have to take speed into account, and try to make our packages as small and efficient as possible. During this phase you are still allowed to send large variables, such as float values, if you need the extra precision. How you construct your messages is of course dependant on your own style of coding as well as the application you're coding. One way of doing this initial data transfer can be found in Example 15.2, where the MSG_TERRAIN structure is used to transfer the heightmap across part by part.

Sending Messages During Gameplay

This is the trickiest part of any multiplayer game, especially a real-time game. During this phase, we need to send messages with any changes we do so that as the users play the game, the game state is still the same for all of them. There are many approaches to this problem, some of which are listed here:

Send All Units Across: This is the simple, brute-force approach that comes intuitively when people face this problem for the first time. A client simply sends the health, position, rotation, and animation for all his units across to the server. The server updates these units and relays the information onward to the other clients. These messages are sent with a nonguaranteed delivery method. This is done because if a message should fail, then a new one will be sent shortly anyway. The messages are sent with a certain time interval, which is usually set to several times per second. This method works, of course, and the great thing about this approach is that all other players have a completely accurate view of your units. This method is also very intuitive and easy to implement. However, the downfall of this method is the huge amount of data that must be transferred with each update. So this approach is only suitable for a demo or game intended for multiplayers over an LAN network; otherwise, it might be too expensive.

Send Delta Units Across: This approach is an improvement over the previous method. Here we only send units across that have been moved or otherwise changed, like damage, animation, and so forth. This greatly reduces the traffic, since any stationary units don't get sent across to the server. While this is still a great improvement, potentially it can still be as bad as the previous method should all the units be moving. It also adds some complications when updating the correct units and so on. However, this is still a pretty straightforward method that can be easily implemented.

Send Orders Across: Variants of this approach are used by some commercial multiplayer RTS games. In this approach, we only send user orders across to the server (which relays the orders to the other clients). Then we execute the orders separately on all machines and hope they are executed in the same way. While this method sends the least amount of information across the network, it is also by far the most difficult method to implement. Usually, small discrepancies caused by network latency result in orders that are executed with different results across the connected computers. For instance, the order "Unit #45 move to position (23, 3)" can then be carried out using different paths. While this may not always be noticed by players, sometimes this can result in confusions—for example on one computer, Unit #45 is killed by a flesh-eating rabbit, while on another computer, Unit #45 just manages to escape. This is of course something that cannot be allowed because keeping the players' game states concurrent is our number-one priority.

Send Time-Stamped Orders Across: This method takes the previous approach one step further. To ensure that all orders are carried out at the same time, the server sends out time messages to all the clients with the current game time. A client then sends an order scheduled for a future game time. The point is that the order should reach all the other clients before the scheduled game time. An example of this type of order is: "Move Unit #12 to position (32, 76) at time #245." When the server sends a message to all the clients with a game time of #245, all clients execute the order at the same moment. Discrepancies still happen of course, but now orders are much more likely to be carried out concurrently for all players. For a good article covering this approach, see [Bettner01].

No matter what approach you decide to use, you will always have to make sure that the game state is the same for all players. Deciding what approach to use and implementing it is a very complex part of creating an RTS game. It takes a lot of resources and time to do correctly.

Example 15.2

This example connects players using the same lobby interface as in Example 15.1. It then transfers the initial game data to make sure that all the players have the same terrain and other objects. In this example, you can only move the units of the different teams around. It's up to you to implement all other aspects of your multiplayer RTS game, such as attack behavior, projectiles, and so on.

SUMMARY

In this chapter, we looked at how to create a multiplayer application using the DirectPlay API. We covered the server-client model and built our own NETWORK class to handle all network-related issues, and made it easy for external objects to send data across the network. Even though we didn't cover the peer-to-peer model at all, you should easily be able to implement a peer-to-peer application with the help of the DirectX documentation.

Once you have created your multiplayer game, you also need to test it properly. To do this, you need at least three computers at your disposal. It's important that you also check that information gets relayed correctly from one client to another via the server. Learning how to set up an application to send data over the network is a simple feat compared to figuring out what data to actually send. Hopefully this chapter will serve as an introduction to the very complex topic of creating a networked real-time strategy game. Chapter 16 will tie our bag of components together, and we will implement the final touches needed to create our RTS demo.

EXERCISES

- Implement a lobby that allows the player to select a team color, start location, and other player data. Send this data together with a name across to the other computers, and make sure no two teams have the same color.
- In the Join Session room in the lobby, add how many players are in each active session as well as the latency time of the host.
- Implement all other aspects of a multiplayer RTS game.

REFERENCES

[Bettner01] Bettner, Paul and Mark Terrano, "1500 Archers on a 28.8: Network Programming in *Age of Empires* and Beyond." Available online at: *http://www. gamasutra.com/features/gdcarchive/2001/terrano_1500arch.doc,* 2001.

FURTHER READING

Royer, Dan, "Network Game Programming." Available online at: *http://www. flipcode.com/articles/network_part01.shtml,* 1999.

16 Putting It All Together

We have now reached the final stage of this project: putting all the components together into a real-time strategy game. We have covered how to create random terrains, manage teams of units and buildings, fog-of-war, visual effects, and sound and network connections. Before we put all these things together into our final game, there are a few final touches we need to add. We will start by taking a look at creating a user interface for our game. Then we'll move onto playing Audio Video Interleave (AVI) files for introductions, cut scenes, and end scenes. Finally, we'll look at the game we have so far and see what else can be done to it. We'll look at what pieces are missing from the game, as well as some of the many technical improvements that can be made.

USER INTERFACE

We've already had a look at how to put a user interface together in Chapter 15, where we covered the lobby interface that connects players together prior to multiplayer gameplay. We also had a look at the minimap in Chapter 11, which is an important part of the user interface in an RTS game. In this section, we will take a look at how the user can navigate the world, selecting units and giving orders. We'll mostly discuss what a player expects from an RTS game-user interface. By designing your user interface roughly according to the "standard," you will make it easier for a new player to learn how to play your game.

Camera Control

Traditionally, real-time strategy games have been in 2D, with the camera watching the battlefield from straight overhead. As RTS games were implemented in 3D, the traditional camera viewpoint was relaxed somewhat, and the user was given more control over the camera. However, even today most RTS games don't give the user total freedom, and the camera is limited to fairly perpendicular angles to the terrain. This of course makes sense because it gives the player the best strategic viewpoint of the battlefield. Here are some user-control techniques:

Scrolling: Scrolling (i.e., moving the camera focus) is almost always done by moving the mouse cursor to the edge of the screen. The direction in which the focus moves is determined by what edge of the screen you move the cursor to. Alternatively, scrolling can be done with the arrow keys on the keyboard.

Zooming: Not all RTS games allow the player to zoom in and out. But for those that do, it is usually done with the mouse wheel. Alternatively, this can be done by pressing both mouse buttons and dragging the mouse forward or backward, but this is a somewhat older method.

Camera Rotation: The rotation of the camera is another thing that some RTS games let the user control; others don't. Locking the rotation makes it clearer to the player what direction is north (up) in his view. This makes it easier for the player to navigate the world at the cost of not being able to view the game world from all angles. Changing the camera rotation can also be done, for example, by pressing the CTRL or SHIFT key together with an arrow key.

In addition to these methods for moving the camera, we also have a small measure of camera control with the minimap. By clicking in the minimap, we move the camera focus to the corresponding location on the map.

Selecting Units

In Chapter 5, we covered how to select units using the mouse. We had two selection schemes: selecting a unit by clicking it, or by clicking-and-dragging a selection area on the screen while selecting all units within it. Today, this is the most accepted scheme for selecting units in an RTS game. Some older games require you to hold a key, like CTRL, to make an area selection. In addition to these unit-selection methods, there are other ways to select units.

> **Selecting Similar Units:** Some RTS games have a function where you can select (or deselect) units of similar types. Usually this is done using a key like CTRL or SHIFT in combination with clicking on a unit of the type you would like to select. All units within the viewing volume of similar type are then selected.

> **Grouping Units:** The user can make a complex selection of units and then assign these units to a group. This group can then be selected at any time with the press of a single button. Creating a group is almost always done in RTS games using CTRL in combination with a numeral key (0–9). Later, if the user would like to select the same units again he would only have to press the numeral key that the group had been assigned to. Should the user double-click this numeral key, the camera usually centers on the group, making it easy to find it.

Giving Orders

Orders are given to any selected units by right-clicking the target position or the target unit. If the user right-clicks a patch of terrain, the selected units will make it their task to move to this location. Should the user right-click an enemy target, then the units will take that as an attack order and pursue the target.

That covers the easy and basic move-and-attack order. More-complex orders, like what building to construct or what spell to cast, require a menu of some sort. The same goes for buildings—usually a building can produce one or more units, technology upgrades, and so on, and therefore needs a menu, as well. There are different paradigms concerning how the menu should work. Some games change the options available in the menu depending on what unit you have selected. Other games always show all available options of what units can be produced and what buildings that can be constructed (e.g., the *Red Alert*™ series). As with all choices, both methods have their ups and downs. The first method forces the user to select the building he wants to produce a certain unit, which of course can cost the player some extra time. But on the other hand, what buildings and units do becomes very clear with this method. Also, only the necessary choices are presented to the user. An example of this type of menu can be seen in Figure 16.1.

FIGURE 16.1   Example of a menu.

In our rather simplistic RTS game, we only need four different choices (most games use at least nine). As you can see in Figure 16.1, the menu shows different options depending on what building/unit is selected. The style and functionality of the menu used in a game is, of course, dependant on the game being created. Remember to keep it simple; don't give the user too many options—and not too few, either.

AVI FILES

AVI files are used to store and play digital video and audio sequences. Many developers use high-quality prerendered movies as introductions or cut scenes in their games. These movies usually contribute to the "wow" factor of the game, but they also work to advance the story in a game. From a game developer point of view, it can be quite tricky to manage AVI files and display them on the screen.

In this section, we want to be able to stream data from an AVI file to an IDirect3DTexture9 object, which we then can map to a 3D object or simply draw with a sprite interface to the screen. There are several approaches to displaying AVI files in a game. The most advanced way to do this is by using a DirectShow filter to render the movie. You can find an example of this in the DirectX samples accompanying the DirectX SDK (the Texture3D9 sample). A somewhat simpler approach is to use the Video-for-Windows (VFW) API. The Video-for-Windows API allows developers to easily read, play, and store AVI files using the AVIFile interface. To use this interface, you must link the winmm.lib and vfw32.lib libraries to your project. You must also include the vfw.h header file in your code. Before we can access any of the AVIFile functions in the Video-for-Windows library, we must call the AVIFileInit() function:

```
//Init the AVIFile interface
AVIFileInit();
```

The AVIFile interface is initiated as simply as that. We must also remember to call the AVIFileExit() function when we are done with the API.

```
//Close the AVIFile interface
AVIFileExit();
```

Opening an AVI file

This section will cover how to open an AVI file, retrieve any audio and video streams stored in the file, as well as how to retrieve their format. To open a AVI file, we use the AVIFileOpen() function:

```
STDAPI AVIFileOpen(
    PAVIFILE * ppfile,       //Handle to AVI file
    LPCTSTR szFile,          //Filename of AVI file
    UINT mode,               //Access mode (read, write etc)
    CLSID  pclsidHandler     //Custom handler
);
```

If this function works, it will return zero. We use the AVIFileOpen() function like this:

```
//New AVI file handle
IAVIFile *aviFile = NULL;

//Open AVI file
if(AVIFileOpen(&aviFile, "movie.avi", OF_READ, NULL) != 0)
{
    //Opening the AVI file failed
}
```

The AVIFileOpen() function retrieves a handle for the AVI file we specify. There are a couple of different ways we can access a AVI file; in this example we use the OF_READ flag, which of course means that we will only read from the AVI file. Other flags are OF_CREATE, OF_WRITE, and OF_READWRITE. Assuming that all went okay, we now must retrieve and read the different streams stored in the AVI file. (An AVI file may contain more than one video and audio stream.) We do this using the following function:

```
STDAPI AVIFileGetStream(
    PAVIFILE pfile,        //AVI file handle
    PAVISTREAM * ppavi,    //Pointer to new stream interface
    DWORD fccType,         //Type of stream to open
    LONG lParam            //which stream to open
);
```

The fccType parameter indicates what stream type we want to retrieve. This can be set to either streamtypeAUDIO, streamtypeMIDI, streamtypeTEXT, or streamtype VIDEO, depending on which stream type to acquire. If all went well, the function returns zero, and the ppavi parameter points to a new stream interface. From a video stream, we will also need an IGetFrame object to extract and decompress a specific frame. We get an IGetFrame object using the following function:

```
STDAPI_(PGETFRAME) AVIStreamGetFrameOpen(
    PAVISTREAM pavi,                    //Stream
    LPBITMAPINFOHEADER lpbiWanted  //Wanted format
);
```

Okay, we've covered the function that opens an AVI file. We've also covered how to extract different streams from this AVI file and also how to get the IGetFrame object that can decompress a specific frame from a stream. The following code shows how to get all video streams from an AVI file:

```
int streamNo = 0;
do
{
    //Create a new stream and getFrame object for each stream
    PAVISTREAM stream = NULL;
    PGETFRAME getFrame = NULL;
```

```
//Get video stream
if(AVIFileGetStream(aviFile, &vs->stream,
                    streamtypeVIDEO, streamNo++) != 0)
{
    //we've reached the end and there are no
    //more streams to retrieve
    break;
}
else        //A valid stream was retrieved
{
    //GetFrame object
    getFrame = AVIStreamGetFrameOpen(stream, NULL);

    //Store stream and getFrame objects here
}
}
while(true);
```

This piece of code retrieves all video streams until the AVIFileGetStream()
function returns something other than zero (i.e., no more streams to retrieve).
Then we get the IGetFrame object for this stream using the AVIStreamGetFrameOpen()
function. Store the stream and IGetFrame object in a list or array so that you can
access them easily during playback. The audio streams are retrieved in exactly the
same way, only you'll have to specify streamtypeAUDIO instead of streamtypeVIDEO in
the AVIFileGetStream(). You also don't have to get an IGetFrame object, of course.
Remember also to release the stream and IGetFrame object like this:

```
//Release a getFrame object
if(getFrame)
    AVIStreamGetFrameClose(getFrame);

//Release a stream object
if(stream)
    AVIStreamRelease(stream);

//Release AVI handle
if(aviFile)
    AVIFileRelease(aviFile);
```

That concludes how we open an AVI file and load all the streams it contains.
Next, all we have to do is play it.

Playing an AVI file

To play an AVI file, we use the IGetFrame object of a certain stream to retrieve the frame (still image) we want. But before we do this we, must calculate which frame we should extract. For this we can use the following function:

```
STDAPI_(LONG) AVIStreamTimeToSample(
    PAVISTREAM pavi,                    //Stream to sample
    LONG lTime                         //Time in milliseconds
);
```

This function returns what frame to use for this specific time, as shown here:

```
//Retrieve frame to use after 3.7 seconds
long frame = AVIStreamTimeToSample(stream, 3700);
```

This function returns −1 if the time is outside the range of the stream or if the function failed for some reason. Once we have figured out what frame to use, we can extract it by using the AVIStreamGetFrame() function:

```
STDAPI_(LPVOID) AVIStreamGetFrame(
    PGETFRAME pgf,                     //IGetFrame object
    LONG lPos                          //Frame to extract
);
```

This function returns NULL if lPos isn't a valid frame. We use this function like this:

```
//Bitmap to store frame in
BITMAPINFOHEADER *bip = NULL;

//Cast the result of AVIStreamGetFrame() to a bitmap
bip = (BITMAPINFOHEADER*)AVIStreamGetFrame(getFrame, frame);
```

The frame has now been extracted and stored as a bitmap in memory. All we need to do is create a texture of it, and we can use it in any way we want. Luckily, there's a D3DX library function to help us do just that. The D3DXCreateTexture FromFileInMemoryEx() function creates a texture from memory and is defined as follows:

```
HRESULT D3DXCreateTextureFromFileInMemoryEx(
    LPDIRECT3DDEVICE9 pDevice,        //Active device
    LPCVOID pSrcData,                 //Source image in memory
```

```
    UINT SrcDataSize,              //Size of the image
    UINT Width,                    //Image width
    UINT Height,                   //Image height
    UINT MipLevels,                //Mip levels to create
    DWORD Usage,                   //Texture usage
    D3DFORMAT Format,              //Texture format
    D3DPOOL Pool,                  //Memory Pool
    DWORD Filter,                  //Creation Filter
    DWORD MipFilter,               //How to create mipmaps
    D3DCOLOR ColorKey,             //Transparent Color
    D3DXIMAGE_INFO *pSrcInfo,      //Image description
    PALETTEENTRY *pPalette,        //Palette, if used
    LPDIRECT3DTEXTURE9 *ppTexture  //The resulting texture
);
```

This function can be used together with the AVIFile interface in the following fashion to load the frame into an IDirect3DTexture9 object:

```
BITMAPINFOHEADER *bip = NULL;
bip = (BITMAPINFOHEADER*)AVIStreamGetFrame(getFrame, frame);

if(bip != NULL)
{
    IDirect3DTexture9 *newFrame = NULL;

    //Image size in bytes
    int size = bip->biSize + bip->biWidth *
               bip->biHeight * bip->biBitCount / 8;

    D3DXCreateTextureFromFileInMemoryEx(
        Device,                //Device
        bip,                   //Source Image
        size,                  //Image Size
        bip->biWidth,          //Width
        bip->biHeight,         //Height
        1,                     //Mipmaps
        D3DUSAGE_DYNAMIC,      //Usage
        D3DFMT_R8G8B8,         //Format
        D3DPOOL_DEFAULT,       //Memory Pool
        D3DX_DEFAULT,          //Filter
        D3DX_DEFAULT,          //Mipmap Filter
        0,                     //ColorKey not used
        NULL,                  //Image Desc
```

```
        NULL,                  //Palette
        &newFrame);            //Output...

    //Use the newFrame here...
}
```

Once the bitmap is loaded into an `IDirect3DTexture9` object, we can map it to a 3D object or just draw it on the screen using a sprite interface. Also, remember that once the frame is stored in an `IDirect3DTexture9` object, we can scale, rotate, and translate it using the sprite interface. You will find the full AVI source code in Example 16.1, where a wrapper class has been created for the `AVIFile` interface. Also, make sure that you read [Nix99] if you want a more-detailed dive into the `AVIFile` interface.

In addition to the `AVIFile` functions and structures we have covered in this section, there are many other things you can do with the Video-for-Windows API. For example, see [Dougherty04], where a movie is created from a game in real time, using the `AVIFile` interface.

THE GAME

This big moment is upon us. Example 16.1 contains a single-player RTS game that combines the components presented in this book. Figure 16.2 shows a screenshot of our RTS demo program:

Example 16.1

You will find this final example on the companion CD-ROM. If you should find the AI opponents too easy to beat, then you could, for example, give them discount prices when purchasing units.

FIGURE 16.2   A screenshot of the RTS demo.

Disclaimer: Remember that this is only a demo program and not a commercial game. It will therefore most likely contain a lot of bugs and unexpected/unwanted behavior. So without any further ado, let the bug hunt begin!

WHERE TO GO FROM HERE?

I'm sure you'll agree that what we have so far still leaves a lot to be desired before our game is perfect. In this section, some of the most common features of an RTS game that for some reason have been left out will be briefly discussed. Whether you implement some or all of these features is now up to you.

Terrain Resources

The most obvious component missing from our RTS game so far is resources. This is what the player fights the other players over. The resources are in almost all RTS games used to purchase more units and buildings. In that way, resources benefit the player's ultimate goal of domination. In most RTS games, the resources are limited—this ensures that sooner or later the game will end. Examples of terrain resources are trees, gold, food, oil, iron, stone, and so on. Some games like, *Dune II* or the *Command and Conquer/Red Alert* series, use patches of special terrain that can be harvested. Other strategy games use a capture-the-flag approach. In these games, the players get more resources based on how many terrain flags they control.

Walls

Building walls to defend your base is another common concept many RTS games use. Walls allow the user to seal off certain passages and limit the amount of possible approaches an enemy can make. The enemy can still attack the walls, but this also gives the player time to prepare for the attack. This is a pretty easy component to implement from the player's point of view. It's slightly harder to create a good wall-building AI. Check out [Grimani04] for a guide on AI wall building.

More Units

At the moment we just have three different types of units in our game. Most RTS games have at least 10 different types, and some have many more. The type of units you add to your game is of course dependant on the setting of your game. Let's take another look at the unit categories (check the Unit section in Chapter 2 for the full description of these categories):

- Engineering units
- Resource gathering units
- Short-range units
- Long-range units
- Supporting units
- Mounted units
- Siege units
- Stealth units
- Air units
- Transport units
- Heroes

Have a look at this list and see if any unit type is missing in your game. Perhaps break tradition and come up with your own type. Some games also reward units for experience in vanquishing enemies and upgrade them (e.g., make the unit more powerful) as they gain more experience.

Technology Upgrades

Another common component of real-time strategy games is technology upgrades. These are almost always done from a building. This can be anything from increasing the damage your units do to increasing the amount of resources your worker units can gather in one go.

Player Alliances

Allow the players to form alliances with each other. This is an essential part of any real-time strategy game, especially if playing in multiplayer mode. Two allied players' fogs-of-war are combined so that they can see what the other one sees. In an alliance, things like resources can be transferred between players (usually at a cost). The players in an alliance can usually also send chat messages to each other without sending them to the enemy players. This allows players to plan surprise attacks and so on. In some games, the alliances are determined in the chat room of a multiplayer game. Other games allow you to make (and break) alliances in the game during runtime.

Game Tutorials

Most real-time strategy games have both complex user interfaces as well as complex game rules. The easiest and most effective way for the user to learn these is by playing a few short tutorials that demonstrate the different functions and rules of the game. In some games, the tutorial is actually a part of the game that you have to play through when starting a new game. Most games allow you to skip the tutorial completely.

TECHNICAL ISSUES

The previous section covered some theoretical components that you might want to add to your game to make it more "complete." This section will look at technical issues that you will have to address if you want your game to more closely resemble a commercial product. These are the "boring" but necessary parts of a game that are usually left to last. The most important issues are: porting the game to older graphical hardware and hunting down any bugs still in the game.

Support Old Hardware

Many vertexshaders and pixelshaders used in this project have been aimed at graphic cards supporting version 2.0. Unfortunately, not everybody has a graphic card that supports this version. This means we must include vertexshaders and pixelshaders that perform the same (or similar) effects on older graphic cards. Luckily, there's a framework for just this in DirectX. We can create an effect file (.fx extension) that can contain many different shaders. An effect file is usually created to render one specific effect—say for example, our terrain texture splatting. As you might recall, there were a number of different ways to do this, even one that didn't require a shader at all. A certain way of rendering the same effect is called a "technique." In the terrain texturing example, we can use the faster shader technique on computers that support it, while we will have to use the slower, fixed function pipeline technique for older computers. Some effects require that we render the same object more than once. For this purpose, the effect framework has "passes." A technique must have one or more passes. In a pass, we specify what rendering states we want to use, as well as what vertexshaders and pixelshaders to use. The effect file contains all shaders and input/output structures needed for the effect, and since it can be stored as a simple text file, it is easy to edit the effect with having to recompile the game. The use of effect files is outside the scope of this book, but once you get used to them, you will find them much more convenient than separate vertex/pixelshader files. Check the DirectX documentation for more information about using effect files.

Multithreading

The next generation of computers are specifically designed for multithreading—not only computers, but also consoles like Playstation 3 and Xbox 360 can execute multiple threads at the same time. At the moment, our whole game runs in one single thread, which on a multiprocessor machine would be a serious waste of resources. To make the most of multiple processors, we should place heavy calculations like pathfinding and AI in their own threads. We can create a new thread using the following function:

```
HANDLE CreateThread(
    LPSECURITY_ATTRIBUTES lpThreadAttributes,//Security
    SIZE_T dwStackSize,                       //Stack size
    LPTHREAD_START_ROUTINE lpStartAddress,    //thread function
    LPVOID lpParameter,                       //thread argument
    DWORD dwCreationFlags,                    //creation option
    LPDWORD lpThreadId                        //Identifier
);
```

We can start new threads only if functions are defined as follows:

```
DWORD WINAPI ThreadProc(
    LPVOID lpParameter              //thread data
);
```

The thread data `lpParameter` is the data sent to the `CreateThread()` function's `lpParameter`. The following code shows how to create a new thread:

```
DWORD WINAPI AI_Thread(LPVOID lpParameter)
{
    //Do AI Stuff here...
    return 0;
}

DWORD WINAPI Game_Thread(LPVOID lpParameter)
{
    //Have game loop here...
    return 0;
}

void main()
{
    //Start Game Thread
    CreateThread(NULL, 0, Game_Thread, NULL, 0, NULL);

    //Start AI Thread
    CreateThread(NULL, 0, AI_Thread, NULL, 0, NULL);
}
```

Starting new threads is, however, a simple task compared to the task of managing data shared by different threads, deadlock problems, and so on. See [Garces06] for a good introduction to writing a multithreaded AI.

Optimization!

This is another big thing you need to look at. Almost all code in this book has been written with the purpose of conveying ideas and concepts, not making an optimized game. When you start the process of optimizing a game, the most important question to ask yourself is: What part of the program will benefit most from being optimized? The answer is, of course, that part of the program that is run most often. This is also known as the 80-20 rule—or in other words, 80 percent of the CPU cycles are used up by 20 percent of your code. It therefore makes sense to focus your optimization on the 20 percent of your code that runs most often. A good example of one piece of the puzzle that fits into this 20 percent is your pathfinding code (which in its current state could be improved a lot).

FINAL WORDS

In this chapter, we had a look at what a player expects from a real-time strategy game user interface. We also covered how to play AVI files using the Video-for-Windows API, something that is commonly used for intros and cut scenes in many games. We also took a look at many issues that could be implemented to make the game better or run smoother.

The end is near! We have covered quite a lot of ground in this book. Hopefully you were able to take most of it in and get a better understanding of what goes on behind the scenes of a real-time strategy game. This book may be over, but hopefully you will continue creating RTS games (or other games) on your own. After all, the only real way to learn something new is by doing it.

REFERENCES

[Dougherty04] Dougherty, James, "Designing a Screen Shot System." Available on-line at: *http://www.gamedev.net/reference/articles/article2063.asp,* 2004.

[Garces06] Garces, Sergio, "Strategies for Multiprocessor AI." *AI Game Programming Wisdom 3,* Charles River Media, 2006.

[Grimani04] Grimani, Mario, "Wall Building for RTS Games." *AI Game Programming Wisdom 2,* Charles River Media, 2004.

[Nix99] Nix, Jonathan, "Working with AVI Files." Available online at: *http://www.gamedev.net/reference/articles/article840.asp,* 1999.

Appendix | **About the CD-ROM**

The companion CD-ROM to *Programming an RTS Game with Direct3D* contains all of the examples referred to in the book. You can use any of the code and/or art found on this CD-ROM in your own projects.

FOLDER CONTENT

Examples: This folder contains all examples referred to in the text. You will find the examples ordered by chapter and example number. In each example folder, you will find the source code and VC++ project file. There is also a Debug folder, where you can find the executables and example resources. It's recommended that you copy the examples to your hard drive before viewing or editing them.

Images: In the Images folder on the CD-ROM, you will find all the images from the book, ordered according to chapter.

Plugins: In this folder you will find the Panda DirectX exporter plug-in for 3ds Max. Copy the plug-in file to your 3ds Max plug-ins folder. Then start (or restart) 3ds Max for the plug-in to be loaded.

USING THE EXAMPLES

Visual Studio: Copy the entire example you want to run to your hard drive (including the Debug folder containing the example resources). Open the VC++ project file (.vcproj) in Visual Studio.

3ds Max: Some examples contain 3ds Max models (.max files). Use 3ds Max 6.0 (or greater) to open, view, and edit these files.

System Requirements

- Windows XP
- DirectX 9.0c
- Graphics card that supports vertexshader and pixelshader version 2.0
- 1200 MHz processor
- 512 MB RAM

Index

A